DATE DUE

#47-0108 Peel Off Pressure Sensitive

J. G. HERDER ON
SOCIAL AND POLITICAL CULTURE

Cambridge Studies in the History and Theory of Politics

J. G. HERDER ON
SOCIAL AND POLITICAL
CULTURE

TRANSLATED, EDITED AND WITH AN
INTRODUCTION BY

F. M. BARNARD
Professor of Political Science, University of Saskatchewan, Saskatoon

CAMBRIDGE
AT THE UNIVERSITY PRESS
1969

Published by the Syndics of the Cambridge University Press
Bentley House, 200 Euston Road, London N.W.1
American Branch: 32 East 57th Street, New York, N.Y.10022

Library of Congress Catalogue Card Number: 69–11022
Standard Book Number: 521 07336 7

Printed in Great Britain
at the University Printing House, Cambridge
(Brooke Crutchley, University Printer)

CONTENTS

CONTENTS

CONTENTS

vii

PREFACE

Commentators (especially German scholars) have tended to divide Herder's most important works into roughly two categories: (i) those falling into the Enlightenment mode of thought; and (ii) those presaging Romanticism. Since to many of them Romanticism was the more significant element in modern thought, they associated Herder's alleged anti-rationalism and historicism with the earlier, 'most vigorous' part of his intellectual creativity. Herder's later writings were attributed to a growing enfeeblement, a 'regression' to the more 'facile' ideas of the Enlightenment. One purpose of this volume is to suggest that these labels are not very meaningful in view of the richness and complexity of Herder's thought. I also feel that these periodizing interpretations misleadingly imply that the undeniable shifts in Herder's thinking follow a distinctly chronological pattern, whilst in fact they are frequently traceable within any single work regardless of its date. Moreover, the emphasis given to these shifts is liable to blur the essential continuity of Herder's thought. To bring this over-all consistency into sharper focus, I decided in an earlier work (*Herder's Social and Political Thought*) to adopt the topical rather than the chronological method of analysis. Since the present book includes works extending over practically the whole of Herder's writing career, in strictly chronological order, the reader is in a position to judge for himself whether or not my view concerning Herder's essential unity of thought amidst the diversity of its expression is adequately warranted. If it is, Herder's work presents a telling example of the operation of the principle of unintended consequences. For Herder was anything but a conscious system-builder.

The other, and intrinsically more substantive concerns of this volume will, I hope, be discernible from the Introduction. The texts selected contain Herder's most original and stimulating ideas on the significance and function of language, tradition, customs, values and beliefs in the formation of social and political cultures, and on the problem of their persistence and change. Although these ideas are of interest in their own right, their relevance to current sociological and political problems will scarcely escape the modern reader.

Herder's *Letters for the Advancement of Humanity* (1793–7), though of undoubted interest (in particular for the light they throw on his attitude towards the French Revolution), have not been included in the text, to avoid repetition and undue length. I have, however, added short excerpts in footnotes to the Introduction wherever this seemed pertinent.

Herder's manner of writing is vivid at all times. Not infrequently it is also lucid, presenting the most complex ideas with succinct precision. Yet there are occasions when he is vexatiously diffuse or when he resorts to stylistic devices that are overly fanciful, rhetorical, ejaculatory or elliptic. Here the task of the translator is not an easy one. In his choice of an apt equivalent to what defies literal translation, he can but hope that he has done justice to the spirit of the thing.

I should like to express my gratitude to the University of Saskatchewan in Saskatoon for its generous financial support towards clerical expenses and to the Canada Council for a research grant which enabled me to spend a period of study in Weimar where I benefited from discussions with Dr Wilhelm Dobbek, the eminent Herder scholar. In non-financial, but no less tangible, terms I am indebted to Miss Janet Fyfe for her valuable assistance with translation problems and in the compilation of the Index. Last, not least, I have reason to thank the publishers for their interest in this volume. It was their initiative which prompted its production.

F.M.B.

Saskatoon, 1968

NOTE ON THE TEXTS

The selection and translation of the texts are based on Herder's *Sämtliche Werke*, ed. B. Suphan, 33 vols., Berlin, 1877–1913. The figures within square brackets after the subheadings refer to the volumes and pages of this edition. Herder's own footnotes are denoted by asterisks. An editorial comment is sometimes added within square brackets.

BOOKS ON HERDER IN ENGLISH

Nevinson, Henry, *A sketch of Herder and his times*. London, Chapman and Hall, 1884.

Ergang, Robert, *Herder and the foundations of German nationalism*. New York, Columbia Univ. Press, 1931.

McEachran, F., *The life and philosophy of Johann Gottfried Herder*. Oxford, Clarendon Press, 1939.

*Gillies, A., *Herder*, Oxford, Basil Blackwell, 1945.

Lovejoy, Arthur O., 'Herder and the enlightenment philosophy of history', in *Essays in the History of Ideas*. Baltimore, Johns Hopkins Press, 1948, pp. 166–82.

*Clark, Robert T., Jr., *Herder: his life and thought*. Berkeley and Los Angeles, Univ. of Calif, Press, 1955.

Wells, G. A., *Herder and after: a study in the development of sociology*. The Hague, Mouton and Co., 1959.

*Barnard, F. M., *Herder's social and political thought: from enlightenment to nationalism*. Oxford, Clarendon Press, 1965, corr. rep. 1967.

Berlin, Isaiah, 'Herder and the enlightenment', in Earl R. Wasserman (ed.), *Aspects of the eighteenth century*. Baltimore, Johns Hopkins Press, 1965, pp. 47–104.

PREVIOUS ENGLISH TRANSLATIONS OF TEXTS INCLUDED
IN THIS VOLUME

Churchill, T. *Outlines of a philosophy of the history of man*, London, Johnson, 1800. (Translation of the *Ideen*.)

Harrison, J. F. *Johann Gottfried Herder: Journal of My Travels in the Year* 1769. Ann Arbor, University Microfilms, 1952. (Columbia University, Ph.D. thesis.)

* These books contain detailed bibliographies of Herder's writings and of studies on Herder.

INTRODUCTION

INTRODUCTION

HERDER AND POLITICS

John Stuart Mill, in one of his essays, speaks of Herder as one of 'that series of great writers and thinkers . . . by whom history, which was till then a "tale told by an idiot, full of sound and fury, signifying nothing", has been made a science of causes and effects; who, by making the facts and events of the past have a meaning and an intelligible place in the gradual evolution of humanity, have at once given history, even to the imagination, an interest like romance, and afforded the only means of predicting and guiding the future, by unfolding the agencies which have produced and still maintain the Present'.[1] This somewhat exuberant assessment of Herder's contribution to historiography could no doubt be questioned on several points of detail. Nonetheless it bears witness to the reputation which Herder enjoyed as a philosopher of history throughout the nineteenth century, a reputation which has not been seriously challenged since. Much the same can be said about his work in the field of language, folklore and literature generally, and about his pioneering ideas on national consciousness, the impact of which is still palpably felt throughout the world.

As a socio-political thinker, however, Herder has been less successful in gaining recognition. That this should be so is not really surprising, if it is borne in mind that many of the questions which interested Herder and which currently occupy political thinkers were dismissed as of little or no relevance to political life less than three decades ago. Herder's essentially 'cultural' approach to politics, his negative attitude to such concepts as 'state', 'sovereignty', 'power' and 'progress', his hostility to the traditional contract and natural right theories, and, not least, his cavalier treatment of procedural government 'machinery', could have had but little appeal to political scientists of nineteenth or early twentieth-century vintage. This is not to suggest, however, that Herder was first and foremost a political thinker. His interests

[1] J. S. Mill, *On Bentham and Coleridge*, ed F. R. Leavis (London, 1950), p. 131.

were too heterogeneous (ranging from literary criticism, aesthetics, philology, folklore and history to psychology, anthropology, philosophy, and theology) for that. The political conditions of his time, and his (often embarrassing) position as court preacher and chief clerical and educational administrator in Bückeburg and Weimar, no doubt also had some bearing on the extent to which Herder could publicly turn to political affairs.

In contrast to England, eighteenth-century Germany was a political desert. None of the major or minor states that composed the only nominally-existing empire offered any scope for shared political activity. There was no effective parliamentary life, no political parties, few, if any, political clubs, and merely the semblance of a free press. These conditions, coupled with the prevailing social structure, in particular the absence of an economically vigorous and politically conscious middle class, resulted in a situation in which 'politics' was virtually tantamount to personal rule by the princes, assisted by councillors who frequently were so privy, so anxious to keep their secrets to themselves, that no one ever heard them speak.[2]

Though not ignorant of the situation in Germany, this *terra obedientiae* as he called it, Herder, like other men of the Enlightenment, cherished hopes of gaining the ear of the princes. At least he did so in his younger years. The *Travel Diary* of his voyage to France in 1769 is full of projects which, he felt, could not but appeal to an enlightened monarch. To be sure, Russia, rather than Germany, was uppermost in his mind, partly because he considered Frederick II far too unimaginative a ruler in comparison to Catherine II,[3] and partly because Riga, to which Herder

[2] Thus wrote F. K. von Moser, one of the outstanding publicists of the period, best-known for his challenging tract *Der Herr und der Diener* (Frankfurt, 1759) (cited in A. Fauchier-Magnan, *The small German courts in the eighteenth century* (London, 1958), p. 55). Regarding the political and intellectual background of Herder's Germany, see Leonard Krieger, *The German idea of freedom* (Boston 1957), pp. 8–80; W. H. Bruford, *Culture and Society in Classical Weimar* (1775–1806) (Cambridge, 1962) and F. M. Barnard, *Herder's social and political thought: from enlightenment to nationalism* (Oxford, 1965), corrected reprint 1967, pp. 1–30.

[3] A poem which Herder wrote on the occasion of Catherine's coronation (in 1765) reveals the ardour with which he looked forward to her reign. (XXIX, 24–7; see also R. Haym, *Herder, nach seinem Leben und seinen Werken*, Berlin, 1880, vol. I, p. 108.)

intended to return, was then—as it is now—part of Russia. His later hopes centred on Joseph II, but by then he was no longer quite so confident of bridging the gap that separated his aspirations from their likely realization.

Oddly enough, however, it was not primarily disappointment over Catherine II or his profound distaste of political conditions in Germany—of which Herder's direct experience was so far limited to his native East Prussia—which caused Herder to question the prevalent faith in reform from above, but rather the impressions which the twenty-five year old traveller gained during his sojourn in France. French social and political life aroused his greatest misgivings. He met a number of eminent writers, such as Diderot, d'Alembert and Barthélemy, and devoted much time to the critical study of Montesquieu's *Esprit des Lois*, but the 'taste for encyclopedias, dictionaries, and extracts' only endorsed his belief that French culture was mortally sick. Instead of rejoicing over the fact that the despised Germans were read at all, Herder diagnosed their being read in translation as the most convincing proof of France's intellectual poverty, her humiliating decline.[4]

It was in this atmosphere of gloom that Herder confided to his notebook an observation which proved crucial for his subsequent political thinking. 'Political reform', the note says, 'has to come from below'.[5] That this realization was wrought with a sizeable measure of frustration and self-questioning is evident enough from his *Travel Diary*. Bold aspirations towards a life of active politics mingle with doubt and resignation. If it was scarcely conceivable for a man of humble birth to gain access to court circles, was it not plainly hopeless to expect to make any headway by putting one's trust in the will and ability of 'the people' to raise itself by its own boot-straps? What is he to do? Should he stop being an author, an 'inkpot and purveyor of pedantic scribblings', and become instead a second Calvin in order to root out the prevalent barbarism, ignorance, and servility?[6] Yet the very moment he contemplates a life of action another mood overtakes him. He resolves to write a comprehensive treatise on psychology, based on case studies taken from all ages and cultures, and insists that 'everything else is to be set aside' while he is engaged in this gigantic task.[7]

[4] IV, 413.   [5] XXXII, 56.   [6] IV, 347 and 363.   [7] IV, 364.

Clearly, Herder is as much aware of the external obstacles that lie in the path of a political career as of his inner uncertainties. In torment over these inner conflicts—which he never quite succeeded in resolving—he exclaims:

O God, who knoweth the elements of human souls and hath fitted them to their bodily vessels, was it necessary only for the design as a whole, or also for the happiness of the individual, that there should be souls which, having as it were entered this world in timid confusion, never know what they are doing or what they are about to do, never arrive where they wish to go and thought they were going, who never really *are* where they happen to be, and only rush from one mental state into another in a haze of feverish activity, astonished by their own whereabouts? . . . Father of men, wilt thou vouchsafe to instruct me?[8]

What Herder later saw at the German courts, in Eutin, Brunswick, Darmstadt, but, above all, in Bückeburg, did little to rekindle his faith in reform from above. Yet, whether or not the life of an active politician was ever a really deep-felt aspiration, whether or not he had the making of a politician even under more propitious circumstances, Herder finally decided that, if any battles were to be waged, his weapon was to be his pen, after all.

Even as a writer, however, dependence on the princely employers imposed limitations on his freedom of expression. Herder's most radical political views, therefore, are not to be found in his published writings—except here and there in unexpected contexts or ingenious disguises—but rather in private letters and unpublished drafts.[9] Among his published writings there is, indeed, no single major work that could unequivocally be classified as a political treatise. The nearest Herder comes to such a work is his prize essay on the interaction between the arts and sciences and political institutions. Many of his most original and suggestive ideas are, instead, contained in writings (such as those included in this volume) that are not obviously political in the narrower

[8] IV, 348.
[9] I have, in an earlier work (*Herder's social and political thought*) attempted a presentation of Herder's political views by drawing on these diverse sources. Herder's *Vom Geist der Ebräischen Poesie* (The spirit of Hebrew poetry), published in 1783 is perhaps the best example of a work where one least expects to find an expression of his political creed. See F. M. Barnard, 'The Hebrews and Herder's political creed', *Modern Language Review*, LIV (1959), 533–46, or 'Herder and Israel', *Jewish Social Studies*, XXVIII (1966), 25–33.

sense in which this word has up to recently been commonly understood. From a reading of these, the contemporary student of political science will hardly fail to observe how astonishingly relevant a good deal of what Herder has to say still is to current concerns. Indeed it would seem that Herder's multi-dimensional and essentially psychological and sociological, conception of 'politics' has gained rather than lost in significance in the period separating his time from our own.

Herder's central political idea lies in the assertion that the proper foundation for a sense of collective political identity is not the acceptance of a common sovereign power, but the sharing of a common culture. For the former is imposed from outside, whilst the latter is the expression of an inner consciousness, in terms of which each individual recognizes himself as an integral part of a social whole. To the possession of such a common culture Herder applies the term nation or, more precisely, *Volk* or nationality. The principal source of both its emergence and perpetuation is language. It is through language that the individual becomes at once aware of his selfhood *and* of his nationhood. In this sense individual identity and collective identity become one. Such close identification between the non-political and the political self unmistakably reveals the influence of Rousseau's philosophy of the General Will, yet at the same time it also signals its transcendence. For Herder's notion of a shared culture is meant to render the concepts of both sovereignty and contract superfluous. Also, by substituting a 'common language' for the 'general will', it stipulates an empirical and historically derived basis for socio-political association in place of a metaphysical and moral absolute.

The political structure of Herder's *Volk*-state is conceived on anarcho-pluralistic lines. There is no single focus of power, for government is not vested in any one permanent administrative authority. Government must be impersonal and non-physical if it is not to be a burden upon a healthy community. The institution of a centralizing power constitutes not the beginning but the collapse of politics; it is the symptom of social decay and political bankruptcy. The *Volk*-state is a territorial unit in which men conscious of sharing a common cultural heritage are free to order their lives within a legal framework of their own making. It is the

7

area of a nation's political self-determination *and* the social framework within which various individuals, groups and institutions
operate and co-operate. Government is virtually reduced (or
rather elevated perhaps) to what Herder in the *Ideas for a
Philosophy of the History of Mankind* calls *Zusammenwirken*, joint
endeavour.[10]

It is remarkable how consistent Herder was in his hostility to
the institution of central administrative bodies. For he opposed it
not only on the national, but also on the international level. In
contrast to the prevailing cosmopolitanism of the Enlightenment,
Herder did not recommend the abolition of nation states in favour
of the creation of a world government, since he believed that even
the mere attempt to institute such an international organization
would exacerbate rather than alleviate international tension.
Whilst aiming to unite people, it would actually divide them
further. Herder referred to such schemes as 'utopian phantoms'
which were not only pointless but also harmful in that they
deceived people into thinking that international unity was merely
a matter of political organization.[11] His own doctrine of *Humanität*
advocated instead (among other things) a loose and informal
linking of autonomous and co-operating nations.

Herder believed such national and international conditions to
be attainable without an essential breach of historical continuity,
because he envisaged the process leading to them as a tendency
inherent in human society no less than in nature: the tendency of
diversity towards unity. Similarly optimistic was his belief in the
gradual transformation from the dynastic 'machine' state into the
'organic' *Volk*-state. He saw this political process in terms of the
evolution of two complementary, yet opposing tendencies: decay
from above (the aristocratic power élite) and growth from below
(increasing popular participation). He was realistic enough, however, to recognize that growth from below was not a necessary
corollary of decay from above. Hence he stressed the need for a
transitional period of educational development (*Bildung*) in which
popular leaders—whom he called aristo-democrats—would help

[10] XIV, 227. Herder's insistence on the diffusion of power between diverse
sectional bodies and interests is in marked contrast to Rousseau's open
hostility to any form of pluralism.
[11] See his *Letters for the advancement of humanity* (XVII, 125 and XVIII, 283 and
346).

all members of the nation to achieve that degree of political maturity which would render their further leadership dispensable.[12] Like Plato's guardians, the aristo-democrats are expected to be men of intellectual excellence rather than men of property. But unlike Plato's philosopher-kings, Herder's popular leaders are only a transitional expedient, the assumption being, of course, that these leaders, in their desire to relinquish power at the earliest possible opportunity, would do everything to hasten the attainment of universal civic consciousness within the nation. In this Herder saw the ultimate goal of the transformation from aristocratic to popular rule, from tutelage to self-determination. This ultimate stage was to witness the disappearance of the state as an administrative machine, and its replacement by a pluralist diffusion of government associated with Herder's concept of 'nomocracy', under which spontaneous 'joint endeavour' and 'self-determination' would dispense with violence and coercion.

Herder was moved to write in this vein by his deeply-felt aversion towards the bureaucracy of German petty absolutism which had already disturbed him in his native Prussia. He feared that it would reduce politics to the regimentation of the barracks square, breed uniformity, and promote a dull, lifeless form of social existence, in which men would become mere cogs in a vast bureaucratic machine. But, unlike Max Weber, who was to express similar fears over a century later, Herder was not satisfied merely to dissociate the 'mechanical' from the 'political'; he opposed all forms of centralized power. In this he shared the apprehensions of another eighteenth-century community theorist, Justus Möser (1720–94), who felt that centralism would destroy the distinctive cultures and traditions of local communities. Herder, however, went both beyond and against Möser in his outspoken hostility to dynastic rule and the hereditary nobility. That those as yet unborn should be destined to rule over others not yet born, simply by virtue of their blood and accumulated wealth, seemed to Herder the most unintelligent proposition that human language could devise, and the most blatant example of unreason in the history of human reason.[13]

[12] See both the *Ideas* (XIII, 149) and the *Letters* (XVIII, 300 and 339).
[13] XIII, 377.

Whereas Möser accepted the existing social and economic structure and, indeed, judged property ownership to be a necessary qualification for exercising the right of citizenship,[14] Herder insisted on the right to political participation for all members of a community—although such activity was clearly envisaged in a much broader sense than that in which Möser used the term. In this radical, populist demand, Herder not only went beyond the traditionalist Möser but also beyond most of his progressivist Enlightenment contemporaries who were more concerned that men should be governed with benevolence and competence than that they should govern themselves, and hence had no serious objection to aristocratic privilege, nor even to absolutist rule, provided the rulers heeded their enlightened pleas for toleration, for a more humane treatment of criminals, and for the provision of education and welfare measures for the poor. Herder, on the other hand, whilst conceding that absolute equality was neither realizable nor desirable, nonetheless felt that the degree of natural inequality was by no means so marked as the inequality actually prevailing.[15] When he therefore advocated co-ordination rather than subordination as the operative principle of a 'healthy community', he wished to stress the mutual interdependence of parts within a whole which combined a high degree of horizontal differentiation with a minimum of vertical differentiation, where all were 'masters' in *some* sphere, but none were masters in *all* spheres.

In this pronounced anti-élitism, Herder did not even shrink from attacking his erstwhile teacher Immanuel Kant, the idol of the age. Whilst Kant, though upholding the principle of self-determination in the moral sphere, argued that man in the realm of politics was like an animal needing a master to rule and control him,[16] Herder, extending the principle of self-determination to politics, contended that man was only man in the true sense when

---

[14] 'It is manifest violence', Möser maintained, 'if members of the lower class unite and attempt to claim the same rights to property as members of the higher class by simply basing such claims on a common human origin'. Justus Möser, *Werke*, Abeken ed. (Berlin, 1842–3), v, 182.

[15] XIII, 295 and 381; see also *Letters* (XVII, 127) where Herder points out that even if equality could be attained in one generation it would scarcely survive it, quite apart from the unforeseeable problems it would pose in terms of freedom.

[16] Kant, *Idee zu einer allgemeinen Geschichte in weltbürgerlicher* Absicht (1784) in *Schriften* (Preuss. Akad. d. Wissenschaften ed., Berlin, 1923), VIII, 23.

he no longer required a political master to rule him.[17] When we remember the tremendous prestige that Kant enjoyed and remember, too, the political conditions of Herder's Germany, which forced more timid minds to confine their Kantian 'idealism' to the safer sphere of symbolic poetry or moral philosophy, Herder's radical and deliberate departure from vague and apolitical interpretations of freedom stands out as an intrepid act of intellectual courage and integrity.

What is equally worth stressing (in view of Herder's somewhat utopian conception of his *Volk*-state) is that Herder was not blind to the dangers of conferring political freedom on a people (such as the eighteenth-century Germans) virtually devoid of political experience and conspicuously deficient in a sense of common identity. In both *Yet Another Philosophy of History* and his treatise *On the Reciprocal Influence of Government and the Sciences* Herder squarely faces up to the problem of the seemingly conflicting pulls of order and freedom. Given the alternative of more efficient government by an enlightened despot and the possibly less efficient and less orderly political arrangement in which the people are free to participate in politics, he unhesitatingly opts for the latter.

Now, is it better, is it healthier and more beneficial for mankind, to produce only the lifeless cogs of a huge, wooden, thoughtless machine, or to arouse and activate living energies? Even if institutions are not perfect, even if men are not always honest, even if there is some disorder and a good deal of disagreement—it is still preferable to a state of affairs in which men are forced to rot and decay during their lifetime.[18]

---

[17] XIII, 383. Herder's repudiation of élitism and centralized power need not, however, be taken as a denial of the relevance of leadership or power to political life. For power, in the sense of influence (as distinct from physical coercion), provided it is widely diffused and/or derived from sentiments of solidarity, and leadership, in the sense of chosen and accountable authorities, are notions very much in evidence in his pluralist scheme. Indeed, in stressing the diffusion of power rather than its concentration in a totality such as Rousseau's 'sovereignty of the people', Herder's democratic ethic reveals in this respect a truer understanding of what political analysis is essentially about.

[18] V, 516; see also XIII, 340–1. Clearly, *legitimacy* matters more to Herder than *effectiveness*, to speak in current sociological terminology. At the same time he doubts that there is a necessary polarity involved here. 'Those who feel they are accountable to no-one', Herder writes in the *Letters*, 'must shoulder the blame for our political disorders.' A state cannot be a healthy polity unless all its members share a sense of civic responsibility (XVIII, 309).

In place of the 'paper-culture' (as he calls it) of the few, Herder pleads for the 'humanization' of the many, by which he understands the provision of basic standards of welfare and the gradual transformation of social values and traditions through a process of educational dissemination to which he applies the term *Bildung*. In contrast to the Enlightenment conception of *Bildung*, however, (and, for that matter, to the still widely accepted meaning of the word), Herder understands by it not something specifically intellectual, or something external (like instruction) to which the individual is merely passively related, but rather an interactive social process in which men influence each other within a specific social setting and in which they both receive from and add to their distinctive historical and communal heritage. This interactive and reciprocal building up of new societal and political goals *within* a socio-cultural continuum represents for Herder the true purpose of human association, the creative, *continuous* development of man. *Bildung*, thus understood, provides the alternative to abrupt socio-cultural discontinuities attending the replacement of traditions and values through their prior destruction rather than their transformation. In view of this, Herder, though hailing the French Revolution as the most momentous event since the Reformation, could not help feeling that it was a regrettable alternative to *Bildung* as he conceived it.[19]

[19] Of German contemporaries, Goethe perhaps comes closest to Herder's conception of *Bildung*, although he views the process in wholly apolitical and individualist terms, as 'self-improvement'. (See Bruford, *Culture and society in classical Weimar*, p. 236.) Herder's faith in the power of *Bildung* to engender in a people the will and ability to govern itself reflects, of course, the influence of Rousseau's educational gospel which in like manner came to dominate Jefferson's democratic creed. Regarding Herder's attitude to the French Revolution, see his letter to Jacobi, dated 11 November 1792 (Düntzer, *Aus Herders Nachlass*, Frankfurt a.M., 1856–7, II, 298–301). A day later, in a letter to Gleim, Herder writes: 'Do we not live in a unique period in which we almost have to believe in the Apocalypse?' (Düntzer, *Von und an Herder*, Leipzig, 1861–2, I, 152). His *Letters for the Advancement of Humanity* leave little doubt concerning Herder's sentiments about the French Revolution. 'Let us hope', he writes in one of the earlier *Letters*, 'that the world spirit is hatching out a gigantic ostrich egg, and that it is helped in this by the burning sand and the all-powerful sun; it should prove a happy event!' (XVII, 81). Although he expresses himself more cautiously in later *Letters*, he still adheres to the view that the Revolution was an epoch-making event which might well render obsolete earlier political theories—such as those of Aristotle and Rousseau—which maintained that republics are only realizable in small states. Herder is most anxious that the new

The basic prerequisite for *Bildung*, according to Herder, was freedom of thought and expression. His advocacy of political freedom in the essay *On the Reciprocal Influence of Government and the Sciences* forcibly recalls Milton's pleas in his *Areopagitica*, as it also foreshadows Mill's central arguments in his essay *On Liberty*.

All inquisition is prejudicial to the republic of learning. A book which must first be passed by ten censors before it reaches the light of day is no longer a book but the hackwork of the holy Inquisition, a mutilated thing, scourged with rods, a muzzled wretch and always a slave. . . . In the sphere of truth, in the realm of ideas, no earthly power should or can give judgment; the government cannot do it, let alone its cowled censor.[20]

Whilst conceding the need for restrictive laws under certain circumstances, Herder also warns that every restriction inevitably courts the danger of stifling the very sap of human creativity. More often than not such laws do not serve the state, but the 'blind and leaden goddess of dullness'.[21] For they tend to reject everything which is new, simply because it fails to conform to habitual ways of thinking. Yet if governments close their eyes to new ideas, if they insist that everything must remain just as it is, they invite, rather than prevent, violence and disorder. If the greatest masterpieces in the arts and sciences require constant checking and overhaul, why should the state, this most imperfect product of human creation, be thought to thrive on apathy and inactivity? Much is still to be discovered, many prejudices, still accepted as truth, to be discredited. Let us not, therefore, close windows and keyholes to light and air anxiously trying to reach us! The sounder a state is, the more orderly and strong within itself, the less risk it runs of being shaken and blown about by every breath of opinion, by every lampoon of an angry writer. Only tyrants are suspicious; only secret evil-doers timorous. Governments, like all other human

political order should be given a chance to establish itself and repudiates the idea of foreign intervention (XVIII, 314 and 318). Nonetheless, he fears that, lacking a sufficiently extensive preliminary process of *Bildung*, it may fail, like all sudden revolutions, to attain its humanitarian ends. (XVIII, 313. See also *ibid.* 314–20 and 331–32.)

[20] IX, 357–8.
[21] IX, 360.

institutions and endeavours, can only gain in the end by every examination and scrutiny. Truth will not wait on them; they must serve truth or else prove unworthy of their existence. Freedom of thought is the fresh air of heaven in which all plants of a polity thrive best. There can be no monopoly of wisdom.[22]

So much for Herder's central political doctrine. Stated in this summary form it does scant justice to the fullness and complexity of Herder's thought. Nonetheless it reveals sufficiently the principal source of Herder's social and political orientation, his acute dissatisfaction with the *status quo*. Coupled with this dissatisfaction was a sense of deep anguish over the legacy his generation was to leave behind. Few documents constitute so devastating an indictment of the contemporary scene as *Yet Another Philosophy of History*. With the incisiveness of a surgeon's knife it lays bare the sores of the eighteenth-century world in an attempt to deflate its sense of grandeur, its pride and complacent optimism.

Herder reminds his contemporaries that the so-called enlightenment and civilization of the world has affected only a few in a narrow strip of the globe and that even where light has been shed ominous shadows were never far afield.[23] Lands, larger than Europe, have been discovered, coasts full of gold, silver and spices conquered. New tools have opened up new worlds, but they have also ushered in new problems. They have rendered superfluous forces which were formerly necessary and which now rest unused. Civilization has forced people into mines, into treadmills, and into the cities which are fast becoming slagheaps of human vitality and energy. Improved techniques are spreading, but they are

[22] IX, 360–1; Herder writes in the same vein in the *Letters*, when discussing the question of prejudices, esoteric views, and widespread delusions (XVII, 226–33). Whether these are harmless, or, like religious fanaticism or national chauvinism, pernicious, the remedy is never force and brutal suppression. For, morals apart, this will create martyrs who may prove politically more dangerous than the views they espoused. The only effective antidote, Herder maintains, is free inquiry, complete tolerance (*ibid.* 233).

[23] V, 564. Herder's criticism of the Enlightenment is anticipated in the *Travel Diary* (IV, 411–12) where he writes: 'Enlightenment is never an end, but always a means; if it becomes the former it is a sign that it has ceased to be the latter, as was the case in France, still more in Italy and still more in Greece—and finally even in Egypt and Asia.'

controlled by the few who do all the thinking. So much in the arts, in industry, in war and civil life is being mechanized, that the *human* machine is losing its zest to function. Man is becoming alienated from himself: head and heart are rent apart. Slavery, it is true, has been abolished in Europe, but only because our business actuaries have found that slaves are far more costly and far less productive than the labour of free men. Outside Europe it is still a flourishing trade, rendered necessary by the expansion of sugar plantations and the difficulty of attracting labour to the silver mines.[24]

It is the incongruity between the high ideals professed by the few and the dismal misery suffered by the many which prompts Herder to accuse his age of hypocrisy. Its culture is a paper-culture, its ideals mere abstractions, instruments of self-deception. Instead of providing detailed studies and sober appraisals of actual social and political needs, writers excel in bird's-eye views, overall pictures, generalities. 'The principles developed by Montesquieu allow a hundred different peoples and countries to be reckoned up extempore on a political multiplication table.'[25] Dictionaries, digests and encyclopedias abound. These instant philosophies, as Herder calls them, though they are produced in the spirit of the mechanical age—being put together from two or three general ideas—wholly fail to meet its needs. Indeed they serve to obfuscate these by inundating us with fine phrases, lofty concepts, and elaborate systems to an extent 'that almost nobody can see the bottom of the floodwaters'.[26] It is all very well to preach liberty, fraternity, and equality, but who knows, Herder observes well over a decade before the French Revolution, what evils can and may yet be committed in their name. It is all very well to speak of the brotherhood of man whilst more and more Europeans invent methods and tools with which to subjugate other continents, to defraud and plunder them. Yet the time may well come, Herder warns, when these cheated and exploited peoples will use these very same methods *and* our lofty ideals to triumph over us. 'We forge the chains with which they will bind us.'[27]

[24] v, 525, 534, 545 and 550. See also XIII, 372–4.
[25] v, 536. See also Herder's criticism of Montesquieu in the *Travel Diary* (IV, 418–19).
[26] v, 537 and 541.
[27] v, 576 and 579; see also XIII, 263–4.

This intense involvement in the ills of his time did not, however, cloud Herder's vision. With a perspicacity which perhaps we can only now truly recognize, he saw and foresaw the magnitude and perilous consequences of ethnocentrism, racial discrimination and colonialism, of political oppression and economic exploitation and the various forms of social disorganization such as alienation or *anomie*. Admittedly, Herder's rejection of any form of political élitism, no less than his refusal to concede the need for a permanent administrative authority to co-ordinate his pluralist scheme, may strike us as exceedingly unrealistic, especially in view of what political sociologists tell us about the inevitability of oligarchic and hierarchical tendencies in all human associations. But it was perhaps not quite so unrealistic within the context of the contemporary scene.[28] Eighteenth-century Germany was riddled with administrative centres of the most hierarchical type. It had also not been short of administrative theories ever since the rise of Cameralism. And yet it was, as an entity, a politically underdeveloped country; a geographical area, not a nation. That these circumstances, coupled with the prevalent social and cultural fragmentation made administrative considerations seem less relevant and vital to Herder than the creation of a sense of collective identity and self-esteem, is not really so astonishing, even if it is granted that he need not have gone as far as he did in dismissing the former.

In repudiating centralism in favour of pluralism, and in replacing the notion of a negotiated *contract* by that of a shared *culture*, Herder did not rule out, however, the possibility of conflict.[29] What he did wish to deny was the idea of an *a priori* tension between the centrifugal and centripetal forces within a polity, which underlies the concept of the social contract, and which also serves as the justification or legitimation of the institution of a central power. At the same time it cannot be gainsaid that Herder's essentially normative model of a polity free from centralizing control and governmental coercion lends itself to abuse when it is made contingent on the existence of complete social harmony,

[28] It may not be without interest to note that recent thinking on administrative processes and 'stateless communities' comes significantly close to Herder's notion of co-ordination free from norms of centrality and hierarchy.
[29] This point will engage our attention in subsequent sections.

or invoked as an ideological device for enforcing such consensus. The concept of *power* may be irrelevant to a theory which views a political community as the outcome of shared cultural traditions and as a network of spontaneous 'joint endeavour'. Yet when actual conditions widely diverge from those envisioned by such a theory, the application of its terminology may easily help to disguise the realities of power politics.

LANGUAGE, CULTURE AND COMMUNITY

On the Origin of Language was Herder's first major philosophical work. The adjective 'philosophical' is used here in a broad sense for the treatise also comprises ideas of considerable psychological and sociological significance. Herder had for some time been meaning to comment publicly on the controversy which the subject was arousing, and the question set by the Royal Academy of Sciences in Berlin in 1769 offered a suitable occasion to do so.[30] Though chiefly concerned to refute Johann Peter Süssmilch's thesis that language was a direct gift of God,[31] Herder was also resolved to deny Condillac's and Rousseau's theories which traced the emergence of human speech to animalistic origins. For both hypotheses were fundamentally in conflict with his own thinking about the nature of man and the basis of human culture. If language was not the product of the human mind, then nothing else was, since language was the seed of all human endeavour. To postulate a divine origin, therefore, was tantamount to a denial of human creativity.[32] By the same token, if language was native to man in exactly the sense in which the hoarding of honey was to the bee, the notion of human culture was a meaningless notion, for its existence presupposed a process of conscious and progressive *development*.[33]

But whilst insisting on the distinctly human origin of language and on the universal capacity for speech among individual members of the human species, Herder denied the operation of both the

---

[30] For the question set see *Travel Diary*, note 25.
[31] *Versuch eines Beweises, dass die erste Sprache ihren Ursprung nicht von Menschen, sondern allein vom Schöpfer erhalten habe* (Berlin, 1766).
[32] v, 146; see also the *Ideas*, where Herder speaks of language as the 'prototype' of man's diverse creative endeavours (XIII, 367).
[33] v, 135; see also 25, 98–9, and XIII, 116–17.

principle of universality and the principle of individuality in the development of any given language. Since there was neither one language uniform throughout the world nor one that was exclusively peculiar to any single individual, the source of diversity had to be sought in the existence of distinct social entities, which constituted specific cultural configurations, in and through which individuals came to share a common language. Conversely, such socio-cultural entities only survived as communities *sui generis* as long as they succeeded in preserving their language as a collective inheritance.[34]

Language, culture, and community, then, are concepts that are inextricably interwoven in Herder's thinking. However, for the purpose of analysis we shall take each of these concepts in turn, chiefly drawing upon Herder's language essay except where references to his other writings seem more pertinent.

Herder draws a basic distinction between what he calls natural language on the one hand and human speech on the other. To agree about the animalistic elements in the former is one thing; to trace the origin of the latter, however, to these elements is quite another. Herder does not dispute that man expresses his strongest emotions in sounds and inarticulate cries in a manner indistinguishable from that of an animal. But what does this prove? Are not speech and sounds two totally different phenomena?[35] Take the sounds of natural language: the weak 'ah' is the sound of languishing love as well as of disheartening despair; the ardent 'oh' is a sudden outburst of joy as well as of explosive rage, of increasing admiration and also of overwhelming pity. Yet these sounds are not 'the main thread of human speech, not its roots, but merely the sap that vitalizes these'.[36] All animals give expression to their sensations, yet not even the most developed of them have as much as the beginnings of human language. Children utter emotional sounds not unlike those of animals, but is not the language they learn of a very different kind?[37]

That neither Condillac nor Rousseau could convincingly account for the transition from primitive sounds to intelligible speech did

---

[34] v, 140; see also 122–4 and 129–34. A nation's self-respect, Herder writes in the *Letters*, no doubt hinges on its ability and willingness to defend itself; but it is wholly inconceivable without its own language (xviii, 346–7).
[35] v, 20.   [36] v, 9.   [37] v, 18.

not surprise Herder since he saw no justification for postulating such a jump. Man was *fundamentally* different from the animal. It was utterly misleading to speak of him as a 'rational animal', as if reason were some sort of entity or 'faculty' that was simply superimposed on his animal nature. For it was not a matter of 'more or less', but rather a *qualitative* difference, in view of which man must be seen as a being *sui generis*, whose energies were developed in a wholly different direction. Herder warns, therefore, against using such terms as 'reason', 'intellect', or 'consciousness', to denote man's distinctiveness. For in using them we are not talking about reality, but in terms of disconnected phantom 'powers'. Man's capacity for speech is a function of the *totality* of his powers, the manifestation of the 'entire economy of his perceptive, cognitive and volitional nature'.[38] To this totality of interacting human energies Herder applies the term *Besonnenheit*, best rendered perhaps as 'reflective mind'.

By virtue of this wholly different direction of his entire energies man is no longer 'an infallible mechanism in the hands of Nature'.[39] Although not endowed at birth with conscious self-awareness (*Besinnung*), the innate possession of a reflective mind (*Besonnenheit*) enables him to attain *Besinnung*, that is, a state of development—denied to the animal—in which he can 'mirror himself within himself' and thus discover the nature and scope of his self-realization.[40] Whilst the animal is wholly a creature of nature, and confined to that sphere of activity for which it is equipped by its natural instincts, man, not thus determined, is also a creature of freedom. His perfectibility or corruptibility—a propensity not shared by the animal world—is closely bound up with this distinguishing feature.

[38] v, 28; Herder consistently adheres to this point throughout his writings. It receives its most systematic exposition in the *Metakritik*, but is already developed in the *Ideas*. 'We name the powers of thought', he writes there, 'according to their different relations, imagination and memory, intellect and judgment; we distinguish the impulse of desire from the pure will, and the power of sensation from that of movement. But the most casual reflection tells us that these faculties are not locally separated, as if judgment resided in one part of the brain, memory and imagination in another, the passions and sense perceptions in a third. The thought processes of our mind are undivided entities, producing in their totality the diverse effects or manifestations which we treat as separate faculties . . . Every creature is in all its parts one living co-operating whole' (XIII, 124 and 127).

[39] v, 28.   [40] *Ibid.* and 95.

Man alone has made a goddess of *choice* in place of *necessity* . . . he can weigh up good against evil, truth against falsehood; he can explore possibilities and choose between alternatives. . . . Even when he most despicably abuses his freedom, man is still king. For he can still choose, even though he chooses the worst; he can rule over himself, even if he legislates himself into a beast.[41]

The vital medium in and through which man can arrive at this consciousness of freedom is language. For the essence of language formation is not the creation of *external* sounds, but the *internal* genesis of word symbols. 'If this point about the genesis of language is missed', Herder warns, 'the area of error . . . is immense.'[42] Vocal expression is only superficially the same as language. Similarly, communication—as the term is generally understood—although it makes use of language, cannot be regarded as its primary source or function. It is Herder's central thesis that language is first and foremost an indispensable requirement for the operation of the human mind, an integral part of thought. Thinking is inconceivable without the use of distinguishing symbols. Language, therefore, 'must be regarded as inherent in, or the natural corollary of, the very first act of human reasoning'.[43] By 'reasoning', however, Herder, in contrast to Süssmilch and the Rationalists generally, does not mean a process separate from, or superior to, feeling and willing, nor does he regard it, as Rousseau did, as a mere 'potentiality'. Reasoning involves the human machine as a whole, the interplay of all senses, and not any one single sense organ or 'faculty' operating in isolation. The mind *in its entirety* works from obscure feelings to conscious awareness and, in arriving at this point, consciously experiences a sense of freedom for the first time.[44] Herder agrees that there are 'obscure

[41] XIII, 110 and 146–7.   [42] V, 46.   [43] V, 39.
[44] V, 42 and 95–6. Herder accords an important function in this process to the mediation of the ear between sight and touch. The ear is said to bring about the coincidence of these senses without which the mind could not perceive the most distinguishing characteristic of an object. This emphasis on the primacy of oral language and on the auditory element involved strikingly anticipates modern linguistic studies. The *Ideas* again stress that reason, like freedom, is not something that man possesses *a priori*. 'Far from being an innate automaton, as so many modern writings tend to imply', Herder remarks, 'reason in both its theoretical and practical manifestations, is nothing more than something *formed by experience* . . . an aggregate of the experiences and observations of the mind' (XIII, 145 and 345).

feelings' that may well be inexpressible, but, he asks, 'are those dim experiences the whole of man? Is a pedestal the whole statue? Is man's whole nature like an oyster only dimly aware of sensations?'[45] As soon as we *perceive* these sensations we do so by means of a *word*. Consequently, there is no conscious state of the human mind which is not actually defined in words.

Only the obscure visionary or the brute, the most abstract prophet or the monad lost in dreams might think entirely without the help of words. Such a condition is not possible in the human mind, neither in dreams nor in deranged minds. To assert that man feels with his mind and speaks as he thinks may sound rather bold; yet I believe it to be perfectly correct.[46]

The development of language, therefore, Herder concludes, is 'as natural to man as his nature'.[47] The first moment of conscious awareness also occasions the first internal emergence of language.

That these first moments of man's self-awareness and self-direction may be governed by Providence is an issue which the philosopher should not feel called upon to decide, for it is not the task of the philosopher to explain the supernatural. Philosophy, Herder points out, is not in a position to explain man's creation; it accepts him in the state in which he can first act voluntarily, and it interprets this situation on a purely human basis.[48] To attempt a solution to the problem of 'origin' would therefore by its very nature be a barren undertaking. That Herder was fully aware of this is evident enough from the content, though not from the title, of his treatise. The latter was clearly a misnomer and may well have been chosen with tongue in cheek. A more appropriate title would have been 'The Nature and Function of Language', for these were Herder's real concerns in what was undoubtedly the most comprehensive treatment of language up to his period.

The dearth of empirical data, Herder correctly realized, did not permit him to present a science of comparative languages. But he felt sufficiently assured that the process of language formation and language transmission was inseparable from the general development of human society. Far from having been 'invented' by some scholar in his ivory tower or by the man of leisure, 'free

[45] v, 100. [46] *Ibid.* [47] v, 101. [48] v, 95.

from urgent needs and provided with all the amenities of life',
language was rather the product of *social* needs, the corollary of
the strains and stresses inherent in the growth of social cultures.[49]
Herder takes up this theme (as so many others in the language
essay) in the *Ideas* and adds;

Were I to confine everything to the individual and deny the chain that
connects one to the other and to the whole, I should equally fail to
come to grips with the nature of man and his actual history. For no one
of us became man by himself alone.[50]

Language, therefore, is viewed by Herder as both the medium
through which man becomes conscious of his inner self *and* as
the key to the understanding of his outer relationships. It unites
him with, but it also differentiates him from others. Imperceptibly
it also links him with the past. By means of language he is able to
enter into communion with the way of thinking and feeling of his
progenitors, to take part as it were, in the workings of the ancestral
mind. He, in turn, again by means of language, perpetuates and
enriches the thoughts, feelings and prejudices of past generations
for the benefit of posterity. In this way language embodies the
living manifestation of historical continuity and the psychological
matrix in which man's awareness of his distinctive social heritage
is aroused and deepened.[51]

The mode of transmission, however, is not simply one of blind
imitation, but of *learning*. Herder makes some very interesting
observations on the nature of this transmitting process, both in the
language treatise and in the *Ideas*. 'Would a child', he asks,
'really *learn* anything by merely repeating words parrotlike without understanding their meaning?'[52] Monkeys always copy others,
but no monkey has ever *consciously* imitated. For if he had ever
done so, if he had ever appropriated to himself a single imitation
and deliberately perpetuated it in his species, in that same moment
he would have ceased to be a monkey. Despite his appearance of a
monkey and without uttering a single word, he would inwardly
have become a speaking man.[53]

---

[49] v, 140. The *Travel Diary* amply illustrates this point. See in particular IV,
422–6, and 428–31.
[50] XIII, 346. See also XIII, 159, 253, and 320–2. Herder anticipates this point in
almost identical terms in the language essay; e.g. v, 113, 114, 116.
[51] v, 117, 125 and 136.   [52] v, 41.
[53] v, 45. See also XIII, 142, 183 and 345–7.

In the *Ideas* Herder applies to this transmitting process the
term *tradition*. This is significant. For 'tradition' used in this
sense denotes not an accumulated *stock* of a set number of beliefs,
customs and ways of doing things, but an ongoing *process* which,
by its very nature (as Herder describes it) entails the continuous
merging of the old and the new. The 'imitator' must have powers
to receive and *convert* into his own nature what has been transmitted to him, just like the food he eats. What and how much he
receives, where he derives it from, and how he applies it to his own
use, is determined by his own receptive powers. It follows that
the inter-generational process of transmission involves not only
the assimilation but also the reappraisal of what is handed on, and
hence necessarily entails a certain dialectic in its operation. In
view of this, Herder speaks of the process as a continuous spiritual
genesis, investing it with both 'genetic' and 'organic' attributes.
It is genetic, by virtue of the manner in which the transmission
takes place, and organic by virtue of the manner in which that
which is being transmitted is assimilated and applied. The result
of this transmission at any given point of time and within any given
social context Herder calls *culture*.[54]

In his treatment of culture Herder makes no distinction
between 'material' and 'non-material' manifestations of man's
creativity; between what he *does* and what he *thinks*. Both are
integral parts of tradition, i.e. of the transmitting process between
the generations. Art, technology, industry and commerce form as
much part of culture as do ideas, beliefs, values and myths. For
culture is held to derive from both the physical and spiritual
nature of man. Formed to walk erect, man has his hands free to
manipulate objects and is thus capable of making tools, weapons
and objects of art. The skills he develops are in turn passed on and
developed further by successive generations.[55] In contrast to the
prevailing outlook of the Enlightenment which tended to identify
culture with intellectual and artistic sophistication, Herder applies
the concept to a wide and varied range of human phenomena,
insisting, however, that there is no single standard of 'culture' in
terms of which these could be judged. If, for example, we take the

[54] XIII, 348. Herder is using these terms in a metaphorical rather than a biological sense. This will become more clearly evident when we discuss his
theory of community.   [55] XIII, 137.

idea of European culture for our standard, we should not expect to find it applicable outside Europe, let alone use it as a criterion for distinguishing cultured from uncultured peoples, for there is no such thing as a people devoid of culture. The difference between so-called enlightened and unenlightened or cultured and uncultured peoples is a purely relative one, of degree and not of kind. 'The picture of nations has infinite shades, changing with place and time. But as in all pictures, everything depends on the point of view or perspective from which we examine it.'[56]

That Herder had no illusions about the enigmatic and elusive nature of the concept of culture is evident from the very first pages of the *Ideas*. 'Nothing', he writes, 'is more indeterminate than this word, and nothing more deceptive than its application to all nations and periods.'[57] In view of the diversity and complexity attending the term 'culture', he feels that it would be more accurate to speak of specific cultures (in the plural) rather than of culture in general. For this would enable one to pay heed to the distinctive culture patterns arising from social, economic, political or climatic differences. Clearly, Herder points out, there are diverse cultures existing side by side even within one nation, owing to differences in occupation, social class, religion and so on, and thus we can speak, for example, of the culture of intellectuals as distinct from the culture of craftsmen and traders.[58] Likewise, the same occupations may reveal entirely different cultural traits among different nations.

It is customary to divide the nations of the world into hunters, fishermen, shepherds and farmers, not only to determine accordingly their

---

[56] XIII, 348. The very thought of a superior European culture Herder considered as a 'blatant insult to the majesty of Nature' (XIII, 342). See also XIII, 370–2. Herder reiterates this point in the *Letters*: 'There is no such thing as a specially favoured nation (*Favoritvolk*) on earth . . . there cannot, therefore, be any order of rank . . . the negro is as much entitled to think the white man degenerate as the white man is to think of the negro as a black beast . . . Least of all must we think of European culture as a universal standard of human values. To apply such a standard is not just misleading; it is meaningless. For "European culture" is a mere abstraction, an empty concept. Where does, or did, it actually exist in its entirety? In which nation? In which period? Besides, it can scarcely pose as the most perfect manifestation of man's culture, having—who can deny?—far too many deficiencies, weaknesses, perversions and abominations associated with it. Only a real misanthrope could regard European culture as the universal condition of our species. The culture of *man* is not the culture of the *European*; it manifests itself according to place and time in *every* people' (XVIII, 247–9).

[57] XIII, 4.   [58] XIV, 34–5.

24

level of cultural development, but also to suggest that culture as such is a necessary corollary of a given occupation or mode of life. This would be most admirable, provided the diverse modes of life were defined in the first place. Since these, however, vary with almost every region and for the most part overlap, it is exceedingly difficult to apply such a classification with accuracy. The Greenlander who harpoons the whale, hunts the reindeer and kills the seal, is engaged in both hunting and fishing, yet in quite a different manner from that of the Negro fisher or the Arancoan hunter. The Bedouin and the Mongol, the Lapp and the Peruvian are shepherds; but how greatly do they differ from each other, with one pasturing camels, the other horses, the third reindeer, and the last alpacas and llamas. The farmers of Whidoh are as unlike those of Japan as the merchants of England are to those of China.[59]

Moreover, different forms of culture may develop at different rates, some attaining their optimum level or 'maximum'—as Herder puts it—before others. He illustrates this point by comparing the political culture—a term which Herder seems to have been the first to use—of the Greeks and the Hebrews.[60] Owing to these differences in the form and rate of development of social cultures, the degree of balance or integration between cultures, especially within given political entities, becomes a crucial consideration. It is therefore of interest to find Herder remarking that it is not the *number* of cultural maxima, nor the degree of perfection achieved in any single cultural sphere, but rather the *balanced relationship* of a people's diverse social cultures that is *politically* most significant.[61] When certain forms of culture are widely out of step with other forms, in particular if 'techniques' and 'values' markedly diverge, alienation results.[62]

[59] XIII, 310.
[60] Unlike the Greeks, Herder observes, the Hebrews failed to attain maturity in their political culture (XIV, 67). See also Herder's remarks on diverse political cultures in the *Travel Diary*.
[61] XIV, 149.
[62] Herder gives a vivid illustration of alienation in his description of the encounter between natives and Europeans. 'Wherever natives and Europeans met, the latter were treated with awe and deference because they appeared superior by virtue of their tools and weapons. But when the natives realized that the European was vulnerable, mortal, liable to disease, and indeed inferior in prowess to themselves, they reacted differently. They continued to dread the European's techniques, but they slew the European; *for his techniques were no part of himself*' (XIII, 371).

Although Herder stressed the closest interrelationship—including conflict—between material and non-material elements in the development of cultures, he was particularly interested in the latter, that is, in the role of ideas, beliefs and values. What struck him most forcibly was the intermixture of notions that are rationally analyzable and/or empirically verifiable with those that are neither, yet equally potent in moulding social cultures. Words, he observes in the essay on language, do not merely describe or classify certain objects; they also transmit feelings, and they do this not only explicitly but also implicitly *via* emotional overtones which they aquire in the process of transmission. In picking up his first words, the infant imperceptibly absorbs the emotional flavour given to them by his parents. He repeats therefore, with every newly acquired word not only certain sounds but also certain feelings. This is why we associate the strongest sentiments with our mother tongue. It is the medium by which our minds and tongues were first moulded and by which images were transplanted from the hearts of our parents into our own. Every word we learn during this early phase carries with it secondary associations which we re-kindle in our minds every time we use the word. Frequently it is these secondary ideas which sway the mind more powerfully than the main concepts with which they were associated, and thus vitally determine the peculiar character of a family, kinship or national mode of thought. Indeed, these 'companions of the dawn of life' permeate social cultures far more than we are able (or willing) to recognize, and frequently prove more effective than 'all political contracts and theories recounted by the philosopher'.[63] 'Reason', he records in his *Travel Diary*, 'a later and ephemeral manifestation, cannot destroy the dreams and deepseated beliefs of childhood.'[64]

These first images of the human mind help to support and perpetuate prejudice and myths and induce man to revel in the miraculous. How relative, indeed, Herder notes, is the question of probability. So much depends on our first impressions; their strength, form and multiplicity, the duration and frequency of subsequent experiences, on chance happenings and circumstances in our immediate social milieu.

[63] V, 118.   [64] IV, 359.

One people's estimate of probability is different in both form and degree from another's. We may laugh at Greek mythology and yet each of us, perhaps, makes up his own. The common people have a mythology in a thousand things. Is their sense of what is improbable the same as that of the sceptical philosopher or the inquiring scientist?[65]

The mythology of a people is for Herder above all an index of the distinctive way it views nature, and he sees it as a function of such interrelated variables as economic factors, climate, and a people's creative imagination. He wholly disagrees with the 'rationalist' thesis that magicians, shamans and priests invented myths to blind the people.

By dismissing them as cheats one is inclined to think that one has explained everything. They may well have been cheats in many or most places, but this should not induce us to forget that they themselves were people too, and the dupes of myths older than themselves.[66]

Herder deplores that so little has been done to investigate myths and religions as sociological phenomena although he concedes that of all the powers of the mind the imagination is the most difficult to explore.[67]

Undoubtedly the most significant feature characterizing Herder's conception of culture—as of history and politics—is the notion of relativism and the admission of the plurality of values which it entails. He is determined to keep aesthetic considerations and value judgments out of the discussion. Myths, beliefs, idiosyncracies in language—such as synonyms, genders, modes of address etc.—diverse achievements in art and the sciences, are all seen as functions of diverse social cultures without the slightest hint of superiority or inferiority being attributed to one or the other. The same art that raised Grecian palaces is held to be displayed by the savage in the construction of his forest hut.[68] Each level of culture reveals to Herder the operation of one and the same creative force: the *striving for development*.

Unlike the animal which is perfect within its limited range of existence, man is the most helpless and ignorant creature when

---

[65] IV, 361.   [66] XIII, 307.

[67] *Ibid.* Herder's early interest in the nature of the imagination is evident from his observations in the *Travel Diary*. See the section on 'Reflections on Myth, Prejudice and the Imagination' (IV, 356–65, 448–60). See also as regards Herder's treatment of religion XIII, 162–4.   [68] V, 142.

coming into the world. Yet from the very first moment that he learns to come to grips with his environment he does so in a manner wholly different from the animal. By virtue of the posses-sion of a mind—and the capacity for speech which this implies for Herder—he perceives nature not directly but through the mediation of ideas which he is in a continuous process of forming. What is more, he learns nothing for one moment only, but connects everything with what he already knows in order to store it up for future use. Also, as he collects impressions, he incessantly evaluates the supply collected. His mind not only receives stimuli but also reacts to them, and, in so doing, *creates* a situation that has not existed before. Thus the activity of the mind entails by its very operation a continuous and cumulative process.

One activity is increased by another; builds upon, or evolves from, the foregoing. . . . Such a chain runs through the life of man until death. We are always growing out of childhood, however old we may be; we are always in motion, restless and dissatisfied. The essence of life is never fruition, but continuous becoming, and we have never been men until we have lived our life to the end. The bee, on the other hand, was a perfect bee when building her first cell.[69]

Man's striving for development, accordingly, would seem to be analyzable into four closely inter-connected elements: (1) the imperfection inherent in the human condition; (2) the recognition of this condition; (3) the ability to transform this condition; and (4) the capacity for transforming it in a chosen direction. The two decisive elements implicit in Herder's concept of human develop-ment, then, are man's sense of imperfection and his sense of freedom. Without either of these, culture would be inconceivable.

We may deplore at times, as Kant did, Herder's failure to offer clear definitions of his categories of thought, but we can scarcely complain of a dearth of indications concerning his conception of culture or accuse him of obscuring the complexities inherent in this notion. In both his philosophy of language and his philosophy of history Herder shows himself quite alert to the different modes and dimensions of interaction and to the crucial question about the ways in which causal determinants relate and interact in any given culture. He was intent, however, not only to provide a

[69] v, 98. See also XIII, 182.

sociological and historical analysis of culture, but also to advance a theory of community in which 'language' and 'becoming'—the key concepts of his philosophy of human development—would jointly supply a basis for the most 'natural' unit of social and political association.

Although the development of a community's distinct collective consciousness, to which Herder also refers in terms of 'national character' and 'national spirit', forms one of the central themes of the *Ideas*, it already engages his interest in the essay on language where, significantly enough, it is closely linked with the phenomenon of conflict.

Far from advocating war as the teacher of man—as some political Romanticists did—Herder nonetheless recognized that conflict can perform a positive function in strengthening the internal cohesion of collectivities. 'The more a group is threatened' he remarks to this effect, 'the more it will turn in upon itself and the closer will be the ties of its members. To avert dispersion they will do everything to strengthen their tribal roots.'[70] This does not mean simply or chiefly, however, that they will adopt warlike postures, but rather that they will seek to maintain their sense of collective identity by treasuring and perpetuating the memory of a common past and all that this entails. They will extol the deeds of their forefathers, observe tribal customs and rituals and, above all, preserve the distinctiveness of their own language.[71]

It was these essentially spiritual elements which constituted for Herder the *organic* forces (*Kräfte*) of social and political cohesion, since they united men from *within*. He saw therefore in most of the contemporary dynastic states mere artefacts, lifeless assemblies of aggregates whose parts, though they were functionally related like those of an organism, nevertheless depended in their operation on an *external* source of power. A mechanism, moreover, is the

---

[70] V, 141.
[71] *Ibid.*; see also *Yet Another Philosophy*: 'If, in this development of particular national tendencies towards particular forms of national happiness, the distance between the nations grows too great, we find prejudices arising . . . Similarly, prejudices, mob judgment and narrow nationalism, arise when the dispositions and spheres of happiness of two nations collide. But prejudice is good, in its time and place, for happiness may spring from it. It urges nations to converge upon their centre [and] attaches them more firmly to their roots' (v, 510).

product of manufacture, whereas an organism is the product of growth. Activity in the latter is self-generated: in the former it is not. A social and political whole resulting from organization from outside, therefore, whilst it may qualify for recognition as a 'body politic', is nonetheless an artificial whole as compared to a community bound together by the inner consciousness of sharing a common cultural heritage. Neither iron and blood nor political fiat and administrative manipulation can engender such an inner consciousness. A state can perish, but the *Volk* remains intact provided it retains the consciousness of its distinctive cultural traditions.[72]

At this point it would seem pertinent to enquire more closely into the nature of the organic model which Herder used as his heuristic construct. In particular we want to establish (*a*) how closely his organistic paradigm can be said to approximate to an actual organism, and (*b*) to what extent the biological metaphor sheds light on the ideas he wished to convey when he applied it to *Volk*, his basic unit of social and political community life.

It will help our enquiry, I think, to adduce here the distinction St Thomas made between a substantial whole and an accidental whole.[73] A composite, yet coherent substance, such as the human body, represents for him a substantial whole. An accidental whole, on the other hand, is not a thing or substance at all, but rather (to use the terminology of psychology) a *Gestalt*, or configuration, contingent on the relation between the constituents forming it. A political community for St Thomas is not a physical body or unitary thing, and hence not a substantial whole. Its coherence and unity is contingent on the peculiar relationship of its members. It is they who are the substances. Men are not material particles forming a physical mass, but discrete individual entities. St Thomas, in advancing his distinction between substantial and accidental wholes, is no less anxious than Aristotle was to point to the obvious difference between the concrete unity of a physical body and the discrete unity of the body politic.

---

[72] xiv, 87; see also xiii, 172–3. Herder makes here an interesting distinction between different levels of a political system. A more detailed account of his contribution to nationalist thought will be found in Carlton J. H. Hayes, 'Contributions of Herder to the Doctrine of Nationalism', *The American Historical Review*, xxxii (1927), 719–36; and Robert Ergang, *Herder and the foundations of German nationalism* (New York, 1931).

[73] I am indebted on this point to Thomas Gilbey's *Between community and society* (London, 1953), esp. pp. 113–23.

Herder, too, seems perfectly aware of the difference between the organic unity of a physical whole and that of a social whole. His conception of the *Volk* community closely corresponds to St Thomas's accidental whole or to Aristotle's notion of the state as a composite. The *Volk* is an organic whole by virtue of the peculiar interrelationship of its members which alone confers upon it a *Gestalt* of its own, a unity *sui generis*. Indeed, in order to underline the composite nature of a social whole, Herder speaks not in terms of a single organism, but rather in terms of a complex of organisms, each of which is an active whole in itself comparable to the Leibnizian monad. Unlike the Leibnizian monad, however, the Herderian monad *has* windows. This is an important qualification. For though the individual units of the whole are distinct entities, deriving their source of activity from within, they are nonetheless considered by Herder as being not wholly self-contained but interconnected. Moreover, the nature of their interconnection is not that of an external link, but rather embodies an *internal* propensity towards interconnection and interaction with other units. In the case of a *Volk*, the decisive interconnecting link is the consciousness of a shared culture and historical tradition.

A *Volk*, accordingly, is not a substantive entity in any biological sense, a *thing* with a corporate existence of its own over and above, or separate from, the individuals who compose it, but a relational *event*, a historical and cultural continuum. An individual's consciousness of belonging to a distinct community, likewise, is not a biological fact, but a derivative social and cultural process, the result of the continuous interaction—in both a temporal and a spatial sense—between the self and the socio-cultural setting of its environment. The individual, far from being enclosed within himself or genetically constituted to be a German, or Italian, or Greek *a priori*, derives the awareness of himself as a member of a particular national community from the social milieu into which he is born, from his contact with the world around him.[74]

What is more, and this too is of crucial significance, Herder's

---

[74] Herder's theory of climate—which in several important respects transcends Montesquieu's doctrine of environmental causation—is particularly relevant to this passage, although, once again, the language treatise is pivotal. For further reference regarding Herder's philosophy of organism see his *Metakritik* (1799) a work that was intended as a criticism of Kant's *Critique of Pure Reason* (see esp. XXI, 152 and 182).

'holism' comprises multiplicity and diversity as well as unity. Indeed, uniqueness and diversity are posited as the necessary condition for interaction between constituents of a social whole. That the social realm, no less than the world of nature, consists of diverse interrelated and interacting organisms, each of which is necessary to the whole, is the principal notion of Herder's theory of social organism. It clearly reflects his concern to forge a synthesis between the individualist ideology of the Enlightenment and his own philosophy of community. In spite of Herder's use of biological similes—particularly in the *Ideas*—his main purpose is to identify socio-cultural traits which could form the basis for the existence and continuity of a distinct community. It is not in racial characteristics or in inherited physical factors as such that he sees the determinants of a *Volk*, but in language, traditions and customs, folklore and folksongs and the numerous other things included in what Sumner called 'folkways'.

Herder wished to emphasize that for a political community to be an organic social whole that would endure in time, it had to be the result of spontaneous *growth* out of, and within, a specific cultural environment. Although he applied biological terms like 'genetic' and 'organic' to this process of growth, he did not think of it in an essentially biological sense. He held the transmission of social cultures to be genetic because *Bildung* (i.e. education in the widest sense) made it possible to link a *Volk's* cultural heritage from one generation to another, and organic by virtue of the creative manner in which it was assimilated and reapplied. The very fact that he explicitly identifies this process of transmission as a *spiritual* genesis[75] leaves no doubt whatsoever that Herder's paradigm of the organically integrated community—which he opposed to the mechanistic model of the bureaucratic state—was in essence a normative rather than a positive form of organicism, if I may borrow Werner Stark's classification.[76] That Herder nowhere stipulates a subordinate organic relationship such as that of a leaf to the tree, or of a limb to the human body, is also significant, for it reveals a remarkable degree of consistency between his imagery and the idea of functional co-ordination which is central to his advocacy of a non-hierarchical form of social pluralism.

[75] XIV, 84.
[76] Werner Stark, *The fundamental forms of social thought* (London, 1962), see esp. chaps. II and III.

CHANGE AND PROGRESS

Underlying Herder's interest in social and political cultures was a twofold quest, the desire to come to grips with the forces shaping human history, and the desire to re-define the nature of the historical process itself. Coupled with, if not implicit in, this quest was Herder's dissatisfaction with contemporary approaches to the study of history and politics. *Yet Another Philosophy*, the treatise *On the Reciprocal Influence of Government and the Sciences*, and his most ambitious work, the *Ideas for a Philosophy of the History of Mankind*, sprang in varying degrees from the same polemical impulse which prompted the writing of the essay *On the Origin of Language*. Moreover, the chief targets of Herder's criticisms were the very men whose ideas formed the earliest influences on his historical and political thinking, such as Voltaire, Rousseau, Montesquieu and Kant.[77] At the same time the considerable degree of consistency that characterizes Herder's thought in these writings does not suggest that his ideas were a reflection of merely momentary or passing moods, or that the polemical impulse was the sole source of his intellectual contribution to historical and political thinking. Not only can a number of dominant themes be traced as far back as 1769 when Herder sketched many of his later works (in the *Travel Diary*), but they also constitute the logical corollary of his organismic *Weltanschauung*. It would, in a sense, not be

[77] Even when Herder claimed to be a follower of such thinkers as Spinoza, Leibniz, Shaftesbury, or Georg Hamann, this did not always prevent him from applying their views in a markedly divergent manner. Where the parallelism of thought, especially on such questions as the origin of language, national cultures and historical relativism, seems closest, there is some doubt concerning the degree of direct or indirect influence. I am, of course, referring to Vico whom Herder did not mention in his published work until 1797, and even then the reference, whilst eloquent in praise, does not suggest that he was very familiar with Vico's thought, let alone conscious of its similarity to his own (XVIII, 246). It would seem that Herder arrived at his philosophy of history quite independently of Vico, but the matter merits further enquiry. (In this connection, see Robert T. Clark, Jr.'s searching article 'Herder, Cesarotti and Vico', in *Studies in Philology*, XLIV (1947), 645–71.) On the question of Herder's intellectual background in general, the *Travel Diary* is most instructive. See also Robert T. Clark Jr, *Herder, his life and thought*, Berkeley and Los Angeles, 1955, ch. 1, Barnard, *Herder's social and political thought*, ch. 1, and Isaiah Berlin, 'Herder and the enlightenment' in Earl R. Wasserman (ed.), *Aspects of the eighteenth century* (Baltimore, 1965), pp. 49–53.

wrong to say that Herder's originality lies in the very manner in which his own thought epitomizes the dialectic mode of interaction between the old and the new which he applied to the historical process as a whole.

Herder's opposition to the more facile forms of rationalism, its *a priorism*, its abstractionism, its love of system-building, its dogmatism and, above all, its 'faculty' psychology, is already evident in his prize essay on language.[78] It stems from the conviction that things, above all, human events, are far too interrelated to lend themselves to arbitrary separation. In conformity with his organismic conception, Herder views social and political cultures as wholes or 'systems', without however denying the individuality of their constituents and the complexity of their interrelationship. Moreover, since he thinks of wholes in terms of *events* rather than in terms of *substances*—as we had occasion to observe earlier—the existence of wholes is inconceivable unless 'existence' is envisaged in the form of continuous activity. The problem of *unity* accordingly, is, for Herder, inseparable from the problem of *continuity*. The relation between the 'parts' and the 'whole' and that between the 'now' and the 'later', constitutes the heart of the matter. As Herder correctly realizes, a philosophy of history, or, indeed, the very notion of history, is inconceivable, unless change, in spite of discontinuities, time lags, and incongruities, also entails an essential element of continuity.[79]

The central thesis of Herder's philosophy of history and politics is that, metaphorically speaking, the road from diversity to unity, from the fortuitous accidents of change to the purposeful continuity of human activity, is a tortuous one and not an obvious unilinear path of 'progress'. But, in order to establish this thesis, Herder felt he had to clear some undergrowth first. *Yet Another Philosophy* was to do the clearing.

---

[78] It is worth noting, however, that the German Enlightenment (*Aufklärung*) was by no means as rationalistically oriented as it is frequently thought. The break with the orthodox rationalist tradition can be traced to such leading *Aufklärer* as Christian Thomasius (1655–1728), commonly regarded as the 'father' of the *Aufklärung*, Christian Wolff (1679–1754), and Moses Mendelssohn (1729–86). For an elaboration of this point see F. M. Barnard, 'Christian Thomasius: Enlightenment and bureaucracy', *American Political Science Review*, LIX (1965), 430–8.

[79] XIII, 345.

Its starting point is the repudiation of the prevalent notion of the immutability of human nature. With the possible exception of Adam Ferguson—whose historical works reveal a remarkable degree of sociological insight—even 'relativist' writers such as Helvetius and Montesquieu and 'positivists' such as Hume, never doubted that, as Voltaire put it, 'man in general has always been what he is'.[80] Herder could never accept this proposition. As early as 1769 he laid down what remained the basic principle of his relativism. 'Human nature under diverse climates is never wholly the same.'[81] *Yet Another Philosophy* is first and foremost an elaboration of this principle. If, Herder asks, we can scarcely express the individuality of one man, determine what specifically distinguishes him, how he feels and experiences things, why should we presume to be able to survey 'an ocean of entire peoples, times and countries' at one glance, with two or three descriptive categories, and without making the slightest effort to enter into the spirit of their thoughts and deeds?[82] Why should we take for granted that their beliefs were the same as ours and their standard of happiness identical to our own? Should we not rather remind ourselves that 'human nature is not the vessel of an absolute, unchanging and independent happiness, as defined by the philosopher; [that] everywhere it attracts that measure of happiness of which it is capable; [that] it is a pliant clay which assumes a different shape under different needs and circumstances'?[83] Who can, therefore, compare the different forms of satisfaction perceived by men in different times and different worlds? Who can compare the shepherd and the Oriental patriarch, the ploughman and the artist, the sailor, the merchant, and so on? Each man, each nation, each period, has its centre of happiness within itself, just as every sphere has its centre of gravity.[84]

This principle of plurality has revolutionary implications. We can no longer think in terms of an ideal man or of an ideal people, or, indeed, of one absolute standard of value. Each historical event, each generation, each culture and civilization carries within itself its own immanent validity. It follows, likewise, that it is both pointless and presumptuous to judge the past, its errors and achievements in the light of some supra-historical absolute or in

---

[80] Voltaire, *Oeuvres*, Lequieu ed. (Paris, 1820), XI, 19.
[81] IV, 38. [82] V, 502. [83] V, 509. [84] *Ibid.*

terms of the standards that happen to be prevalent at any particular time or place. Each event has to be viewed within the context of its total cultural setting, and that may mean including features which seem of little or no value or significance to the present-day historian. Did not, or could not, a patriarch have other tendencies besides those which we attribute to him?[85] Unless we make every effort to understand the values that are operative in a given historical context we shall scarcely be able to understand the facts. For 'facts' and 'values' are inseparable. A chronicle of causally unrelated facts is not history. We want to know not only *what* happened, but *why* it happened as it did. Historical *understanding*, therefore, presupposes more than the collection of data. To grasp the purposive direction of past events, we must attempt to relive them, to feel ourselves into the situation surrounding them, taking into account the times and circumstances. This requires both empathy and analytical imagination. At every step we have to ask ourselves if events could have occurred differently than they did before we apportion praise or blame. Herder insists on a careful blending of factual enquiry and imaginative theoretical interpretation. The historian must guard against naïve factual empiricism, no less than against drawing glib analogies—since no two moments in the world are ever identical—or the fitting of facts to *a priori* theories.

The philosopher of history cannot start off with an abstraction; his views must be firmly grounded in historical facts. At the same time he has to connect the innumerable facts within some generalizing framework in order to arrive at relatively meaningful conclusions.[86]

Furthermore, recognition of the multiplicity of values necessarily implies the acceptance of their possible incompatibility. In other words, tensions and conflicts must be accepted as the price of diversity. Their recognition, rather than their denial, affords the only possibility of coming to grips with human history and human affairs generally. *Yet Another Philosophy* emphasizes the difference between historical constellations and logical systems. To project the latter into the former seemed to Herder the malaise of contemporary historiography. To explain away all 'prejudices', moral inconsistencies, and irrationalities as deviations, regrettable

---

[85] V, 503.   [86] XIII, 290; see also V, 504.

aberrations, intended to serve subsequent generations as lessons, was to misconceive the very nature of history, its manifest richness and variety.

A nation may have the most sublime virtues in some respects and blemishes in others, show irregularities and reveal the most astonishing contradictions and incongruities. These will be all the more startling to anyone carrying within himself an idealized shadow-image of virtue according to the manual of his century, one so filled with philosophy that he expects to find the whole universe in a grain of sand. But for him who wants to understand the human heart within the living circumstances, such irregularities and contradictions are perfectly human.[87]

Arbitrary verdicts of praise and blame in the light of some invariant law of morals or psychology are, therefore, out of place. Good is diffused in a thousand different forms; the summit borders on the valley, and defects and virtues always dwell together under one human roof. Paris is not Europe, and Europe is not the entire universe. What an abyss there is between even the finest general truth and the least of its applications to a given sphere, to a particular purpose, and in any one specific manner![88]

Finally, if plurality is the operative principle of history and human affairs generally, it cannot be excluded from the sphere of politics. If it is absurd to apply absolute standards in the former, it is equally absurd to speak in terms of a best or ideal form of constitution in the latter. Montesquieu is taken to task for applying empty generalizations to so varied and complex a phenomenon as the political organization of man and reducing the infinite multiplicity of its manifestations into three neat heaps. All that man has achieved—or failed to achieve—in ordering his life in society is made to hang on 'three weak nails'.[89] It is Herder's ambition to show that governments, like other human institutions, are subject to continuous change, that such change involves a host of interactions of varying forms and degrees—and not merely the influence of climate—and that arbitrary labels such as 'despotism', 'mon-

[87] v, 506.
[88] v, 508, 510, 511, 541, 542. Clearly Herder sees interpretative understanding rather than the formulation of generalizations or causal laws as the crucial characteristic of historical method, or, indeed, the method of all social enquiry. [89] v, 566.

37

archy' or 'republic' not only do scant justice to political reality, but also positively distort it. Both the treatise on government and the *Ideas* aim to remedy this, the former by dealing specifically with the interaction of government and the sciences, the latter by viewing social and political development within the interrelated totality of physical, biological, psychological and historical forces. In both, Herder's relativistic principle of plurality fully comes into play.

The validity of Herder's theory of correlation between political development and the development of the arts and sciences may well be a matter of debate. What, however, chiefly bears on our purpose here is his approach to the problem of change. Let us note first how Herder himself poses the problem. What caused, he asks, the irregular and fitful changes in human endeavour in different parts of the world? Was it climate? If so, how did it come about that countries where the sciences flourished and faded changed their climate not at all, or only slightly? Egypt, Rome and Greece stand where they stood, yet how different is the condition of their literature, sciences and arts to what it once was! And if it was not climate that had altered appreciably, was it perhaps national character? If the latter is defined in terms of physical heredity, it must, Herder feels, be taken as a constant. Neither climate as such, then, nor national origin, is held to constitute an independent determinant of historical change. Instead Herder suggests a mode of interaction that is at once highly imaginative and most instructive. 'Climate', he says,

may be regarded as the soil in which the seed of human knowledge grows, where it thrives better in one place than in another; national character may more closely determine the kind of seed; whilst the political constitution of a nation in its widest sense—its laws, government, customs, and civic traditions—undoubtedly represents the close tilling of the soil, the sowing of the seed and the influence of all those natural factors without which nothing can prosper and grow.[90]

This formulation of interaction is of interest not only because it illustrates in a most vivid manner Herder's conception of politics as political culture, but also because it reveals an unusual

[90] IX, 311, 312.

perceptiveness of the distinction between 'interaction' in the strict sense and 'interaction' in the broader sense of the word. Clearly, 'interaction' in the former sense presupposes some form of *human* activity (including thought and its product, ideas), for only men are capable of inter-*acting* within any setting of human relationships, either 'horizontally', in so far as at any given time men influence each other directly or indirectly, or 'vertically', in so far as this influence involves a temporal dimension. On the other hand we may speak of 'interaction' in a broader (and less precise) sense when referring to interrelations, interconnections, or forms of interdependence, where the reciprocal influence is that between a human and a non-human factor. From Herder's formulation it is evident that interaction in the strict sense is confined to distinctly human spheres involving the operation of such man-made factors as laws, customs, civic traditions and administrative decisions, whilst climatic and biological influences come within the category of interaction in the broader sense. That Herder made this distinction quite deliberately is borne out also by his treatment of climate and the 'genetic force' in the *Ideas*, and there can be little doubt that in both instances he was anxious to refute Montesquieu's theory of correlation between climate and government which he considered grossly oversimplified.

We shall return to Herder's ideas on political development when we come to discuss his conception of progress. At this point it may be desirable to inquire more closely into Herder's theory of historical causation and his attempt to equate change with continuous interaction.

The keynote of Herder's theory of causation is the notion of 'becoming'. In Herder's use this notion has both a metaphysical and an empirical connotation. Metaphysically, 'becoming' is seen as the unfolding of something that in itself is not susceptible to observation or further analysis. To this irreducible 'something' Herder applies the term genetic force or energy (*Kraft*). It signifies the prime and *inner* source of all that is alive and the dynamic principle of its continued existence.[91] Whilst it is ration-

---

[91] XIII, 172–88 and 274–7. For a fuller discussion of the notion of *Kraft* see Robert T. Clark, Jr., 'Herder's conception of Kraft', *Publications of the Modern Language Association of America*, LVII (1942), 737–52 and Barnard, *Herder's social and political thought*, pp. 38–9 and 44–53 where Herder's views are compared with those of Rousseau, Locke, Spinoza and Leibniz.

ally inexplicable in terms of its origins, it can nonetheless, Herder maintains, be observed and described by virtue of the manifestations which embody the process of its functioning. Its effects, therefore, are the proper subject of empirical enquiry. And since these effects are identified with a *process*, namely the process of continuous development, they necessarily entail the dimension of time. It follows that the empirical enquiry applicable to the study of becoming, must be historical in orientation. Now, in human, as distinct from natural, history, the *direction* which this process assumes is not purely, or even chiefly, the product of biological, physical, or geographical determinants. Man, by virtue of the characteristics that distinguish him from plants and animals, is capable not only of recognizing a chain of development, but also of consciously participating in the forging of this chain. At the same time, the very characteristics that distinguish man from other living creatures make the existence of a chain in which he forms a link indispensable, since his development is inseparable from the social heritage into which he is born.

In this lies the principle of the history of mankind, without which no history could exist. Did man receive everything from himself, and develop everything independently of external circumstances, we might have a history of *one* man, but not of man as a species. Since our specific character derives from being born almost without instinct, it is only by training and experience that our lives as men take shape; they determine both the perfectibility and the corruptibility of our race.[92]

Hence, Herder concludes, the history of mankind is necessarily a relational 'whole', a chain formed from the first link to the last by the moulding process of socialization and tradition.

But, granted that human development or 'becoming' assumes the form of interaction within a social and cultural continuum as Herder describes it, what causes it to be characterized by change, if by 'change' we mean the coming into being of new and specifically *different* situations or ideas and not merely the replacement of one set of conditions by a new set of the same specific type, or simply the biological changes associated with ageing in any natural process? The answer to this question must be sought in Herder's theory of culture transmission. We have

[92] XIII, 345.

indicated earlier that the two operative terms in this theory, 'genetic' and 'organic', are not to be understood in a biological sense. This is further borne out by Herder's discussion of the 'conflict' between climate and the 'genetic force' in the *Ideas*. He goes out of his way to assure us that by insisting that the genetic force is the mother of all creations on earth to which climate can only contribute, favourably or unfavourably,[93] he is not thinking in terms of racial characteristics. Much to the chagrin of Kant, he bluntly declares that he has no use for the concept of race.

Some . . . have thought fit to employ the term *races* for four or five divisions, according to regions of origin or complexion. I see no reason for employing this term. Race refers to a difference of origin, which . . . either does not exist or which comprises in each of these regions or complexions the most diverse 'races'. For every distinct community is a *nation*, having its own national culture as it has its own language. The climate, it is true, may imprint on each its peculiar stamp, or it may spread over it a slight veil, without destroying, however, its original national character. . . . In short, there are neither four or five races, nor exclusive varieties on this earth. Complexions run into each other; forms follow the genetic character; and in *toto* they are, in the final analysis, but different shades of the same great picture which extends through all ages and all parts of the earth. Their study, therefore, properly forms no part of biology or systematic natural history, but belongs rather to the anthropological history of man.[94]

It is evident, then, that Herder identifies the manifestation of the 'genetic force' in social development with distinct *cultures*, that is, with the result of an historical process in which ideas, beliefs, and ways of doing things, are passed on within a given collectivity of men characterized chiefly by a common language.

If we also bear in mind that the adjective 'organic' refers to the dialectic mode in the transmission of social cultures, which implies, as we noted, not only the acceptance, but also the re-appraisal and challenging of what is passed on by successive generations, it is not difficult to see that change is, so to speak, a

[93] XIII, 274.
[94] XIII, 257-8. I have quoted this passage in full because, surprisingly enough, Herder has been presented as a racialist by some commentators. Herder's distaste for the very concept of race provoked a rather severe stricture from Kant who castigated him for his 'inadequate and unsympathetic treatment of race' (Kant's review of the *Ideas* in the *Allgemeine Literaturzeitung* of 15 Nov. 1785).

built-in characteristic of historical interaction. It is at once part of a given continuum *and* the instrument of its transformation. This being so, the factors operative in historical causation are as much temporal antecedents as emerging directional goals. To explain an historical process we must, accordingly, not only look backwards to that which occasioned its coming into being, but also forwards to the end towards which it is tending. For 'becoming' not only reflects its past but also foreshadows its future.[95] Whether or not this dialectic interaction of the old and the new can be equated with 'progress', in the sense of a continuous amelioration of the human condition, is another matter. We shall see from the next section that Herder had serious doubts about the validity of such an equation.

To assume that human destiny is forever marching forward in giant steps; to believe that depravity is a necessary precondition for improvement and order; to argue that there must be shadow in order that there be light, that to unravel the knot of events it must first be tied, that to produce a clear nectar, fermentation must first remove the impurities: these were the assumptions which aroused Herder's ire against what he called the 'pet philosophy' of his century. According to this philosophy, 'so many corners had first to be forcibly rubbed off before the round, smooth, pretty thing that we are could appear'.[96] According to this philosophy, too, progress is a continuous advance towards greater virtue and happiness. To support this idea, facts are embellished or invented, contrary facts minimized or suppressed, words are taken for works, enlightenment for happiness, and greater sophistication for virtue. The result is the fiction of the 'general, progressive amelioration of the world' which few believe, least of all the true student of history and the human heart.[97] No doubt, Herder scathingly adds, we derive much pride and comfort from this fiction, for does it not conjure up in almost superhuman splendour a world of

[95] For a more detailed analysis particularly of Herder's approach to the problem of determinism see G. A. Wells, *Herder and after* (The Hague, 1959), pp. 262–9; and F. M. Barnard, 'Herder's treatment of causation and continuity in history', *Journal of the History of Ideas*, XXIV (1963), 197–212. See also Lewis W. Spitz, 'Natural law and the theory of history', *Journal of the History of Ideas*, XVI (1955), 453–75, for a most penetrating study of Herder's conception of historical laws.

[96] V, 527.   [97] V, 511.

infinite achievements, a century superior to all the previous centuries? We look down on Orientals, Greeks, Romans, especially on the Gothic barbarians of the Middle Ages! From what a height we look down upon the world! How diffused our enlightenment becomes with every day! Soon there will be European colonies everywhere! Savages all over the world will become ripe for conversion to our culture and become good, strong and happy men just like us![98]

To speak of a 'law of progress' in these terms is to misconceive the nature of the historical process. This much both *Yet Another Philosophy* and the *Ideas* make abundantly clear. Judaism was not merely the preparation for Christianity, the Middle Ages were not just a passage to the modern era, evil politics were not a prerequisite for achieving political bliss. One did not follow from the other like the morning sun out of the night of darkness. For nothing is merely a means; everything is both a means and an end simultaneously. The individual exists neither merely for the state, nor for the good of the species, and his generation is not simply intended to live for the benefit of posterity. Men who have perished over the ages have not lived solely to manure the earth with their ashes. Each link in the chain has its own place. Each epoch, each culture is unique in its own way. No nation succeeding another, even inheriting all its adjuncts, ever becomes what the other was. All the rudiments of its culture may be the same, but the culture itself could not be so, lacking the original influences which helped to shape its former nature. Greek learning, absorbed by the Romans, became Roman; Aristotle became an Arab and later a Scholastic.[99]

History, then, *is* progress, but not in the uniform and unilinear sense in which Herder's contemporaries most commonly conceived it. Human history is also characterized by striving for perfection. But, again, such striving is not divorced from specific circumstances of time and place; it is not the manifestation of some inexorable supra-historical law, but rather a tendency of human activity in given social and cultural concatenations. It can, moreover, assume different forms, and different degrees of intensity,

[98] v, 546.
[99] v, 527, 559, 564. See also xiii, 339–42. 'To set goals beyond the grave harms rather than promotes the welfare of mankind', Herder writes in the *Letters* (xvii, 120; similarly xviii, 329).

not only at different times and within different cultures, but also within one particular period and culture, amongst the individual members of a given society.

No-one will deny that Europe is the repository of art and the accumulated knowledge of man. . . . But this is not tantamount to saying that everyone who made use of them [the inventions] has also therefore had the intellect of the inventor. On the contrary, the easy access to inventions has to some extent blunted the European's inventiveness.[100]

What is more, progress and the striving for perfection may yield results that can as easily conflict as harmonize with each other. Every discovery in the arts and sciences, in technology and industry, knits a new pattern of society. New situations create new problems, and every increase in wants is not necessarily conducive to an extension of human happiness.[101]

But Herder's critical and relativist view of progress and the striving for perfection should not be interpreted as an expression of utter scepticism. Although he attempts a relativist interpretation even of the inherited universal of *Humanität*, insisting that the tracing of its *manifold* expressions within diverse cultures is the true function of social philosophy, he is as critical of those who deny all progress and all objective standards of morality and happiness, as he is of those who link the promotion of these with every step into the future.[102]

Similarly, Herder's strictures of the complacently optimistic progressivism of his age display no traces of nostalgic romanticism. 'Orientals, Greeks, Romans, only existed once; only at one point were they to touch the electric chain held out by destiny.'[103] We

---

[100] XIII, 372.   [101] XIII, 372–3.
[102] V, 511–12 and XIII, 161. Herder's theory of perfectibility is further elaborated in the *Letters*. The subject is treated in the form of a discussion between imaginary correspondents. One of the feigned correspondents is made to ask whether the whole idea of a continuously progressing perfection of mankind is not a mere dream. 'What,' he asks, 'is its path and purpose? And the aim of perfection? Is the line leading to it an asymptote, an ellipse, a cycloid, or some other curve?' To which Herder replies that 'perfection' must be conceived in a relative sense only. It does not aim at the development of 'superman' or at producing 'extra-human' beings (*Ueber- oder Aussermensch*). If that were the case, Herder remarks, there would be no point in writing even a single line on the subject. Perfection simply means the process by which a thing becomes what it can and should (XVII, 112–15).
[103] V, 554.

are heading for failure if we wish to be Orientals, Greeks and Romans all at once. There is no country where civilization has been able to take a backward step and become for the second time what it was before.[104] Although Herder did much to transform the prevalent image of the Middle Ages, he showed no inclination to idolize the period, let alone to advocate a revival of its institutions, as some of his 'successors', the political Romanticists did. It was not his aim 'to defend the perpetual migrations and devastations, the feudal wars and attacks, the armies of monks, the pilgrimages or the crusades', but rather to try to understand the spirit 'which breathed through it all', to feel the ferment permeating it.[105] Had Voltaire, Hume, Robertson or Iselin gone some way in this direction, they could not have missed noticing how men struggled during this allegedly barbaric age to overcome their defects and to attain such perfection as seemed attainable to them. But, alas, they failed to do so, and history is the poorer for it.[106]

Herder attempts to apply the same dispassionate approach to the development of government. Following Hume, he denies both a pre-political state of nature and the formation of civil society on the basis of a social contract. The human race, he maintains in his essay on government and the sciences, has never been without government; it is as natural to it as its origin and the grouping together of its members within families. As soon as there is a family there is a form of government.[107] And since the nation-state is held to be but an extension of the family—the same sort of 'plant' only with more branches[108]—'family' and 'state' are not differentiated in kind but merely in degree. This denial of a *fundamental* difference between the family and the state is in marked contrast to Aristotle's conception of the state if not to his account of its emergence, with which Herder's bears some obvious

---

[104] v, 565.
[105] v, 526.
[106] v, 524. The same attitude is already evident in the *Travel Diary* where Herder criticizes Rousseau for extolling ages which no longer exist. 'In every age—though in each in a different way—the human race has had happiness as its objective; we in our own times are misled if, like Rousseau, we extol ages which no longer exist and never did exist, if we make ourselves miserable by painting romantic pictures of these ages to the disparagement of our own' (IV, 364).
[107] IX, 313.   [108] XIII, 384.

similarities.[109] Whilst this denial involves Herder in a number of perplexities (which I have discussed elsewhere),[110] it also signals an important departure from the still common identification of the political with one specific type of organization such as the state. For the rejection of the Aristotelian 'state and non-state' distinction as *the* criterion of what is or is not political introduces a new and potentially fruitful dimension into political theorizing, which makes it possible to view political developments of diverse cultures in terms of a continuum.

The rejection of this dichotomous distinction stems not only from Herder's essentially cultural approach to politics, but also from his refusal to reduce the manifold ways in which men regulate their lives within collectivities to a limited number of conceptual categories or 'ideal types'. Whilst he concedes that abstract images of government may prove useful at times—and abstract *ideals* even desirable if not necessary—he doubts if actual governments can ever be found to correspond to them. All we can expect in the real world is this or that characteristic, occasioned by such or such a factor, and arising from specific historical, geographic and climatic circumstances. 'Government in the abstract has not yet appeared on our ever-rotating globe and probably is nowhere likely to appear.'[111] Political analysis, therefore, cannot dispense with the most careful empirical enquiry. Moreover, if such an enquiry is to pay heed to the ubiquity of change, it must not lose sight of the historical dimension. Unless we realize that classification into a few broad categories is not only too general to do justice to the complex variables involved but also that these categories are themselves subject to changes in meaning, we shall inevitably fail to analyze correctly the effects produced by the dynamics of historical interaction. Concepts rarely, if ever, retain the meaning which they originally had. Often, after the briefest of periods, even in the same place, they assume a completely different significance.

No two republics or monarchies have yet been identical. . . . Time itself changes each of these at each moment, and philosophical history has no

---

[109] Aristotle was emphatic in stressing that the distinction between a family and a state is not a simple, numerical difference, but a difference in kind (*Politics* I, chs. I, 3 and III, ch. 4).

[110] See Barnard, *Herder's social and political thought*, ch. IV, esp. pp. 84–6.

[111] IX, 371.

46

choice but to observe each detail most carefully and take account of it. I wish we had such a philosophical history of the sciences as well as of governments, and also of their influence on each other,

Herder remarks in his essay *On the Reciprocal Influence of the Government and the Sciences*, which is clearly intended as a groping effort in this direction.[112] Since Herder himself succinctly sets out the hypotheses which he arrives at, there is no point in repeating them here. But the reader will scarcely fail to observe the subtle distinctions that are adduced, the wealth of illustrations, and above all the acuteness of insight which his treatment of interaction reveals. Nor will he fail to note where Herder's own sympathies lie. 'The boldest, most sublime ideas of the human spirit have been conceived in republics and likewise the finest plans and works have been accomplished in them.'[113] At the same time he should bear in mind that Herder undoubtedly refers here to the actual mode of functioning rather than to the purely formal structure of a polity.

The central aim of the chapter on government in the *Ideas* is to determine the degree to which man's *actual* progress in ordering his social and political life constitutes a *natural* development. Since the attribute 'natural' has both positivistic and normative connotations, it is not surprising to find Herder's arguments oscillating between description and prescription. When these arguments are not too scrupulously kept apart—and they rarely are—the 'is' and 'ought' tend to get confused; detachment alternates with partisanship. Broadly speaking, Herder's positivistic or descriptive arguments are concerned with the sociological question of what political structures 'go with' what social cultures; whilst his normative or prescriptive arguments are concerned with the double question of (1) what is the most natural unit for men to live in and (2) what type of government is most compatible or least incompatible with the nature of man and his society.

---

[112] IX, 372; see also Herder's criticism of Montesquieu's typology of governments in one of the unpublished drafts of the *Ideas*: 'The terms applied to diverse forms of government, particularly in the case of modern states (since they are the most changeable political systems), are the most deceptive shadows on earth. What is often called a monarchy, is in actual fact the most oppressive aristocracy or oligarchy. A "republic" may in reality be a cloak for the worst form of despotism where the most stupid and extravagant of tyrants holds unbridled sway' (XIII, 451).

[113] IX, 376.

47

Evidently, familial and *ad hoc* structures of political authority—the first and second order of government in Herder's terminology—are perfectly natural in that they correspond to the social and cultural needs of given collective entities at certain stages of their development. They are not necessarily 'the best'—Herder speaks here as the pragmatic relativist—but they have proved the most stable and enduring in spite of, or perhaps because of, the diffusion of authoritative functions, particularly in the second form.

A nation of hunters, for instance, may feel the need for a leader when embarking on the chase. Such a leader, however, will only be a leader of the hunt. His election as leader will be determined by his reputation as a skilful hunter, and his electors freely choose to obey him only because his expertise serves their common interests.[114]

All the other leaders or 'functionaries' are elected on the same basis. Their sphere of competence and range of power starts and ends in carrying out the limited task that has been allotted to them.

But what about the 'third type of political order', as Herder calls it, the institution of hereditary government? Since 'Nature does not distribute her noblest gifts in families',[115] Herder offers two explanations for this peculiar development, of which the second seems to me the more sophisticated. His first explanation is that conquest and violence usurped the power of law: the stronger took what the weaker could not keep. The result was utter weakness on the one side and monopoly of power on the other. Cunning and trickery did the rest. Once absolute rule or despotism was established, even the noblest nation turned into a rabble of slaves, of cringing base creatures and shameless flatterers. Dissolute luxury and unlimited arrogance on the one hand contrasted with abject misery on the other.[116] The second explanation, curiously enough, is found in one of the unpublished versions of the chapter on government. Unlike the first explanation, it seeks to account for the emergence of hereditary government in 'functional' terms, and hence is more in keeping with Herder's sociologically orientated arguments. It attributes the development of this third type of political order to the growing need felt by a collectivity of men for symbolic representation. The monarch is, as it

[114] XIII, 376.   [115] XIII, 377.   [116] XIII, 376–82.

were, the abstracted symbol of the whole nation. All honours and distinctions that were conferred upon the person of the first elected monarch were insignia, by means of which external recognition could be given to the collective values of the political artefact. Once it is recognized that the status of the monarch is that of an *office*—and not of a deity—and that the monarch therefore is only a functional part of the machine of state, it matters little whether the personal qualities of the hereditary successors measure up to those of the first elected monarch. For such a recognition would entail the maintenance of vigilance on the part of all other members of the state to ensure that even the worst monarch can do little or no damage to the machine as a whole.[117]

Herder's prescriptive arguments have engaged us in an earlier part of this Introduction, and we may recall that Herder questioned Kant's view that man always needs a political master to rule him. Nature, Herder maintains, has designated no master to the human species; only brutal vices and passions render one necessary.

The wife requires a husband; the untutored child requires the instruction of the parents; the sick need the services of a physician; conflicting parties select an umpire, and the herd a leader. These are natural relations; they are inherent in the very notions themselves. The notion of despot, however, is not inherent in the notion of man. It presupposes man to be weak, under age, and hence incapable of managing his own affairs . . . or a wild, detestable creature, demanding a tamer or a minister of vengeance.[118]

We would take a poor view, Herder adds, of a father who keeps his children permanently under age, or of a physician who keeps his patient in a wretched state to ensure that his services are not dispensed with. But, apparently, we think nothing of being treated as sick children by our political rulers.[119]

We may recall also that, in Herder's view, nothing short of a complete regeneration could enable a nation to rise again from such an 'abyss of habitual slavery'.[120] The lines on which this regeneration was to come about have been sketched earlier and there is little that needs to be added here. Herder confidently

---

[117] XIII, 453–4. This is intended by Herder as an explanation, but not as a justification of hereditary monarchy.
[118] XIII, 383–4.   [119] XIII, 384.   [120] XIII, 382.

believed that the time would come when, as he puts it in an un-published draft of the *Ideas*, class distinctions would wear down to such an extent that even the most misguided of subjects would realize that the monarch is no god.[121] But in advancing the notion of the popular—or populist—nation state, based on common language and 'folkway' traditions, in place of the absolutist—and frequently multi-national—dynastic state, Herder does not lose sight of the fact that even the 'democratic' nation state remains *qua* state a mechanical contrivance as long as it cannot dispense with élitism however popularly based. Nonetheless he held such a state to be preferable to the multi-national dynastic state because in the latter 'the causes of disintegration are inherent in its very structure'.[122]

Whilst it is obvious enough that Herder's prescriptive argu-ments concerning the nature of political development are in-separable from a conception of history in which progress con-stitutes a force pressing towards the attainment of desired ends, they do not therefore invalidate, or conflict with, the notion of progress as a dialectic process. For there is no necessary contra-diction between belief in progress in terms of perfection and the sober realization that progress cannot be thought of as a smooth and continuous advance towards absolute and unchanging goals. Nevertheless, Herder's vision of a social and political transforma-tion necessitated a philosophy of traditionalism that could not dispense with the idea of progress. If social and political life had so far failed to emerge in a form that befitted the nature of man, it was because, so Herder believed, the process of development had been artificially arrested. Traditions had become warped because growth was denied to them. Instead of opposing tradition and progress, therefore, Herder regarded both as interdependent variables in the process of socio-political development. One with-out the other had only a shadow existence. Progress, to have real and enduring significance, had to be a concomitant of social growth; it had to emerge out of a given social culture and historical tradition. Without tradition, progress was like a plant without roots. Conversely, a living tradition was inconceivable without the progressive emergence of new goals. If progress without tradition was like a plant without roots, tradition without progress

---

[121] XIII, 454.   [122] XIII, 455; see also XIII, 385.

was like a plant without water. Indeed, Herder describes such stagnant traditionalism as a real opium of the spirit and as the death-knell of states and individuals alike.[123]

In this conjunction of progress and tradition Herder's ability to reconcile apparent opposites again becomes evident. We have seen how he attempted to forge a synthesis between individualism and his own philosophy of community. Similarly, in his theory of historical change he tried to fuse the prevalent progressivist ideology of the age with his own traditionalism in order to demonstrate that 'progress' and 'perfection' must be envisaged as processes where the *telos* is not beyond but *within* a generation's social development. Whilst each generation may have to seek anew the goals of its self-development and amelioration—for these cannot be achieved once and for all—it can do so only within its own specific cultural and historical context.

Herder's stress on the interplay rather than on the polarity between tradition and progress, his organismic terminology and, particularly, his conception of social development in terms of *growth*, are features commonly associated with political conservatism. It might not be out of place, therefore, to devote this final section to a brief comparative analysis of traditionalist thought following in the wake of the French Revolution *vis-à-vis* that of Herder in order to point up how substantively the former differed from the latter in spite of the close similarity in political vocabulary. For the purpose of this comparative analysis we propose to consider Burke's traditionalism in particular and that of political Romanticism in general.

Burke, and most conservative political thinkers who have invoked his organismic mode of argumentation, sought to provide a rationale for maintaining the status quo and/or for preventing those changes that radically seemed to threaten it. Burke, however, appears to have shown greater insight than some of his followers in recognizing the limits of the growth concept as a rationale for

---

[123] xiv, 89. This view has recently been expressed in similar words by George Grant in his lament over the supposed demise of the Canadian nation. 'A nation', Grant writes, 'does not remain a nation only because it has roots in the past. Memory is never enough to guarantee that a nation can articulate itself in the present. There must be a thrust of intention into the future' (*Lament for a nation*, Toronto, Montreal, 1965, p. 12).

4-2

conservatism. It is no accident that Burke, after making ample rhetorical use of the metaphor of organic growth when dealing with the British constitution up to the beginning of his own century, makes much less use of it when dealing with contemporary institutions. Growth was good imagery for the formative period of the constitution; it had little relevance to the finished or virtually finished product, or, to use biological terms, to something that had attained the stage of maturity. For Burke the British constitution had grown up; it had reached manhood. To have pursued the organismic imagery beyond this point would necessarily have implied either that maturity had not really been achieved or that decay had already set in. Neither implication would have been palatable to Burke, since he was convinced that only slight changes, if any, were desirable in so perfect an instrument as the British constitution. Not change, but preservation and permanence were the chief *desiderata*. Burke, therefore, as far as the present and future were concerned, felt no compunction in abandoning biological imagery in favour of mechanical imagery, in particular the imagery of architecture. Buildings suggested greater durability than organisms. There was infinitely more scope for keeping buildings in a state of good repair and thus for prolonging their lives almost indefinitely than there was for preventing the decay and death of living things. *Repair*, not change, was the operative notion of Burke's political philosophy. When he did make use of the concept of growth, therefore, he certainly did not imply a process of *continuing* change or progress.

Herder, too, preferred 'gradual, natural, reasonable evolution' to revolution.[124] Yet he saw this gradual evolution, which he identified with growth, in terms of *continuing* change. Philosophical considerations apart, there were good political reasons for the different interpretation and application of the growth metaphor in Herder's, as distinct from Burke's, political vocabulary. Unlike Burke, Herder found little in his country's political institutions worth preserving. His traditionalism was essentially cultural, not political. It was centred on language and literature, on folklore and

[124] XVIII, 332. With editorial permission from the *Canadian Journal of Economics and Political Science* I have included in this final section material from an article which I published in the *Canadian Journal*, XXXII (1966), 281–301, under the title 'Metaphors, laments, and the organic community'.

folksong, on customary ways that have evolved within community life outside the political 'perimeter'. Political life as he envisioned it was yet to emerge out of this culture; hence there was plenty of scope for progress and 'growth', for the seed had barely been sown.

Unlike Burke's 'static', and Herder's 'progressivist' conception of tradition, the orientation of the political Romanticists was distinctly 'reactionary', in the most literal sense of this much-abused word.[125] Disenchanted with the results of the French Revolution, they saw the best hope for mankind in a return to the type of society which they associated with the Middle Ages. In their craving for order and stability they projected into the past what they most fervently desired in the here-and-now. The French Revolution, they held, was but the climax of a process of social atomization which could be traced in its origins to the destruction of the values, groups, and institutions of the mediaeval epoch, an epoch in which men, beliefs and customs were insepar-ably related elements in a tightly knit social system. The Middle Ages, in short, provided for the Romanticists the model of an organic community in which, in contrast to the Enlightenment, the social group, and not the individual, was the irreducible unit of society, and in which social order rather than individual freedom constituted the most basic inspirational value animating society.

The political Romanticists have often been acclaimed as followers of Herder, and it cannot be denied that a number of their ideas derived from Herderian sources. The sympathetic treatment of the Middle Ages (which hitherto had been dismissed as a dark and barbarian era); the viewing of history as a force no less powerful and real than that of nature; the notion of the uniqueness of creative activity within a specific context of time and place; the organic wholeness of social cultures; the denial of Natural Law, of social contract, and of a pre-political state of nature; the affirmation of language as the most vital source of a people's collective consciousness: all these are ideas which the political Romanticists shared with Herder. These shared ideas

---

[125] Although political Romanticism did not represent a solid and unified ideology, the features that we shall single out for discussion were common to the views of most leading representatives of this school. The men we chiefly have in mind here are Novalis, the brothers Wilhelm and Friedrich Schlegel, Adam Müller, Schleiermacher, and Savigny in Germany, Bonald, Lamennais, and De Maistre in France, and Coleridge in England.

have undoubtedly led commentators to identify closely the political thought of the Romanticists with that of Herder and even to hold him responsible for the different forms of perversion which Romanticism has undergone.[126] But such close identification wholly blurs crucial differences in political content. Because of their almost compulsive obsession with the Middle Ages the Romanticists preferred to think of their ideal community structure in strictly hierarchical terms. Herder's notion of pluralism was not abandoned, but transmuted. In place of Herder's novel conception of co-operative pluralism within the context of an essentially undifferentiated society (undifferentiated in the vertical sense), the Romanticists put the much older notion of functional subordination. In contrast to Herder's advocacy of *multiple* affiliations where individuals can move between, and belong to, a diversity of groups, the Romanticists revived the mediaeval notion of social immobility and of the total and exclusive submission of a member to a single group. Metaphorically, this divergence from the Herderian community model is reflected in the Romanticists' return to a wholly anthropomorphic image of organism. The State, said Novalis, was a *macro-anthropos*, the anatomy of which was composed of the different social orders that formed a polity. The guilds were its limbs and the source of its physical strength, the nobility represented the moral element, the priests the religious, the teachers the intellectual, whilst the king embodied its will.[127] According to such a conception of the body politic, the inequality of social orders is a necessary presupposition and obedience and subordination natural corollaries. Some men were born to rule and others destined to serve; each had to perform the role that Providence had assigned to him. Obedience to authority does not degrade. On the contrary, there is joy in obedience.[128] The soul

---

[126] See, for example, R. G. Collingwood, *The idea of history* (Oxford, 1946), pp. 86–92; K. R. Popper, *The open society and its enemies* (2nd ed., London, 1952), II, 52; H. S. Reiss, *The political thought of the German romantics* (1793–1815) (Oxford, 1955), pp. 2 and 8; Max Rouché, *La philosophie de l'histoire de Herder* (Paris, 1940), p. 554; or (approvingly) Benno von Wiese, *Volk und Dichtung von Herder bis zur Romantik* (Erlangen, 1938), p. 18 and his 'Der Gedanke des Volkes in Herder's Weltbild', *Die Erziehung* (1939), pp. 121 and 137.

[127] Novalis, *Werke*, ed. Carl Seelig (5 vols, Zürich, 1945), IV, 158; see also II, 193: 'The State is a person like any individual'; and similarly III, 298.

[128] Novalis, *ibid.* V, 32–3.

craves for elevation in voluntary surrender; it finds freedom in complete submission to the fatherland.[129] The land-owning nobility was generally identified with the natural ruling class and favourably contrasted with commerce and trade as the most reliable custodian of order and stability.[130] Not obedience, but disobedience, was degrading and the most common source of alienation. As man moves away from order, anguish presses around him. He is the king of his own misery, a degraded sovereign in revolt against himself, without duties, without bounds, without society.[131]

Allied with this glorification of the mediaeval social structure was a somewhat incongruous notion, the idea of the supremacy and all-pervasiveness of the state. The state was represented as an all-embracing organic whole, outside which human existence was wholly inconceivable. Adam Müller spoke of the state as the interest of all interests, as the supreme end, and as the totality of all human affairs. Man entirely belonged to the state, in mind and in body, and with all his earthly possessions. It was not, therefore, for man to question the purpose of the state, for to do so implied that there was a purpose beyond the state which the state itself should serve—a utilitarian notion too despicable even to con-template.[132] The state was not simply an institution serving particular human needs; rather it was an idea outside and beyond the sphere of ordinary empirical experience. Thus Müller, writing before Hegel, conceived of the state as the extremely moving realm of ideas.[133] For Schleiermacher the monarch was the

[129] Adam Müller, *Elemente der Staatskunst* (Berlin, 1809), III, 327.
[130] See, for example, S. T. Coleridge, *The constitution of church and state* (London, 1829), pp. 20–32, and his *Lay Sermon* (London, 1817), p. 414.
[131] Lamennais, *Oeuvres* (Brussels, 1839), II, 150–1, cited in Robert A. Nisbet, 'Conservatism and sociology', *American Journal of Sociology*, LVIII (1952–3), 170.
[132] Müller, *Elemente*, I, 62–8; II, 85. See also Novalis, *Werke*, IV, 225 and 274.
[133] Müller, *Elemente*, I, 63. In speaking of the state as an idea, Müller wished to distinguish it from a concept. The latter, he held, was susceptible to rational analysis; the former was not. For concepts refer to purely static conditions, to the composition of events at any particular point of time. Ideas, on the other hand, refer to dynamic phenomena, to objects that 'move and grow'. To gain true knowledge of the state, therefore, the analytical method of the sciences is wholly out of place. What is required is not observation, classification, the construction of hypotheses and the formulation of definitions, but direct intuitive insight (see Müller, *Elemente*, I, 20).

embodiment of the divine idea of the state.[134] Like Müller, he also denied the validity of a utilitarian or empirical justification of the state, judging it to be beyond definition because it was entirely beyond the grasp of the logical or empirical processes of the mind. Indeed Müller went so far as to regard this inherent indefinability as the most profound and distinctive hallmark of the state.[135] By endowing the state with a mystique and transcendance of its own the Romanticists wished to distinguish it from all other forms of human organization, as something ontologically unique and superior.

Admittedly, on logical and theoretical grounds, the Romanticist conception of functional subordination is as valid as Herder's conception of functional co-ordination, for both conceptions are compatible with the image of an organism. One may, of course, legitimately question the adequacy of the organic analogy in either conception as a description or explanation of social and political structures. But the point at issue here is whether the *diverse* claims made by the political Romanticists for the political community do not involve an almost absurd overextension of the metaphor originally chosen. Clearly, when we think of an organism we do not think of the whole as being on an ontologically higher level than its parts. The political Romanticists, on the other hand, maintained both: (*a*) that the political community is an organism; and (*b*) that it is on an ontologically higher level than its members. And they seemed to think that the first statement entailed the second, or more precisely, they invariably argued as if the two claims were identical. Similarly, it does not follow from the analogy of organism that the state cannot be conceived in an instrumental sense. One can legitimately hold the state to be an organism (or, rather, like an organism), without holding also that it is an end in itself. Conversely, one can legitimately uphold the belief that the state is something final, in the nature of an absolute in some metaphysical or transcendental sense, without committing oneself to the view that the state is an organism. There simply is no necessary connection between these two beliefs.

A further confusion arises from the Romanticists' attempt to

---

[134] F. Schleiermacher, *Vorlesung über den Staat* (1829), translated in Reiss, *Political Thought of the German Romantics*, p. 198.
[135] Müller, *Elemente*, I, 27.

identify the image of an organism with that of a person. For not only is the unity of a person a wholly different conception from that of the unity of an organism; it is also difficult to see how one can speak of the *parts* of a person. One may conceivably argue that the state is an organism made up of other co-ordinate organisms (as Herder did) or of subordinate organisms (as the Romanticists did), but it is more difficult to understand how one can maintain that the state as a person is made up of other or lesser persons. Although both the organic model and the model of a person may or may not be regarded as methodologically fruitful devices for political analysis, nothing but confusion can result from the mixing or identification of these two models.[136]

Finally, even if it is conceded that in terms of the organic model the parts can only be explained in reference to the whole, this does not imply that their *value* is derivative from the value of the whole. For clearly, ethically speaking, the members of a social whole may be more or less valuable than the whole, or of equal value. Again Herder, in contrast to the Romanticists, seems to have recognized this point by upholding the notions of both *Volk* and *Humanität* as equally relevant value considerations.[137]

In the light of these observations one may wonder whether the political organism of the Romanticists was not essentially a pseudo-organism. By making the sort of claims for the state which they did, they both distorted and obscured the image of organism as a political model. Herder, by refraining from associating such claims with the organic model, was in this sense a more consistent organicist than his Romanticist 'followers'. Also, by insisting on functional co-ordination rather than subordination, he suggested the possibility of an organic community theory that was both democratic and pluralistic.

[136] I feel indebted here to H. J. McCloskey's article, 'The state as an organism', *Philosophical Review* (July 1963), pp. 309–24.
[137] For Herder neither the nation or *Volk*, nor the nation-state, has an exclusive claim on man's loyalty. It is the very task of *Bildung* to reconcile patriotism with a respect for mankind at large, with *Humanität*. Herder's 'categorical imperative' decrees: 'Serve the state, if you *must*, but serve humanity if you *can*' (XIII, 456). Herder decisively repudiates national chauvinism and treats with the utmost contempt the belief that any one nation can claim superiority over another. There is no such thing as a 'historical nation' (as Hegel would have it) for Herder. The idea of master-nations or master-races simply has no meaning for him (see XIII, 252, 257, and XVII, 115).

It may undoubtedly be argued that, by opposing the atomization of society into what is commonly referred to as mass society, the political Romanticists revived the belief in the importance of intermediary groups as buffers between the omnipotent Leviathan and the individual citizen. By possessing an independent group life within diverse associations, non-élites, it may be maintained with some plausibility, are less accessible to the manipulation of élites. But what can less plausibly be maintained is that a theory which lays as much stress on the hierarchy of status as the Romanticist theory of community did leaves enough scope for autonomous groups to serve as effective brakes upon central autocracy, especially if such a theory is overlaid—as it frequently was—with transcendental images of the state that confer upon it an absolute pre-eminence over every other form of social organization. It would therefore seem that the Romanticists' conception of pluralism was as much out of keeping with the notion of social pluralism, as it is commonly understood today, as was their image of organism with that of a social whole or body politic. Even if it is conceded that the Romanticists were imbued with a Christian ethos and that they cherished the hope that those who govern would do so with a paternal concern for the governed, it nonetheless remains true that they allied this faith with a complete trust in the rulers to be the infallible arbiters of what was best for the ruled. In effect, therefore, if not necessarily in intention, their political theories came to provide an ideological sanction for authoritarian, if not totalitarian, forms of government.

Some of the most reactionary Romanticists were at the time of the French Revolution its most enthusiastic supporters. Herder did not live to witness the events that followed in its wake. The Romanticists whose views we outlined did. They became reactionaries not because they favoured absolutism—many in fact opposed it—but because they felt betrayed by the principles in which they had placed their trust. Their lament over the gods that failed kindled their post-Revolutionary faith in the idols of the past. Disillusioned over the eagerly hoped-for reform from below, they reverted to the belief that political initiative could only be expected from above, and what is more, that it would only be effective if it was glorified and invested with mystique.

Terms such as 'mass society' and 'alienation' have by now acquired such strong emotional overtones that their cognitional status has been seriously impaired. It yet remains to be demonstrated that the 'forces' alleged to have brought in their train the alienation of man, from himself no less than from his community roots, have not also brought about his liberation from servitude to community traditions and customs. The men of the Enlightenment, indeed, believed implicitly in such liberation, but the truth may well lie between these two extremes. It was the merit of Herder and the Romanticists to have caught the first glimpses of this possibility.

As with all 'might-have-beens', it is no doubt futile to speculate what the course of the history of ideas and events would have been had the political Romanticists developed Herder's progressivist traditionalism. As it was, his political legacy found no immediate heirs. What seems less fanciful, however, is to suggest that Herder's ingenious attempt to resolve dichotomies commonly thought to be irrevocably opposed to each other—individualism *versus* collectivism; reason *versus* feeling; nature *versus* culture; state *versus* non-state political cultures; uniqueness *versus* generalization; fact *versus* value; conservation and tradition *versus* change and the progressive emergence of new goals; nationalism *versus* internationalism—has lost none of its relevance to current discussions in politics, history and sociology.

That in spite of his imaginative treatment of polarities, Herder left many perplexities unresolved, that he was occasionally imprecise and rarely systematic: all this cannot be denied. Yet these defects, I feel, are less important than his positive achievement. Herder was one of the first of modern thinkers to combine most effectively the historical and sociological method and to recognize that the question of persistence and the question of change essentially constituted one inseparable problem. This is particularly evident from his treatment of *Bildung* in terms of nonreplicative socialization and of tradition as a dialectic continuum. His conception of culture, likewise, is remarkably modern in its emphasis on relativism, pluralism, historism, a non-deterministic form of causalism, and a type of holism which embraces diversity as well as unity. It presents culture not merely as a relational attribute of a social group but as its existential hallmark. At once the product and the source of a group's shared activities, ideas, symbols, values and artefacts, in short its collective way of life over time, culture is seen as the inescapable bedrock of a polity that is a social as well as a legal entity. This is not to say, however, that Herder's notion of *political* culture is devoid of a specifically political content. The importance attached to the political constitution 'in the widest sense' in his essay on government clearly bears this out. Though civic norms and traditions are held to be embedded in the social infrastructure, they nonetheless embody an ethos *sui generis*. It is in and through this specifically political ethos that Herder's democratic ethic of participation is intended to be realized and nurtured.

Finally, in his insistence on uniqueness, diversity, and continuous change, he went far beyond contemporary thinking. Indeed, by denying that the standards and goals of human development can be subsumed under any single immutable universal, Herder challenged one of the major premises of western thought. At the same time—and this needs emphasizing—this challenge did not imply a denial of the authenticity of universals as such. Concretely perceived, 'within the actuality of the particular' (to borrow Cassirer's apt phrase),[138] ethical norms could and, Herder fervently hoped, would assume the status of meaningful universals, in terms of which men would come to recognize the standards of mutuality to which they ought to aspire as human beings. Nonetheless, Herder's admission of the plurality of values was a timely corrective to glib universalism and to the tempting desire to underrate the problematic tension that characterizes the relation between diverse human goals.

'I hope to blaze several new trails,' Herder confided to his *Travel Diary* of 1769.[139] Aspirations such as these are not uncommon in a twenty-five year old. Yet I think it no undue exaggeration to say that in the study of the social and political culture of man—as in other realms—Herder did manage to blaze a number of new trails, opening up regions as yet uncharted or but poorly charted.

[138] Ernst Cassirer, *The logic of the humanities* (New Haven, 1961), p. 25.
[139] IV, 444.

JOURNAL OF MY VOYAGE
IN THE YEAR 1769

JOURNAL OF MY VOYAGE IN THE YEAR 1769

I. AUTOBIOGRAPHICAL REFLECTIONS[1]

[IV, 345–351; 437–447]

I. DEPARTURE FROM RIGA

Every farewell is bewildering. One thinks and feels far less than one anticipated. The intensity with which the mind focuses on the future blurs the sensibilities towards what is left behind. If, in addition, the farewell is too drawn out, it also tends to become wearisome, not unlike the one described in the *London Merchant*.[2] Only after departing does one begin to reflect on the past and to regret lost opportunities. Thus I found myself confessing that I made far from the best use of the library.[3] It would have been of obvious advantage to me had I drawn up a systematic plan of study in the subjects for which I was responsible and made the history of their respective domains my chief concern. O God, how infinitely fruitful, had I studied mathematics in its diverse aspects and surveyed from this base the other sciences—physics and natural history—in the most thorough fashion and with the aid of all the relevant data! Likewise, my studies could only have gained in illumination had I made fuller use of the books that were illustrated by engravings. Above all, I should have concentrated far more on the French language. It would have enabled me to read men like Hénault, Velly, Montesquieu, Voltaire, St. Marc, Lacombe, Coyer, St. Réal, Duclos, Linguet, much earlier and more thoroughly; even Hume I could have read in French. Next Buffon, D'Alembert, Maupertuis, La Caille, Euler, Kästner, Newton, Keill, Mariotte, Torricelli, Nollet and the like; and finally the original stylists—Crébillon, Sévigné, Molière, Ninon, Voltaire, Beaumelle, and so on. That would have been making use of my

---

[1] Since Herder did not publish the *Journal of My Voyage*, I have felt free to rearrange the text under headings of my own.
[2] The *London Merchant*, by George Lillo, 1731, was translated into German in 1755, and became widely known in Germany.
[3] Herder had been appointed assistant librarian at the city library of Riga in 1765.

position [as librarian] and proving worthy of it. It would have enriched my education in the most agreeable manner, and prevented it from being neglected or becoming wearisome. If only I had included in my studies mathematical drawing, historical exposition, practice in speaking French! God, how much one loses in those years through violent passions, through levity and through allowing oneself to be carried away into the paths of chance, years that can never be regained.

I deplore the loss of those years of my mortal life; yet was it not entirely up to me to make better and more rewarding use of them? Had not Fate itself offered me ample dispositions towards this end? Had I chosen the studies mentioned, had I made French, history, natural science, mathematics, drawing, social intercourse and the aptitude for lively discussion my principal objects, into what society could they not have brought me? How much they could have facilitated the enjoyment of subsequent years! Then, thank God, I would not have become an author, and how much time I would have saved by this! How often I would have been spared from losing myself in audacious ventures and vain preoccupations! How much false honour, ambition, irritability and false love of learning; how many hours of mental confusion, how much folly in my reading, writing and thinking I would have avoided! Then too I would probably not have become a preacher, or at least not yet, and to be sure I would have lost many opportunities in just that sphere where I think I have made the best impression; but there too what an awkward situation I would have escaped! I would have learned to enjoy my life, to acquire thorough, practical knowledge, and to apply all that I learned. I would not have become an inkpot, a purveyor of pedantic scribblings, a dictionary of arts and sciences that I have not seen and do not understand; I would not have become a bookcase full of papers and books, whose only place is in the study. I would have avoided situations which confined my spirit and thus restricted it to a false, *intensive* knowledge of human nature, whereas it should rather have learned to know the world, men, societies, women and pleasure *extensively*—with the noble, fiery curiosity of a youth, who enters the world and runs quickly and tirelessly from one experience to another. How different a dwelling for how different a soul! Tender, resourceful, rich in experience rather than in booklearning, cheerful, lively and youthful, maturing into a happy manhood and a happy old age! Oh, what irreparable damage it does, the desire—the compulsion—to affect fruits when one should bear only blossoms! The fruits are artificial and premature; they not only fall off, but bear witness to the corruption of the tree! 'But then I would not have become what I am!' Well, and what would I have lost by that? How much I would have gained!

O God, who knoweth the elements of human souls and hath fitted them to their bodily vessels, was it necessary only for the design as a whole, or also for the happiness of the individual, that there should be souls which, having as it were entered this world in timid confusion, never know what they are doing or what they are about to do, never arrive where they wish to go and thought they were going, who never really *are* where they happen to be, and only rush from one mental state into another in a haze of feverish activity, astonished by their own whereabouts? When, o God, Thou Father of souls, will these find rest and philosophical poise? In this world? At least in their old age? Or are they destined to end their lives prematurely through just such a feverish, night-marish activity, without ever really having achieved anything or enjoyed anything properly, snatching at everything in haste like hurried, frightened vagrants, only to embark in death on a new pilgrimage not unlike that of their lives? Father of men, wilt Thou vouchsafe to instruct me?

Thus one thinks when one moves from one situation into another; and what a wide scope for thought a ship, suspended between sky and sea, provides! Everything here adds wings to one's thoughts, gives them motion and an ample sphere! The fluttering sail, the ever-rolling ship, the rippling waves, the flying clouds, the broad, infinite atmosphere! On land one is chained to a fixed point and restricted to the narrow limits of a situation. Often this point is a student's chair in a musty study, a place at a monotonous boarding-house table, a pulpit, a lecture-desk. And the situation is often a small town, where one is the idol of an audience of three, to whom alone one pays attention, and a mono-tony of occupation in which one is jostled alike by conventionality and presumption. How petty and restricted do life, honour, esteem, desires, fears, hate, aversion, love, friendship, delight in learning, professional duties and inclinations become in such circumstances; how narrow and cramped the whole spirit in the end! But let a man suddenly retire from this scene—or rather be thrown out, without books, writing, occupation, or homogenous society—what a different prospect! Where is the solid land on which I stood so solidly, and the little pulpit, and the armchair, and the lecture desk at which I used to give myself airs? Where are the people of whom I stood in awe, and whom I loved? O soul, how will it be with you when you leave this little world? The narrow, firm, restricted centre of your sphere of activity is no more; you flutter in the wind or float on a sea—the world is vanishing from you—has vanished beneath you! What a changed perspective! But such a new mode of looking at things costs tears, remorse, the extrication of one's heart from old attachments, self-condemnation! I was no longer satisfied with myself even as regards my virtue; I saw it as nothing but a weakness, an abstract name which everyone learns from his youth onward to transform into a reality. Whether it was the sea air, the effect of the food on board, restless sleep, or whatever else, I had hours in which I could not comprehend any virtue, even the virtue of a wife, which I had always thought the highest and truest. Even as regards man's improvement—individual cases apart—I found only weakening of character, self-torture, or the old faults in new disguise. Oh, why is man deluded by language into thinking that abstract shadow images represent solid bodies, existing realities? When will I reach the stage at which I can destroy in myself everything I have learned so far and rediscover, in my own convictions alone, what I have really learned, what I really think and believe? Companions of my youth, how much I will have to tell you when I see you again, when I can enlighten you about the darkness which at this time still hung over me! Nothing is virtue but human life and happiness; action is the only thing that matters; everything else is a shadow, is sophistry. Too much chastity, when it weakens a man, is just as much vice as too much unchastity; every renunciation should be negation only: to make it into privation for its own sake, and then to make this into a positive element of one's chief virtue—where will this lead us? ...

Our first conversations are naturally family conversations, in which we learn to know characters that we did not know before; in this way I came to know a tormentor, a spoiled boy, etc. Then, one readily throws oneself back on ideas to which one has been accustomed, and in this way I became a philosopher on the boat—but a philosopher who had as yet learned imperfectly how to philosophize from nature without books and instruments. Had I this ability, what a vantage point I would have had, sitting at the foot of a mast on the wide ocean, from which to philosophize on the sky, the sun, the stars, the moon, the air, the wind, the sea, the rain, the currents, the fish and the ocean floor, and to discover the physical laws governing all these from within, as it were. Philosopher of nature—that should be your position with the youth whom you are teaching! Place yourself with your pupil on the wide sea and show him facts and the real properties of things; and do not explain them to him in words, but let him explain everything for himself. And I myself, when I read Nollet and Kästner and Newton,[4] I too will place myself at the foot of the mast, where I once sat, and will trace the course of the electric spark from the impulse of the initial wave to the thunderstorm, link water pressure to atmospheric pressure, follow the motion of the ship, embraced by the waters, in relation to the form and motion of the stars, and not stop until I know everything from immediate personal conviction, as now I know nothing.

2. ARRIVAL IN FRANCE

With all my French, I could understand neither the pilot nor the innkeeper nor the old women. A classical scholar would be in exactly the same position if he went to Greece today. O you pedants, read Homer as though he were singing in the streets; read Cicero as though he were holding forth before the town council!

The first sight of Nantes was sheer bewilderment: I saw on all sides what I never saw again—a distortion almost to the point of the grotesque. This is the habit of my eye—and is it not the habit of my thinking too? Whence does it come? A friend whom I asked about his first reactions to this same sight was taken aback and said that his impression also had been one of vastness, but of vast

[4] Nollet, Jean Antoine, 1700–70. French abbé and physicist; credited with the discovery of endosmosis, improvements on the Leyden jar, and the invention of an electroscope. Kästner, Abraham Gotthelf, 1719–1800. German mathematician and epigrammatist.

regularity and of great beauty. This man must have either colder blood than I or, if I may put it this way, a differently tailored perspective. Did my first entrance into the world of feeling produce sensations of the same sort [as those I experienced at Nantes]—a shudder instead of a calm feeling of satisfaction? To judge by the temperaments of the people responsible for my being, this might well have been so; and if so, it would have set the original tone, the original mood of my soul, and would have given the initial impulse to that feeling which now returns only too often. Even now, at certain moments, when I open my feelings to something new and, as it were, impart a new intensity to them, what do I experience but a sort of shudder, and not exactly one of voluptuous pleasure. Even the strongest impulses which man can experience arise in me in this manner. Were I to set to work in these moments, is it not more than likely that I would implant these very sensations into what I was doing? And would I not thus pass on my own unhappy, warped nature to others? Or is it no misfortune to have such a nature? Will other feelings and sensations be in store for me in riper years, in marriage, in hours of true and tender love? How am I to know? Meanwhile the tendencies that I find in myself now have their effect on everything I do. A first work, a first book, a first system, a first visit, a first thought, a first design or plan, a first conception—these always assume in my mind gothic dimensions, and much in my plans, designs, works, conceptions, has either not yet passed from this gigantic style into one of finer proportions, or else has vanished at the first stage. A feeling for the sublime, then, is the bent of my soul; it determines my love, my hate, my admiration, my dreams of happiness and unhappiness, my resolution to live in society, my expression, my style, my deportment, my physiognomy, my conversation, my occupation—everything. When I am in love, for example, my emotions border on the sublime, to the point of tears. How powerfully separation affects me, whereas to the Angolas only the present moment matters! How a single misfortune of my loved one, a single tear in her eye, can move me! What attached me to her more closely than this? What has ever moved me more than separation from her?—From this same source comes also my taste for speculation and for the sombre in philosophy, poetry, stories and ideas! From this comes my fascination for bygone ages and

68

the shades of antiquity, my liking for the Hebrews, considered as a nation, for the Greeks, Egyptians, Celts, Scots, etc.! From this also resulted my early dedication to holy orders. Beyond a doubt, local prejudices of my boyhood played a large part in this; but so, with equal certainty, did my impressions of church and altar, of pulpit and sacred eloquence, of the church service and religious reverence. From this came my first series of undertakings, my youthful dreams of a water-world, my favourite pursuits in the garden, my solitary walks, the shudder which accompanied my psychological discoveries, with their revelation of new thoughts in the human soul, my half-comprehensible, half-sombre style, my perspective of *Fragments, Groves, Torsos, Archives of the Human Race*—everything![5] My life is a passage through gothic arches or an avenue full of green shadows. The prospect is always awe-inspiring and sublime; the entrance into it a sort of shudder, the exit full of perplexities and confusion—then the avenue suddenly leads into wide open country. It is then that I have to put my ideas to the best use I can; to tread thoughtfully but also to notice the sun breaking through the leaves and painting shadows that are all the lovelier for the rays being broken by the leaves; to see the meadows with their bustle of activity; and yet, all the time, to keep to the path . . .

What have I done in the past that I should be fated always to see shadows instead of experiencing real things? I enjoy little, or rather, I enjoy too much, to excess, and therefore without relish. The sense of touch and the world of sensuous pleasures—these I have not enjoyed. I see and feel *at a distance* and put obstacles in the way of my own enjoyment through over-eager anticipation and through weakness and foolishness in the moment of experience itself. In my friendships and my contact with society I feel in advance a premature anxiety or a strange, excessive expectation; the first makes it difficult for me to enter into a relationship, while the second always deceives and makes a fool of me. So in every situation my imagination, swelling up in advance and turning away from the realities of the situation, kills my enjoyment, makes it jaded and dull, and only afterwards allows me to see that I have

[5] Herder is referring to some of his earlier works: *Ueber die neuere deutsche Litteratur: Fragmente* (1767); *Über Thomas Abbts Schriften; Torso* (1768); *Kritische Wälder* (1769); *Fragmente zu einer 'Archäologie des Morgenlandes'* (1769).

not enjoyed my experience, that it has in fact been jaded and dull. So I am even in love, which I feel platonically, in absence more than in the present moment, in fear and hope more than in enjoyment; in abstractions, intellectual conceptions, more than in realities. So I am in my reading: how I burn with eagerness to read a book, to possess it, and how my spirits sink when I do read it, when I do possess it! How many even of the best authors have I read through—purely for the sake of factual information, absorbed in the illusion of their systems, carried away by the work as a whole, interested only in the surface content—without pausing to fully savour the spirit of the work! Thus do I read, plan, work, travel, write; thus I am in all things!

Feelings of this kind led me, like Walter Shandy, to the notion of thinking out a work *on the youth and aging of the human soul*, in which—partly from my own sad experience, partly from the example of other souls that I have had the opportunity of knowing —I would teach men how to avert such premature old age, to rejoice in their youth and to enjoy it as they should. This plan had already taken shape in Riga, in gloomy days when the whole organization of my mind was, as it were, paralysed, when the driving wheel of external experience was motionless, and my mind, penned in its own wretched ego, had lost the happy longing to gather in fresh ideas and pleasures and notions of perfection. I went around stupid, unthinking, apathetic and idle, talked nonsense, etc., took up a hundred books only to throw them away again and still to know nothing. Then I suddenly thought of the noble Swift, who shrugged his shoulders at the old, wretched, gray-haired man he saw in his mirror and in contrast portrayed—for himself and for me—the young, happy world of Plato and Socrates, in which, amid jests and play, men exercised and trained their minds and bodies and made them slender, strong and firm, like beautiful olive trees at the rim of a spring.[6] I thought of the old and ever-young Montaigne, who always knew how to rejuvenate himself in his old age, and I stood there perplexed, bewildered and old in my youth.

[6] This seems to refer to the apparently apocryphal story which describes the mad Swift seeing himself in a mirror and crying out 'O poor old man!' In this as in several other references, John Francis Harrison's *Johan Gottfried Herder: Journal of my Travels in the year 1769* (University Microfilms, 1952) proved helpful.

II. THE VOYAGE: REFLECTIONS ON MYTH,
PREJUDICE AND THE IMAGINATION
[IV, 356–65; 448–60]

The sea-faring folk still remain particularly attached to super-stition and the marvellous. Since they have to attend to wind and weather, to small signs and portents, since their fate depends on phenomena of the upper atmosphere, they have good reason to heed such signs, to look on them with a kind of reverent wonder and to develop as it were a science of portents. And since these things are supremely important, since life and death depend on them, what man will not pray in the tempest of a dark and fearful night, in a violent storm, in places where pale death beckons? Where human help ceases, man always assumes the reality of divine aid, if only for his own comfort—especially the ignorant man, who out of every ten phenomena of nature sees only one as natural, and who is terrified by the fortuitous, the sudden, the amazing, the inescapable. Oh, he will believe and pray, even if he is coarse and dissolute otherwise. He will have pious formulas in his mouth where things of the sea are concerned, and will not ask, 'How did Jonah get inside the whale?' For nothing is impossible to almighty God, even if the man thinks himself otherwise quite capable of making a religion for himself and sets no store by the Bible. The whole language of shipboard life, the reveille, the calling of the hours, is therefore framed in pious stock phrases and is as solemn as a chant from the bowels of the ship itself.—In all this lie data which explain the earliest ages of mythology. When man in his ignorance of nature listened to signs, nay, had to listen to them, it is scarcely surprising that for sailors coming to Greece, unfamiliar with the waters, the flight of a bird was a solemn matter—as indeed it still is in the vast expanse of air and on the desolate sea. Likewise the lightning of Jupiter gave cause for anguish and fright—as lightning still does at sea. Zeus thundered through the sky and forged bolts to strike sinful groves and waters. With what awe did men then worship the silent silver moon, which stands so huge and solitary and so powerfully affects the air, the seas and the seasons. With what avidity did men then look to certain help-bringing stars, to Castor and Pollux, Venus, etc., as seamen still do on a foggy night. Even I, who from youth on had seen and known all these things in an entirely different perspective, have found that the flight of a bird and the lightning on the sea and the silent moon in the evening made impressions on me that were quite different from those they had made on land —so what must have been their effect on a seafarer who, ignorant of the sea—perhaps as an exile from his homeland, as a youth guilty of some crime—was seeking a strange land? How readily he would kneel before thunder and lightning and eagles! How natural for him to see Jupiter's seat in the sphere of the upper air! And how comforting for him to feel he could influence these things by his prayers! How natural for him to paint the sun sinking into the sea with the colours of chariot-driving Phoebus and to deck Aurora in all her beauty! A thousand new and more natural explanations of mythology, a thousand more profound appreciations of its most ancient poets, come to mind when one reads Orpheus, Homer, Pindar—and especially the first—on shipboard. Sailors brought the Greeks their earliest religion; all Greece was a colony on the sea coast. Hence she could not have a mythology like that of the Egyptians and Arabs beyond their sandy deserts, but developed a religion of foreign lands, of the sea and of sacred groves. Therefore her mythology must be read at sea. What would I have given to have been able to read Orpheus and the *Odyssey* on board! When I do read them again, I will throw myself back into their times. How far the Greek imagination went in matters relating to the sea is illustrated by their stories of dolphins. There is nothing beautiful or friendly to men in the appearance of these creatures; but their gambols around the ship, their swift pace in calm weather, their leaping and diving, gave occasion for legends about them. To say, 'a dolphin abducted him' was as much as to say, 'Aurora stole him away': two circumstances occur together and one must therefore be the result of the other. So the transformed ships in Vergil,[7] the nymphs, sirens, tritons, etc. are both easily explicable in terms of the sea, and also perfectly credible, especially if one imagines the terror of night, and fog, and so on . . .

With what reverence stories are listened to and told on board! And how strongly a sailor is inclined towards the adventurous

[7] Cf. *Aeneid*, IX, 119.

element in them! Himself as it were half-adventurer, a man seeking strange new worlds, what fantastic things does he not see at the first startled sight? Have I not myself experienced the same on approaching an unfamiliar coast, a new country, or even a particular period in history? How often have I asked myself: is what you saw at first sight actually there? Since the very first impression is one of utter amazement it quite naturally gives rise to gigantic tales, such as *Argonauticas, Odysseys,* and Lucianesque travel narratives.[8] The striking thing about these twilight first impressions is their ambivalence: what can one not read into them? A sailor is very susceptible to such initial auguries. When he longs to see land, a new, strange land after his long voyage—what auguries will he not imagine there! With what amazement did I myself board ship! Did I not at first find everything more wonderful, larger, more amazing, more fearful than afterwards, when everything became familiar to me once I had walked through the ship? With what a passion for novelty one approaches land! How one stares at the first pilot with his wooden clogs and his great white hat! One thinks that one sees in him the whole French nation, right up to their king Louis the Great. How avid one is for the first face—the first faces—be they only those of old women; now they are foreign rarities, Frenchwomen! How prone one is to form one's first conceptions from a single household, from a few people, and how slowly one reaches the point at which one can claim to know a country! Now if you combine this desire to see wonders with the inclination of the eye to find them at the very first encounter: it is not hard to see how poetical the narrative becomes. In this sense Herodotus, without wishing to lie, becomes a poet too. How novel to read him, or Orpheus, Homer, Pindar and the tragic poets, from this point of view!

A sailor, long accustomed to such adventurous tales, believes and spreads them; they are avidly listened to and repeated by sailors and children and fools. How many tales one hears today from the East and West Indies, the names in them half-garbled and the stories surrounded by an aura of the wonderful! We hear of great heroes of the sea and pirates whose heads somehow

[8] The *Argonautica* is an epic poem by Apollonius Rhodius (third century B.C.). The *True History*, a mock travel narrative by the Greek satirist Lucian (c. A.D. 120–200), was the archetype of books like Swift's *Gulliver's Travels*.

managed to run about after their deaths! The result of all this is the emergence of a mentality which finds tales of the Knight of the Swan, of John Mandeville,[9] and so on, credible and possible, which repeats such tales, and even believes and recounts them when it no longer finds them possible. Why? Because they were read in youth, they fitted in with all the adventurous expectations one entertains at that age; they aroused the mind of a future sailor, fashioned its dreams, and in this way remain incorruptible. Reason, a later and ephemeral manifestation, cannot destroy the dreams and deepseated beliefs of childhood. Every slightly similar tale which we have heard told as true (although heard from ignorant men, from semi-adventurers) has confirmed these early stories; every adventurous experience of our own confirms them— who will disprove them? How hard it is to demonstrate that there is no paradise guarded by fiery dragons, no Mandevillean hell, no Tower of Babylon [i.e. Babel]! That the Emperor of Siam with all his gold is not what he appears to be in such fictions! That the white swans and their knight are delusions! A man says at most, 'It is hard to believe'—and goes on telling the story; or he argues in its favour more vigorously than he would for the Bible. But is such a credulous person therefore a fool, a stupid ass in every respect? Surely not. Apart from such dreams and delusions, which his occupation, his upbringing, his education and his general habit of thinking have helped to form, he may be a very sensible, active, capable and intelligent fellow.

To start with, we could look upon these observations as the germ of a philosophical theory which seeks to explain belief in myths and fictitious stories. Though it may find that the mythology of Jews and Arabs, Greeks and Romans, differ from one another, it may also discover that all mythologies derive from one common source: the prejudices of childhood. The tendency to identify early impressions with fairy tales, the avid desire to hear them (especially if the occurrences of our own experience so predispose us), the ease with which we grasp them, the habit of

---

[9] In German epic, the Knight of the Swan is Lohengrin, son of Parzival. Led by a swan to rescue Elsa, a dispossessed princess of Brabant, he then marries her. When she asks his name, in violation of a pledge, he has to return to the castle of the Grail. The swan comes to fetch him, and is revealed as Elsa's brother Gottfried. Sir John Mandeville (c. 1300–72) was an explorer whose highly exaggerated *Travels* are a classic of travel literature.

mind that is formed by having told them repeatedly and been believed: these are the props which sustain such early prejudices. Inadequate as real explanations they might well be, nonetheless they do at least help to explain away some things if only by such moral truisms as 'nothing is impossible to God'. Yet, surely, it would be worth while to enquire further into the factors that support and perpetuate prejudice. A host of phenomena concerning the human mind suggest themselves here: the first images formed by the imagination; dreams that we silently cherish so long in childhood; the impression of every sound which supports and strengthens that impetuous inward tone which finds a dim echo in ideas only darkly perceived; the inclination to revel in the miraculous; the cumulative effect which the addition of someone else's belief has on one's own; the facility with which we recount the memories of our youth—a thousand phenomena, for each of which one could easily find a precedent in the fables of the primitive world, and which could help to account for much that is subjectively felt by the individual mind and objectively expressed in ancient poetry, historical legend and fable. This would offer a theory of fable, a philosophical history of daydreams, a genetic explanation of the inclination towards the miraculous and adventurous derived from human nature, a logic of the poetic faculty. Extended over all ages, all peoples, all types of fable and legend from the Chinese to the Jews, from the Jews to the Egyptians, Greeks and Normans, it could provide a great and immensely useful work. It would explain what *Don Quixote* mocks at, and, at the same time show how great an author Cervantes really was.

Secondly, we would discover how relative the question of probability and improbability actually is. So much depends on our first impressions: their strength, form and multiplicity, the duration and frequency of experiences confirming them, and on a number of chance happenings that influence them according to time, circumstance and social milieu. One people's estimate of probability is different in both form and degree from another's. We may laugh at Greek mythology and yet each of us, perhaps, makes up his own. The common people have a mythology in a thousand things. Is their sense of what is improbable the same as that of the sceptical philosopher or the inquiring scientist? Is

Klopstock's the same as that of Hume or Moses Mendelssohn?[10]
What an individual way of measuring improbabilities every
formulator of a hypothesis has: Hermann von der Hardt and
Hardouin;[11] Leibniz and Plato, the two greatest minds for
hypotheses in the world; Descartes—how sceptical, how distrust-
ful, and what hypotheses! The sense of probability, then, takes a
peculiar form according to the proportion of the different powers
of the mind—of imagination to judgment, of penetration to
intellect, of understanding to the initial liveliness of impressions,
etc. What a theory of the human soul, following Hume, Moses
(Mendelssohn), Bernouilli and Lambert![12]

Every class, every way of life, has its customs: Hume in his
history and his political essays has described many such characteristics very vividly. I shall learn to know classes and people from
individual men. Take a sailor, for example: what a mixture of
superstitious timidity and foolhardiness; of rugged earnestness
and uselessness; of confidence in himself and enmity towards
others. In many traits one can recognize a hero of antiquity: the
way he talks about himself, boasts of his strength, thinks his own
book-knowledge infallible, believes that all possible discoveries
have already been made, holds Holland above all other nations,
retails his amorous adventures—as improbable as they are coarse—
his heroic deeds, and so on and so forth . . .

What a great study concerning the imagination and the understanding, the heart and the emotions! A man from Judaea, a Job
from Arabia, a seer from Egypt, a Roman hero, a friend of the
clergy, a crusader, a virtuoso of our own century: all set alongside
each other and each of them revealing the spirit of his age, the
nature of his mind, the manner his character was formed, and the

---

[10] Klopstock, Friedrich Gottlieb, 1724–1803, German poet. Mendelssohn,
Moses, 1729–86, German Jewish philosopher, friend and collaborator of
Lessing, and author of *Philosophische Gespräche* (1755) and *Phädon* (1767).

[11] The theologian Hermann von der Hardt (1660–1746) believed that all
Semitic languages were derived from Greek, and the Jesuit Jean Hardouin
(1646–1729) believed that most of the works of classical literature were
actually forgeries produced by thirteenth-century monks under the direction
of Severus Archontius.

[12] Bernouilli, Jacques, 1654–1705, professor of mathematics at the University
of Basel. His *Ars conjecturandi* was posthumously published in 1713. Lambert,
Johann Heinrich, 1728–77, philosopher, physicist, mathematician and
astronomer. He was the author of the *Neues Organon* (1764).

way he conceived of virtue and happiness. These would constitute significant fragments about the morals and the religions of all peoples, cultures and periods, of value for current studies which, if I were to produce them, would leave the *Bruckers*, the *sermon-book preachers* and the *Mosheimian moralists* far behind.[13] What a work for the entire world such a great undertaking would be when completed! But why am I worrying about the world, when I have myself and my own world and my own life to worry about, and so must draw on the resources of my own life? What to do then? Observe and study this life in all its scenes! Pay attention to the first workings of the youthful imagination and the first strong impressions received by the impressionable, sensitive mind; learn from the former how to explain much in the history of our taste and modes of thought, and from the latter how to make use of all that can stir and excite men . . .

The human mind has its ages like the body. Its youth is curiosity, and therefore childish belief, an insatiable desire to see things, especially wonderful things; it is the gift of learning languages— provided that they are taught only on the basis of firm conceptions and real things; it is youthful flexibility and vigour, etc. An old person who has this sort of curiosity is always contemptible and childish.

The child cannot take much real interest in all the things he learns through his curiosity: he merely sees, wonders and admires. Hence his reverence for old people who seem to him really worthy of veneration. Hence the depth of his impressions, which are as it were driven into him by wonder and admiration. But the more our minds and bodies grow, the more the sap increases and wells up in both, the closer we approach the objects of our experience or the more strongly we attract them towards ourselves. We colour them with the fire of our blood—and this is *imagination*, the dominant trait of youth. Love in all its aspects becomes the enchanted world in which it roams. In solitude it evokes the poet in us and the craving for poetry, for stories of the distant past, for

[13] Brucker, Jakob, 1696–1770, pastor and historian. His 15-vol. *Historia Critica Philosophiae* (1742–4) was the first history of philosophy in Germany. Mosheim, Johann Lorenz, 1694–1755, professor at Göttingen and writer on ecclesiastical history. He was also well-known as a preacher and moralist. Unlike Gibbon, Herder had not even mild praise for Mosheim's *Geschichte Servets*, finding it unreadable.

romances. It kindles our first enthusiasms, as those of friendship, and paints them in didactic or poetic colours. It fashions our world of pleasures, our sympathies and tender feelings. Even the world of learning assumes in the youthful imagination the form of images, of sensations, of upsurging delight. All this is natural to youth. In an old greybeard such ardent, fiery feelings are as foolish as they are trifling.

The youth becomes a man and a member of society—but primarily the latter—and thus, as our world demands, the strong sallies of his imagination are stifled: he learns to adapt himself to the ways of others, and at the same time to distinguish himself from them; that is to say, he develops wit and discrimination. He becomes a part of the social world and learns all the refinements of social polish, refinements to which he is encouraged by love, by the desire to please his fair one and cut a worthy figure in her eyes; by friendship, which is mostly a social matter with us; by pleasures, which are never so universal unless they are social—in short, by everything . . . Through becoming part of society at large the youth develops into manhood, the latter being the really important stage, to which the former merely constitutes the preliminary process: a process that is indispensable, yet not to be lingered over. In the man, *bon sens* and wisdom in affairs predominate. He has traversed the paths of curiosity and has found that there is much in life that is empty, that deserves a first glance and nothing more; he has lived through the age of the passions and feels that they are good insofar as they teach him about life and the world, but he must beware lest they come to dominate the rest of his life for then everything is lost. Hence he must acquire calmness, genuine kindness, friendship, wisdom, usefulness, in short, *bon sens*. This is the most crucial age in a man's social life, the period when his mental and physical activities are at their peak. It is during manhood that man can be a true philosopher of action, of wisdom and experience.

The old man is a prater and a philosopher in words. He recites his experiences in the form of dull, long-winded lessons, completely devoid of focus and exactitude, mere commonplaces. He has a great store of these because he thinks himself rich in experience, and pontificates about the laxity of present-day youth from which he is too far removed to be able to join in. This is the age of rest.

The mind is scarcely open to new impressions any more and little disposed to new experiences. As it closes its gates, so to speak, it also becomes more timid, more rigid, incapable of benefiting from instruction, satiated, as it were, with lessons and precepts. What previously was soft, the cartilage of movement, has become the bone of repose. The mind recalls with enjoyment the life it has led and lives out the remainder of its days; and this retired timidity is a good thing, for the old man hardly has the energy and strength any more to move out of his oyster shell. Such is old age.—Aristotle, Horace, Hagedorn, have all portrayed the ages of man's life,[14] but their portrayal must be traced back to certain basic psychological concepts if it is to be applicable to the mind, and these concepts are curiosity, imagination and passion, wit and *bon sens* and finally the reason of old age. And from these can be developed just such a systematic view of human life as Montesquieu has constructed for the various forms of government.

Every man must pass through these stages, for they develop out of each other; and *one can never enjoy any given stage if he has not enjoyed the preceding one*: the first always contains the data necessary for the second, and the whole series proceeds in geometric, not arithmetic progression. Only in the totality of its sequences can one enjoy life and only by reviewing it as one continuous whole can one also enjoy a tranquil old age. *One can never wholly annul what has gone before (even by way of improvement) without sacrificing the present.*

But, on the other hand, if a man 1) fails to do justice to the stage of life in which he finds himself, 2) goes on too soon to the next, 3) tries to live them all at once, or 4) returns to a stage he has already lived through, then the order of nature is upset: then we have prematurely aged souls, young greybeards, greybeard youths. And the prejudices of our society afford many chances for such monsters to develop. These prejudices assume some stages of life prematurely, encourage regression in others and thus subvert the whole nature of man. Our education, our instruction, our whole way of life is like this. A single voice raised for truth and humanity would be a blessing here; it could ensure

[14] Herder refers to Aristotle's *On the Generation of Animals* and Horace's *Ars Poetica*, 11, 156–78. The German poet Friedrich von Hagedorn, 1708–54, wrote four poems on the ages of man.

the enjoyment of the whole of a human lifetime—it would be invaluable. And this the book must do!

First part: *According to the Capabilities of the Mind, and so According to the Ages of Man.*

First section: *Of the Training of the Senses;*—and therefore *Of the Soul of Childhood.*

One loses one's youth if one *does not use one's senses.* A mind abandoned by sensation is in the most barren of all deserts and in the most painful state of annihilation. Momentary occurrences of this condition—the most irksome in human life—often follow long periods of abstract thought. The mind is barren and stupid; it has no thoughts to collect nor any inclination even to attempt thought; it has no preoccupation, nor the inclination to seek any, not even in the form of amusement. These are moments of purgatory, of total annihilation, a state of weakness so intense that one cannot even desire anything.—We prepare the mind of a child to find itself in this state some day if we force upon it abstractions without a trace of the living world, learning without knowledge of real things, words without thoughts—unnatural thoughts, as it were, divorced from real objects and truth. There is no greater torture for the mind of a child than this. To *extend* his ideas will never be a torture. But to imagine that he has ideas where there is actually only a shadow of thought without reality, precept without example, abstract propositions without facts, words without meaning—this is torture, this ages and warps the mind. (All virtues and vices are abstractions of this kind, generalized from thousands of actual cases, the subtle result of many subtle conceptions.)

Go into a school for grammarians and you find a world of weary souls under a superannuated teacher! Everyone should really invent his own language, understand the idea underlying each word as thoroughly as if he had discovered it himself. A proper school of language instruction will not teach the pupil a word that he cannot understand within the context of his own experience. Go through a German dictionary and see how much of our own language we understand in this way; go through a foreign language—a thousand times less! A child learns a thousand words, a thousand nuances of abstract meaning, of which he has absolutely no real conception, and a thousand others of which he has only a half-formed idea. In both cases he is tortured, his mind is exhaus-ted and made old for life. This is where our age so badly fails. Men long ago invented language; a thousand generations before us have enriched it with subtle concepts. We expect to learn this language, to comprehend by means of a two-minute recitation of vocabulary the significance and nuances of a language our fore-fathers invented and developed over the course of centuries—and in fact we learn nothing in the process. We grow old peering into grammars, dictionaries and discourses that we do not understand; we have put ourselves on the wrong track for life.

Away then with grammars and grammarians! My child shall learn each dead language as a living one and each living one as though it were just being discovered. Montaigne and Shaftesbury learned Greek as a living language, and how much more feeling they had for their Plato and Plutarch than do our pedants! And he who would learn his mother tongue in so lively a way that each word would come to him at the very same time he saw the object and conceived the thought—what an accurate and philosophical head he would have! What a young, flourishing mind! Such were those who had to invent their own languages—Hermes in the wilderness and Robinson Crusoe. In just such a wilderness should our children be! Talk nothing but childish talk to them! The first abstract, uncomprehended idea is poison to them, is like food which cannot possibly be digested and so, unless nature gets rid of it, weakens and corrupts the body. If nature did not let a kindly oblivion relieve us of most of this educational stuffing, I shudder to think what would become of us. How the school, education, instruction—everything—changes in the light of this! What a method of teaching a language! What labour and precision it will cost to write the textbook—and, still more, to read about a science and teach it in this way! Teacher! In philosophy, physics, aesthe-tics, morals, theology, politics, history and geography *let there be no word without a concept, no concept prematurely assumed! Teach as much as a human mind can grasp at any given time by its own powers*—and that means that in early youth nothing but ideas received through the senses should be introduced.

Limited to these, how the human mind will revive! No more compulsion, no more artificial learning! Learning will spring from curiosity, it will become a pleasurable activity, a joy and a delight.

To exercise one's faculties—to see—to see things in a wonderful new way—what happiness it would bring to youth! A plan for this—what the boy must learn in all the sciences and how he must learn it in order always to remain young—would be a service to mankind.

Just look at the wretched pupils who in their whole lives learn nothing but metaphysics in language, the arts and the sciences, who torture themselves with things they do not understand and dispute about things they have not understood in the first place! Just look at the many wretched teachers—and textbooks, too, for that matter—who themselves often do not understand a word they teach. Into what a wilderness of nominal concepts and definitions our textbooks stray! No wonder our age produces nothing great, nothing new. It is like a miser: it has everything and enjoys nothing. I need only go through my own education to find a wealth of sorry examples. A child must act of himself and according to his own motive, which is curiosity; this must be led and guided, but no foreign motives that he has not yet acquired—e.g. vanity—should be implanted. For though from these a child can be induced to study much, he will learn nothing in the right place or at the right time. To restore the youth of the human mind through true education, to kill the swarm of prejudices in religion, politics, philosophy, etc. that covers the world: what an undertaking that would be! But I doubt whether it is entirely feasible in our society. Everyone learns the whole mass of a hundred other men's thoughts and grows old in doing so.

This is not to say that man living in society should not profit from the thoughts of others. For insofar as he is a human being, man is a gregarious animal. The gravitation of the planets towards the sun is as natural as the centrifugal force which pulls them away from it. But gregariousness must not entirely kill our individuality, only put it on a different and nobler basis. In this way society will be able to give us a thousand times more ideas than we would have if we were alone. However let them be ideas that we can understand, that we can call our own. Our mentor and guide is to shorten our path, but he must let us do our own walking; he must not attempt to carry us lest we should thereby become paralysed!

It is a difficult matter to trace every concept of each science and every word of each language back to the senses, in which and for which they arose; and yet this must be done for every science and every language.

Moreover, we have to make use of all our senses. The sense of touch, for example, is dormant in our time, and the eye takes its place, though often only very inadequately. There is a whole series of modifications of the sense of touch which can hardly be comprehended in the sum of the five senses as we have hitherto known them, and in the use of which youth must be cultivated and trained. In general there is no axiom more noteworthy, and almost none more often forgotten, than this: without the body, our mind will not function; if the senses are crippled, the mind is crippled too; if all the senses are used vigorously and in proper measure, the mind, too, is invigorated. There are indications that in the noble sensuality of ancient times, especially in the East, men's minds had, as it were, a wider orbit in which to work than ours. They could perceive both new phenomena and old ones in a far more vivid manner.

To produce original men, let them experience many things in their youth and let them perceive these in the manner that is natural to them, without compulsion and without prejudicing them in any particular direction. Every sensation received by the youthful mind embodies experiential data which remain of consequence for a lifetime, since they are constantly worked over in later years. The diverse tangible and vivid sensations, spontaneously perceived in the most uniquely individual manner, constitute the basic components of a sound human frame and the very foundation of that characteristic which we principally associate with original genius: strong, lively, creative ideas independently formed. The most propitious situations and ages for the emergence of genius have been those in which the minds of men were fertilized by a great number of strong and extraordinary experiences: in great republics, in times of patriotic zeal, during revolutions, liberation movements and political upheavals generally. These ages are past for us; we live in the century of ordinary experiences, of law and orderly government, of refinement and comfort, in which we must think like others because we learn to see what they see and as they see it and are forbidden by our religion, our political organization, the tone of our society, etc. to think as we ourselves might want to. We see few real phenomena in our youth—at the very time when we should see them if they are to remain alive in our minds. And those we do see are mostly weak, commonplace, trivial—phenomena of a comfortable, luxurious world, in which the government of states and all the great actions of the human race are secret or concealed or have even vanished entirely, so that the sight of them can no longer kindle great deeds. We are so smothered by words and by learning alien, generalized ideas that we pay no attention to these great actions, or at least cannot pay attention to them with the full fire of our souls. The most moving scenes of nature are nothing to us any more. Thus we receive only feeble, monotonous shocks; our youthful sensations tell our souls little; and the soul expires.

Oh, give me an unspoiled youthful soul, not smothered by abstractions and words, in all its fullness of life, and place me in a world in which I can give it all the impressions I wish: how it will live! . . . The thoughts which we elaborate later always derive from such early impressions, visions, feelings, sensations and phenomena, though they are often hard to rediscover. Childhood, in its long deep dream at the dawn of life, works on such impressions and modifies them in every way it can . . .

All the images we see are painted in our eye, in our brain; some traces—perhaps material ones—remain, and these constitute memory. These traces, revived and brought to bear on the realities of the present, constitute imagination. How do they become painted in the brain? Physically this problem is as yet inadequately solved. The observations on the brains of criminals, which Maupertuis proposes, would help. Then the world of material ideas would, as it were, come to life. How do these images remain in the brain and not be obliterated by others? Huarte has given us some sophistries on this subject which, for all their ingenuity, only show that no solution to this problem can come from merely brooding over it.

How can the images be awakened again in the brain? That is one of the three incomprehensibles which Scaliger could not solve—let us abandon metaphysics and speak practically.[15]

[15] Maupertuis, in his *Lettre sur le progrès des sciences* (1752) suggested that experiments should be performed on the brains of criminals who had been condemned to death. Huarte, Juan, *c.*1520–92, Spanish physician and author

Whilst the brain, or tablet of the mind, is soft and tender and receives all new images in their full strength, in all their colours and nuances, with all fidelity, freshness and flexibility, it reveals a receptive, tender, youthful soul . . . Gradually, however, the mind becomes closed, that is to say, it works over its earlier ideas; it applies them as often as it has the opportunity, and thus, by being constantly recalled and constantly more deeply imprinted they harden and become more rigid. Finally, precisely because of this constant powerful renewal, these ideas become the only ones in the mind and are fixed for life. They recur constantly, and the mind cannot think of anything without their recurrence. Naturally enough, these ideas in the end prevent the entrance of others and the mind finds it increasingly difficult to come to grips with novel situations. Novelty creates more strain than the mind can bear and hence it prefers to lean on what is old and already familiar; these are the ideas it revisits; here it is at ease. This timidity about entertaining new ideas, this attachment to old friends, is a sign of age.

Finally one gets to the point of talking about one's ideas until one forgets oneself in the telling and offers in one's words only feeble and dull copies of what one is actually thinking and imagining. Just as a habitual liar finally lies without even noticing it, so also a habitual talker talks without knowing what he is saying. He no longer pays any attention to whether or not what he says is full, emphatic, complete enough to make an adequate impression on one who has not seen or heard the things the speaker is talking about, or who has not heard them talked about as often as he himself has talked about them. O youthful epoch of the soul, which speaks as strongly as it sees and feels! With each repetition a touch of attentiveness disappears; with each repetition an image is weakened and becomes a mere imitation, a mere second copy, until finally it is the feeblest product of the mind.

O you great masters of all time, you Moses' and Homers! You sang from inspiration! You planted what you sang in eternal metre, in which it was held fast; and thus it could be sung again for as long as men wanted to sing it. We in our dull, uncertain prose, at

of the *Examen de ingenios para las sciencias,* which Herder is here referring to. Scaliger, Julius Caesar, 1484–1558, Italian physicist and scholar. Herder is referring to the *Exoticarum exercitationum liber quintus decimus de subtilitate* (1557).

the mercy of ourselves and of every passing moment, repeat ourselves and drone prosaically on until at last we say nothing any more. This is what happens to an old professor who has read the same old stuff too often; to an old preacher who has taught, spoken and conducted services too often in the same old way; to an old wit—he becomes feeble in the end: the sting has gone, and what should be delicacy becomes mere *finesse*.

All this suggests one master rule: *Make the images of your imagination so enduring that you do not lose them, yet, at the same time, refrain from recalling them at inappropriate moments!* This may serve as a rule for preserving the eternal youth of the mind. He whose earliest images are so weak that he cannot express them strongly—with exactly the degree of strength in which he received them—that man is feeble and old. This is what happens to all widely read men and to men who read too much, who either never have the chance to recall in a strong and lively manner what they have read, or who do not have sufficient vivacity to read as though they themselves saw, felt, experienced and applied what they were reading; or, finally, who sacrifice their own individuality through excessive, sporadic, scattered reading!

III. THE VOYAGE: REFLECTIONS ON SOCIAL
AND POLITICAL CULTURES

[IV, 354–64; 401–45]

The ship is the archetype of a very special and severe form of government. Since it is a small state which sees enemies everywhere around it—sky, storm, wind, sea, currents, cliffs, darkness, other ships, the shore—it requires a government which comes close to the despotism of the early hostile ages. Here is a monarch with his prime minister, the helmsman; everyone below him has his appointed place and duties, and any neglect of these—especially any rebellion against them—is very severely punished. There are two reasons, then, why Russia does not as yet have a good navy. First, there is no discipline on their ships—just where it should be strictest unless the whole ship is to be lost. Anecdotes from Peter's life show that even he had to submit to this state of affairs and allow himself to be thrust, sword in hand, into his cabin, because he commanded unjustly. Secondly, instead of everyone having his assigned place, anyone is used for anything. The decrepit old soldier who no longer has the desire or the ability to learn any-thing new becomes a sailor, and soon thinks himself a real seaman when he can hardly clamber up the rigging. In bygone days, when navigation as an art was scarcely known, when ships con-sisted of oars and hands, men and soldiers, and nothing more, this state of affairs might have been feasible. But nowadays there is no art more complex than navigation. Everything may depend on a single oversight, a single case of ignorance. The Russians, therefore, would have to become accustomed to the sea from their youth and learn from other nations before they practice . . . No nation is more eager to imitate, to adopt the ways of others than they; but then, when they think they know everything, they never investigate further and so always remain bunglers in every-thing they undertake. It is not only as seafarers that they try to copy others. They show the same facile tendency when they pre-tend to assume French manners and the French language. The same is true of their handicrafts, their manufactures and their arts. But in all these spheres they stop short of really becoming *proficient* imitators. They never get beyond a certain point. All the same, I see in this desire to imitate, in this childlike passion for innovation, nothing but the healthy disposition of a developing nation—a tendency in the right direction. Let it learn, imitate and compile from all sides; let it even remain for a time less than fully developed. But let there also come a time, a monarch, a century which will lead the nation to the stage of fruition. What a great intellectual under-taking we have here for a statesman—to consider how the energies of a youthful, half-savage people can be brought to maturity so that it becomes a genuinely great and original nation. Peter the Great will always remain the creator who brought about the dawn of a new day; but the noontide is yet to come, and the great work of 'civilizing a nation to perfection' is yet to be accomplished . . .

One imagines that as one glides past countries and continents at sea one will think a great deal about them; but actually one does not see them. They are only mists lying in the distance, and so, for the most part, are the ideas which ordinary minds form of them. It makes no difference whether these are Courlandish,

Prussian, Pomeranian, Danish, Swedish, Norwegian, Dutch, English or French waters; as we navigate today, it is just sea everywhere. In this respect the navigation of the ancients was different: it showed the sailor coasts and races of men. In their battles we hear characters, real men speaking. Today everything is a science— battles, war, navigation, everything. I wanted to enlist the aid of travel-books so that I could form an opinion about the countries whose coasts we were passing, as if I had seen the countries themselves; but this too was in vain. I found nothing on the ship but lists of landfalls and saw nothing but distant coasts.

Livonia, thou province of barbarism and luxury, of ignorance and pretended taste, of freedom and slavery, how much would there be to do in thee! How much to do to destroy barbarism, to root out ignorance, to spread culture and freedom, to be a second Zwingli, Calvin or Luther to this province! Can I do this? Do I have the disposition, the opportunity, the talents? What must I do to attain this end? What must I destroy in myself?—Do I need to ask? I must give up writing useless criticisms and pursuing dead researches; raise myself above disputations and literary fame; dedicate myself to the benefit and the education of the living world; win the confidence of the administration, the imperial government and the court; travel through France, England and Italy with this in mind and acquire the French language and *savoir-faire*, the English sense of reality and freedom, the Italian taste for subtle invention, the German thoroughness and knowledge, and lastly, where it is necessary, Dutch erudition; arouse others to a high opinion of me and myself to great plans; conform to the age in which I live and acquire the spirit of commerce and polity; dare to examine everything from the point of view of politics, the state and finances; not expose myself to any further ridicule and try to make good as quickly as possible my previous mistakes in this respect; concentrate night and day on becoming this guiding genius of Livonia, on getting to know the country from A to Z, on thinking and acting practically in all things, on accustoming myself to talk persuasively to society, the nobility and the common men and win them over to my side.

But is all this really dormant within you, noble-minded youth? Is it just a matter of neglect, a case of having failed so far to translate it into reality? The narrowness of your education, the slavery of your native land, the petty, trifling spirit of your century, the uncertain state of your career, have all combined to limit you, to debase you so that you scarcely recognize yourself. You are wasting the fire of your youth, the finest heat of your genius, the strongest part of your ambitious passion in useless, coarse, wretched critical groves.[16] You have a soul as sluggish and slack as all the fibres and nerves of your body. Wretched man, what manner of things do you busy yourself with? How do they compare with the things which you should, and—since the occasion, the opportunity and the obligation are there—*could* be doing? O that a Fury would appear in my groves to frighten me, to chase me out of them forever and banish me to the useful activity of the great world! Livonia is a province given over to foreigners! And many foreigners have enjoyed it in the past, but only in their merchants' way, in order to get rich from it; to me, also a foreigner, it is given for a higher purpose, that I may develop it! . . . Let my first prospect be the study of the human soul, in itself and in its manifestations on this earth; its strains and stresses, its hopes and satisfactions, its influence on a man's character and on his conception of his duties; in short, let me discover the springs of human happiness. Everything else is to be set aside whilst I am engaged in gathering materials for this task and in learning to know, arouse, control and use every motive force in the human heart, from fear and wonder to quiet meditation and gentle daydreaming. For this purpose I will collect data from the history of all ages; each shall yield to me the picture of its own customs, usages, virtues, and vices, and of its own conception of happiness; and I will trace them all down to the present and so learn to use it rightly. In every age—though in each in a different way—the human race has had happiness as its objective; we in our own times are misled if, like Rousseau, we extol ages which no longer exist and never did exist, if we make ourselves miserable by painting romantic pictures of these ages to the disparagement of our own, instead of finding enjoyment in the present. Seek then even in biblical times only that religion and virtue, those examples, those forms of happiness, which are appropriate to us: become a

[16] Herder is referring to his own *Kritische Wälder*, of which three parts had appeared earlier in 1769 and a fourth was in preparation while he was in Nantes.

preacher of the virtue *of your own age!* Oh, how much I have to do to achieve this! . . .

I sailed past Courland, Prussia, Denmark, Sweden, Norway, Jutland, Holland, Scotland, England and the Netherlands to France: here are a few political sea-dreams. *Courland*, the land of licence and poverty, of freedom and confusion, now a moral and literary desert. If certain [of my] plans succeed, could it not become the seat and repository of freedom and learning? If the rights and power of the nobility were well used, if their acquired taste for luxury were directed to great ends? A library is the prime necessity here; other things can develop out of it . . . How would it be possible to persuade the Livonian nobility to support great and good institutions? The nobility of Courland could be approached through Masonic lodges; the Livonians through a sense of honour, the respect due to my cloth, my fame as a scholar, and my usefulness to the province. In this way, then, I can work for the improvement of the Lyceum, for the acquisition of a collection of scientific specimens and instruments, for the founding of new teaching appointments in drawing, French, Italian etc.[17] The good social relations of the preachers in Courland should also be a model for me! What a prospect these regions of western and northern Russia will afford, if ever the spirit of culture visits them! The Ukraine will become a new Greece; the beautiful sky under which these people live, their happy disposition, their musical nature, their fertile land, etc. will awake some day; from so many small, savage peoples—as the Greeks too once were—will develop a civilized nation, whose territory will extend to the Black Sea and thence throughout the world.[18] Hungary, its peoples, a portion of Poland, and Russia will share this new culture, and its spirit will spread from the northwest over Europe, which now lies asleep, and make a spiritual conquest of it.

All this lies ahead and is bound to happen; but how, when, and by what means? What seeds lie dormant in the spirit of these people that will give them a mythology, a poetry, a living culture? Can the Catholic religion awaken them? No, and it will not, to judge from

[17] Herder was to succeed the incumbent rector of the Imperial Livonian *Lyzeum* in Riga.
[18] Herder's interest in the Slavs recurs throughout his subsequent writings, reaching a climax in the *Ideen.*

its condition in Hungary, Poland, etc., from the spirit of toleration which is spreading to an ever greater extent even in this and the Greek religion, and from its apparent inability to make any further conquests. Our [Protestant] religions, on the other hand, with their tolerance, their refinement, their tendency to merge in a common deism, will just fall asleep and peter out like the ancient Roman religion that adopted every foreign god. Their once potent ferment will be revived from its slumber and arouse people in another corner of the earth. And which will be the first people to be aroused? What form will the awakening take? What will be the ingredients of their new way of thinking? Will their culture develop in an essentially aggressive manner, or peacefully and quietly? What is there in Europe that will endure by virtue of book printing, the countless inventions and the habits of thought among its nations? Can one not make conjectures on all this from the condition of the present-day world and on the analogy of past centuries? And can one not influence these things in advance? Would it not prove extremely rewarding to show Russia that she could develop a truly national culture of her own? Anyone able to do this would be more than a Bacon; he would display a vision greater than that of a Newton. But he would have to observe with the spirit of a Montesquieu, write with the fiery pen of a Rousseau and have Voltaire's good fortune in catching the ear of the great. Our century is the time for the task: we have Hume and Locke, Montesquieu and Mably; we have an Empress of Russia who can be attacked through the weakness of her code of laws, as Voltaire attacked the King of Prussia; and who knows what will come out of the present war in those regions?[19] I want to make an attempt in this direction. Schlözer's Russian annals, supplements and curiosities, Miller's collections and the former's history of Moldavia shall be my model in thinking, or at least in expression;[20] and the Empress' code of laws shall form at least the frame of my picture 'Concerning the True Culture of a People, and Especially of Russia'.[21]

[19] Herder is referring to the Russo-Turkish war of 1768–74.
[20] The works referred to are August Ludwig von Schlözer's *Annalen von Russland*, part I, 1767, *Probe Russischer Annalen*, 1768, and *Beilage zum neuveränderten Russland, oder das Leben Catharina der Zweyten*, 1769–72, and Gerhard Friedrich Müller's *Sammlung russischer Geschichte*.
[21] Catherine called a convention in Moscow in 1767 to formulate new laws.

I. In what does true culture consist? Not merely in providing laws but in cultivating morals and customs, especially if the laws are derived from imported foreign principles. And in framing legislation for Russia, should 'honour' be of high priority? What image does Russia project as a nation? Its laziness is not as bad as it is made out to be; up to a point it is also perfectly natural: every nation went through such a sleepy stage before its true awakening. Its cunning, its passion for imitation, its frivolity: do these not also contain seeds of good? How are these seeds to be nurtured into germination? What are the obstacles one might meet? Which path leads to freedom gradually, since sudden freedom might prove harmful? What form should the institutions take? Could not the sudden acquisition of colonies present a real danger? Would it not prove equally hazardous to be too quick in adopting other countries, such as Germany, as models? The excellence of good institutions counts for more than the best of laws and certainly as much as any example set by the court, especially in such spheres as agriculture, family life and housekeeping. I would comment on the dependence of the subjects, their taxes and their general way of life, and make some proposals for a new economic order of society more in keeping with the spirit of the Russian economy. No other country—not even Sweden—can always serve here as a model. Concerning luxury, I would argue that mere decrees are of no avail whatsoever; mention of the evil consequences of such decrees in Riga should drive this point home. The example of the court [in this respect] is only valid at the court, though even there its prestigious advantages are not without disadvantages. Many individual examples taken from the diverse provinces or, better still, from individual households should prove more relevant and effective. I would show also that as a result of a number of Russian gentlemen lining their pockets in Petersburg, the state of Petersburg is degenerating into tasteless splendour—though the Empress is working against this. In France conditions are somewhat different because of the constant visits of foreigners and the different nature of the institutions; but even there the country is faced with exhaustion largely as a result of the bad example set by provincial governors and by the supervisors on farms and in the factories.

II. Next I would point out that neither English, nor French,

nor German legal minds can legislate for Russia; and that neither
Greece nor Rome can be taken as models. Is it not obvious enough,
how mistaken Russia was to imitate Sweden? There are peoples
in the East from whom Russia can learn far more: Persians,
Assyrians, Egyptians, Chinese and Japanese. The principles underlying legislation must, moreover, pay heed to the character of
Russia's nations, their multiplicity and their various levels of
culture: there are regions which are highly developed, but there
are also those which are still very primitive or underdeveloped.
The laws which the latter need for their development are the basic
laws of mankind generally—the laws of crude primitive times.
Russia can make excellent use of her underdeveloped peoples.
The semi-developed regions require laws that will in the first
place do no more than turn them into governable provinces. The
differences between the spirit and culture in the provinces and
in the capitals must also be kept in mind. Clearly, the capitals
and commercial cities need laws of their own. In all this Montesquieu could serve me as a guide. I would first describe the primitive peoples on the borders; then the semi-developed areas of the
interior; and finally the developed regions along the seacoast. The
Ukraine would command my particular attention: here I would
mention my former plans.

III. The material content of the laws and the contribution
made by each to the development and education of the people
would form the third part of my study. I would treat everything according to Montesquieu's method, briefly and with
examples, but without his system. The errors of Russian legislation will be freely criticized, and its good points freely praised.
Plenty of examples, reports and facts will be adduced. It should
be a great work! And if it achieved its purpose: what a calling
to be a legislator for princes and kings! This is the moment to
act in Russia: the age, the century, the spirit, the very taste
demand it.

The States of the King of Prussia will not be happy until they
become autonomous parts of a large fraternal [German] union.
How far can a man [like Frederick] go through his own unaided
efforts? How great it would be to follow him along all the secret
paths of his mind! How great if he could write his political testament

without deserving the epigram he himself wrote on Richelieu![22] Whatever we may think of him now, how will he appear to posterity? What will his Silesia mean then? Where will his empire be?—Where is the empire of Pyrrhus now? Does not Frederick greatly resemble him?—Beyond a doubt, his greatest traits are negative—defensive ability, strength and endurance; and only his truly great institutions will prove lasting. His Academy, however, what has it accomplished? Have his Frenchmen brought as much benefit to Germany and its states as people thought they would? No! His Voltaires despised the Germans without knowing them, while the Germans for their part took as much interest in them as they would have taken in anything emanating from France. His Academy has contributed to the decline of philosophy. His Maupertuis', Prémontvals, Formeys, D'Argens'[23]—what kind of philosophers are they? To what kind of writings have they awarded prizes? They have misunderstood Leibniz and Wolff and have hatched out Prémontval's essay on chance, Justi's monadology, Reinhard's free will, Maupertuis' moral philosophy and cosmology and Formey's style.[24] And what is Formey in comparison to Fontenelle? What are the philosophers themselves, with all their fine style, in comparison to men like Locke and Leibniz?—Admittedly, in philological studies the Academy has recently become more of an asset. Michaelis and Prémontval have done some good work in this field; the current problem posed by the Academy has aroused considerable attention;[25] but nothing great has been

[22] Frederick II had described Richelieu's *Testament Politique* in an epigram addressed to Voltaire as the result of the temporary eclipse of an otherwise great mind. Frederick himself did in fact write two political testaments, one in 1752 and the other in 1768, but they were not published in full until 1920.

[23] Maupertuis, Pierre Louis Moreau de, 1698–1759; Prémontval (assumed name of André Pierre Le Guay), 1716–64; Formey, Johann Heinrich Samuel, 1711–97; D'Argens, Jean Baptiste de Boyer, *Marquis*, 1704–71; were all members of the Berlin Academy. Maupertuis was president from 1746, Formey was perpetual secretary from 1748, and D'Argens was Director of Fine Arts.

[24] Prémontval's *Du Hasard* appeared in 1755. Johann Heinrich Gottlob von Justi, 1720–71, best known for his contribution to cameralism, had attacked Leibniz's *Monadologie* in an Academy prize essay in 1748. Adolph Friedrich von Reinhard, 1726–83, German philosopher. He wrote a prize essay in 1755 comparing Pope and Leibniz as metaphysicians.

[25] Michaelis, Johann David, 1717–91, theologian and orientalist, professor of philosophy at Göttingen, editor of the *Gelehrte Anzeigen* from 1753 to 1770, and librarian of the University of Göttingen. His philological writings

94

achieved to date. Mathematics has had its Euler, but he would have developed under any circumstances, just as Le Grange educated himself in private.[26] Unfortunately the Academy's discoveries lack that great practicality in application by means of which nations learn and philosophers improve their theories in order to carry them into execution. The Voltairean taste in history, which Frederick also followed, did not spread through his efforts; his subjects were too far beneath him and Voltaire to take the former as their model: they were too German, too ignorant or unsophisticated, too submissive. Frederick's and Voltaire's philosophy has spread, but mainly to the detriment of the world. Frederick's personal example, however, has proved even more harmful than his philosophical theories. Was he not completely ignorant of his Germans? Did he not thoroughly despise Prussia? He may have refuted Machiavelli in print, but this did not prevent him from following him in practice. There may well be prospects for the happiness of his subjects after the division of his territories.

Sweden: I see the rock of Olaus![27] What an age it was in which he lived and died! His grave, shrouded in clouds and mist, and washed by the waves, calls to mind a host of magnificent ideas about the enchantment and mystery of his times. How the world has changed! What a contrast between the three ages—the ancient Scandinavian world, the world of Olaus and the poor, economic, enlightened Sweden of our times. It was here that Goths, pirates, Vikings and Norsemen once sailed; that the songs of their skalds resounded! Here they performed their wondrous deeds! Here heroes like Lodbrog and Skille fought! What a different age!

consisted of grammars of the Hebrew, Syriac and Chaldee languages. The 'current problem posed by the Academy' was its 1769 prize essay on the subject: 'En supposant les hommes abandonnés à leurs facultés naturelles, sont-ils en état d'inventer le langage? et par quels moyens parviendront-ils d'eux-mêmes à cette invention?' Herder submitted his *Abhandlung über den Ursprung der Sprache*, which won the prize.

[26] Euler, Leonard, 1707–83, celebrated Swiss geometrician. From 1741 to 1766 he lived in Berlin, having been invited by Frederick II to assist in the formation of the Academy. Lagrange, Joseph-Louis, 1736–1814, eminent geometrician, director of the mathematical section of the Academy from 1766 to 1787.

[27] Olaf Tryggvason, a Viking chief, was defeated in a naval battle in A.D. 1000 at Svoldr which, according to tradition, was an island in the Baltic near Rügen. When all hope was lost, Olaf is said to have hurled himself into the sea.

In future I will read their songs in just such dark, gloomy regions as these and will hear them as though I were on the sea; then I shall feel them more deeply than Nero felt the epic he sang when Rome burned. How different from these times was the time when the Hanseatic cities ruled over this sea! Visby, where are you now? Ancient splendour of Lübeck, when a dance with the queen cost Bornholm and you gave Sweden her Gustavus Vasa, where are you now? Ancient freedom of Riga, when the alderman left his hat in the town hall and hastened towards Sweden to defend the city, where are you now?[28] Everything has relapsed: weakness, falsehood, inactivity and political servility have been introduced along with effeminate manners; the spirit of the Hanseatic cities is gone from northern Europe, and who will reawaken it? And is it not a great and historically important question for each of these towns— Hamburg, Lübeck, Danzig, Riga—*how* this spirit was lost? It is not how their trade, their privileges, etc., diminished and finally departed from Europe which is significant historically, so much as the loss of their very *spirit*? And do we have such histories of the Hanseatic towns? Willebrand should write them, if he were not too pious, and all the Hanseatic towns should read them aloud at their public assemblies![29]

Take Riga, what is it now? Poor, nay more than poor, wretched! The town has nothing and must lay out more than it has to maintain its paltry, useless, expensive splendour. Its town militia costs money, and what does it do? Its walls and its keys to the city cost money, and what do they do? The dignity of its aldermen costs them so much trouble in their relations with others, and all the benefit they derive from it is that they can give themselves airs and offend the citizens.... It must not remain a sham republic, but must become a free state with privileges and rank within the larger [Russian] empire, a republic within a republic, as it were.

[28] Visby was the commercial centre of N. Europe in the early days of the Hanseatic League. It was conquered by Sweden and later by Denmark but restored to the League in 1370. It declined in importance with the rise of Lübeck. After complicated negotiations, the city of Lübeck acquired the island of Bornholm from the Danish crown in 1526. The Swedish king, Gustavus Vasa, had been supported by Lübeck during Sweden's war of liberation against Denmark, 1521–3. Riga was attacked by Sweden under Gustavus Adolphus in 1621.

[29] Willebrand, Johan Peter, 1719–86, wrote a *Hansische Chronik*, in 1748 and a *Betrachtung über die Würde der deutschen Hansa* (1768).

What a happy man he would be who could bring this about! He would be more than Zwingli and Calvin—a liberator and at the same time a citizen! Are there no possible ways of doing this? If not now, perhaps later, through pressure at court? I have hitherto been in the service of the city, have associated with advocates, the chancellery and the council; now I am to come under the crown, and I will get to know this department too, will investigate both—will this not be advantageous to me? Let me but make use of Campenhausen, Tesch, Schwarz and Berens, let me work quietly, and perhaps one day I shall be able to speak a word in the ear of the Empress![30] What Morellet has accomplished in France, can I not accomplish elsewhere?[31] To this end I will cultivate my gift for both phlegm and ardour, develop the knack of first expressing myself in cold, clear proposals, only later supporting them with enthusiasm, and thus quietly prepare myself to be useful some day. I will turn away as completely as I can from the spirit of authorship and accustom myself to a life of action!—How great if I can make Riga a happy city!

The third stage on the Baltic is the Dutch domains. Holland, this miracle of a republic, has only one driving force—the commercial spirit—and I should like to read a history of this spirit: how it succeeded the spirit of the feudal wars, transplanted itself from America and Asia to Europe and created the spirit of a new age. It was not the same as the spirit of exploration—Portugal and Spain did not make full economic use of their discoveries. It was something quite different: the spirit of a new European economy, to which a poor, needy, industrious republic raised itself out of the marshes. And what a great concatenation of circumstances accompanied Holland's rise to good fortune—to the good fortune of Europe! Everyone learned from the Dutch; the same spirit spread everywhere: to England with its Navigation Acts, to France, Sweden, Denmark, etc. Now Holland is on the verge of declining, though of course only gradually. The author of *Le*

[30] Baron Johann Christoph von Campenhausen was head of the Russian provincial government in Riga. Tesch, Schwarz and Berens were prominent citizens of Riga and friends of Herder.
[31] Morellet, André, 1727–1819, friend of Voltaire, Rousseau, Diderot and D'Alembert, contributor to the Encyclopedia and author of many works on political economy.

Commerce de la Hollande has demonstrated this;[32] but his exped-ient of finding a remedy by discovering the fifth continent will not work. The spirit of exploration is one thing; that of commerce is quite another. In view of this, Holland has shown little inclination to even contemplate such an undertaking. But even assuming it had undertaken such a task, it would scarcely have been possible for the Dutch to take possession of the new territory and bring it under their rule; eventually they would lose it as surely as they lost Brazil and Portugal lost its East Indian possessions. This decline is hardly avoidable any more; the whole constellation in Europe is such that it virtually demands it, and Holland itself is in no position to prevent it. Its shipping is no longer profitable; the shares of the East India Company are falling; the republic weighs less in the balance of Europe and must continue to weigh less or it will decline still further. It enriches itself from the goods which it receives from others to make a profit on, and these others are giving it less and will eventually want to make money out of Holland themselves. A time will come, perhaps in my own lifetime, when Holland will be nothing but a lifeless warehouse which is being emptied but not replenished, and hence goes out of business like a fancy-goods stall that fails to replace its stock. The foreign exchange market, however, should manage to continue longer than the market in goods, unless England, with its national debt, should suddenly go bankrupt. By this means Holland should be able to maintain itself for some time to come; for all Europe needs a moneychanger, and this moneychanger must be connected with sea transport, must have precision as its national characteristic —and lo, that country is Holland! A republic, in the centre of Europe, born to the sea, industrious and nothing more, exact and fair in its accounting as in its cash transactions, it will remain the moneychanger for a long time, but what will it be beyond this? Not a sea power, but a servant of the sea; no longer a trading nation, but the servant and instrument of trade; what a great change! Then the world will see what weaknesses are inherent in a commercial spirit which is nothing but a commercial spirit; no brooding philosopher, but the actual events themselves will drive home this realization, and they will teach this lesson, not by

---

[32] Herder read *Le Commerce de la Hollande* by Jacques Accariague de Sérionne, 1709–92, during the voyage.

words, but by deeds, in one great example for all Europe given by a whole nation. Then people will see how the unadulterated commercial spirit kills or restricts the spirit of valour, of great undertaking, of true statesmanship, wisdom, learning, etc.; one can see this to some extent even now in Holland. Is there any true genius here? I make an exception of the honest Frisians—this province is not Holland; for the rest, as far as publications are concerned, be they Latin, Greek, Hebrew or Arabic studies, medical works or commercial treatises, though one must acknowledge them to be very good, indeed excellent and exemplary by the standards of our [German] literature, they nonetheless lack genius. The Dutch get further than the Germans and the French, who devote themselves to everything indiscrimately, and not as far as the English, who always combine genius with their practical experiments—and indeed often exaggerate the former. Everything in Holland is for sale: talents, which therefore become mere industry; learning—and that too becomes industry; humanity, *honnêteté*, everything is formed by the commercial spirit. For all that, I want to see Holland first, for, genius apart, I believe it to be the best of all countries in which to memorize the stock-in-trade of methodical scholarship.

But what will succeed the commercial spirit of Holland? The spirit of faction—characteristic of the internal economic competition of many a country? For a while, I think, this will prevail: everything in Europe points to it. Or the spirit of faction in the sense of incitement to rebellion? This is an inevitable consequence of the former. One of the great commercial powers—England, for example—will stir up another nation that is still primitive and will be ruined itself in the process—and could not this primitive nation be Russia? Or will we see the spirit of complete savagery—heathenism and the submerging of nations? How do I know? . . . No one in Greece said a word about Rome until Rome conquered it; it was the same with Greece and Egypt, Egypt and Persia, Assyria and Media. With Rome and the barbarians it was, however, different: there, to speak in common parlance, the word had been getting around for a long time. Maybe, in our age, the word has to get around for longer still, but the outbreak will be all the more sudden.

After all, what do all our arts of war amount to? . . . One new invention which supersedes all previous ones, can put all that went before into shade. What of all our erudition and learning, our printing presses, our libraries, and so on? One general calamity, one inundation of barbarians—even a Moravian spirit in the pulpits, which makes learning a sin and a want of religion, and philosophy the source of ruin—can bring in the spirit which burns libraries and printing presses, abandons the regions of learning and becomes ignorant for piety's sake. So with our deism, with our philosophizing about religion, with our too-refined cultivation of reason itself, we are working ourselves into ruin. But this is inevitable in the very nature of things. The same material that gives us strength and turns our cartilage to bone ends by turning to bone even that which should remain cartilage; and the same refinement which makes the populace civilized eventually makes it old, weak and useless. Who can oppose the nature of things? The wise man continues on his way, enlightening human reason, and only shrugs his shoulders when fools talk of this enlightenment as a final goal, as an eternal state. One must, therefore, refute political thinkers like Diderot . . . or—since to do so might go too much against the anti-Rousseauistic temper of our times, incur the charge of merely spinning fables and, being premature, fail to produce any tangible results—make at least one's own mental reservations. Enlightenment is never an end, but always a means; if it becomes the former it is a sign that it has ceased to be the latter, as was the case in France, still more in Italy and still more in Greece—and finally even in Egypt and Asia. If those who lack enlightenment are regarded as contemptible barbarians, what about the monks of Lebanon, the pilgrims to Mecca, the Greek monks (real vermin from the rottenness of a noble horse)? The Italian academies, like the one at Cortona, show us the relics of their ancestors and write long books—*mémoires*, quartos and folios—about them to prove their right to show them to us.[33] In France things will soon be as bad; when men like Voltaire and Montesquieu are dead, others will water down their spirit and that of Bossuet, Racine, etc. until there is nothing left of it. Now they are making an encyclopedia: even men like Diderot and D'Alembert lower themselves to it;

[33] The Etruscan Academy at Cortona, founded in 1727. For Herder's attitude to Academies see also *Vom Einfluss der Regierung auf die Wissenschaften und der Wissenschaften auf die Regierung*, IX, 351–7.

and this very book, which the French regard as their triumph, is to me the chief sign of their decline. They have nothing to write, so they make *abrégés*, *dictionnaires*, *histoires*, *vocabulaires*, *esprits*, encyclopedias, etc. Original works are not produced. That a people once started on the wrong road loses itself all the more completely because of its intellectual refinement is shown by the incomparable Montesquieu in the case of the Greeks, who because of their intellectual refinement became all the more deeply entangled in the speculation about religion which overthrew their whole structure.

England—Is it going to ruin itself through its trade? Will its national debt cause the decline of the whole country? Will it not be injured by its American colonies? How does it fare in competition with other nations? Or, on the other hand, how much more intense can this competition become? Is England then in a commercial decline or will it rise still higher? Will not its spirit of manufacture, of arts, of sciences maintain itself for a long time to come? Is not the country protected by its sea-girt situation, by its institutions, its freedom, its brains? And—especially if it should turn out to be the country which stirs up future conquering nations—will it not at least gain a respite for itself and save itself from ruin for a long time?—

France: Its age in literature is finished—the century of Louis XIV is past; men like Montesquieu, D'Alembert, Voltaire and Rousseau are past also; the nation is living on the ruins. What significance have the present-day singers of heroides, the little writers of comedies and the makers of little songs? The taste for encyclopedias, dictionaries, extracts and 'spirits of the writing' shows the lack of original writings. So does the taste for foreign writings, the laudatory articles on them in the *Journal étranger* etc.; in translation these writings must always lose their true expression, their stamp of authenticity, and if they are read in spite of this it is a sign that their intrinsic worth, the nature of their thoughts, is in itself rich enough so that they do not need stylistic beauty. And since the French make so much, indeed everything, of the latter; since the turn of phrase, the expression and the clothing of the thought in general is all in all to them; the fact that the despised Germans—who depart so far from the turns of phrase and the beloved finery of the French—are read nonetheless, is in itself a clear indication of the poverty of the country, of its humiliating decline . . .

How can the French manner be imitated in German? It cannot—so much the less since we know little of this monarchy, these courtly conditions, this *honneur* in literature; since we cannot have these things and, where we do have them, buy them at a loss. The Frenchman knows nothing of the reality of metaphysics and cannot comprehend that there is anything of real significance in it. In his philosophy he knows and seeks only what is socially conventional; we on the other hand love abstract truth, which we think lovable in itself, and the concrete is to us not merely the main concern but the *conditio sine qua non*. So also in physics, etc. In Fontenelle everything is smothered under conversation; in his eulogies all the material content is buried under fine turns of phrase, so that science itself becomes a matter of secondary importance. Much the same is true of social philosophy: in Rousseau everything must have a paradoxical turn, and this spoils him, seduces him, leads him to make commonplace things new, small things great, true things untrue and untrue things true. Nothing is just a simple statement with him: everything has to be new, striking, wonderful. Thus what is in itself beautiful becomes exaggerated, what is true becomes too generalized and ceases to be true; its false ornamentation has to be stripped away, it has to be brought back into our world: but who can do this? Is the common reader capable of it? And is it not often more trouble than it is worth? Thus does not Rousseau, for all his greatness, become by his very brilliance useless or even harmful?—Finally, even Voltaire—what is history to him but a supplement to and an occasion for his wit, his mockery, his sardonic observation? This last is fine in itself—it can be especially useful in educating the Germans—but can it be imitated? Be imitated in history? Be a model for history? With or without Voltaire's brilliance?—Never! History is distorted with this brilliance and would be still more so without it. Read him then as 'Voltaire's Occasional Notions on History'! This is the right way, and one can learn much by it. This applies still more strongly to his writings on the abstract sciences, Newtonian philosophy and most of all metaphysics . . .

Finally Montesquieu: Is even he entirely free from the *faux-*

brillant? Note how often he is unrecognizable in translation, and to some extent must be so on account of both the virtues and the vices of his diction. Nor is he entirely free from the pseudo-philosophical. The way he translates into our more philosophical language is a striking demonstration of this.—One can see the trouble he takes to be abstract and profound, to abbreviate ideas so as to give the reader much to ponder over and to make it appear that he himself has thought even more than he has expressed. For instance, he will include comments on minor juristic cases and phenomena under the pretext that they provide a broader perspective, that they are continuations of his main subject, relevant observations, preparatory remarks, etc. Even his basic principles, true, subtle and fine as they are, are not complete and are subject to endless variations. There are democratic aristocracies and vice versa; aristocracies and democracies, the latter at various stages of culture, the former at various stages of power and prestige; aristocratic monarchies and monarchist aristocracies, the latter represented by Rome, Florence, etc., the former by Sweden and Poland—and how different from each other even these last two examples are! And they appear even more different if one considers their institutions, their customs, their culture and the power of their respective aristocracies and kings. Then we have monarchic despotism, in which the latter term is merely tempered by the former, as in France under Louis XIV and Richelieu; despotic monarchy, as in Prussia and, less obviously, in Denmark; aristocratic despotism as in Russia and democratic despotism as in Turkey; democratic-aristocratic monarchy as in Sweden, monarchic-aristocratic democracy as in England, etc. Who can go through all the smaller republics and state constitutions—in all times, in all lands, in all their changes? Even Rome alone—how much it contained! When was it consistent with itself? Never! What a fine work remains to be written by Montesquieu (*Spirit of the Laws*) about Montesquieu (*Spirit of the Romans*)—a work which neither he nor Mably has produced![34]—How necessary it is,

---

[34] In his [unpublished] notes 'Thoughts on reading Montesquieu' written at the same time as the *Journal of my Voyage*, Herder further elaborates his criticisms of Montesquieu's *Spirit of the Laws*. He points out, for example, that Montesquieu knew too few political systems and that even those few which he dealt with he did not analyse sufficiently to arrive at universal principles (IV, 465–6).

then, to understand and supplement him, to fill in the gaps and apply him correctly! Yet how difficult it is, too, especially the latter! The provision of a constitution for Russia shows this very clearly. Had Montesquieu produced a work by which he could be remembered after his death as a lawgiver to this, the greatest empire in the world, how great would be his reputation! It is great enough now, so far as popularity is concerned; but has he proved himself really worthy and really useful? I do not know.

[*Russia*] The Empress of Russia has assumed in her legislation a motive which is alien to her language, her nation and her empire: honour. Read Montesquieu on this matter, and point for point the Russian nation and constitution are the reverse of what he has to say; read him on despotism and fear, however, and point for point it fits the Russian scene. The question he does not settle is whether honour and despotism can exist simultaneously.

Honour demands that a man distinguish himself from his fellow citizens, that he perform noble, great, extraordinary actions; a Russian cannot have this motive, for he has no fellow citizens: he has not even a word for 'citizen' in his language. The young Russian of rank sees in citizens nothing but servants; of this I myself have known a telling example or two. The young Russian of no social position thinks only of clever tricks whereby he can advance himself. These tricks constitute the real spirit of the nation; for it is they, and not greatness of mind, which net in material advantage. Thus the man of wealth and social standing raises himself to political prominence by successful rebellion, whilst the poor man supports him because he hopes to grow rich in the process. Both, as slaves, risk their all—failure or success— fear or hope! Their gambling conflicts in every respect with the concept of honour! Is it honourable to be a deceitful merchant, a flatterer, a rebel, a regicide? The Russian is all these things by nature!

Honour demands that one shall not flatter basely; the Russian is never anything other than base in his flattery, which he uses in order to become great at the expense of others; that is, he is a slave in order to become a despot. Honour demands that one speak the truth when *honnêteté* requires it; the Russian speaks it then least of all, and lies for the most paltry of advantages. Russian politeness is coarsely despotic—for example in drinking, kissing, etc. It shows a crude idea of honour and is itself mere coarse habit or even hypocrisy. No Russian is refined simply in order to show that he is not coarse or base: for then he would always be refined, even towards servants and subordinates, whereas it is precisely to these that he is a despot . . .

Not only, then, does this motive not exist, but its opposite, slavish fear, is all the more operative. How then can honour be used as a motive force for legislation? If it is so used, the court will deceive itself, the laws will not be maintained and complete savagery will set in. It will be impossible to anticipate, restrain, or control fear and the heinous deeds it inspires—because the laws are too mild! On the other hand, laws will never infuse honour into the country, and therefore will never make it operative; the state, then, will have no motive force. It will remain a despotic aristocracy, or at best a democratic-aristocratic despotism, and will fall into a great revolution as soon as the code of laws and not the person of a prince rules. It is the prince who now rules, but will he do so for ever?

The Empress, in order not to detract from her nation, does not want to recognize despotism in looking for a motive force for the laws of the country; and perhaps she also fails to recognize it in its actual effect: for, no matter *how* and *in what way* and *from what place* she rules, she is not a despot and cannot be one. But does she not see any despots above herself? Does she not see a senate, nobles etc. to whom she has to accommodate herself? And what is worse than aristocratic despotism? She sees in the senate nothing but an aristocratic republic: she honours it with the name of a repository of laws, etc.; she takes the rules of a republic and tries to apply them to it. Great Empress, how wrong you are!—Do these gentlemen represent your empire? Have they been chosen from the entire nobility of the country? Did they obtain their seats by proper means? Are they the guarantors of the laws, when Russia has no laws? Do they have the necessary power to oppose unjust proposals, or the necessary motive to speak for the whole empire? What is their empire? Their subjects? These are mere slaves. Your empire, great Empress? No! Their palaces, estates, luxury, wants, interests, obtained as gifts from the crown—that is their empire, the empire they serve, for which they will do anything—for which they will act like servants before you in order to be despots over you and your empire. What a commonwealth! What a dissipation of energies! Well now, and where is Montesquieu; or a second Montesquieu to apply his teaching! . . .

———————

In France: Yes, everyone here speaks French, even pilots and children . . . Thus, if we examine the Greek language in Homer let us bear in mind that it was spoken by all the children, understood by everybody, sung in the streets by poets and fools. The gods were the gods of the people, even of the rabble! History and heroic deeds were things possessed and treasured by the people, by the children—accent and metre the creation of the people, of the whole nation! Hence one must read them, hear them, sing them, as if one were hearing them in Greece, as if one were a Greek! I know what a difference there is between a living language and a dead one. One reads the latter with the eye, sees it instead of hearing it; one does not pronounce it—often one cannot pronounce it, although one understands it. Thus one misses all the living sound, and in a poet—a Greek poet—all the living euphony, all the power of portraiture in the sound of the words, all the force of the metre, the sound and the charm. As little as I can feel all the suavity of Voltaire's metres, as much as I still have to learn to feel it in him and Gresset[35] and Racine, it is a thousand times harder with the Greek language, which, living, resounding, vitally musical as it is, is in its very liveliness remote from us. What magic is needed in order to sing it—not to declaim, but to sing, to hear, as Plato's Ion sang and heard and felt—and who can do this? . . .

Second, all living accent disappears from a dead language—the expletives and connectives on which the spoken language relies; though these may only be such words as 'eh bien', 'ma foi', etc., they can so clearly be heard as to make the difference between life and void in the language. Thus in French we have 'n'allez pas', 'je m'en vais' etc. and a thousand other expressions, and many phrases, connectives, etc. must exist in Greek also . . . I wish I could find a native Greek or could get to Greece—even in its present condition—to hear this living tone of the sense, this

[35] Gresset, Jean Baptiste Louis, 1709–77, French poet and dramatist.

accentuation of expressions, etc., to learn to speak like a born Greek. How many thousand small distinctions there are in constructions, tenses, particles, pronunciation, which one hears only through the living speech! The French, for example, seem to speak with entirely different and higher organs than we; ours seem to lie lower down in the mouth and throat, as do those of the Dutch and English; the French speak higher, open their mouths more; this becomes especially noticeable in singing. Therefore the higher the organs with which one speaks, the more musical one becomes and the more closely one approaches song. Thus the Germans sing little or not at all, the French more, the Italians, in accordance with their language and vocal organs, still more, and the same applies even more to the Greeks who truly sang when they spoke. To have heard this, to be able to speak in this way, to know the language thus, in all its accents of passion—that is to know Greek. Oh, if I could read Homer as I do Klopstock! If I would not have to scan him mechanically, what a different poet he would be for me! If I knew how to scan him for passion and spontaneous nature, how much more would I hear then! What intensification, what suspensions, what tremulousness, what agitation, etc.! O that Homer, Pindar and Sophocles could sing to me!

Third and last, the sense and content of speech: God, what difference there is among nations in their favourite expressions and descriptions, their favourite turns of phrase and their individual modes of thought! Thus the Frenchman loves the *joli*, always speaks of the *amusant*, of *honnêteté*, which means to him something quite different from what it means to us. What did the spirit of the Greek and Latin languages have to designate these ideas? The question is not what a word can mean according to a few dictionaries, but what it means in the consciousness of living people—here, now, in all its capriciousness . . .

Languages, no less than governments, depend in this on the spirit of the age: this becomes striking to the point of being obvious, if one makes comparisons. The same spirit of monarchic manners which Montesquieu so strikingly portrays in his own person dominates his language also. Like the French nation, it has little real virtue, little inner strength; it makes as much as it can out of little, as a machine is moved by a small driving wheel. National strength, the idiomatic quality which clings to its native soil, originality—these it does not have in large measure; the concept of honour, however, without which no person, no book and no phrase is complete—features most prominently in it. A certain nobility of thought, a certain freedom of expression, a *politesse* in the manner of using words and in turning phrases— these are the stamp of the French language as of French manners. The chief concern is not with what a writer should teach others, but with what he himself excels in and what he feels he owes it to himself to teach others. Nobody knows this better than Voltaire and Rousseau, however strongly the latter denies it and however immensely they may differ even in this respect. They show it all the same: the first is vain and bold about his own accomplishments, the second proud and arrogant—both seek for nothing so determinedly as for distinctiveness. Only Voltaire thinks he has already distinguished himself, and merely seeks to show off his wit, while Rousseau continues to search for the novel, the unheard-of, the paradoxical, often to an intolerable degree. However strongly Rousseau may combat the *philosophes*, he too appears to be less concerned with the validity, the intrinsic quality, the reasonableness and applicability of his ideas, than with their greatness, their extraordinariness, their novelty, their striking effect. Where he can find these qualities he is a sophist and an apologist. Reasons such as these account for the fact that the French have produced so few philosophers, political writers and historians since for these truth is the prime requirement. Voltaire, however, will gladly sacrifice it to a brain-wave, Rousseau to a novelty, and Marmontel to a turn of phrase.

Nowhere is gallantry more finely developed than among this nation. It characterizes the French novel and accounts for the coquetry of the French style generally. Underlying it is a concern with polished rather than deep emotions, with the outward manifestation rather than the inner experience of feeling. Mode of expression, capacity for making instant conquests: these are the all-important considerations. The French style is constantly at pains to show that it knows the secret of the art of living, of the art of making conquests. The subtlety of turns of phrase may mean absolutely nothing, yet it cannot fail to demonstrate the writer's command of style . . . It is the same with the compliments of the journalist; no nation can frame them better, more deliberately, more precisely, more richly than the French; but again this is intended more to show that they can thus frame them—that they are educated people, that they are not coarse like the Germans—than to express an upsurge of sincerity and feeling. Gallantry is the language not of emotion and tenderness but of convention and social intercourse; it indicates that one knows the world.

So it is also with the language of censure: this is always calculated to show that the writer is *hardi* and free and clever enough to be able to censure, not that the censure itself is indispensable, useful, necessary, good or thorough. To speak plainly and to the point would be the way of the *hoi polloi*, which speaks the truth out of sheer simplicity and for its own sake.

Much the same can be said about the French conception of good breeding. The hallmark is *politesse*; its mode of expression a sizeable superfluity of words, and its prime motive the desire to please. It is supposed to denote *savoir-faire*, knowledge of polite usage, ease of social intercourse, ability to make fine distinctions and, above all, that delectable skill of being generous with praise without at the same time compromising one's own superiority. This arrogant courtliness has shaped the language internally and externally and has given it its polish. Taste is the main concern, and is a thousand times more important than genius, which is banned, mocked at, or at least disparaged in favour of taste. The constant superfluity of new writings and amusements makes nothing a major virtue but innovation; people are tired of truth—they want something new; hence the most baroque taste must prevail in order that it may be provided. This craving for novelty, this determination to appeal and amuse, is the keynote of everything. In literature, in everyday speech, the *honnête homme* is the leading spirit. There are a thousand expressions to illustrate this, even in the mouths of the common people, and they give the French language a refined and cultivated air which other languages do not have. Everyone will speak of his honour, of *honnêteté*, etc., and will express himself on this subject so well—often so sensitively, so delicately—that one is struck with admiration. In this the nation is a model, and it would be an excellent thing to write about the spirit, the sense of *savoir-faire* and honour and the politeness of the French language and French culture.

But let us look now at the reverse side of the coin: where is genius; or truth; or spontaneous vigour; or virtue? The philosophy of the French, which resides in their language with all its wealth of abstractions, is *learned*; it is only vaguely defined, almost wholly descriptive, and hence hardly philosophy at all in the proper sense. If the French were not so readily satisfied with only approximating to truth, they would have to pay much closer attention to each expression, each idea, each definition. Instead of taking things for granted, they would have to discover them for themselves. As it is, they assume them to have been already discovered and only in need of being learned and applied. They know things *praeter propter*, and use them in the manner that others understand them or understand them approximately as others use them. Hence they never write tersely, exactly, or fully in accordance with reality. The philosophy of the French language hinders the philosophy of thought.—What pains Montesquieu took in this respect! How often he found it necessary to stick to one word and closely determine its meaning or create a new one only to avoid ambiguity! How tersely, drily, compactly and economically he tried to write in order to adhere closely to reality, and yet he did not always succeed, chiefly on account of the French language which prevented him from being really exact. Indeed his very craving for exactitude only led him into the other extreme of becoming too abbreviated, too concise, and hence, to be perfectly frank, unreadable to the French. Helvetius and Rousseau, each in his own way, provide even more striking confirmation of what I say. Are we to conclude, then, that French cannot serve as a language of philosophy? Certainly not. The French language could be perfectly philosophical were it not used by, or written for, Frenchmen. That is to say, it would have to be written as a dead metaphysical language. And in this case it would be better to take in place of the outlandish language which French would then become, another still more outlandish one, which was not invented by Frenchmen, has not changed as French has, is dead, metaphysical and well-defined—Latin. But it must be admitted that no language is better than French for treating lively social intercourse with some *teinture* of philosophy. It has a wealth of subtle and delicate abstractions among its nouns, a great number of adjectives by which to designate quality, especially in matters of taste, a uniformity in its constructions which guards against ambiguities and a greater brevity in its verb forms than German; it is the best language for practical philosophy . . .

The [French] turns of phrase require particular attention. They are always twisted around; they never express what they want to say, but always form a relationship between the speaker and the one spoken to, and thus relegate the main issue to a subordinate position. The relationship itself becomes the principal concern— and does not this best indicate the etiquette of social intercourse? It seems to me that the origin of turns of phrase has not been sufficiently studied yet in this light although it manifestly calls for philosophical treatment. In this respect the French language diverges from all the older ones and strikes out on an entirely new path; in this respect it has become so much a model for other languages, including German; in this respect, and in this alone, it is the original language of Europe. The ancients knew nothing of this business of gallant circumlocutions . . . The Greek language knew no more of these turns of phrase expressive of nothing but social status than the oriental tongues—as their language of love, of social intercourse, of feeling, their style in letters and speeches, all show. Hence the pitiful contrast between the speech of Greek lovers in Euripides and Racine, between that of the heroes of Corneille and Sophocles. With the Greeks, everything is meaning; with the Frenchmen, everything is just a matter of social convention and social adroitness . . .

How did this spirit of social gallantry take shape among the French, how did it originate? Did it derive from the native genius of the people who, so Saint-Foix claims, honoured the fair sex even in bardic times and even under Julius Caesar were known for their lighthearted gaiety? Or should we attribute it to the feudal spirit of the ancient Franks? If Montesquieu sees the genesis of the laws of political honour and monarchy in this epoch, may we not also trace the genesis of the laws of social honour and etiquette in language to the same period? . . .

But when the French acquired this spirit of gallantry and decorum, they almost entirely lost the capacity for spontaneous emotion. The regularity of their language is constantly distorted on this account, and they never express themselves directly and bluntly. Decorum blocks their very spirit. Their 'vive le roi' is words—a mere expression, which they feel, as they feel everything, frivolously, without thinking or judgement, superficially, without any real basis; and they are happy in this—they praise him, serve him, do everything *pour le roi*—even when they run away in battle! The Germans brood more, grumble when their king discharges and pensions off disabled soldiers (a device constantly resorted to by the French king); grumble when they are refused permission to leave the country (whilst the French make it a point of honour not to want to leave their country); grumble at imposts and the farming-out of taxes, when in France everything is farmed out! In short, everything in France—right up to the name 'Louis the Well-Beloved'—is a matter of patriotic honour, of which one is inclined to write: 'they know not what they do or why they do it.' And what about French generosity? Is it real, thorough friendship, readiness to involve oneself in another's situation, or is it not rather mere *politesse*? Their pleasures, too, are but facile amusements and sheer diversions, lacking in real depth . . .

Finally, the French nation itself, its customs, its general nature, its specific traits, its government, its overall condition: what impact do these have on its literature, on its social culture? What *is* this culture, what is its history? What has the native character of the French people contributed to their culture? By what ways have they become the nation of *honnêteté*, of manners, of *savoir-vivre* and *amusements*? And having become such a nation, how much of more substantial value has been lost in the process? How much have they deprived—are they depriving—other nations in their development by communicating their culture—and with it their follies—to them! . . .

I return to my Germans, who think a great deal, yet think of nothing original. Nothing is more true and more untrue than this proposition, looked at from two different sides. Nothing more untrue: the discoverers of the air pump, of gunpowder, of the orbits of the planets, of the differential calculus, of the art of copper engraving, etc. are Germans—Guerike, Kepler, Schwartz, Leibniz, Dürer, etc.—but against these few discoveries what a mass of [abstract] systems we have evolved! In theology: have we a commentary on the Bible? Have we men like Poole, Locke, Benson, etc.? In law and history: there we exist only as compilers. In medicine: are our real observers the equals of men like Boerhaave and Sydenham? And finally in philosophy: how much in

Wolff is mere system, arrangement, form, method![36] Aesthetics is
a good example: how much thinking we seem to have done here,
yet how little we have effectively contributed to thinking!

I, for instance, have done some work in aesthetics and believe
that what I have to say is really new; but to what extent? Only in
the proposition that our sight perceives only planes and our sense
of touch feels only solid forms. But this proposition is already
well known from optics and geometry, and it would be a misfortune
indeed if it had not already been proved. Only its application,
then, would remain to my credit: that painting is for the eye and
sculpture for the sense of touch—a discovery that in its present
form is insignificant and that could, if it were extended too far,
lead to conclusions which would seem ludicrous in our present age,
when we use sight for touch and are accustomed to doing so.
Therefore let this proposition be merely a signpost pointing towards many more practical experiments with the senses of sight
and touch! I must become a blind man, dependent on my sense
of touch, in order that I may explore the philosophy of this sense!
In this I think I am following several new paths . . .

Diderot can be a model for my experiments,[37] but I must not
solely build on his experiments, and construct a system from them!
A work of this sort can become a basic psychology—and in addition, since all sciences are derived from this one, a philosophy or
encyclopedia of them all. But, above all, I want to resist the
German disease of deriving everything, whether it really follows
or not, from purely formal propositions.

[36] Guericke, Otto von, 1602–86, German physicist who made the first air pump.
Schwartz, Berthold, German chemist and Franciscan monk, is said to have
invented gunpowder about 1330. Poole, Matthew, c.1624–79, English non-
conformist divine; author of *Synopsis Criticorum Biblicorum* (5 vol., 1669–76).
Herder is referring to Locke's *The Reasonableness of Christianity as delivered
in the Scriptures* (1695). George Benson, 1699–1763 was the author of
numerous commentaries on the Bible. Hermann Boerhaave, 1669–1738, was
a Dutch physiologist and chemist. His physiological theories were further
developed in Albrecht von Haller's *Elementa physiologicae corporis humani*
(1757), a source which considerably influenced Herder's own biological and
psychological thinking. Thomas Sydenham, 1624–89, was a renowned
English physician, the founder of modern clinical medicine. Wolff, Christian
von, 1679–1754, German philosopher and mathematician, who developed
a deductive rationalistic system of philosophy, considerably influenced by
Leibniz.
[37] The reference is to the *Lettre sur les sourds et les muets* (1751).

ESSAY ON THE ORIGIN OF LANGUAGE

which received the prize awarded by
the Royal Academy of Sciences for
the year 1770

Vocabula sunt notae rerum. *Cic.*

BERLIN, 1772

ESSAY ON THE ORIGIN OF LANGUAGE

PART I

WAS IT POSSIBLE FOR MAN TO INVENT LANGUAGE SOLELY BY HIS OWN NATURAL FACULTIES?

SECTION I

[v, 5–26]

Even as an animal man has a language. All strong sensations of body or mind, especially the most violent, those of pain as well as those of the passions, are spontaneously expressed by cries, sounds, and by wild inarticulate noises. A suffering beast, no less than the hero Philoctetes in his agony, will wail and groan even if abandoned on a desert island where there is neither sight, nor trace, nor hope of help from a fellow creature.[1] It seems that a creature breathes more freely when giving vent to the burning anguish of its mind, as if part of its pain escapes and it draws new strength from the empty air to bear the suffering while charging the deaf winds with its groans. Nature certainly did not create us as isolated rocks or egoistic monads. The most delicate chords of animal feeling (I am forced to use this comparison for the mechanics of sentient life, as I know no better one), the tones and intensity of which are not the result of voluntary control, nor of slow deliberation, and whose very nature the probing of reason has so far been unable to fathom, are utterances essentially directed towards other creatures. This is not to say they are thus *motivated*, for they may stem neither from the consciousness of the existence of other creatures nor from a belief in their sympathy. The chord, when struck, cannot but vibrate. It invites the echo of sympathetic

---

[1] In Greek myth, Philoctetes was the famous archer in the Trojan War to whom Hercules bequeathed his arrows. In the Island of Lemnos his foot was bitten by a serpent and became so offensively ulcerated that the Greeks abandoned him there. Later he was sent for when an oracle declared that Troy could not be taken without Hercules' arrows. He slew Paris, and Troy fell.

117

vibrations even when these are not likely to be forthcoming, expected or hoped for.

If physiology is to succeed in providing a comprehensive theory of the mind—the likelihood of which I seriously doubt—it would have to undertake a most careful analysis of the nervous system. Such an analysis might, however, go too far and leave us with minute, unconnected fragments too obtuse to be of any significance. We shall, therefore, work here on the assumption that the mind constitutes a single entity, and postulate the following hypothesis: *A sentient being cannot confine any vivid sensation within itself; it must give utterance to it at the first moment of surprise, without deliberation or intention* . . . These utterances are a form of language, the language of the emotions, expressive of an original force of nature.

That man has this language in common with the animal may be proved nowadays only by certain remnants in language. These remnants, however, are unmistakable. Our artificial language may have superseded the spontaneous language of nature; our urban civilization and our social conventions may have checked, dried up and diverted the flood and the ocean of passions. And yet, in a moment of violent sensation, no matter where or how it may occur, the spontaneous element in language will reassert itself in its original force in everyone's mother tongue. The quick-rising storm of passion, a sudden joy or pleasure, pain or sorrow, ploughing deep furrows through the soul; an overwhelming feeling of vengeance, despair, rage, fright or horror, etc.; each has its own voice, and the sounds are diversified according to the emotions. There is a sound for every emotion of which our nature is capable.

It would appear that the greater the affinity between man and beast in the structure of their nervous systems the more they can understand each other's natural language. Being creatures of the earth ourselves we are better able to understand land animals than those of the sea; among land animals we can interpret the gregarious better than the maverick; and among the gregarious we understand best those closest to us. However, even here the degree of understanding will depend largely on such matters as frequency of association and force of habit. It is natural that the Arab, who, as it were, forms one being with his horse, should understand it better

THE ORIGIN OF LANGUAGE

than anyone mounting a horse for the first time. He converses with it almost as well as Hector of the Iliad did with his horse. The Arab of the desert, with no living companion but his camel and perhaps a few stray birds, is more likely than we are to understand his camel and the shrill voice of the birds. The son of the forest, the hunter, understands the voice of the hart, and the Lapp that of his reindeer. Such at least is the general order of things, to which, no doubt, there are exceptions. In a sense there is a natural language community for each species, and so also for man.

The sounds of such natural languages are, however, very simple, and when they are articulated and written on paper as inter-jections, the most contrasting emotions have one and the same expression. The weak 'Ah' is the sound of languishing love as well as of disheartening despair; the ardent 'Oh' is a sudden outburst of joy as well as of explosive rage, of increasing admiration and also of overwhelming pity. But are all these sounds intended to be drawn on paper as interjections? The tear that fills these sad, sunken eyes, yearning for consolation—how touching a portrayal of sorrow in its proper setting! Taken by itself, it is but a cold drop of water. Examine it under the microscope, and what do we see? Isolate this dying breath, this languishing sigh on lips drawn with pain, from all its vivid accompanying elements, and it is but a percussion of the empty air. In their living context, within the scene of creative nature and accompanied by many other pheno-mena, the diverse expressions of emotion are pathetic and suffi-ciently expressive, but severed from all these and disconnected, bereft of life, they are nothing but letters . . . Their purpose was to call attention to the scene and let the scene speak for itself, to sound not to describe. In any case, do not, as Socrates maintained, intense joy and pain touch on the same borderland? In emotional matters nature appears to have joined the extremes, and what can the language of emotions do but indicate such points of contact?—

In all original languages the remnants of these natural sounds can still be heard. They are, however, not the main thread of human speech, not its roots, but merely the sap which vitalizes these.

A precise metaphysical language developed by later ages can only be looked upon as a scion of the fourth degree of the original mother tongue of any given community. Such an offspring of reason and society can know little or nothing of its original ancestry once it has undergone a myriad variations through centuries of refinement, civilization and humanization. But the ancient, the primitive, languages embody more of it the closer they are to the origin. I should not, however, at this stage dwell on the development of human speech, but merely confine myself to its raw materials. Let us assume, then, that not a single word exists as yet, but only sounds that may form into a word expressing an emotion, though we may note in passing that in their interjections, in the roots of their nouns and verbs, many languages have retained relics of these sounds. Thus the most ancient oriental languages are full of exclamations for which we nowadays have nothing but blanks or dull and mute misconceptions . . .

I can only explain most of these phenomena in their proper connexion later on. Here I would just make one further point. A defender of the divine origin of language demands admiration for the divine organization which makes it possible to reduce the sounds of all known languages to about twenty symbols.* The fact, however, is incorrect, and the conclusion even more so. Not a single language pregnant with life can be rendered completely in symbols, much less in twenty symbols. This can be demonstrated by any language. The articulations of our organs of speech are so numerous, each sound is pronounced in so many ways that, as Mr. Lambert has rightly pointed out in the second part of the *Organon*, we have far fewer symbols than sounds and hence the former can only give a very indefinite expression of the latter.[2] If this is true of the German language, which in its written form has taken no account of the variety of sounds, nor of the differentiations of dialects, what about languages which are nothing but such living dialects? What causes the peculiarities and anomalies of orthography but the inability to write as we speak? What living language can be learned as it sounds from the written letter symbols? What dead language can be thus revived?

The less a language has been forced into written symbols, the more closely it approaches the full flowing sounds of nature. Hence, the more vitality it has, the less it can be written at all, let

* Süssmilch, Johann Peter. *Versuch eines Beweises dass die erste Sprache ihren Ursprung nicht vom Menschen sondern allein vom Schöpfer erhalten habe* . . . Berlin, 1766.

[2] Lambert, Johann Heinrich, 1728–77. *Neues Organon* . . . (Leipzig, 1764).

alone with only twenty letters. In fact, it is quite often unpro-
nounceable for foreigners. Father Rasles, who spent ten years
among the Abenakies of North America, complains that despite
paying the closest attention to pronunciation he often repeated
only half the word and made a fool of himself.[3] How even more
ridiculous it would have been, had he tried to write the language
with the French alphabet! Father Chaumont, who lived among the
Hurons for fifty years, and who even attempted to write a Huron
grammar, complains of their guttural sounds and of the impossi-
bility of pronouncing them correctly: 'In many instances, two
words containing the very same letters were entirely different in
meaning.'[4] Garcilasso de Vega reports of the Spaniards that they
completely distorted, corrupted and falsified the sounds of the
Peruvian language and that, merely as a result of these falsifica-
tions, they attributed the grossest crimes to the Peruvians[5] . . .
But why refer to people from the remote ends of the earth? Our
small remnants of primitive nations in Europe, the Esthonians,
Lapps, etc., often use sounds as semi-inarticulate and incapable of
being transmitted to script as those of the Hurons and Peruvians.
Russians and Poles, though their languages have been written and
transformed for writing, still aspirate to such an extent as to make
it impossible to render the true sound of their tones by means of
letter symbols. What pains the English take to write their sounds,
yet how far is he who can understand written English from having
a command of the oral language! . . .

The facts, and the conclusion drawn from them, do not point to
a divine origin of language, but to the very opposite, namely, that
language has its origin in our animal nature. Consider the so-called
divine first language, Hebrew, from which the greater part of the
world inherited their symbols. It is evident from its grammatical
structure, from its frequent mistaken use of similar letters, most
especially from its complete lack of written vowel sounds, that it
was replete with *living* sounds in the beginning, which could be

---

[3] Rasles, Sebastien, 1657–1724. Jesuit missionary in North America. The
Abenakis belonged to the confederacy of thirteen Algonquian tribes occupying
Maine and parts of New Brunswick and Quebec.
[4] Chaumont, Pierre Joseph Marie, 1611–93. Jesuit missionary who lived among
the Hurons from 1639–48 and again from 1663–92.
[5] Garcilasso de Vega, 1539–1617. Peruvian historian, who wrote about the
Conquest of Peru and the history of the Incas.

written only imperfectly. How is one to explain the peculiarity that its letters are only consonants, and that the very elements of the words, upon which everything depends, the vowels, originally were not written at all? This mode of writing the unimportant, and of omitting the essential, is so contrary to the laws of logic and reason that, if grammarians were in the habit of comprehending things, it ought to be incomprehensible to them. We consider vowels of primary importance. They are the door-hinges of the language, as one might say, but the Hebrews do not write them. Why? Because they could not be written. Their pronunciation was so subject to change, so delicately organized, their aspiration so spiritual and aetherial, that it faded away and could not be imprisoned in written symbols. It was only the Greeks who strung these living aspirations together in formal vowels which had still to be supplemented by the *spiritus*, etc., since with the Orientals speech was altogether *spiritus*, the breath or spirit proceeding from the mouth, as it is often called in their descriptive poetry. It was the breath of God, a breeze received by the ear; the dead letters which they drew on paper were only the corpses into which the spirit of life was breathed in reading. This is not the place to point out the enormous influence this fact has on the understanding of their language; but it is evident that these aspirations betray the origin of their language. Is there anything less transmittable into script than the inarticulate sounds of nature? And when a language is all the more inarticulate the closer it is to its origins, what conclusion can be drawn but that it was not invented by a Higher Being to suit the twenty-four letters, that the twenty-four letters were not invented at the same time with it, but were a far later experiment to set up a few marks as an aid to memory, and that the language is not derived from symbols of a divine grammar, but from the primitive sounds of natural organs. Otherwise it would be odd that the very letters from which and for which God invented the language, by means of which He taught the first man a language, should be the most imperfect of their kind in the world . . .

Since in all original languages natural sounds are intended to express our innermost passions, it is scarcely surprising or unnatural that they should constitute the basic elements of feeling as such. Whose heart would remain untouched by the contortions and moans of one under torture, by the groans of the dying or even by the whinings of an animal, when the whole machine is suffering? Who would be such an insensible barbarian? . . . How much hardening of fibres, how much power to block the avenues of sensibility, is required for man to turn a deaf ear to the cries of a sufferer? Diderot thinks that a man born blind ought to be less impressed by the moans of an animal in pain:* I think the opposite is sometimes true. No doubt the touching display of the wretched quivering creature is hidden from him. Experience, however, teaches that for this very reason the sense of hearing is less distracted, hence more intense and piercing. See him listening in darkness in the quiet of his eternal night: each moan touches his heart more closely and piercingly, like an arrow . . .

Despite their civilization or over-civilization, Europeans have been deeply moved everywhere by the primitive wailings of the aborigines. Léri tells us how, in Brazil, his people were moved to tears by the heart-rending, discordant yell expressive of the love and kindness of these Indians.[6] Charlevoix and others say that they cannot adequately render the gruesome impression made upon them by the war songs and the magic of the North American Indians.[7] When later we shall take the opportunity of showing to what extent the ancient poetry and music were still animated by these primitive sounds, we shall be in a position to explain more philosophically the effect which, e.g., the ancient Greek songs and dances and the ancient Greek theatre once had, and which music, dancing and poetry as a whole still have upon aborigines. The same may be said about us. Often, it is true, reason dethrones sensations and the language of society the sounds of nature. Yet the sublimest thunder of rhetoric, the most powerful strokes of poetry, and the magic power of action are closely allied to this natural language through imitation. What is it that in the assembled crowd works miracles, penetrates the hearts and revolutionizes the souls? Intellectual speeches and metaphysics? Comparisons

* Diderot. *Lettre sur les Aveugles à l'usage de ceux qui voyent.* London, 1749.

[6] Léri, Jean, 1534–1611. French Protestant who was a missionary in Brazil from 1556 to 1558. Author of *Histoire d'un voyage fait en la terre du Brésil* (La Rochelle, 1578).

[7] Charlevoix, Pierre François Xavier de, 1682–1761. Jesuit traveller in America. Author of *Histoire et description générale de la Nouvelle France* (Paris, 1744), and other works.

and figures of speech? Artifices and cold conviction? Much has to be done by these if the enthusiasm is not to be spent uselessly; but do these artifices of rhetoric accomplish everything? Whence came the overpowering moment of blind enthusiasm? From a power of a very different nature. These tones, these gestures, those simple movements of the melody, these sudden changes, this touching voice, and I know not how many other things. With children and primitive people, with women, and highly sensitive persons, with the sick, the lonely, the aggrieved, they are a thousand times more effective than truth itself would be if her soft fine voice were heard from heaven. These words, these sounds, the intricacy of this gruesome romance interwoven with a whole multitude of concurrent ideas, awe, solemnity, fright, fear, joy, transfixed our soul when we heard them the first time in our childhood. The word falls from the lips, like a troop of ghosts suddenly rising from their graves in sombre majesty. They dim the clear transparent meaning of the word which could be grasped only when held apart from them. The word is no more, but the vibrations of emotion remain. Obscure emotions overwhelm us; even the thoughtless tremble—not at thoughts, but at syllables, at sounds of childhood. It was the magic of the speaking voice, of the poet, which transformed us again to children. There was no reflection, no weighing of thoughts, there was but this basic law of nature at the root of it all: *the vibrations of emotion tend to transpose the sympathetic creature into the same key.*

If we are to call these spontaneous expressions of feeling language, then I find its origin is very natural indeed. It is evidently not superhuman, but of animal origin: the natural law of a sentient mechanism.

At the same time, I cannot conceal my amazement that philosophers, that is to say, people who look for clear concepts, could conceive the idea that these cries of feeling completely explain the origin of human speech. For is not speech obviously something rather different? All animals, down to the mute fish, give expression to their sensations; nevertheless, no animal, not even the most perfect, has as much as the beginnings of a human language properly so-called. We may develop, refine and organize these cries as we will, but if reason and the understanding do not intervene to enable us to make conscious use of the sounds, I do not see how a human language could ever evolve. Children utter emotional sounds like animals, but is not the language they learn from man of a very different kind?

Abbé Condillac is to be counted among these interpreters.* Not only has he presumed the invention of this whole thing called language even before the first page of his book was written, but I find on every page descriptions of events in the course of the formation of language which could not possibly have taken place. As the basis of his hypothesis he places 'two children in a desert before they know the use of any sign'. Why does he postulate all this? 'Two children', who must either perish or become animals; 'in a desert', where the difficulties of keeping alive and of inventing anything are increased; 'before the use or even the knowledge of any natural sign', but even the infant of a few weeks has such knowledge. Now why, I ask, should the author postulate such unnatural contradictory data as the basis of an hypothesis whose purpose is to investigate the natural development of human knowledge? However, I undertake to prove that an explanation of the origin of language cannot be built upon it. His two children meet ignorant of any sign, and behold, at the first moment 'they have already established a mutual relationship'. (§ 2) Yet it is by means of this mutual relationship that they learn 'to link with these emotional cries the thoughts of which these are the natural signs'. To learn the natural signs of emotion through a relationship? To learn thereby what thoughts are to be linked with them? And yet to form a relationship at the very first moment of meeting, to be able to learn what thoughts are to be linked with certain signs before having a knowledge of what even the most stupid animal knows? I do not understand this at all. 'Owing to the recurrence of similar circumstances they form the habit of connecting thoughts with emotional sounds and the various bodily signs. No doubt their memory is exercised. No doubt they can command their imagination, and no doubt they are able to accomplish upon reflection what a moment ago they did by instinct only'. (§ 3) Yet, we have already seen that they could not do it before their relationship. I can understand this still less. 'The use of these signs enlarges the activities of the mind, and these in turn perfect the signs. (§ 4) It was therefore emotional cries which developed

* *Essai sur l'origine des connoissances humaines*. Amsterdam, 1746. Vol. II.

the powers of the mind (§ 5); emotional cries which established the habit of connecting ideas with arbitrary signs (§ 6); emotional cries which served as a pattern to formulate a new language, to articulate new sounds, to develop the habit of calling things by names.' I repeat all these repetitions and understand none of them. Finally, after the author has based the prosody, the declamation, the music, the dances, and the poetry of the ancient languages upon this childish origin of language, and has now and then made some good comments which, however, have no bearing to our purpose, he resumes his topic. 'In order to understand how men could agree upon the meaning of the first words which they wanted to use, it is sufficient to say that they were used under circumstances where each was bound to link them with the same ideas' (§ 80) etc. In short, words were formed because words existed before men existed. It seems to me of little value to follow the thread of this interpreter any further, since it is completely broken.

Perhaps it was Condillac's empty explanation of the origin of language which afforded Rousseau an opportunity to give this problem new impetus in our century, along his own sceptical lines.* Though it required no Rousseau to have doubts about Condillac's explanation, it did require the sweeping and radical turn of mind of a Rousseau to deny point blank the very possibility of man's inventing language. But does it follow that because Condillac gave a bad explanation, no explanation could be given? Because a human language can never grow from emotional sounds, does it follow that it can have had no other origin?

Rousseau's own plan makes it evident that he was misled by this covert paralogism: 'What if, after all, language had perhaps evolved by human means as it ought to have done?' Like his predecessor, he begins with the natural cries from which human language is said to have originated. I cannot see how it ever could have originated from them, and I am astonished that the acumen of a Rousseau could for one moment have placed the origin of language there...

As man is the only creature we know of as possessing a language, and as he is distinguished from all animals by language, where could the investigation begin more properly than with the ex-

---

* *Discours sur l'origine et les fondemens de l'inegalité parmi les hommes.* Amsterdam, 1755.

periences of the differences between man and animals? Condillac
and Rousseau must have been in error over the origin of language
because they were in error over these various well-known differences, the former making animals into men, the latter men into
animals.* I must therefore begin farther back.

It is certain that man is vastly inferior to animals in the power
and reliability of his instinct; it may even be said that we do not
possess at all what in many species of animals we call 'inborn
capacities and natural aptitudes'. But just as philosophers, and
lately one of the profoundest of German philosophers,† have not
been successful in offering an explanation of these instincts,
neither has clear light been thrown on the true reason for the lack
of them in human nature. To me it seems that a main point of
view has been overlooked which, though not furnishing a complete
explanation of the nature of animals, will at least allow us to make
some remarks on it which may throw light on human psychology,
as I hope to show in a different place. This point of view is 'the
sphere of the animals'.

Every animal has its sphere to which it belongs by birth, into
which it instantly enters, in which it continues all through life,
and in which it dies. Now it is a curious fact that the more intense
the senses of an animal are, and the more marvellous its natural
aptitudes, the narrower is its sphere and the more uniform is its
structure. I have investigated this relationship and I find that a
strange inverse proportion can be observed between the slightest
extension of their movements, their food, their preservation, their
mating, their training, and their fellowship on the one hand, and
their instincts and natural aptitudes on the other. The bee in
its hive builds with more wisdom than Egeria could teach Numa;[8]
but apart from these cells and from its proper occupation in these
cells, the bee is nothing. The spider weaves with as much skill as

* Condillac. *Traité des animaux* . . . Amsterdam, 1755. Rousseau. *Discours sur
l'origine et les fondemens de l'inégalité parmis les hommes, op. cit.*
† Reimarus, Hermann Samuel. *Allgemeine Betrachtungen über die Triebe der
Thiere, hauptsächlich über ihre Kunst-Triebe.* Hamburg, 1760. For some
opinions on it see *Briefe die neueste Litteratur betreffend.*

8 In Roman mythology, Pompilius Numa was reputed to have been the second
king of Rome, renowned for his wisdom and piety. He received instruction
about forms of worship from the Nymph Egeria who visited him in a grove
near Rome.

did Minerva, but all its skill is woven into this narrow sphere: this is its universe. How marvellous is the insect yet how narrow the sphere of its activity!

On the other hand, the more manifold the work and purposes of the animals are, the more their attention is divided among various objects, the more variable their modes of living. In short, the greater and the more diversified their sphere is, the more we observe that their sense activity is divided and weakened. It is beyond the scope of the present work to demonstrate this great proportion which ranges through the realms of all living beings. I leave the test to my readers. I must refer them to a later opportunity and continue my arguments.

According to probability and analogy it is thus possible to explain all the instinctive capacities and natural aptitudes by reference to the imaginative faculties of the animals, without having to stipulate blind determinism. (Reimarus assumed this, but such an assumption would wholly run counter to all philosophy). How penetrating the senses must become when, finely discriminative, they are confined to a narrow circle and to one single object, and when all the rest of the world does not exist for them! How strongly the active powers of the imagination must work if they are confined to a narrow circle and are endowed with an analogous intensity of the senses! If, finally, senses and imagination are concentrated on one point, what can develop from such a situation but instinct? It is from them that the sensitivity, the natural aptitudes and the instincts of animals, according to their varieties and species, are developed.

Hence I may state the following thesis. *The sensitivity, aptitudes, and instincts of animals increase in power and intensity in an inverse ratio to the size and multiplicity of their sphere of activity.*

Man has no such uniform and narrow sphere in which only one operation is to be performed; a world of activities and purposes surrounds him. His senses and his organization are not adapted to one single thing; his senses have to serve all his purposes, and hence for each individual thing they are weaker and duller. The powers of his mind embrace the whole world, hence his imagination is not focused upon one single thing. Consequently he has no instincts, no native skills—and, which is more pertinent to our case—no instinctive language.

What are the sounds which in some species we call animal language and which extend beyond the utterances of a sentient 'machine' as previously mentioned? They are, as a corollary to the observations I have just recorded, intimations of an obscurely felt agreement among members of a species about their purposes or roles within a given sphere of activity.

The more limited the sphere of the animals, the less need is there of a language. The keener their senses, the more their imagination is focused on one thing, and the more compelling their instincts, the more limited is the range of sound, signs or utterances which they may use. It is a sentient mechanism of governing instincts which speaks and which listens. How little speech is necessary for it to be understood!

Animals of the narrowest sphere are therefore even without the sense of hearing; for their own world they are all touch, smell or sight, a single image, a single trait, a single performance; they have no language or very little.

The larger the sphere of an animal, the more diversified its senses are—yet why repeat what has been said? With man the whole aspect changes. Of what use would the language of animals, even of those that command the greatest variety of sounds, be to him, even in his most primitive state? Of what use could the indistinct language of all animals as a whole be to man's sporadic yearnings, to his widely wavering attention, to his dimly perceptive senses? It is neither rich nor definite, neither does it specify many objects, nor is it adapted to his organs; for—if we do not wish to play with words—what is the proper language of any creature but the one adapted to the sphere of its needs and its operations, to the organization of its senses, the direction of its imagination and to the strength of its desires. And with respect to man, which animal language meets these requirements?

However, even this question is superfluous in a sense. For what language, apart from the above-mentioned mechanical language, does man possess so instinctively as each animal species does its own, within and according to its sphere? The answer is brief: none. It is this short answer which is decisive.

With every animal, as we have seen, its language is an expression of such strong sensual imaginations that these develop into instincts. Hence, language, like senses, imagination and instincts, is inborn and therefore spontaneously natural. The bee buzzes in like manner as she sucks; the bird sings as it nests; but how does man speak by nature? Not at all! Just as he does not act, or very little, from pure animal instinct. If we exclude the cries of its sentient nature, a new-born infant is mute. He expresses neither concepts nor impulses by sounds as every animal does in its own manner. Surrounded by animals only, he would be the most abandoned child of nature; naked and exposed, weak and needy, shy and without weapons, and, to cap his wretchedness, bereft of all guidance as to what to do with his life. Born with such distracted and weakened sensibilities, with such indefinite slumbering faculties, with such divided and enfeebled drives, depending upon a thousand needs, he is evidently destined for a larger sphere, and yet he is so orphaned and abandoned that he is not even endowed with a language to allow him to utter his wants. No, such a contradiction is most decidedly not the economy of nature. There must be within him other powers to take the place of instincts.

SECTION 2

[v, 28–47]

. . . If man's senses, applied to a limited patch of the earth, to activity and enjoyment within a narrow sphere in the universe, are inferior in acuteness to the senses of the animal that lives within its own sphere, they gain by this very fact the *boon of freedom*. Just because they are not intended to serve in so restricted a sphere, the senses of man are oriented in a far more general manner . . .

There is not a single human task which could not be improved. Man has ample scope to exercise his powers in many ways, and hence the opportunity to perfect himself. An idea is not the immediate operation of nature and for that very reason is capable of becoming man's own creation.

Thus, if instinct, which developed merely from the organization of the senses and the sphere of the imagination, had to be discarded, the blind determination of nature could no longer be said to operate. The loss of instincts is, however, compensated in man by the gain of *greater clarity*. If he falls down, he does not obtusely remain prostrate on that spot but raises himself to erect and free stature. Moreover, he can seek a sphere of self-reflection, can mirror himself within himself. No longer an infallible mechanism in the hands of Nature, he becomes to himself purpose and goal of improvement.

It matters not what one may call the entire disposition of his powers: reason, intellect, consciousness, etc., as long as these names are not to denote disconnected powers or merely a higher degree of animal powers. *It is the totality of the organization of all human powers, the entire economy of man's perceptive, cognitive and volitional nature,* or rather, *it is the sole positive power of thinking which, combined with a certain organization of the body, is called mind in man just as it becomes natural aptitude in animals; in man it gives rise to freedom, with animals it constitutes instinct. The difference, however, is not one of degree or of a 'more or less' of given faculties or powers, but rather that of a wholly dissimilar direction and development of all powers . . .*

All those who have raised difficulties against this position have been deceived by erroneous conceptions or by unclear notions. Reason has been construed as an additional, entirely disconnected faculty of the mind, with which man has been endowed as with a special gift, in preference to the animal: a kind of fourth rung of a ladder over and above the three lower ones, destined to be singled out for separate consideration. But to speak of reason in this manner is to talk philosophical nonsense, even if the greatest philosophers do the talking. All individual faculties of our mind or of that of the animal are nothing but metaphysical abstractions, elaborations. They are considered separately because our weak intellect could not study them as a whole; they are arranged in chapters, not because they naturally operate in such divisions but rather because the student finds it easier to study them in this way. The fact that we classify some of their functions by means of such terms as wit, sagacity, imagination, reason, does not mean to say that 'esprit' or reason could possibly operate separately as a single function of the mind, but we classify them in this manner only because we primarily discern in the act that abstraction which we call esprit or reason, e.g. in comparison, or definition of ideas; but everywhere the individual mind acts in its totality. If man could ever perform a single act in which he thought wholly as an animal, he would most decidedly not be a man any more, nor would he be capable of performing any human acts. Were he ever for one moment devoid of reason I cannot see how he ever in his life could think reasonably. If that could be the case, his whole mind, the entire economy of his nature, would have to be changed...

If man had the senses of animals, he would have no reason. For the intense susceptibilities of his senses and the perceptions these would force upon him would wholly stifle his capacity for calm reflective choice. But conversely, in view of the laws of balanced interrelation that govern the economy of nature, it must follow that, in the absence of the confining powers of animalistic drives and sense perceptions, a different creature, distinctive and free, would manifest itself: a creature, not only *capable* of cognition, volition and action, but also *conscious* of knowing, willing and acting. Its positive powers would operate in a much wider sphere owing to its more complex organization and its capacity for conscious discernment. This creature is man, and, in order to avoid the ambiguities inherent in the notion of distinct and separate faculties, we shall call this whole disposition of his nature *mind*.[9]

From the same natural laws of interrelation it also follows that, since such expressions as sense perception and instinct, imagination and reason are connotations of one and the same vital force (*Kraft*) in which opposites cancel each other out, man, unless he was intended to be a creature dominated by animalistic instincts, had to be a reflective self-conscious being by virtue of the possession of a positive dispositional capacity for freely choosing his activities.

By extending the chain of these syllogisms a little further, I may be able to anticipate some later objections.

If reason is not a separate faculty operating in isolation, but rather an integral element of the entire economy of man's nature [*i.e.* his mind], which confers upon his species a peculiar direction of its own, then *man must have been endowed with it from his very origin, in the most primeval stages of his existence as man*. Just as an insect is manifestly an insect from the very outset, the mind of man is revealed as such in the first thought of the child. More

---

[9] Herder uses the term *Besonnenheit* here. I have translated it as 'mind' in preference to 'reflection' because this is much closer to Herder's intended meaning. (When Herder interprets it as reflection he specifically indicates this. See, e.g. v, 34.) For further discussion of this point, see my *Herder's Social and Political Thought*, pp. 39–44.

than one writer has been unable to grasp this through a mis-
conception. To use one's mind does not necessarily mean to use a
perfectly developed mind. An infant thinks with his mind: does
that mean he reasons like a sophist at the lecturing desk or like a
statesman in his cabinet? Blessed and thrice blessed is the child
that is yet ignorant of this wearisome chaos of subtleties. Is it not
obvious, however, that this objection does not deny the existence
of a positive mental power, but only a certain use, or a more or
less developed use of it? And what fool would claim that man in
the first moment of his life should use his mind in the same manner as after years of practice, unless he would deny a development
of all powers of the mind and thereby confess he is an ignoramus.
The notion of development (in the sense of easier, more vigorous
and more diversified functioning) presupposes the existence of
something to which this development could be applied. Is not the
whole tree already contained in the seed? Just as the child is not
born with the claws of a vulture nor with the mane of a lion,
neither can it think as a vulture nor as a lion. However, if it does
think in a human manner, then it must possess a mind—that is to
say, a capacity for determining all its powers towards a given
direction in the first moment as well as in the last. Within this
sensitivity the mind reveals itself so definitely that the Allknowing
who created it beheld in its first state the maze of the activities
of a whole life, just as a surveyor, one might say, finds the whole
proportion from one term of a progression according to a given
class.

'But at this early stage was not the mind more a potential
power (*réflexion en puissance*) rather than actual power?' This
proviso means nothing. Pure, naked capability which, even without impediment, is still no real power but only capability, is like an
empty sound, or like 'plastic forms' which give form, yet themselves are not forms. If the most negligible amount of positive
power is not combined with the capability, then there is nothing—
the word is a purely academic abstraction. As we shall see,
the modern French philosopher who presented the concept
'*réflexion en puissance*'*—this sham concept—in so dazzling a
manner has, when all is said, only presented a dazzling air-bubble

---

* Rousseau, *Discours sur l'origine et les fondamens de l'inégalité parmi les
hommes.*

which he pursued for a while but which burst suddenly and unexpectedly in his path. Now if this potential power is but an empty power, and hence no power at all, how is it ever to enter the human mind? And if it cannot enter it in its earliest stages of existence, how can it ever become actualized in a million subsequent stages? It is a fallacy that use could ever change potentiality into power, something purely possible into actuality; for, if there exists no power to start with, it cannot later be used or applied. Moreover, what sense does it make to stipulate both a separate potential power of reasoning and an actual power of reasoning as faculties of the mind? One is as incomprehensible as the other. Place man into the universe as the being he is, endowed with a degree of sensitivity and organization: the whole universe will impress itself on his senses, yet causing sensations in *human* fashion. For, unlike animals, man is a thinking being not dominated by instincts. He has scope to manifest his power with more freedom, and this freer relationship is termed 'rationality'. Where is pure potentiality, or a separate faculty of reason to be found? It is the one positive power of the mind, which acts on the principle that the more sensual is the less reasonable, and the more reasonable the less vivid. But man's most sensual condition is still a *human* condition, implying the operation of a mind in a more or less perceptible degree, whilst the animal's least sensual condition is still an *animal* condition in which no possible clarity of its thought could produce a human idea. But let us not play with words any further.

I regret having lost so much time merely defining and classifying concepts. However, this was a necessary task, since this part of psychology has been badly ravaged in recent years. French philosophers, in particular, have thrown things into the greatest possible confusion by pointing to this or that peculiarity which supposedly distinguishes man from the animal. The German philosophers, on the other hand, have classified most concepts of this kind to suit their system and viewpoint without bothering about the ambiguities they created in the public mind. Thus I can scarcely be accused of having wasted time, especially if I can show that my preliminary steps have in fact brought us practically to the heart of the matter, which I may formulate in the following proposition: *Man, endowed with mind—a characteristic peculiar to himself alone—*

has by his very first act of spontaneous reflection invented language.
But what is reflection; what is language? . . . Let us now elaborate
these two concepts.

Man reveals reflection when the power of his mind acts so
spontaneously that, in the vast ocean of sensations rushing in on it
by way of the senses, it can isolate and retain one single wave, so
to speak, fix its attention on it, and be wholly conscious of doing
so. He reveals reflection when from the fleeting dreams of images
which flit past his senses, he can rouse himself to a moment of
alertness, concentrate deliberately on one image, observe it quietly
and clearly, isolate some characteristics of it, and identify it as this
object and no other. Thus man exhibits reflection not only by
recognizing clearly or distinctly the qualities of objects that are
before his mind, but also by realizing the characteristics that
distinguish one from another. This first act of apperception renders
a clear concept: it is the first judgment of the mind.

How was this apperception brought about? By the act of
consciously isolating one quality which impressed the mind as a
distinguishing quality. The first indication of this conscious
activity of the mind was a *word*. With it, human language was
invented! . . .

Most writers who wrote about the origin of language did not
search for it in the one point where alone, according to my
opinion, it may be found; and thus many have been disturbed by
numerous doubts as to whether it could be found anywhere within
the human soul. It has been sought in the better articulation of the
organs of speech, as if an orang-utang with the same organs could
ever have invented a language! It has been sought in the emotional
cries, as if animals did not possess these cries, and as if any animal
had ever developed a language from them! Others have postulated
a principle by which man would be led to imitate nature and
hence also her sounds, as if reasoning could be combined with
such a blind propensity! And as if the monkey gifted with the
same inclination, or the blackbird so skilled in imitating voices,
had invented a language! The greater number posited a mere
convention, a contract; and it was against these that Rousseau
argued most vigorously; for after all, what an obscure, tangled
expression it is: a natural contract to make language! These
numerous fallacies concerning the human origin of language

have contributed to make the opposite theory almost universally held. I hope it will not remain so. It is not an adaptation of the mouth that created language, for even a man dumb for life, once he was a man and had the use of his mind, would form a language in his mind. It is not the utterance of sensations, for it was not a breathing machine that invented language but a conscious and reflective creature. Nor was it a principle of imitation; the incidental imitation of nature could be a means to one end and to one end only, as will be explained later. Least of all can it be an agreement, an arbitrary social convention. The solitary savage, the hermit in the forest, would have been bound to invent language for himself though he had never spoken. It was an agreement between his mind and himself, as inevitable as he was man. While to others it seems incomprehensible how man could have invented language, it is incomprehensible to me how a human mind being what it is could avoid inventing language, even without either tongue or society.

It is the objections of opponents which will most convincingly vindicate this origin.* Because he penetrated below the surface which others merely grazed, the most profound and circumstantial defender of the divine origin of language almost becomes a defendant of the true, human origin. He stopped short at the very point of the proof, and his main objection, interpreted somewhat more correctly, proves to be an argument against himself, verifying the opposite, *i.e.* the possibility of a human origin. He claims to have proved 'that the use of language is indispensable for the use of reason.' Had he succeeded in doing so, then I do not know what other truth could have been proved by it but that 'as the use of reason is the characteristic of man, so the use of language must be the same'. Unfortunately, he did not prove the statement. He only demonstrates in a very painstaking manner that so many subtle intricate activities as attention, reflection, abstraction, etc. cannot be carried out expediently without symbols on which the soul depends; however, the 'not being expedient, not easy, not probable' does not exhaust the subject. Just as we can only to a limited degree think in terms of abstractions, *i.e.* without the help of sense symbols, in view of our limited powers of abstraction, so other beings might well be able

* Süssmilch, chapt. 2.

to think more without such symbols. At least it is conceivable that abstract thought *as such* is possible without sense-symbols. I, on my part, however, have established that the use of human reason without a distinguishing symbol pertaining to a significant characteristic [of the object of thought] is not only improbable but actually impossible; that without it not even the simplest definite concept, nor the most elementary judgment of the human mind, is conceivable. For the difference between two things can be determined only by means of a third. It is this third which constitutes the significant characteristic and which fashions the identifying symbol we apply to it within our mind. Hence, language is inherent in, or the natural corollary of, the very first act of human reasoning.

Mr. Süssmilch is anxious to propound that the higher applications of reason could not take place without language, and to this end adduces statements by Wolff, although the latter only speaks on this point in terms of probabilities.* In any case the point has actually no bearing on my argument. For the higher applications of reason, as they occur in the speculative sciences, were not indispensable for the early foundations of the structure of language. Just the same, even this proposition, which might easily have been proved, is only asserted by Süssmilch, whilst I believe that I have proved that even the first elementary operation of the reasoning power of the mind is inconceivable without the use of language. But if he then concludes that 'no man can have invented language for himself, because the invention of language requires reason; consequently language must already have existed before the mind was used', I make a break in this vicious circle, and consider it closely, and behold! it proves an entirely different thing: Ratio et Oratio! If reason was impossible without language, then indeed the invention of the latter was to man as natural, as old, as original and as characteristic as the use of the former.

I have called Süssmilch's syllogism a vicious circle: for I can turn it against him as aptly as he can turn it against me, and the play becomes a constant turn about. Without language man can have no reason, without reason no language. Without language and reason man is not capable of receiving divine instruction, and without divine instruction he has neither reason nor language.

* Süssmilch. *Ibid.* p. 52.

Where is this reasoning going to land us? How is it possible for man to learn language through divine instruction if he has no reason? Yet without language he cannot enjoy the least use of reason. Is he supposed to have language before he has it, or is capable of having it? And can he become a rational being without in the least using his mind? Before receiving the first syllable of divine instruction he must be man, as Süssmilch himself concedes, that is to say, he must have been able to reason distinctly; and with the first distinct concept language was already in his mind, hence it was invented through his own resources and not in a mechanical manner through divine instruction.

The instruction which parents give their children is usually thought of as divine instruction. It must, however, be recognized that such is not the case here. Parents never teach their children language without the concurrent inventive activity of the child; the former only draw the children's attention to the differences among objects by means of certain word syllables, in this way promoting and facilitating, but not substituting speech for the use of reason. To posit supernatural assistance for some extraneous reason does not touch my purpose here. Man may well exercise his powers under a higher guidance but this does not affect the point I wish to make, namely, that it was not God who *invented* a language for man, but that man himself had to *find* a language by operating his own powers. In order to receive from the mouth of God the first word as a word, that is to say as a distinguishing mark of the mind, reason was indispensable; and in order to conceive this word as a word man had to apply his mind as much as if he had invented it himself. If so, then all the weapons of my opponent turn against himself. Man needed the actual use of reason to learn a divine language. Would a child really *learn* anything by merely repeating words parrotlike without understanding their meaning? Could it in 'learning' in this manner be properly considered a worthy pupil of God? Could learning of this sort ever have led to the emergence of our rational language?

I flatter myself that my worthy opponent, were he still living, would acknowledge that his objection more definitely interpreted is the most convincing proof against himself, and that, unintentionally, he collected in his work material for his own refutation. He could not hide behind the phrase 'potentiality of reason which is not yet reason' in any proper sense. Turn it as you may, there are contradictions. A rational creature without the least use of reason, or a rational creature without language! An irrational creature to whom instruction can impart rationality, or a creature capable of being instructed which is still without reason! A creature without the slightest use of reason, yet a human being! A being which by its own natural powers could not use its mind, and which nevertheless learned to use it naturally in the course of supernatural instruction. A human language which was not human, that is to say, which could not be invented by human powers, and a language which is so human that without it none of his specific powers can operate! A thing without which he was not man, yet a state in which he was man and did not possess this thing, which thus existed before it existed and manifested itself before it could manifest itself, etc. These contradictions become evident as soon as all the nonsense contained in the phantom notion of 'potentiality' (potentiality of being human, of having a mind, of possessing a language) is unmasked and we begin to realize that man, mind and language denote actualities and not potentialities . . .

Take Rousseau's phantom, 'man in the state of nature'. This freak has to be satisfied with a mere potentiality of reason, whilst it is invested on the other hand with a degree of perfectibility enabling it to learn from all species of animals. How much has been conceded to man by Rousseau in this proposition! More than we ask for or need. There is reflection already in his first thought, 'Behold, this is the nature of the animal: the wolf howls, the bear growls' (this thought already is reflection considered in the light that it could be linked with the second, 'I am different'); then follow the third and fourth, 'Very well, this is also in keeping with my nature, I could imitate this, I will imitate it! And by it I will perfect my species.' What a range of fine logical discrimination and reflection such a creature must be assumed to possess, for in order to be able to comprehend the very first distinction it requires a mind and a language in which to think. It must accordingly *already* have possessed the art of thinking and, with it, the art of speaking, since the former entails the latter in its operation. Monkeys always copy others, but no monkey has ever consciously imitated. It never said to itself in its mind, 'This I will imitate, in order to perfect my species'; for had he ever done so, had he ever appropriated to himself a single imitation and deliberately and intentionally perpetuated it in his species: had he been capable of making a single such reflection a single time—in that same moment he would have ceased to be a monkey. Despite his appearance of a monkey, without a sound of his tongue he would inwardly have been a speaking man who was bound sooner or later to invent also an external language. The orang-utang has organs of speech very similar to those of man, but was there ever one who has uttered a single human word?

There are still in Europe, it is true, primitivists who say, 'Yes, perhaps—if he wanted to speak or if he came into circumstances where he had to speak!' Both 'if's' are sufficiently refuted by the history of animals; nor is the ability of the monkey impeded by its organs* His head within and without resembles ours: yet did he ever speak? The parrot and the blackbird learned human sounds: but did they ever conceive a human word? Moreover, we are not concerned yet with the external sound of a word; we are examining the internal genesis of a word as its essential characteristic which we associate with the existence of a clear and distinct *consciousness* . . . If this point about the genesis of language is missed, the area of error in either direction is immense. One direction points to positing language as something so superhuman that God had to invent it, the other makes it appear so non-human that every animal could invent it if it would take the trouble to do so. The goal of truth lies in one point only; from this point we can survey all sides and discover that no animal can invent language, that no God had to invent it, and that man as a human being can and must invent it.

From the viewpoint of metaphysics I will not follow up the hypothesis of a divine origin of language any further, as psychologically its futility has been demonstrated by the fact that in order to understand the language of the Olympian gods man needs both reason and consequently language. Nor can I go into a detailed discussion of animal languages, as all of them, as we have seen, are totally, incommensurably different from human language.

* From Camper's dissection of the orang-utang it would seem that this statement is somewhat bold (see the translation of his shorter writings); yet at the time I wrote this, it was the general opinion of anatomists.

What I regret most is the fact that I cannot follow the numerous avenues from which this genetic point of language within the human mind lead into the vast fields of logic, aesthetics, and psychology; more especially the problem: How far can man think *without* language; what can he think *with* language?—a problem which later in its application expands into all branches of knowledge. It must suffice here to recognize language as the external distinguishing characteristic of our species just as the mind is the internal mark . . .

It is remarkable how this self-created inner sense of the spirit constitutes in its very origin also a means of communication. Man cannot conceive the first thought, cannot form the first reflective judgment, without experiencing a kind of dialogue within his own mind, or without feeling impelled towards engaging in a dialogue with other minds. Essentially, therefore, the first human thought prepares communication with other beings; whatever I grasp distinctly assumes the form of both an identifying symbol for myself and a communicating symbol for others.

> Sic verba, quibus voces sensusque notarent
> Nominaque invenere.   (Horace)

SECTION 3

[v, 51–90]

. . . If an angel or a heavenly spirit had invented language, its structure must needs have borne the impress of the mode of thinking of this spirit. For how could I recognize a portrait as painted by an angel but by its angelic superhuman expression? Where is that to be found in our language? The structure and the first sketch, even the very foundation stone of this edifice, betray humanity.

Is there a single language in existence where supernatural spiritual concepts are first in order of time? Those concepts which, according to the laws of our logical mind, ought to have been first, the subjects, the *notiones communes*, the seeds of our cognition, the points around which everything else turns and to which it returns—are these vital points elements of our language? The subject should precede the predicate, and the simplest subjects should precede the more complex; that which acts and changes should precede that which is done, the essential and the certain should precede the uncertain and accidental—but in our primitive languages the opposite happens. A listening sensible creature is discernible, but not a heavenly spirit; for full-sounding verbs are the first dynamic elements of the most ancient languages. Full-sounding verbs? Actions, yet nothing which acts? Predicates and no subjects? A heavenly genius might find this strange to his nature, not so a sensible human creature; for what moved it more deeply, as we have seen, than actions connected with sound? What is the whole structure of language but a mode of development of man's spirit, the history of his discoveries? The divine origin of language does not explain anything, and nothing can be explained from it. It is, as Bacon says of a different thing, a sacred vestal, consecrated to God but sterile—pious but useless! . . .

Verba developed into *nomina*, but not from them. A child does not call the sheep a sheep, but a bleating creature, and thus changes the interjection to a verb. This phenomenon is explicable in terms of the progressive workings of the human senses, but not in terms of the logic of a higher spirit.

Every ancient and primitive language is replete with signs of this origin; and in a philosophical dictionary of the Oriental languages each root-word with its family, classified properly and naturally developed, would be a chart of the progress of the human mind, and a history of its evolution. A complete dictionary of this kind would provide excellent evidence of the inventive power of the human mind. But could it also serve as a textbook of God's method of teaching man his language? I very much doubt it.

As everything in nature utters sounds, nothing is more natural to man as a sensitive being than to think that nature is alive, able to speak and to act. The primitive man saw the tall tree and its magnificent crown and admired it. The crown rustled: 'This is the breath of God', he said, fell upon his face and worshipped. Two phases of the history of sense-bound man are revealed here: firstly, how *verba* became *nomina*, and secondly, how easily the concrete becomes an abstraction. With the aborigines of North America, for instance, everything is still animated, every object has its genius, its spirit; and the oldest dictionaries and the oldest grammar of the Greeks and the Orientals prove that the same holds true of them; they are a Pantheon, a realm of living and acting beings just as nature was to the primitive inventor.

Man referred everything to himself; things seemed to speak to him and act either for or against him; he, in his turn, felt either in favour or in opposition to them, loved them or hated them, and pictured them to himself in a human manner. Consequently the marks of this human mode of thinking were also imprinted upon the first names. These expressed love or hatred, curse or blessing, sympathy or opposition, and, as is noticeable in many languages, these feelings determined the gender. Everything is humanized, personified to man and woman; everywhere gods and goddesses act as malicious or benevolent creatures. The roaring storm and the gentle zephyr, the clear spring of water and the mighty ocean— their whole mythology is disclosed in these sources, in the *verba* and *nomina* of the ancient languages . . . In this respect, the language of the ancient primitive peoples, like their mythology, is a study in the labyrinth of human imagination and passions. Every word family is like a tangled undergrowth around a sacred oak where traces can still be found of the image—of its dryad in the mind of the inventor. His sensations and emotions are linked together: 'Whatever moves is alive; whatever sounds speaks, and since it speaks for or against thee, it is either friend or foe, god or goddess; it acts from passion like thyself' . . .

It may be easily understood that sounds, noted by the mind as distinguishing characteristics, could become words; but, all objects do not give off sound. How could sensible word-symbols be obtained for objects without sound so that the mind could name them? Who was to teach man the art to convert into sound that which is not sound? Is there any connection between colour or curves and a name which would suggest them as naturally as bleating provides a name for the sheep? The defenders of the supernatural origin of language have an answer ready. 'Divine accident', they say, for 'who can comprehend and who can search the mind of God, why green is called green and not blue? Doubtless, it has been His good pleasure!' and that cuts the argument short. Our philosophy about the origin of language then, hovers uncertainly in the clouds, and every word is a *qualitas occulta*, a wholly arbitrary symbol. I must confess that I do not understand the words 'divine accident' or 'arbitrariness' in this case. The human mind requires for each action a purpose, if only a very slight one, and hence could never invent a language arbitrarily without the slightest motive of selection . . .

To the point, then! How could man left to his own resources invent a language where no tone struck his ear? What connection is there between sight and the ear, colour and word, odour and sound?

There is none between the objects as such. But what are these qualities residing in the objects? They are but sensations within us; and as such do they not all blend into one? We are one single thinking *sensorium commune*, but we are influenced from many different directions. Here lies the explanation.

All senses are associated with feeling and this produces such an intimate, strong and ineffable tie between the most dissimilar sensations that the most peculiar phenomena result from this union. I know of more than one instance where persons, perhaps through some impression in childhood, would spontaneously and indeed quite inevitably, as by some rapid freak, associate a certain sound with a certain colour, a certain appearance with a quite indistinct, dim feeling; things which in the light of slow reason have no relationship whatever with each other; for who can compare sound and colour, shape and touch? Our mind is rich in such associations of the most diversified senses; only we do not notice them except in moments which disturb our balance: in sicknesses of the imagination or in situations that make them conspicuous. The usual flow of thoughts proceeds so fast, the waves of feeling intermingle so obscurely, so many things occupy our minds at one and the same time, that we are scarcely aware of many of our ideas, and resemble a person dozing beside a stream, who may still hear the murmur of the water but only indistinctly, until finally sleep robs him of all conscious sensations. Were it possible for us to break the chain of our thoughts and to search each link for its associations, what peculiarities, what strange analogies of the most diverse sensations would we not perceive! And yet these are the habitual modes which characterize the working of our mind. To a purely rational being we would resemble that class of madmen who think cleverly but make the most incredible and absurd associations.

With sense-creatures who perceive by several senses simul-taneously, this association of ideas is inevitable—for, what are our senses but modes of perception of a single positive power of the mind? We differentiate them, but again only by means of our senses. Hence modes of perception are discriminated in turn by modes of perception. With considerable pains we learn to separate them while employing them; but at a certain depth of our con-sciousness they still act jointly. All attempts at analyzing and classifying man's sensations by Buffon, Condillac and Bonnet are but abstractions.[10] The philosopher must drop one thread of sensation while following up the other; in nature, however, all these threads are one web. The less the mind has learned to use one sense without the other, with ease and facility, the more indistinct and confused will be the impressions which the senses impart to it. Let us apply this to the beginnings of language . . .

Man stepped into the universe: what an ocean rushed in upon him! How difficult it was to learn to differentiate the things around him and the senses within him. Sight is the coldest sense, and if it had always been as cold, as distant, and as distinct as it has become through the labours and the practice of many years, I cannot understand how what is perceived by sight could ever have been converted to sound. Nature, however, took care of it and showed the way . . . Needing a new word in the throng of sensations crowding in upon it, the groping mind perhaps grasped a word pertaining to a neighbouring sense, the sensations of which mingled with those of the former; thus words were created for all senses, even for the coldest. Lightning sounds not; if this messenger of midnight,

> Which in a flash reveals the sky, the earth,
> And ere a voice may say, 'Behold',
> Is swallowed up by darkest gloom of night,

is to be named it will naturally be by means of a word transmitting to the ear the sensation of a flashing, abrupt rapidity which the eye experienced—lightning (*Blitz*). The words fragrance, tone, sweet, bitter, sour, etc. sound as if based on feeling; for, primarily,

---

[10] Buffon, Georges Louis Leclerc de, 1707–88. French naturalist. Author (with others) of *Histoire naturelle* (44 vols., 1749–1804). Bonnet, Charles, 1720–93. Swiss naturalist and philosopher. Condillac's analysis of the sensations is to be found in his *Traité des Sensations* (London and Paris, 1754).

all senses are feeling. But that feeling can be voiced in sound has been shown in the first part to be a direct natural law of the sentient mechanism which needs no further explanation.

Thus all difficulties may be reduced to the following two theses already proved: 1. All senses are modes of perception of the mind; all clear perceptions are gained by means of distinguishing characteristics; with such a characteristic a word-symbol is born. 2. All senses, especially during the infancy of the human race, are modes of feeling of one single mind; and as every feeling has a spontaneous sound according to the law of feeling of animal nature, so this feeling being distinct enough is raised to a distinguishing characteristic in itself, and thus a word-symbol for external speech is created . . .

But man can receive the voice of his tutor, nature, only through hearing, and without the latter he cannot invent language; hence hearing is, as it were, his central sense, the proper gateway to the mind and the bond of association of the other senses.

I shall explain.

Hearing is the centre of the human senses with regard to the range of external stimulation. The sense of touch perceives everything within itself and in its organ; sight projects us outside of ourselves to great distances; hearing is midway between them with regard to communication. Of what significance is this for language? Suppose a creature, a rational creature, even, whose chief sense were touch: how narrow its world would be! And as it cannot perceive the world through hearing, it will never invent a language. Again, suppose a creature be all eye: how inexhaustible is his world of perceptions! How immeasurably far would he be projected out of himself! How distracted would he be by the infinite multiplicity of his experience! His language, of which we can form no idea, would be a series of infinitely fine pantomimes, his writing an algebra of colours and lines; but it would never be a vocal language. Beings that hear, such as creatures possessing hearing as we do, are placed in the centre: we see, and we feel, and nature, seen and felt by us, adds sound. She teaches a language of sounds; we become, as it were, hearing creatures by way of all the senses.

Let us appreciate the advantage of this situation; for through it every sense is made fit to contribute toward speech. It is true, only hearing supplies sounds immediately, and man cannot invent, but only find and imitate. However, in one direction touch is next to hearing, in another sight is the proximate sense: the sensations unite and approach the region where characteristics change to sounds. In this way, what is seen and what is felt is made vocal. The sense for language has become our central sense of associations: we are beings with a language.

Hearing is the central and mediating sense with regard to distinctness and clearness, which again makes it an essential sense for language. How faint is touch; it is drowned by the rush of sensations upon it; it senses all things as in a tangle; with great difficulty only can a characteristic be isolated; it is unspeakable.

On the other hand, sight is bright and dazzling; it furnishes many qualities; the mind falters before the variety of impressions and can isolate perhaps one characteristic only and so dimly that recognition by means of it becomes uncertain. Hearing is in the middle, as far from the faint chaos of touch as from the too fine sensations of sight. A sound suddenly arises from the object which is seen and felt; the marks of the two other senses converge upon it—the sound becomes word-symbol. Hearing reaches out both ways, rendering clear what was too obscure, and agreeable what was too bright. The obscure multiplicity of touch and the dazzling multiplicity of sight are reduced to unity; and thus recognition of a complex by means of one distinguishing characteristic gives rise to language . . .

If I could gather all the ends of the different threads and expose to view the entire web called human nature, it would reveal itself as an organism designed to create language, functioning in a space or sphere adapted to its capacity for thinking in terms of a medium of which the form and material content are determined by the organization of all senses. Man has neither more, nor different senses, thinks neither more clearly nor more dimly, sees and feels neither more keenly, nor more steadily or vividly than this purpose requires. Everything is balanced, economized, compensated, as if it were wisely planned and carefully apportioned to form unity and coherence, proportion and order. It is no less than a complete whole. We may indeed speak of this creature endowed with mind and language, with discerning consciousness and creativity as a *system*. If anyone, after all these observations, would deny the definition of man as a creature of language, he could no longer be regarded as an observer of nature but as its destroyer. He would have to turn its harmonies into discords, batter the magnificent structure of human powers, and pervert his own sensibilities to such an extent that instead of perceiving man as a masterpiece of nature he would see him as a being full of defects and deficiencies, of weakness and convulsions . . .

It may be easily seen how difficult it would be to compose a true etymological dictionary of such a metaphorical language. The divergent meanings of its root words which are to be derived etymologically and reduced to their origin, are connected only through dim feelings, fleeting subordinate ideas, through simultaneous sensations arising from the depth of the mind and are difficult to arrange according to rules. Moreover these connections are so intensely national, engendered according to the peculiar disposition and viewpoint of a people and conditioned by the time and circumstances of a country, that it is almost impossible for a Northerner and Westerner to render these root-words adequately, without having recourse to long, prosaic paraphrases. Furthermore, as they were produced under the strain and stress of life, in moments of excitement, of feeling, and coined when the need of expression was felt, how much luck is required to strike the same feeling. To collect, therefore, in a dictionary of this kind, the words with their different meanings at different periods, under different circumstances and states of mind, to bear in mind these infinite variations, would indeed be a gigantic task, a work of untold labours. Much discernment would be required to penetrate into these circumstances and needs, and considerable discretion to keep the interpretations of different periods within reasonable limits. How much learning and adaptability of mind are necessary to enter into the primitive intellect, the daring imagination, the national feelings of distant ages, and to render them in our own idiom. Such an undertaking would light a torch and illuminate not only the history, the mode of thought and the literature of the country, but also those dark regions of the human mind where ideas cross and intermingle, where the most diverse feelings generate one another, where times of need rouse all the powers of the mind and test its inventive ability to the full. In such a work every step would be a discovery, and every new finding would complete the inductive proof of the human origin of language . . .

Let us proceed to another proposition:

'The more primitive a language is, the more frequent the transposition of feelings, the less can the latter be minutely and logically subordinated to each other. Such a language is rich in synonyms; though lacking in essential parts, it has a wealth of unnecessary expressions.'

The defenders of the divine origin of language who claim to discover divine order in everything are surely at a loss here, and hence they deny synonyms.* Do they deny them? Very well, let us concede that there are some slight variations, long since lost, among the fifty names the Arabs uses for the lion, among the two hundred for the snake, among the eighty for honey, and among more than a thousand for sword—why did these exist if they had to be lost? Why did God invent an unnecessary treasure of words, the entire volume of which, as the Arab claims, only a divine prophet could comprehend. Bearing in mind the great many ideas for which words are lacking, the above must certainly be considered synonyms. Can it be called divine organization when God surveying the realm of language devised seventy names for a stone and none to denote indispensable ideas, interior feelings and abstractions; when he accumulated unnecessary abundance in one place leaving a deplorable scarcity in another, thus creating the need of usurping metaphors and nonsensical speech?

On the human basis the thing can easily be explained. Difficult and rare ideas were indeed seldom expressed, while familiar and easy ones occurred frequently. In proportion as nature was yet little understood, inexperience led man to look at nature from different points of view and yet not recognize her. As language was made by sense experience and not *a priori*, the more was the need of synonyms . . . They were in frequent use with a certain tribe, family or poet: thus it came about, as an Arabian lexicographer says after enumerating four hundred words for misery, that it was four hundred times misery to have to mention them one by one . . .

A comparison of primitive languages confirms my thesis. Each of them is extravagant in expressions, but also insufficient in its

* Süssmilch, chapt. 9.

own way, according to its own nature. As the Arab has many expressions for stone, camel, sword and snake (objects among which he lives), so has the Ceylonese language a profusion of flatteries, titles and pompous phrases in keeping with the tendencies of the Ceylonese. It has no less than twelve different words for woman specifying station and rank, while we impolite Germans, for instance, have to borrow such expressions from our neighbours. But we do have, according to station and rank, 'thou' and 'you' and it is expressed in eight different ways by the labourer as well as by the courtier: this extravagance is our characteristic mode of speech. In Siam there are eight ways of saying 'I' and 'we' according as the master addresses the servant or the servant the master. The Caribs have almost two separate languages for men and women, the most common objects such as bed, moon, sun, bow, being denoted differently by either sex—what a wealth of synonyms! Yet these same Caribs know only four names of colours and must refer all others to these—what dearth! The Hurons use two different verbs when alluding to animate or inanimate objects, so that 'to see a stone' and 'to see a man' requires two different expressions to denote 'see'; if this is traced all through nature— what abundance! 'To make use of one's own property', 'to make use of the property of the person to whom one is speaking' also requires two different words for property—what abundance! In the chief dialect of Peru the two sexes are indicated in so peculiar a manner that the word 'sister' referring to the sister of the brother, and the sister of the sister, the child of the father, and the child of the mother are termed differently; yet this same language has no proper plural! Each of these synonyms is closely connected with the customs, the character and the origin of a people; and everywhere it reveals the inventive spirit of man.

I should like to add now a further proposition.

'The human mind has no recollection of abstractions received from the realms of spirits which it did not arrive at through the medium of the senses; neither has any language abstractions which were not acquired through sound and feeling. And the more primitive the language is, the fewer abstractions, the more numerous are the feelings.'

In this vast field I can again pick only a few flowers.

The whole structure of the Oriental languages demonstrates that all the abstract ideas were primarily conceived as objects of the senses: the spirit was wind, breath, storm of the night; the word 'sacred' meant set apart, 'solitary'; the word 'soul' meant breath; 'anger' the snorting of the nostrils, etc. The more general ideas were later on obtained by abstraction through the intellect and imagination, through comparison and analogy, etc., not one of which originated in the depths of the language.

The same may be said of all primitive peoples. Language is always a function of the general culture. In the Barantola language there was no word for sacred, in the Hottentot tongue none for spirit. Missionaries from all parts of the world complain of the difficulty of communicating Christian ideas to the aborigines in their own language; yet these ideas certainly are not scholastic dogmas but the common ideas of common sense. An insight into these difficulties can be obtained by reading specimens of their teaching in translation and by inspecting the handbooks and dictionaries of these languages. The same holds true even of the undeveloped languages of Europe, such as the Lapp, the Finnish and the Esthonian tongues . . .

Why should one neglect all these traces of the human spirit creating and changing language, and seek its origin in the clouds? Is there proof of a single word which only God could have created? Is there in any language a single purely abstract concept which must have been given to man from above? Is any such at all possible?* On the other hand, there are a hundred thousand reasons, analogies and proofs of the genesis of language in the human mind arrived at by means of the human senses and human modes of thinking. How many proofs of the expansion and development of language along with reason among all peoples, in all zones, and under all circumstances! What ear can refuse to hear this general voice of the nations?

And yet, it is astonishing how Mr. Süssmilch can discover divine order in the same path where I can only discover the most human trails, viz., 'that no language has yet been found that was altogether unfit for art and sciences'.† What may be concluded

* The best essay on this matter that I know of is by an Englishman: *Things divine and supernatural conceived by analogy with things natural and human, by the author of the Procedure, extent and limits of human understanding.* London, 1755, [Peter Browne, D.D., Bishop of Corke and Ross.]
† Süssmilch, chapt. 11.

from this fact but that no language is derived from the animal but that all languages are human? Has there ever been found a people altogether unfit for art and sciences? Is it a miracle? 'All missionaries were able to speak to the most primitive people and to convert them; this could not be done without conclusions and reason: hence their languages must have contained *terminos abstractos*, etc.' And if so, was it divine ordination? Was it not rather the most human action to abstract words when needed? What people ever had abstractions in their language which they had not coined by their own efforts? And have all peoples an equal number of abstractions? Could the missionaries express their teaching everywhere with equal facility, or have we not heard the very reverse from all parts of the world? And how did they express themselves but by adapting their new concepts of language by analogy to the primitive language? And was this done everywhere in the same manner? . . .

Since human reason cannot remain devoid of abstractions, and since no abstractions can be made without language, it follows that the language of every people must contain abstractions, that is to say, must bear the stamp of reason, the tool by which it has been formed. Each, however, counts only as many abstractions as the people could make, and not a single one was made without the help of the senses, as is proved by the original sense imprint which they bear. Hence nowhere can a divine ordinance be detected except indirectly insofar as the language is thoroughly human . . .

I take it that the possibility of a human origin of language has been substantiated, in what I have said, by the internal evidence of the workings of the human mind, by the external evidence of the organization of man, by the analogy of all languages and peoples. Whether considered as a constituent element of speech or in its total progress, language is so obviously tied up with the development of reason that those who do not deny man the possession of reason or, which is the same, who know what reason is, and who also have taken the trouble to think philosophically about language and have carefully studied the character and history of languages throughout the world, can have no doubt concerning the origin of language even were I to add no further word. That the genesis of language lies in the human mind seems to be self-evident, as intrinsically convincing as any philosophical proof could be. Likewise the extrinsic analogy of all ages, languages and peoples contains that degree of probability which any fact of history can provide. Nevertheless, in order to forestall any possible objections and establish the thesis as securely as any philosophical truth can be established, let us prove from all external circumstances and the analogy of human nature that man could not but have invented his own language, and let us describe the manner in which he could most appropriately have done so.

PART II

HOW MAN COULD AND MUST HAVE INVENTED LANGUAGE IN THE MOST APPROPRIATE MANNER

Nature gives no powers in vain. If, then, she not only gave to man the power to invent language, but also made this power the specific characteristic and the dynamic principle of his very being, it is evident that this power is a living and active property, an operative principle, as it were, and hence requires, by implication, a sphere in which to act. Let us now examine more closely some of the circumstances and concerns which induced man to develop a language for himself upon entering the world, equipped as he was with the best disposition for language. Since these circumstances and concerns were many and varied, I propose to subsume them under certain principal laws governing the nature of man and his species.

FIRST LAW OF NATURE

[v, 93–112]

Man is a free, thinking, and creative being whose faculties operate in a continuous progression: hence he is predisposed for language.

Considered as a naked animal without instincts, man is the most wretched of living creatures. Not the dimmest innate instinct guides him towards his natural habitat, his sphere of activity, his sustenance and occupation. No smell or scent forces him to the herbs that will allay his hunger; no blind mechanical tutor builds a nest for him! Weak and submissive, exposed to the struggle of the elements, to hunger and all sorts of dangers, a prey to stronger animals, liable to a thousandfold deaths, he stands, lonely and alone, deprived of maternal instructions and guidance, forlorn on all sides.

Yet, however vividly this picture may be painted, it is not the portrait of man: it exhibits but one superficial aspect of his nature, and even that is set in a wrong light. If intellect and mind are the natural endowment of his species, they must manifest themselves as soon as the weaker sensitivity and the pitiable plight of his deficiencies become apparent. The miserable creature deprived of instinct, born in so forlorn a state, was also from its first moment a rational being, capable of voluntary acts, meant to help himself and, indeed, fully prepared to do so. His defects and deficiencies as an animal urged him to prove himself as man. But the faculties of man are not just weak compensations for the greater perfections of animals denied to him (according to modern philosophy, the great benefactress of animals), but rather something peculiar to his very nature and hence quite incomparable to the powers of the animal. His centre of gravity lies in, and his principal orientation is governed by, the activities of the human understanding, which presuppose the existence of a *mind*, just as with the bee the guiding principle lies in sucking and building.

Given that the human understanding could not operate without employing a word symbol—as we were anxious to prove—it must follow that the first moment of conscious awareness also occasioned the first internal emergence of language.

Allow man as much time as you will for this first distinct act of the mind; let us even presume that, according to Buffon's theory, he only gradually gained the *use* of his mind. Let us not forget, however, that from the very first moment of his existence, man was not an animal but a human being, because he possessed a creative and reflective mind (*Besonnenheit*) even if at his entry into the universe he was not yet a creature endowed with conscious awareness (*Besinnung*). Man was not an unwieldy helpless machine, intended to move but unable to do so because of its rigidity, intended to see, hear, taste, but hindered from doing so on account of watery eyes, hardened ears, and a petrified tongue. People liable to these kind of doubts ought to remember that man did not escape from Plato's cave, where he had sojourned from the first moment of his life, for many years debarred from light and movement, blind with open eyes and inflexible with sound limbs; but rather that he emerged from the hands of nature, his faculties and vitality at their best, with a vigorous, dynamic tendency towards development from the first moment. These first moments of reasoning and self-direction, it is true, must have been governed by creative Providence. It is, however, not the task of philosophy to explain the supernatural of these moments, just as philosophy is not in a position to explain man's creation; it accepts him in the state in which he can first act voluntarily, when he enjoys for the first time the exuberance of a healthy existence; and it thus interprets these situations on a purely human basis.

I may now build upon what has been said before. We argued that it is the human machine as a whole which perceives sensations and not any one single sense organ operating in isolation, for there can be no metaphysical separation of the senses. The mind in its entirety works from obscure feelings to conscious awareness and involves in arriving at this point the mediation of the ear between sight and touch, since it is only through the coincidence of these senses that it can perceive the first distinguishing characteristic of an object. In this lies the genesis of language. It is as spontaneous a process as the impulse of an embryo towards birth. Nature impels man to further this process by developing his faculties towards full manhood. And since language derives its origin from this process, each stage of this process constitutes a link in the chain of continuity in the formation of language.

Let us shed further light on the law governing this natural process.

Animals connect their thoughts dimly or clearly, but not distinctly. The species which are nearest to man in their mode of life and in the structure of their nervous system often disclose a keener capacity of remembering, of memory, in certain cases even a more retentive one than that of man: yet it always remains a sensual memory; and no animal has ever evinced remembrance by an act which would improve conditions for its whole species and would generalize experiences in order to make use of them in the future. The dog recognizes the gesture associated with a beating, and the fox avoids the unsafe place where he was hunted; yet neither can reflect in a general way on how to escape permanently from the threatening gesture and the cunning of the hunter. The individual sense experience remained isolated, and the memory grew to be a chain of such sensual experiences produced and reproduced, but never organized by reasoning: a multiplicity without a unity . . .

Among the many varieties of the animal species there are indeed considerable differences. The more narrow their sphere, the more powerful their sensitivity and instinct, the more uniform their skill and activity, the less progress through experience is perceptible, at least for us. The bee builds in youth as in old age, and will build at the end of the world in the same way as she did at the beginning of creation. Creatures of this kind are single specks, glowing sparks of the light of the Divine Mind, gleaming, however, always as the same single specks. An experienced fox acts differently from a young fox on its first hunt; he knows many tricks beforehand and tries to escape his pursuers; but how does he know them? and how does he try to escape them? Because he finds that certain direct experiences accompany such and such an action and no other. This constitutes the only principle of his behaviour. In no case is distinct reflection at work; for, are not even the most cunning foxes caught today as was the first fox by the first hunter of the world? In man, evidently, a different principle, that of reflective mind, governs the succession of ideas; it operates even in his most sensual states, only less discernibly. Man is the most ignorant creature when coming into the world; but immediately he is apprenticed to nature in a manner in which no animal can be. It is not only that one day teaches the following, but also every minute of the day teaches the next, and one thought the following. It is an essential trait of the human mind, to learn nothing for one moment only, but to connect everything with what it already knew, or to store it up for future associations. Incessantly it evaluates the supply already collected or that to be collected later, thus acquiring the power to collect continually. Such a chain runs through the life of man until death. At no single moment can he be said to be the *whole* man, rather he is always in a state of development, of progress, of becoming. One activity is increased by another, builds upon, or evolves from, the foregoing. Generations and epochs pass which we can name and divide off only by the most obvious characteristics. Were man able to recognize not only the fact that he has grown, but also the minute stages of his growth, he would no doubt be in a better position not only to survey an era as a whole but also to analyze it into its most infinitesimal parts.

We are always growing out of childhood, however old we may be; we are always in motion, restless and dissatisfied. The essence of our life is never fruition, but continuous becoming, and we have never been men until we have lived our life to the end. The bee, on the other hand, was a perfect bee when building her first cell.

This law of becoming, this principle of continuous progression of the human mind, does not operate equally noticeably at all times, but this fact does not refute its continued existence. When dreaming man does not think in the same orderly and clear fashion as he does when awake; yet even then he thinks as man. Though dreaming may constitute a kind of twilight state of thinking, it is fundamentally different from the mental processes of the animal. With a healthy person dreams follow certain laws of association just as thoughts normally do, with the possible exception that they may not be subject to quite the same rules, *i.e.* they may not operate as regularly as when man is fully awake. These very exceptions testify to the validity of the principal rule; sicknesses, unnatural conditions, faints, aberrations of the mind, etc. verify them still more. Thus whilst not every act of thinking is a direct result of conscious awareness, it nonetheless presupposes the existence of a reflective human mind. No such act could be performed by any being other than man in just this manner; man, indeed, would not be man if he did not think according to such a law of nature, peculiar to him alone.

The very first stage of conscious awareness, however, could not emerge without man's spontaneous ability to put his thoughts into words; nor could the mind connect a chain of thoughts without a chain of words. Hence all processes of the mind of which we are consciously aware involve the use of language. The former is indeed inconceivable without the latter.

I do not thereby mean to say, of course, that the most obscure feelings of man require the formation of a word; that he could perceive them only by means of a word. Indeed, it has been proved that what can be perceived only by vague feelings is not fitted to form a word, since it does not possess a distinct characteristic. The first elementary experiences of mankind may well be inexpressible in terms of some arbitrary language. But are those dim experiences the whole of man? Is a pedestal the whole statue? Is man's whole nature like an oyster only dimly aware of sensations? Let us rather consider the entire thought process. It is a process of the mind having no stage which in itself is not mental or cannot be grasped by the mind. Feeling as such does not predominate; rather, the centre of man's nature is in the higher senses, sight and hearing, and these create language for him continually; consequently it follows that on the whole there is no state of the human mind which cannot blossom forth into words or which is not actually defined in words. Only the obscure visionary or the brute, the most abstract prophet or the monad lost in dreams might think entirely without the help of words. Such a condition is not normally possible in the human mind, neither in dreams nor in deranged minds. To assert that man feels with his mind and speaks as he thinks may sound rather bold: yet I believe it to be perfectly correct. As man's thoughts flow on, associating quietly with what went before and with what follows after, every state thus joined by reflection assists him to think better, and hence speak better.

Let man make free use of his senses. As the focus of their application lies in sight and hearing, the former furnishing the characteristic, the latter the word-symbol, every step towards a more refined and skilful use of the senses promotes language simultaneously. Let man enjoy an unhampered use of his mental powers. Since their centre is in the mind and allied with speech, every step towards a more refined and skilful use of the mind promotes language also. Therefore *the development of language is as natural to man as his nature* . . .

The more experience man gains, the more he learns to know diverse things from diverse aspects, the richer grows his language. The more he repeats what he has learnt and the words he gained in doing so, the more permanent and fluent his language becomes. The more he differentiates and classifies, the more it becomes organized. This process, carried on through years of active life, among continual changes, in a permanent struggle with obstacles of all kinds, in ever new surroundings: would not this provide a considerable vocabulary as a beginning of language? Yet this is but the life of one man.

A dumb man—in the sense in which we think of an animal as dumb—who could not think in terms of words because his mind is incapable of forming them, would be the most pitiable, wretched and forsaken, if not absurd, creature of creation. For he would be completely out of harmony with himself and thus be his own greatest adversary. Alone and lonely throughout the whole universe, related to nothing, yet exposed to everything; protected by nothing outside nor within himself, he must either succumb, or dominate all; he must either appropriate everything by means of wisdom of which no animal is capable, or perish. He must choose between freedom and slavery, between language and death. These pressing needs cause the mind to summon its powers, and the whole race strives to realize its manhood: how much can thus be invented, organized, and accomplished!

Our hearts tremble when, social beings that we are, we try to picture ourselves as just such lonely dumb creatures. How, we ask ourselves, can man in such a lonely state defend himself against all the odds? Just by the faculties of reason and reflection? Are these not too slow, too weak and ineffective in face of the many needs and dangers pressing upon him?

Questions and objections of this kind may well be raised and further elaborated; yet they do not so much challenge as support my argument. Society, having brought men together so that their faculties and activities work as a unit, caused certain aptitudes and opportunities to be preferred from youth onwards. Thus society demands from one man only the intelligence required to solve algebraic problems, and from another a stout heart, courage and his fist! One is useful to society by his industry though he is no genius, another is a genius in one department only and can serve in no other. All cog-wheels must be held in proportion and in place or they will not form a perfect engine. But a distribution of mental powers where many are neglected in order to excel in one, is not the state of natural man! A scholar born and bred in society has trained only his head for thinking and his hand for writing. Suddenly he is uprooted from his protected position, deprived of the manifold amenities which society accords to him for the one-sided service he renders. He has to provide his own sustenance in an unknown country, to fight against animals and be in every respect his own protector: what calamities has he to face!

He has neither senses nor powers for the task, nor has he experience to guide him. In the labyrinth of his abstractions he has
perhaps lost the senses of smell, sight, hearing, and quick resource-
fulness, and certainly the courage and rapid decisiveness which
develops and manifests itself only in danger, which requires for
its growth an ever renewed activity. If he has reached the age
when the life-giving springs of his mind have ceased to flow and
begun to dry up, then it will certainly be forever too late for him
to adapt himself to this new sphere.

But is man when forming his own language in such a position?
I think not. The attempts at language which I have discussed were
not philosophical experiments. The specific characteristics of
plants were not intended to serve Linnaeus's classification; the
first experiences were not cool experiments, slowly and carefully
abstracted, like those of the solitary philosopher pursuing the
hidden workings of nature in order to know *how* it operates, and
not *that* it operates. The first inhabitants of this earth were least
concerned about that. There was no demonstration needed to
show him that such and such a plant was poisonous; the lion did
not need to attack him to teach him fear . . . We need no timid,
abstract philosopher to invent language: primitive man who still
has the consciousness of the essential unity of mind and body can
do more than all language-producing academies. Let us not
consider a scholar, therefore, as a specimen of the inventors of
language, and let us not throw dust into each other's eyes in order
to prove that man is unable to see . . .

It is almost incomprehensible how our age could lose itself in
the shadows and dark workshops of artificiality to such an extent
as to be blind to the broad daylight of unrestricted nature of
earlier ages. The great heroic deeds of the human mind, which
could be accomplished and made manifest only through collision
with the world of realities, have degenerated, and have become
subject matter for class exercises in the dust of our gloomy lecture
halls. The masterpieces of man's poetry and eloquence have
deteriorated into childish toys used by old and young children
from which they study phrases and rules. We cherish their forms
and have lost their spirit; we learn their language and do not feel
the throbbing world of their thoughts. And so it is with our
judgments of the masterpiece of the human mind, the formation

of language as a whole. We expect to grasp through dull reasoning the powers which issued from the vital forces of the world and from the spirit and grandeur of creative nature, which animate man, call him from the deep and carry him to perfection. The dull rules formulated later by the grammarians claim our worship, while we forget the truly divine *human* faculty for language, formed in harmony with the *human* mind, however irregularly it may operate. The inventive power for language has taken refuge in the shadows of schools from whence it cannot profit the living world. Are we therefore to conclude that a brighter world never existed in which the first inventors of language lived, felt, worked and created? I appeal to those who can comprehend man, the deep sources of his powers, the force and greatness of primitive languages, and especially the true nature of language as a whole. Hence I continue:

SECOND LAW OF NATURE

[v, 113–23]

Man is by nature a gregarious creature, born to live in society; hence the development of language is both natural and essential for him.

Man is a weak animal exposed under most skies to the rigours of the seasons. The human female has more need of the help of society both during pregnancy and delivery than the ostrich who lays her eggs in the desert.

More particularly, how dependent on human assistance and the sympathy of society is the human offspring upon entering the world! From the most sheltered state in the womb of his mother he comes into the world the weakest and most helpless of all animals, if not nursed at the bosom of his mother and protected by the strength of his father. Who cannot discern nature's plan that man should live in social groups? The necessity is as intimately connected with the vital instincts as is possible with a rational being.

This last point needs some elaboration, for the work of nature is here most evident; this will also enable me to reach my conclusion more directly. If, like crude Epicureans, we explain everything in terms of man's sensuality and undisguised selfishness, how shall we account for the parental feeling and the strong ties thereby established? The poor mortal comes into the world without knowing that he is miserable. He is in need of pity, yet cannot earn it in any way. He cries, but his crying causes as much annoyance as Philoctet's did to the Greeks when they exiled him to a desert island, despite the great services he had rendered to them. In the light of cold Epicurean reasoning natural ties would most easily break just where in actual fact they prove strongest. A mother has been delivered in pain of the fruit borne with so much labour; if new pleasures and satisfactions were her aim, she would dispose of it. The father, whose ardour had cooled off within a matter of minutes, would not be concerned about the mother and child for whom he must now toil; he would rove through the forest in search of new satisfaction like Rousseau's male animal. What a contrast there is between the natures of man and beast! How wisely nature has decreed! Pain and travail increase maternal affection. The love of his parents is intensified by the pitiable appearance of the infant, by his lack of attractiveness, by the frailty of his constitution, by the hardships and annoyances of his training. The greatest affection of the mother rests with the son who has caused her the greatest pain, has frequently threatened to leave her, and for whom she shed many bitter tears; that of the father lies with the boy whom he has early wrested from danger, trained with his most arduous efforts, and on whom he spent most in instruction and training. And thus throughout the human race, nature draws strength from weakness. Man comes into the world in a state of weakness and deficiency, deprived of instincts and natural aptitudes as no animal is, in order to receive a training and education as no animal does, and thereby develop into an intricately connected whole in a manner unknown to any animal species.

Ducklings escape from the hen that hatched them, and, playing in the element to which they are naturally drawn, they heed not the voice of their adoptive mother calling from the bank. Such would be the behaviour also of the infant if it were born with the instincts of a duck. Every bird brings with it from its egg the skill to build a nest, yet carries it also, without passing it on, into its grave. Nature here takes the place of the teacher. Every skill remains a purely individual concern, the direct work of nature.

Hence there is no chain of spiritual progression nor unity in the sense in which nature had ordained it for man . . . The tie formed by education and the transmission of culture—so essential to man —is missing.

Parents accumulate experience not just for themselves but also in order to communicate their store of ideas to the offspring. The son has the advantage, so to speak, of entering his inheritance prematurely, whilst his parents are still in full possession of the accumulated treasures, and he does so long before attaining manhood. By teaching, parents pay their debt to nature; by learning, the children follow the natural bent of their minds. In turn they will repay their debt to nature and pass on the wealth, increased by their own experience, to posterity. Thus *no man lives for himself alone; he is knit into the texture of the whole: he is only one link in the chain of generations, one cipher in the cumulative progression of his species.*

We shall discuss later the significance of this cumulative progression. Here we are merely concerned with the first two links in the progressive chain: (1) *the formation of a kinship mode of thought* by virtue of the manner in which education is first transmitted; and (2) *the development of language* which constitutes the medium of this transmission and which, like the former, is intimately bound up with the spiritual heritage of the family, since it is through the language of the parents that a given mode of thinking is perpetuated.

Why is the infant, weak and ignorant, dependent on the care of his mother and the strength of his father? In order to make him eager to learn and to adopt language. He is weak in order that his species may be strong. By means of language he is able to enter into communion with the way of thinking and feeling of his progenitors, to take part, as it were, in the workings of the ancestral mind. His forefathers took pride and pleasure in passing on the heritage, since in it they saw part of themselves. In picking up his first words, the infant imperceptibly absorbs the emotional flavour given to them by his parents. He repeats therefore, with every newly acquired word not only certain sounds but also certain feelings. Indeed, it can almost be said that a promise to perpetuate these is implicit in every word he learns to utter. Not surprisingly, we associate the strongest sentiments with our native language—

calling it fittingly our mother tongue—for it was the medium by which our minds and tongues were first moulded and by which images were transplanted from the hearts of our parents into our own. These first images of childhood live on for one's remaining life; every word we learn during this early phase carries with it secondary associations which we re-kindle in our minds every time we use the word. Frequently it is these secondary ideas which sway the mind more powerfully than the main concept with which they were associated, and essentially determine the character of what we earlier termed the family or kinship mode of thought . . .

The laws of nature are more effective than all political contracts and theories recounted by the philosopher. Who would not recognize in these words of infancy the companions of the dawn of life in harmony with which our mind was formed? Who would forget them? Our mother tongue embodies the first universe we saw, the first sensations we felt, the first activities and pleasures we enjoyed. Secondary ideas of time and place, of love and hate, and all the flaming impetuous thoughts of youth are perpetuated by it. This perpetuation of thoughts and feelings through language is the essence of tradition . . .

Rousseau and others have written many paradoxes on the origin of, and the right to, private property. But had Rousseau enquired more deeply into the nature of his noble savage, he might have found the solution. What right has the bee to the flower from which she sucks honey? The bee might answer, 'Because nature made me for sucking honey; my instinct guiding me to this flower, and no other, is my dictator who gave me a title to this flower and the garden'. If we ask the first man, 'Who gave you the right to these herbs?' he will answer, 'Nature, because she gave me conscious awareness. I have laboured to recognize these herbs, laboured also to teach their characteristics to my wife and my son. Our lives depend on them. I have a better title to them than the bee that hums among them and the cattle that feed on them, for they had not the toil of recognizing them and teaching others to do so! Every thought I spent on them is the seal of my title, and whoever drives me out of my own, not only takes my life in taking the sustenance of it, but also the value of my past years, my strength, my pains, my thoughts and my language: I have laboured hard for them!' And is not this signature of his soul which the first member of the human race stamped upon an object by recognition, abstraction and language as good a seal as the picture of the monarch on a coin? . . .

What a treasure language is when kinship groups grow into tribes and nations! Even the smallest of nations in any part of the globe, no matter how undeveloped it may be, cherishes in and through its language the history, the poetry and songs about the great deeds of its forefathers. The language is its collective treasure, the source of its social wisdom and communal self-respect. Instruction, games and dances are associated with it. Greek lore tells of the Argonauts, Hercules and Bacchus, of heroes and the conquerors of Troy, the Celts sing of the first chieftains of their tribes, Fingal and Ossian. The songs of the tribes and fore-fathers in Peru and North America, in the Caribbean and Ladrone Islands still betray the origin of the tribal dialects . . . We may note here that several of the peoples that we mentioned have two almost distinct languages: one for the male, the other for the female sex. In these instances the former was considered by national custom as the noble sex and the latter as the servile sex. The sexes lived apart, even at meals, as two separate groups; if the education of the young was chiefly in the hands of the father then the tribal language was mainly that of the male sex, if in the hands of the mother it was that of the female sex.

THIRD LAW OF NATURE

[v, 124–34]

Since the whole human race is not one single homogeneous group, it does not speak one and the same language. The formation of diverse national languages, therefore, is a natural corollary of human diversity.

Properly speaking, no two human beings speak exactly the same language. Even father and son, husband and wife, never speak exactly alike. Take the Oriental languages, for example. There are long and short vowels, various aspirations and guttural sounds, frequent and diversified interchange of sounds formed by the same organs, marks of rests and pronunciation, and many other differentiations hardly possible to represent in writing: tone and accent, stress and its absence, and a hundred other minute details in the elements of the language. They are the result of the dissimilarities of the vocal organs of the two sexes, of youth and age, or even of two similar persons; the structure of the organs is modified by numerous incidents and details, by many a habit so firmly established as to become second nature, etc. Just as there are no two men absolutely identical in their features and physical make-up, so there are no two words even in one language ever spoken in quite the same way by two different people.

Each generation develops in its language a specific home or family idiom: this is the beginning of a dialect at least as far as pronunciation is concerned. Climate, air and water, food and drink, influence the vocal organs and of course also the language. Social conventions and the mighty goddess of fashion will soon introduce through gestures and polite forms this or that peculiarity or variation . . .

So far we have chiefly had pronunciation in mind. But what vast possibilities of language become apparent when we consider the very soul of language, the *meaning* of words. We have seen that most ancient languages were replete with synonyms. This was probably due to the fact that a given synonym made a deeper impression on one person than on another, because he found it easier to remember, or because it accorded better with his point of view and experience, or again because it expressed his sensations more spontaneously. In this way favourite words, special words and idioms took shape. Among one group a certain word was discarded, another was kept or deflected from one meaning to a slightly different one. Declensions, derivations, conjugations, prefixes and suffixes, transpositions and loss of partial or whole meanings help to create new idioms, and this ever on-going process of change is as natural to the growth of a living language as language is to the development of the human mind.

Indeed, the more living a language and the closer it is to its origin, the more changeable it is. A language existing only in books, studied by rules, in use only by scholars and not in real intercourse, denoting a definite number of objects and meaning, its vocabulary being complete and limited, its grammar systematized, its application fixed: such a language may remain virtually unaltered. But a language of a wild and roving life in the midst of the great boundless universe, devoid of well-formulated rules, of books and letter symbols, of classic masterpieces, deficient and incomplete so as to need daily enrichment, which is so young and supple that it admits of daily additions at the first movement of perception, at the first call of passion or sensation: such a language must undergo changes in every new world which it experiences, with every new mode of thought or reasoning. Even Egyptian laws of conformity would not succeed here in decreeing a halt . . .

The separation of kinship groups into nations was certainly not accomplished according to those well-regulated schemes of distances, migrations, new relationships, etc., which the scholar in his ivory tower, compass in hand, marks off on the map, or according to the portentous volumes which have been written on the 'Relationship of Peoples', in which every particular is accurate except the laws which are said to govern this relationship. If we keep our eyes on the throbbing world of everyday life and ignore those who would like to press man into a mould conforming to some favourite scheme of their own, we shall discover motive forces which quite naturally account for the diversity of languages even among the most closely neighbouring nations. Man is not a Hobbesian wolf, nor a lone creature of the forest, as Rousseau would have it; for he has a communal language in which to communicate. But neither is he a helpless lamb, inseparably bound up with one herd, incapable of adjusting to novel surroundings or of developing new dispositions, habits or languages. In short, variations in language among nations are not wholly, or even mainly, attributable to such *external* circumstances as climate or geographical distances, but largely to *internal* factors such as dispositions and attitudes arising from relations between families and nations. Conflict and mutual aversion, in particular, have greatly favoured the emergence of language differentiation.

Without casting aspersions on human nature, it can be said that two or more neighbouring tribes with well-defined family partialities will soon find cause for conflict and friction. It is not only that similar needs will before long involve them in a dispute over food and drink (as happens when two groups of shepherds quarrel over wells and pasture grounds). There is a far more dangerous spark liable to set them on fire: jealousy, ambition, tribal pride and honour. The same family affection which, turned in upon itself, strengthens the unity of the tribe, generates feuds and intensifies family hatred when directed against another kinship group. In the first case it binds many into one by strong ties, in the second it turns two parties into enemies. And it is not simply wickedness or some other despicable vice that can be blamed for such perennial enmities and struggles, but more probably a misguided sense of human nobility coupled with human frailty as such.

The social culture of man in its earlier stages of development is characterized by creativeness and action rather than by acquisitiveness and the desire for private possessions. Hence pride in the former constitutes a far greater point of honour than the distressing pride in property of later and more spineless periods. To be an honest, upright man and to belong to a tribe of honest, upright members meant almost the same thing in those earlier times. For the son inherited his father's virtue and courage, and learned from him to a much greater extent and in a deeper sense than is customary today. What is more, membership of the tribe was tantamount for the individual to being an integral part of a whole where the whole represented the very personification of uprightness, in defence of which every member of the tribe would rise in arms on all occasions, just as the tribe as a whole would fight for the honour of every single one of its members. The slogan, 'whoever is not with us and of us, is below us' was, under these circumstances a fairly natural corollary. The term 'barbarian' was a watchword of contempt, applied to the stranger who, by implication, was considered inferior in every respect. Whatever the norms and standards of the times, the stranger was considered less noble, less courageous and less enlightened.

If it were merely a dispute over property rights, over security of possession, these attitudes would scarcely give cause for war. Indeed, the feeling that your neighbour is less courageous than you should provide grounds for rejoicing. However, precisely because it is not only, or mainly, a matter of clashing material interests—if it is these at all—but a matter of collective opinion and tribal honour, the bone of contention is something far more divisive. Unlike the clash of material interests, the clash of strongly held communal opinions involves public 'face', the pride and prowess of the whole tribe; it causes each side to blow the trumpet of war and to answer its call to patriotic heroism. Since every single member is concerned in the cause of the war and is imbued with the same spirit of righteousness, the feeling of national hatred goes deep. Bitter wars are perpetuated from one generation to another. This state of affairs gives rise to another slogan: 'Whoever is not with me is against me'. The barbarian is not only the despised foreigner, he is also the hated enemy.

Contempt and enmity cannot but lead to complete separation and estrangement. For who would associate with so contemptible an enemy as a barbarian? Who would want to share with him the family traditions, the memory of a common origin and, above all, language, this very symbol of tribal identity? . . .

An Oriental account of the separation and differentiation of languages* (which is considered here merely as a poetic fragment of the archeology and history of the human race) supports by its rather poetic legend what has since been observed about many nations in all parts of the world. For it has been found that languages did not gradually change following migrations, as the philosopher has it. The process resembled far more the poetic tale of the Hebrews. 'Peoples assembled to erect a great edifice; then came disaster and they reeled under a confusion of tongues; they ceased to build and scattered to the four corners of the earth'. Is it not conceivable that so great an undertaking gave ample opportunity for dissension and bitterness, that some slight affront could have aroused family partiality, kindling the spark of discord? Discord, in turn, could have given rise to separation, and accomplished the very thing which their building was designed to prevent: the diversification of their language, the basis of their common origin.

I will not dispute with theology on divine dispensation in this matter. But those familiar with the Oriental bias for symbolism will not fail to recognize the principal idea in the allegorical tale. Distinct nations were formed, each with its own language, not only as a result of migrations, but also because of discord in the course of great common concerns. They are, so to speak, the debris of the confusion of peoples.

But quite apart from this Oriental testimony, which I mention purely as a poem, it is evident that the multiplicity of languages is no argument against a natural human development of language.

* Genesis, xi.

Now and again, it is true, mountains have been thrown up by earthquakes: but must we conclude from this that the earth as a whole with its mountain ranges, streams and oceans, could not have been formed out of water? At any rate, what has been said may caution etymologists not to draw too hasty conclusions as to origin and relationship from the differences in language. Families may be closely related and yet find cause to deny the similarity of their coat of arms. The spirit of discord in the smallest of groups provides sufficient evidence for such an hypothesis.

FOURTH LAW OF NATURE

[v, 134–47]

Since mankind in all probability forms one progressive totality, originating from one common origin within one universal order, all languages and, with them, the whole chain of culture, derive from one common source.

We have observed that man is subject to a peculiar rule that characterizes the workings of his mind: a tendency to build up associations between what it sees and what it has seen. As a result of these associations *the mind creates a progressive unity out of the multiplicity of its states*. This creative process entails *language* and its *continuous growth*.

We have also observed that education provides the chain of continuity between parents and children, so that *the succession of the generations forms a chain of unity as well as a chain of continuity*, in which each link is only inserted, as it were, between two other links, in order to receive and transmit the cultural heritage. This process, too, entails *language* and its *continuous growth*.

Both of these tendencies, then—the creative operation of individual minds and the process of transmitting education from one generation to the next—entail the existence and development of language. It is by virtue of these two combined tendencies that we can speak of *cultural growth* throughout the whole human race in the most meaningful sense.

Each individual as a human being is capable of consciously grasping the chain of continuity within his own life. Each individual is son or daughter, moulded by education; consequently he or she receives from the earliest moments in life part of the cultural treasures of the ancestral heritage. Since son and daughter in turn pass on the heritage transmitted to them, there is, in a sense, no thought, no invention, no improvement, which is not passed on, which is not extended almost into infinity. I can do no act, think no thought, which in some measure has not some effect on the inexhaustible fullness of my own life; neither is there any other being of my species whose acts and thoughts do not in some way affect the whole species and its progressive development. Every act raises a wave, great or small; every thought produces a change in the individual mind, affecting the whole constellation of its previous states. Similarly, changes in one human mind invariably exercise some influence on other minds. The first thought of the first human mind has some bearing on the last thought of the last human mind.

If language were native to man in exactly the same sense as the hoarding of honey is to the bee, the great and magnificent structure of human culture (if it existed at all) would collapse all at once. Every man would bring into the world his own limited stock of language, which in effect means that he would have to invent it for himself. What a pitiable creature he would be, having to invent the rudiments of language every time anew, for his ancestors will have taken theirs into their grave just as the bee takes her skill in building the honeycomb with her when she dies. His successor enters the world, labours with infinite pains at the same beginning, accomplishes just as much, or just as little, dies; and this goes on *ad infinitum* . . . If every individual invents for himself only, vain attempts are multiplied to infinity, and the inventive mind would be bereft of its most treasured prize: *growth*. . .

I entered the world and, in doing so, I entered a world of instruction; so did my father; so did the first son of the first ancestor. And as I develop my thoughts and transmit them to my descendants, so did my father, so my father's father, back to the first of all ancestors. The chain stretches backwards and comes to an end only when the 'first man' is reached. We are all his sons; with him began the race; here originated language and instruction. He began to invent; we invented after him; he first taught; we learned and taught after him, with more or less success. No thought created by the human mind was ever lost. Yet no human skill was ever perfect from the very start. Unlike the skill of the animal, it was always subject to further development, forever in a state of *becoming*. Hence language, too, was no ready-made article like the cell of the bee. As everything else in man, it was forever developing, striving for perfection without attaining it. Thus considered, how sublime is language! A treasure of human ideas, to which every one contributed in his own way, an accumulation of the continuous activity of all human minds . . .

Many have attempted genealogies of languages: I shall not do so. There are many incidental causes which escape the etymologist, which, however, palpably increase the difficulties in tracing the genealogical tree of a language. Among travellers and missionaries there have been so few expert philologists capable of reporting on the spirit and characteristics of tribal languages that we are still on the whole left very much in the dark. What we get in most instances is a list of words. This, clearly, is not a good enough basis for a science of comparative languages. All that can be said with a degree of assurance, therefore, is that the process of language formation and language transmission is inseparable from the general development of human society. I shall make only three main observations here which may add different dimensions to this discussion.

1. It is true that every individual human being has faculties common to the species as a whole, as every nation has those of a plurality of nations. Nonetheless, it cannot be denied that society can invent more than the individual, and the whole race more than a nation, not merely because there is strength in numbers but also by virtue of qualitatively diverse but closely interacting circumstances. It might be supposed that an individual, free from urgent needs and provided with all the amenities of life, would, left to himself, have the leisure to exercise the faculties of his mind, and hence would prove most inventive in all things including the formation of new words. The reverse, however, is the case. Without society man is apt to relapse into a savage state and languish away in inactivity, when having placed himself in circumstances in which his most necessary wants will be supplied he will be like a flower uprooted and torn from its stem, wilting on the ground. But let him be a member of society having many wants; let him be responsible for himself and others. These duties might be supposed to deprive him of the liberty to raise himself, the increased

vexations to deprive him of the leisure to invent. But again the reverse is true. Duties invigorate him; vexations rouse him; restlessness keeps his mind in motion; he will accomplish more, the more astonishing it is that he should do so. Man as a member of a group will contribute disproportionately more to the formation and development of language than an equal number of isolated individuals. Other considerations apart, how little would a lone man on a desert island invent, even if he were a philosopher of language! For this reason *nature elected the development of man in society*.

2. It might be thought that a single isolated tribe enjoying ease and leisure could do more to further its language than one threatened by invasions and wars from other tribes. But this is not so. The more a group is threatened, the more it will turn in upon itself and the closer will be the ties of its members. To avert dispersion they will do everything to strengthen their tribal roots. They will extol the deeds of their forefathers in songs, in patriotic appeals, in monuments, and thereby preserve their language and literary traditions for posterity. The maintenance of tribal languages will therefore be more securely assured if tribes are not isolated. For this reason *nature elected the development of groups among other groups*.

3. A nation which turns in upon itself will, however, in time get set in its own ways. By rigidly containing its needs and interests, it will also retard the development of its language and of its general culture. It will, as it were, isolate itself from within. Many small, so-called barbarian, nations illustrate this state of affairs. Isolated by their self-imposed limitations, they continue for centuries in the most astounding ignorance like islanders who had never heard of fire, unaware of the simplest mechanical skills. It is almost as if they had no eyes to see what is going on around them. This does not escape the notice of other nations who eagerly pronounce such a people stupid and inhuman, even though not so long before they themselves may have been no less backward or 'barbarian'. Many a philosopher, too, raises a deafening alarm about the ignorance and backwardness of primitive peoples as if it were the most incomprehensible thing, whilst in actual fact it is the most intelligible, the most natural, phenomenon according to the analogy of the universal order. Have we Germans not learned

most of what we know as a 'civilized nation' from other peoples? Indeed we have. In this and in many other such cases nature has forged a new chain of transmission, from nation to nation. Arts, sciences, languages, the totality of social cultures, have been developed and refined in a powerful progression in this very manner. This inter-national transmission of social cultures is indeed the *highest form of cultural development which nature has elected.*

We Germans would, like the Indians of North America, still be living contentedly in our forests, waging cruel wars as heroes, if the chain of foreign cultures had not pressed in upon us and, with the impact of centuries, had not forced us to join in. Roman civilization hailed from Greece; Greece owed its culture to Asia and Egypt; Egypt to Asia, China perhaps to Egypt, and so on; thus the chain extends from its first link to the last and will one day encircle perhaps the whole world. The art that raised Grecian palaces is displayed by the savage in the construction of his forest hut; likewise, the first traces of Mengs' and Dürer's paintings can be found in their crudest aspect on Hermann's painted shield. The Eskimo haranguing his army is a Demosthenes in embryo, and a nation in the Amazon valley might produce the Phidias of the future.* Let the nations freely learn from one another, let one continue where the other has left off . . . Egyptians, Greeks, Romans, and some modern nations, merely carried on and developed the heritage handed down to them. Others, such as Persians, Tartars, Goths and Papists arrived on the scene to destroy and lay waste what the former had created. Yet this only helped to stimulate new activity and new creations upon the debris of the old . . .

It should be apparent by now how futile it is to derive a divine origin of language from providing proof of its organization and beauty. To be sure, there is organization, there is beauty; but when, where and how did this come about? Is this or that language which we so greatly admire the original language, or is it not rather the offspring of many centuries and nations? Take any magnificent edifice: have not nations, perhaps even continents and whole epochs worked on it? Does this refute or rather support

---

* De La Condamine. [Charles Marie, 1701–74. French explorer of the Amazon.]

the thesis that a wretched primitive hut could have been the origin of building and architecture? Did God have to teach man to build a palace because man could not build a palace on the very first day of existence? What sort of logic is this? I might as well say that because I cannot quite conceive how this huge bridge here between the two mountains could have been built, I must conclude that the devil must have built it. It takes a certain audacity or ignorance to deny in the face of all the historical and philological evidence—not to speak of common sense—that language, like man himself, had developed in stages, by gradual steps and under varying circumstances. But if there was development, it had to have a beginning. Unless the human mind could develop without language, or language without the human mind, we cannot but conclude that both processes are inseparably connected from their very origin. The only alternative would be to maintain that, without reason or cause, the beginning of these processes was radically different from their development; that whilst the latter was entirely human, the former was entirely divine. To advance such an hypothesis of a divine origin of language seems to me an oversophisticated way of concealing utter nonsense.

Nonsense is indeed a harsh word: yet I use it quite deliberately. Let me, by way of summing up, explain why I do so.

There are three possible reasons for claiming a divine origin of language.

In the first place, it may be argued that language is divine because it cannot be derived from the nature of man. If an opponent says 'I can wholly derive it from the nature of man', who has said more? The former, hiding behind the curtain of ignorance, shouts 'here is God'; the latter, standing on an open platform, proclaims 'look at me, I am a living and active human being'!

In the second place, the champion of a divine origin may continue his argument further by saying that, since *he* cannot explain language as a product of human nature, *nobody* can, and *therefore* it is thus wholly inexplicable. Yet is there logic in his reasoning? His opponent says; 'To me no element of language is explicable, in terms of origin and development, unless it is derived from the human mind. Indeed, I cannot conceive of a human mind separate from, or without, language; I cannot conceive of a human species as a constituent of nature in abstraction from language'.

Who is more convincing? Who has more commonsense on his side?

Finally, there are those who invoke the 'divine' hypothesis positively. They are not content with asserting *that* language could not have originated in the human mind; they have not only *clearly* espied *why*, in view of man's nature on the one hand and the nature of language on the other, the latter could not possibly be traced to a human origin; they also claim to *know*, and know *clearly* not only the nature of language, but also the nature of God. And, fortified by this knowledge, they consider themselves in an incontrovertible position to conclude that only God and God alone could have invented language. This conclusion, to be sure, is a perfectly valid inference from the stated premises. However, it is also a piece of perfectly abominable nonsense. It is as valid as the 'proof' advanced by the Turks in support of the divine origin of the Koran. 'Who', they say, 'but the prophet of God could have written thus.' Indeed! Yet who but a prophet of God can also know for certain that only the prophet of God could write thus? Only God could have invented language! But only God Himself can ascertain that no other than God could have invented it. And what mortal creature dares to measure not merely language and the human mind but even language and Divinity itself?

The 'divine' hypothesis finds no support, not even in the Oriental document which it invokes. For the latter manifestly places the origin of language in the human mind when it speaks of man naming the animals. The postulate of the human origin of language, on the other hand, can claim every fact in its favour: the nature of the human mind; the nature of the fundamental elements of language; the analogous development of language and mankind; actual examples taken from all nations, ages and continents!

The higher-origin-argument, however pious it may seem, is thoroughly irreligious. At each step God is disparaged by the most ignoble, most jejune anthropomorphic conceptions. The theory of the human origin of language, on the other hand, exalts God and His works, for it credits Him with having created a human mind capable of forming and developing language by its own powers. The mind has evolved language because it is necessary to its operation as the most perfect image of the Creator. Thus the

176

origin of language is explained in a truly divine manner only insofar as it is truly human.

The theory of a higher origin is not only without value; it can also prove exceedingly harmful. It destroys the natural propensity of the human mind to probe into the phenomena it encounters by its own efforts and thus militates against all scientific enquiry, particularly in the field of psychology. If language is not the product of the human mind, then nothing else is. For language is the seed of all knowledge. Without it the very beginning of the arts and sciences would remain forever inconceivable. Only by postulating a human origin of language does it make sense to cherish the hope that with every further step man will gain clearer perspectives into, and more fruitful explanations of, the diverse spheres of his existence. Only then does it make sense to expect progress in all branches of philosophy, and, in particular, in the philosophy of language.

It would be particularly gratifying to the author if his treatise would succeed in displacing an hypothesis which has cast, and still casts, a shadow over the human spirit. He has violated the rules of the Academy in not stipulating an hypothesis of his own, because he saw no point in offering an equivalent or substitute to the previous hypothesis. What value is there, after all, in adding yet another hypothesis to the ample stock already in existence? What about those of Rousseau, of Condillac, of all the others? Are they not looked upon merely as philosophical fiction? This author preferred to collect factual data about the human mind, about the organization of human nature, about the structure of ancient and primitive languages and the conditions under which they developed within the total economy of man, in order to establish his thesis as incontestably as any philosophical truth can be established. He hopes, therefore, that by deviating from the rules of the Academy he has served its purpose more directly than he could otherwise have done.

YET ANOTHER PHILOSOPHY OF HISTORY

FOR THE ENLIGHTENMENT OF MANKIND

A FURTHER CONTRIBUTION TO THE MANY CONTRIBUTIONS OF THE CENTURY

1774

YET ANOTHER PHILOSOPHY OF HISTORY

I

... No one in the world feels the weakness of general characterization more than I do. If one depicts a whole people, an age, an area, whom has one depicted? If one groups into one mass the peoples and periods which succeed each other eternally like the waves of the sea, what has one described? To whom does the descriptive term apply? Finally, one brings all of it together into nothing but a *general word*, whereby each individual thinks and feels as he will. How imperfect the means of description! How great the ease of misunderstanding!

Have you noticed how inexpressible is the individuality of one man, how difficult it is to know distinctly what distinguishes him, how he feels and lives, how differently his eyes see, his soul measures, his heart experiences, everything? What depth there is in the character of a single nation which, even after repeated and probing observation manages to evade the word that would capture it and render it recognizable enough for general comprehension and empathy. If this is so, how then can one survey an ocean of entire peoples, times and countries, comprehend them in one glance, one sentiment or one word, a weak incomplete silhouette of a word? A whole *tableau vivant* of manners, customs, necessities, particularities of earth and heaven must be added to it, or precede it; you must enter the spirit of a nation before you can share even one of its thoughts or deeds. You would indeed have to discover that single word which would contain everything that it is to express; else one simply reads—*a word*.

We believe that we still possess the paternal, domestic and human instincts of the Oriental, the loyalty and artistic diligence of the Egyptian, the vivacity of the Phoenician, the Greek love of liberty, the Roman strength of mind—who does not believe himself to share all these dispositions, lacking only the time and the occasion for exercising them? And see, my reader, this is exactly where we stand. The most cowardly villain has still without doubt a remote tendency to become the most magnanimous hero—but what a gulf separates these potentialities from their realization in such a character! And this gulf remains, even if you lack nothing except the time and the occasion to translate your propensities into the actual skills and practices of an Oriental, a Greek or a Roman. For it is these, the *applied* skills and practices, which are the heart of the matter. In order to feel the whole nature of the soul which reigns in everything, which models after itself all other tendencies and all other spiritual faculties, and colours even the most trivial actions, do not limit your response to a word, but penetrate deeply into this century, this region, this entire history, plunge yourself into it all and feel it all inside yourself—then only will you be in a position to understand; then only will you give up the idea of comparing everything, in general or in particular, with yourself. For it would be manifest stupidity to consider yourself to be the quintessence of all times and all peoples.

Take the character of nations! All we can go by are the data we have about their constitution and history. Did not, or could not, a Patriarch have, however, other tendencies besides those which you attribute to him? To this double question, I reply simply; Yes, undoubtedly. Undoubtedly he had other secondary traits which are taken for granted, regardless of what you or I have said or not said, and which I, and perhaps others with me who have his history in mind, have already implicitly recognized in this word. Better still, let us suppose that things could have been quite different—given another place, another time, and taking into account different cultural developments and circumstances— could we not ask then why Leonidas, Caesar and Abraham could not have been celebrities of our century? They could have been, but they were not. These are the questions which history should pose; they should be its prime concern.

I should likewise not be surprised to come across more or less trivial contradictions within the wealth of detail of peoples and times. That no people long remained, or could remain, what it was, that each, like the arts and sciences and everything else in the world, had its period of growth, flowering and decay; that each of these modifications has lasted only the minimum of time which could be given to it on the wheel of human destiny; that, finally, no two moments in the world were ever identical and that therefore the Egyptians, the Romans and the Greeks have not stayed the same through all time—I tremble to think what clever objections could be raised on this subject by clever people, especially historians! Greece was composed of many peoples: were Athenians and Boetians, Spartans and Corinthians, nothing less than identical? Was agriculture not already practised in Asia? Did not the Egyptians once trade as well as the Phoenicians? Were the Macedonians not as much conquerors as the Romans? Did Aristotle not have as speculative a mind as Leibniz? Did not our Nordic peoples surpass the Romans in bravery? Egyptians, Greeks, Romans—rats and mice—were they, are they, not all alike? No, for after all there are rats *and* mice.

How tiresome to address the public when one always has to guard against objections of this kind and worse, and delivered in such a tone, from the vociferous section of the public (the nobler-thinking section keeps quiet!) And yet at the same time one has to bear in mind that the great mass of sheep who cannot tell their right paw from their left will bleat in concert. Can there be a general picture without grouping and arrangement? Can you have a wide view without height? If you hold your face up against the picture, if you cut off this splinter of it, pick out that little lump of paint, you will never see the picture whole—indeed you will not see a picture at all. And if your head is full of one particular group with which you are infatuated, how can you possibly view the flux of ever-changing events as a totality? How can you order them, follow their course, distinguish the essential effect in each scene, quietly trace the influences and finally give a name to it all? But if you cannot do all this, history just flickers and wavers before your eyes like a confusion of scenes, peoples and times. First you must read and learn to see. I concede, however, that to give a general description, to provide a general concept, is inevitably an abstraction. For only the Creator can conceive the immense variety within one nation or all nations without losing sight of their essential unity.

II

So, away with these trivial objections lacking purpose or point of view. Seen as a great sequence in its entirety, how miserable appear some fashionable prejudices of our century drawn purely from general textbook concepts about the advantages, virtues, and happiness of nations so distant and varied.

Human nature, even at its best, is not an independent deity: it has to learn everything, develop through progress, keep on advancing through gradual struggle. Naturally it will develop for the most part, or only, in those directions which give it cause for virtue, for struggle or for progress. Each form of human perfection then, is, in a sense, national and time-bound and, considered most specifically, individual. Nothing develops, without being occasioned by time, climate, necessity, by world events or the accidents of fate. Tendencies or talents slumbering in the heart, therefore, may never become actual accomplishments. A nation may have the most sublime virtues in some respects and blemishes in others, show irregularities and reveal the most astonishing contradictions and incongruities. These will be all the more startling to anyone carrying within himself an idealized shadow-image of virtue according to the manual of his century, one so filled with philosophy that he expects to find the whole universe in a grain of sand. But for him who wants to understand the human heart within the living elements of its circumstances, such irregularities and contradictions are perfectly human. Powers and tendencies proportionally related to given purposes do not constitute exceptions but are the rule, for these purposes could scarcely be attained without them . . .

What right justifies the arbitrary verdicts of praise and blame which we heap on all the earth on account of a favourite people of antiquity with which we have become infatuated? These Romans were as no other nation could be, and did what no one could imitate, because they were Romans. They were at the peak of the world and everything around them was valley. On this peak from youth on, formed by this Roman spirit, they acted accordingly. What was so astonishing about that? And what was so astonishing that a small pastoral and farming people in one of earth's valleys

184

should not be creatures of iron who could act like them? Was it so astonishing, that they should have virtues which the noblest Roman could not have, and that the noblest Roman on his peak, under pressure of necessity, could in cold blood resolve on cruelties foreign to the mind of the shepherd in the small valley? . . . The very machine, which made possible the wide diffusion of vice also raised virtues and extended activities. Is mankind in general, in one particular condition, capable of pure perfection? The summit borders on the valley. Around the noble Spartans dwell the barbarically treated helots. The Roman in triumph, coloured with godly red, is also tinctured invisibly with blood: robbery, sacrilege and debauchery surround his chariot; oppression goes before him; misery and poverty follow him. Defects and virtues, then, always dwell together under one human roof.

To conjure up in superhuman splendour a favourite people of the earth may well pass as fine poetry, and, as such even prove useful, for man can be ennobled by a beautiful prejudice. But what if the poet should also be a historian, or a philosopher, as most pretend to be, modelling all centuries after the pattern of their time (a pattern frequently inadequate and feeble)? Hume, Voltaire, Robertson, classical twilight ghosts, what are you in the light of the truth?

A learned society of our time proposed, doubtless with the best of intentions, the following question: 'Which was the happiest people in history?'* If I understand the question aright, and if it does not lie beyond the horizon of a human response, I can only say that at a certain time and in certain circumstances, *each* people met with such a moment or else there never was one. Indeed, human nature is not the vessel of an absolute, unchanging and independent happiness, as defined by the philosopher; everywhere it attracts that measure of happiness of which it is capable: it is a pliant clay which assumes a different shape under different needs and circumstances. Even the image of happiness changes with each condition and climate. (What is it then, if not the sum of 'satisfaction of desires, realization of ends and a quiet surmounting of

* The gentlemen must have cherished a terribly high ideal since, to my knowledge, none of the philosophical problems they posed ever proved soluble. [Herder is here referring to the Berlin Academy.]

needs', which everyone interprets according to the land, the time and the place?) Basically, therefore, all comparison is unprofitable. When the inner sense of happiness has altered, this or that attitude has changed; when the external circumstances and needs fashion and fortify this new sentiment: who can then compare the different forms of satisfaction perceived by different senses in different worlds? Who can compare the shepherd and the Oriental patriarch, the ploughman and the artist, the sailor, the runner, the conqueror of the world? Happiness lies not in the laurel wreath or in the sight of the blessed herd, in the cargo ship or in the captured field-trophy, but in the soul which needs this, aspires to that, has attained this and claims no more—each nation has its centre of happiness within itself, just as every sphere has its centre of gravity.

Mother Nature has taken good care of this. She placed in men's hearts inclinations towards diversity, but made each of them so little pressing in itself that if only some of them are satisfied the soul soon makes a concert out of the awakened notes and only senses the unawakened ones as if they mutely and obscurely supported the sounding melody. She has put tendencies towards diversity in our hearts; she has placed part of the diversity in a close circle around us; she has restricted man's view so that by force of habit the circle became a horizon, beyond which he could not see nor scarcely speculate. All that is akin to my nature, all that can be assimilated by it, I hanker and strive after, and adopt; beyond that, kind nature has armed me with insensibility, coldness and blindness, which can even turn into contempt and disgust. Her aim is only to force me back on myself so that I find satisfaction in my own centre. The Greek adopts as much of the Roman, the Roman of the Greek, as he needs for himself; he is satisfied, the rest falls to the earth and he no longer strives for it. If, in this development of particular national tendencies towards particular forms of national happiness, the distance between the nations grows too great, we find prejudices arising. The Egyptian detests the shepherd and the nomad and despises the frivolous Greek. Similarly prejudices, mob judgment and narrow nationalism arise when the dispositions and spheres of happiness of two nations collide. But prejudice is good, in its time and place, for happiness may spring from it. It urges nations to converge upon their centre,

attaches them more firmly to their roots, causes them to flourish after their kind, and makes them more ardent and therefore happier in their inclinations and purposes. The most ignorant, most prejudiced nation is often superior in this respect. The moment men start dwelling in wishful dreams of foreign lands from whence they seek hope and salvation they reveal the first symptoms of disease, of flatulence of unhealthy opulence, of approaching death!

The general, philosophical, philanthropical tone of our century wishes to extend 'our own ideal' of virtue and happiness to each distant nation, to even the remotest age in history. But can one such single ideal act as an arbiter praising or condemning other nations or periods, their customs and laws; can it remake them after its own image? Is good not dispersed over the earth? Since one form of mankind and one region could not encompass it, it has been distributed in a thousand forms, changing shape like an eternal Proteus throughout continents and centuries. And even if it does not strive, as it keeps on changing, towards the greater virtue and happiness of the individual—for man remains forever man— nonetheless a plan of progressive endeavour becomes evident. This is my great theme.

Those who have so far undertaken to explain the progress of the centuries have mostly cherished the idea that such progress must lead towards greater virtue and individual happiness. In support of this idea they have embellished or invented facts, minimized or suppressed contrary facts; covered whole pages; taken words for works, enlightenment for happiness, greater sophistication for virtue, and in this way invented the fiction of the 'general, progressive amelioration of the world' which few believed, least of all the true student of history and the human heart.

Others, who saw the harmfulness of this dream without knowing a better one, saw vices and virtues alternating like climates, perfections sprouting and dying like spring leaves, human customs and preferences strewn about like leaves of fate. No plan! No progress, but an endless revolution! Weaving and unravelling like Penelope! They fell into a whirlpool of scepticism about all virtue, about all happiness and the destiny of man, and introduced into history, religion and ethics the latest fad of recent philosophy (especially that of France):* doubt. Doubt in a hundred forms, but almost invariably sporting the dazzling title 'history of the world'! We founder on contradictions as on the waves of the sea; and either we miscarry completely, or the modicum of morality and philosophy that we save from the wreck is not worth talking about.

Does this mean that there can be no manifest progress and development, in some higher sense than we usually think? Do you see this river flowing on, how it springs from a tiny source, swells, divides, joins up again, winds in and out and cuts farther and deeper but, whatever the intricacies of its course, still remains water. A river! A drop of water! Nothing but a drop of water, until it plunges into the sea! Might it not be the same with human kind? Or do you see that tree growing there, or that striving man? He must pass through different ages of life, between which are apparent resting-places, revolutions, changes, and each of which obviously constitutes a form of progress from the one before. Each age is different, but each has the centre of its happiness within itself. The youth is not happier than the innocent, contented child; nor is the peaceful old man unhappier than the energetic man in his prime. The force of the pendulum is the same whether it swings quickly through its widest arc or slowly as it approaches a state of rest. And yet the striving never ceases. No one lives in his own period only; he builds on what has gone before and lays a foundation for what comes after. Thus speaks the analogy of nature, the pattern of God eloquent in all His works; obviously mankind must be similar. The Egyptian could not have existed without the Oriental, nor the Greek without the Egyptian; the Roman carried on his back the whole world. This indeed is genuine progress, continuous development, however little it may prosper the individual! Becoming on a grand scale! History may not manifestly be revealed as the theatre of a directing purpose on earth—of which our shallow histories boast so much—for we may not be able to espy its final end. But it may conceivably offer us glimpses of a divine theatre through the openings and ruins of individual scenes...

* Good honest Montaigne started this trend; Bayle, the rationalist dialectician, whose contradictions in the *Dictionary* neither Crousaz nor Leibniz could resolve, continued it and further influenced the century. Finally, the most

SECTION 2

[v, 513–54]

I

The universal Roman constitution also reached its end, and the bigger and higher the building, the harder its fall. Half of the world was in ruins. Peoples and continents had lived under the tree and now, when the voice of the holy watchman shouted 'Cut it down', what a void ensued, like a break in the thread of world events. Nothing less than a new world was needed to heal the rift.

Now it was the turn of the Northerners. And the simplest explanation which may be devised for the origins and systems of these peoples appears to be the truest. When at peace they were, so to speak, a kind of northern patriarchy. Since in such a climate an oriental pastoral life was not possible, their condition naturally remained ruder, their small societies more divided and more savage. For here more serious needs pressed harder on the human spirit than where Nature worked almost entirely in favour of man. And these graver needs and the Northern air hardened men more than they could be hardened in the warm aromatic hothouses of the East and South. Human ties nonetheless were quite strong, human instincts and human powers richly in abundance. Hence the region could well have been as Tacitus described it. And when this North Sea of peoples set all its waves in motion, waves pressed on waves and peoples on peoples. Walls and dikes around Rome were breached: the Romans themselves had shown them the weak spots and had enticed them thither to repair them. Finally everything gave way to the great inundation of the South by the North. And after all the revolutions and atrocities, what a new south-nordic world!

Whoever takes note of the conditions in the Roman lands in these last centuries (at that time, the cultured universe) will gaze with astonishment at the way in which Providence prepared such a

recent philosophers, Voltaire, Hume and even Diderot have reached the height of scepticism with their daring assertions and have caused our epoch to be the great century of doubt and the high crest of disbelief. [Jean Pierre de Crousaz (1663–1748) was professor of philosophy and mathematics at Lausanne. He was known chiefly as an educationalist.]

189

remarkable reserve of human forces. Everything was exhausted, enervated, thrown into confusion. Lands were abandoned by men or inhabited by spineless men sinking into opulence, vices, disorders, licence and savage pride of war. The fine Roman laws and learning could not take the place of energies which had vanished, restore nerves which had lost their vitality or stir recumbent desires. So death took over and left a debilitated corpse lying in blood. Just then a new man was born in the North. Under a fresh sky, in the wilderness, where no one suspected it, there matured a new growth of strong, nutritious plants which, transplanted to the more beautiful southern lands—now dismal, empty fields—yielded a great harvest for the destiny of the world. Goths, Vandals, Burgundians, Angles, Huns, Heruli, Franks and Bulgarians, Slavs and Lombards arrived and settled, and the whole new world from the Mediterranean to the Black Sea, from the Atlantic to the North Sea, is their work, their civilization, their constitution.

For it was not only human energies, but also laws and institutions, that they brought on to the stage of world development. To be sure, they despised the arts and sciences, opulence and elegance —which had laid waste mankind; but if they brought nature instead of arts, nordic common sense instead of sciences, strong and good, though wild, customs instead of elegance, and all of these in a ferment together, what an event it was! Their laws breathed virile courage, dignity, reliance on common sense, honesty and respect for their gods. Their feudal system, though it undermined the bustling, teeming, wealthy cities, injected new life into the countryside, provided occupation for men's hands, and, in doing so, increased their health and happiness. Their later ideal went beyond needs, aiming at chastity and honour and ennobling the best part of human dispositions. Romance it may have been, yet what a Romance, a real new blossoming of the human spirit!

Consider how these centuries of ferment actually served mankind as a period of rehabilitation, when their powers were exercised through the division of society into small associations, groups, subgroups and innumerable individual members, and when the interaction of one with another brought vitality and energy to the whole. It was indeed this epoch of ferment which for so long held at bay those devouring jaws of despotism, which swallows up everything, not for the sake of order and obedience (as it claims), but in order to crush everything into deadly uniformity. Now, is it better, is it healthier and more beneficial for mankind, to produce only the lifeless cogs of a huge, wooden, thoughtless machine, or to arouse and activate living energies? Even if institutions are not perfect, even if men are not always honest, even if there is some disorder and a good deal of disagreement—it is still preferable to a state of affairs in which men are forced to rot and decay during their lifetime . . .

The spirit of 'Nordic chivalry' has been compared to the heroic age of the Greeks[1]—and, to be sure, points of comparison do exist—but it seems to me that it is really unique in the sequence of the centuries, resembling nothing but itself. Because it comes between the Romans and us—*quanti viri*—some have treated it with derision; others, somewhat adventurously minded, have exalted it above everything, but it seems to me that it is neither more nor less than a 'particular state of the world', whose advantages and disadvantages should not be compared with those of preceding ages: it took its point of departure from these ages, but by ceaseless transformation and aspiration became uniquely itself —on a grand scale!

We can read of the dark sides of this period in any book. Every classical litterateur who takes our regimented century for the *ne plus ultra* of mankind finds occasion to reproach whole centuries for barbarism, wretched constitutional law, superstition and stupidity, lack of manners and taste, and to mock their schools, country seats, temples, monasteries, town halls, guilds, cottages and houses. At the same time, he shouts the praises of the light of our century, or, rather, of its frivolity and exuberance, its warmth in theory and coldness in practice, its apparent strength and freedom, and its real mortal weakness and exhaustion under the weight of unbelief, despotism, and luxury. All the books of our Voltaires, Humes, Robertsons and Iselins[2] are, to the delight

---

[1] Herder refers here to Richard Hurd's *Letters on Chivalry and Romance* (1762).
[2] Iselin, Isaak, 1728–82. Swiss writer who advocated reform in morals, education and legislation. His chief work is *Über die Geschichte der Menschheit* (1761), an attempt at a philosophical interpretation of universal history which did much to provoke Herder's own polemical attempt.

of their contemporaries, full of beautiful accounts of how the enlightenment and improvement of the world, philosophy and order, emerged from the bleaker epochs of theism and spiritual despotism. All this is both true and untrue. It is true if, like a child, one holds one colour against another, if one wishes to contrive a bright, contrasty little picture—there is, alas, so much light in our century! It is untrue, if one considers the earlier epoch according to its intrinsic nature and aims, its pastimes and mores, and especially as the instrument of the historical process. Often in these apparently coercive institutions and corporations there was something solid, cohesive, noble and majestic, which we certainly do not feel, nor are scarcely able to feel, with our refined ways, disbanded guilds yet shackled states, and with our innate cleverness and all-embracing cosmopolitanism. You mock the servitude of these times, the simple country seats of the nobility, the numerous little social islands and subdivisions and all that depended on them. You praise nothing so much as the breaking of these ties and know of no greater good which ever happened to mankind than when Europe, and with it the world, became free. Became free? What wishful thinking! If only it were true! If only you could realize what these earlier circumstances (in the absence of which human ingenuity would have been stultified) did in fact achieve: Europe was populated and built up; generations and families, master and servant, king and subject, interacted more strongly and closely with one another; what one is wont to call 'simple country seats' prevented the luxuriant, unhealthy growth of the cities, those slagheaps of human vitality and energy, whilst the lack of trade and sophistication prevented ostentation and the loss of human simplicity in such things as sex and marriage, thrift and diligence, and family life generally. The mediaeval guilds and baronies engendered pride in the knights and craftsmen, self-confidence, steadfastness and manliness in their spheres of activity, and checked the worst torment of mankind, the enslavement of lands and souls under a yoke which now, apparently, since the earlier social enclaves have been disbanded, everyone accepts readily and wholeheartedly. How could so many warring republics, so many strong and independent cities, spring up later on? Because the vital forces, on whose sad remains we now live, were planted, nourished and nurtured in the rougher climate of an earlier period. Poor, regimented Europe, devourer and sacrificer of your children, if heaven had not ordained that these barbaric times should precede you and had not maintained them for so long, against various kinds of attack and vicissitude, what would you have been with all your erudition and enlightenment?—a desert.

How strange that anyone in the world should find it hard to understand that light does not nourish men, that order and opulence and so-called free thought can be neither the happiness nor the destiny of everyone. Though they may miss their purpose (after all, what, on the human stage has an abiding purpose?), though they may be accompanied by violence and revolutions, by emotions fraught with enthusiasm or fanaticism, capable of becoming brutal or even atrocious, what power and efficacy feelings, tendencies and actions have as tools in the historical process! The heart and not the head is nourished! It is dispositions and instincts of devotion and chivalry, boldness in love and civic vigour, the constitution of the state, legislation, and religion, which have had unifying effects, not sickly thoughts! I am by no means disposed to defend the perpetual migrations and devastations, the feudal wars and attacks, the armies of monks, the pilgrimages, the crusades. I only want to explain them; to show the spirit which breathed through it all, the fermentation of human forces. The whole species underwent a great cure through violent movement, and, if I may speak so boldly, destiny rewound the giant run-down clock, not, to be sure, without a deafening rattle in the wheels, nor without disturbing the weights from their rest.

How differently I see the times in that light! How more prepared I am to forgive, seeing how ceaselessly they themselves struggled against their defects and strove for improvement. How many slanders are obviously false and exaggerated, since the abuses to which they refer were either later invented by the minds of others or, though existing, were then far more innocuous—if not indeed inevitable—than now. Frequently, too, these abuses were accompanied by compensating good qualities, or else they later revealed themselves to us as the tool of a great good in the future which was not recognized as such at the time. Who, reading this history, will not often wonder what has become of the dispositions and virtues of honour and freedom of these times, of their love and gallantry, their courtesy and fidelity? Their depths have been silted up. Their foundations are shifting, silvery sands, where nothing grows. However that may be, in some respects we would willingly take their devotion and superstition, their obscurity and ignorance, their disorder and unpolished manners, in exchange for our light and our unbelief, our enervated coldness and refinement, our philosophical exhaustion and our human misery. As for the rest, mountain and valley certainly have to have a boundary, and the dark, mighty vault could be nothing other than a dark, mighty, *Gothic* vault!

To assume that human destiny is forever marching forward in giant steps; to believe that depravity is a necessary pre-condition for improvement and order; to argue that there must be shadow in order that there be light, that to unravel the knot of events it must first be tied, that, to produce a clear nectar, fermentation must first remove the impurities: this seems to me to be the corollary of our century's pet philosophy. According to this philosophy, so many corners had first to be forcibly rubbed off before the round, smooth, pretty thing that we are could appear. In the Church, so many abominations, errors, absurdities and blasphemies had first to exist, and all the centuries to struggle, clamour and strive for betterment, before our Reformation, or our splendid and enlightened deism, could come about. Evil politics had to run the whole gamut of horror and abomination before our great art of politics, and all that it entails, could emerge like the morning sun out of the night and the fog. What a beautiful portrayal of the natural order and progress in all things we owe to our brilliant philosophers!

Yet I cannot persuade myself that anything in the kingdom of God is *only* a means—everything is both a means and an end simultaneously, now no less than in the centuries of the past . . .

If we penetrate more deeply into the circumstances surrounding the origin of all this so-called enlightenment of the world, we find that chance, destiny and divinity affect both the whole and the details. Every reformation began with insignificant trifles which only later on became incorporated into a colossal, overall plan; indeed, whenever such a plan was deliberately drawn up in advance, it failed. All the great church councils, emperors, kings, cardinals and eminent gentlemen were unable to change anything, but this plain, unsophisticated monk, Luther, could do it. What is more, he could do it through trifles, by means which our philosophers would have dismissed as wholly ineffective, not himself aware of how far he would go. For the most part, he himself achieved very little. He merely inspired others to achievement, encouraged reformers in other lands, stood up and said 'I am moving, therefore movement exists!' By this means there happened what has happened—a transformation of the world. How often before had such Luthers risen and fallen, silenced by smoke and flame or else by the lack of a free atmosphere in which their words could resound. But now Springtime has come, the earth awakes, the sun broods over it and a thousand new plants shoot up. Oh man, how often you have been used, unwittingly, as a mere tool!

'Why,' asks the gentle philosopher, 'could the human spirit not simply have followed its quiet course, instead of changing one evil for another as passions gave rise to new prejudices within the turmoil of heated action?' The answer is that a quiet progress of the human spirit towards the improvement of the world is hardly anything more than a phantom of our minds, and never the working of God in nature. The seed falls to the ground: it lies there dormant until the sun comes to awaken it; then it germinates, its cells grow and divide vigorously and it breaks through the ground; then come the flower and the fruit—hardly the ugliest mushroom grows as you imagine it. The cause of each reformation was always just such a little seed which fell silently into the earth, hardly worth mentioning. It had already been there for some time, but no one looked at it or took notice of it. Now, however, dispositions, manners, a whole world of habits, are changed by it and recreated. How could that be possible without revolution, without passion and without movement? What Luther said had long been known; only now Luther spelled it out. When Roger Bacon, Galileo, Descartes and Leibniz made their discoveries they did so quietly. It was only a ray of light. Yet when their discoveries broke through the darkness and challenged opinions, they changed the world. The ray sparked off a tempest of flame. The passions of the reformer may bear but little on the intrinsic nature of science, but they profoundly affect its propagation. The very fact that the reformer was animated by such passions enabled him to achieve by a trifle what whole centuries had not been able to achieve through institutions, machineries and speculation. This is the credential of his calling.

Many a simple mechanical discovery, long known and toyed with, has now by some quirk of chance been applied in one particular way, and in this specific application has wrought a revolutionary change. Thus the application of glass to optics, of the magnet to the compass, of gunpowder to warfare, of the art of printing to learning, and of the calculus to a whole new world of mathematics, gave a new shape to things. Changed tools discovered new worlds; such is the nature of progress.

Artillery was invented, and gone was the old fortitude of Theseus, of the Spartans, the Romans, knights and giants. War was transformed, and with it how many other things!

Printing was invented! What a transformation to the realm of knowledge! The diffusion of learning was made possible and opened up a new world to all who could read and spell.

Who can count the revolutions in every part of the world which have come about because of the little needle at sea? Lands, larger than Europe, have been discovered. Coasts have been conquered, full of gold, silver, precious stones, spices—and death. Human beings have been forced, through a process of conversion or civilization, into mines, treadmills and depravity. Europe has been depopulated, her innermost resources consumed by diseases and opulence. Who can count these revolutions, or describe them? Who can count or describe the new manners, the dispositions, virtues or vices? The cycle in which, after three centuries, the world moves, is infinite—and on what does it depend? What gives it its impulse? The point of a needle and two or three other mechanical inventions.

II

Hence it must follow that a large part of this so-called new civilization is actually a piece of mechanism. More closely examined, this mechanism is in fact the essential characteristic of the new spirit. If for the most part new methods of every description and in every art changed the world, these new methods also rendered superfluous forces which were formerly necessary and which now (for every unused force decays) are lost in the mists of time. Certain virtues pertaining to science, war, civil life, navigation, government, are no longer needed, since these have been mechanized, and the machine can be controlled by one single person, with one single thought, with one single sign. Therefore so many forces rest unused. The invention of artillery entailed the weakening of physical military strength, of morale, of bravery, loyalty, individual initiative and old-world sense of honour. The army has become a hired machine without thought, force or will, which one man directs from above and which he employs as pawns, as a living wall to dispatch and to intercept bullets. Fundamentally, therefore, the virtues that a Roman or a Spartan would have admired have been burned away in the depths of men's hearts and the wreath of military honour has withered. And what has taken its place? The soldier is the first servant of the state, in the livery of a hero. This is his honour and his profession. He exists—and because of his existence little remains of other individual existences. This allegedly miserable edifice of bad taste, the old Gothic structure of freedom, of corporations, of property, is cast to the ground and destroyed: it is so closely blocked up in its little ruins that, though country, inhabitant, citizen, native land, may occasionally count for something, the master–servant relationship is nonetheless the most pervasive characteristic of our offices of state, of the trades and of all social orders from peasant to minister and from minister to priest. It is always a matter of master and servant, of despot and vassal. This system of relationships finds its most sublime political expression in the new-fangled philosophical concept of *sovereignty*. If you wish to know what this so-called political sovereignty rests on, you only have to look at our coins with their famous sun-eagle, their crowns and royal insignia, their drums, standards, bullets and the caps of the servile soldiery.

What most spiritual offspring of the new philosophy reveal is that in more than one way it is nothing but a mechanism. With all their philosophy and their knowledge, how ignorant and anaemic our enlightened men often are in matters of life and common sense! Whereas in former times the philosophic spirit never existed only for itself but reached out to affairs and hastened to share in them with the single purpose of creating complete, healthy and active souls, it now stands alone and has become a craft apart—consequently, a craft is what it is. What fraction among you considers logic, metaphysics, morals, physics as organs of the human soul, instruments by the aid of which one should act, as precepts which should infuse our minds with a more beautiful pattern of ideas? Instead, we build our thoughts mechanically, we play and juggle with them like street urchins at a ball game. The philosopher does a sword dance on an academic tight-rope to the joy and admiration of all who sit around and acclaim the great artist because he does not break his neck or his bones—such is his art! If there is one thing in the world you want to see badly done, entrust it to the philosopher. On paper, everything is neat, smooth, beautiful and great; in performance it is a disaster. At every step he is astonished and petrified before unforeseen obstacles and consequences. Any child, therefore, would seem to be a great philosopher; for he can count and he also enjoys playing with syllogisms, figures and instruments, thereby producing new syllogisms, new results, and so-called discoveries—the fruit, the honour and the peak of the human spirit—all by means of a mechanic toy!

We had difficult philosophy: now we have an easy and beautiful one. What on earth could be more mechanical than such a transformation! What, indeed, could be more mechanical than the new philosophy itself! It has forced its way into the sciences, the arts, customs and ways of living and is considered the sap and blossom of our century. Old traditions, prejudices in favour of painstaking scholarship, slow maturing, searching inquiry, and cautious judging have been thrown off like a yoke from the neck! At the bars of our courts, in place of minute, detailed, dusty learning and the individual treatment and examination of each case, we now have that elegant, free-and-easy fashion of judging all cases from a couple of precedents, leaving aside everything which is individual and unique in favour of facile or grandiose generalities. Instead of a judge, we now have that flower of the century, a philosopher! In our political economy and political science philosophy has offered us a bird's eye view in place of an arduously acquired knowledge of the real needs and conditions of the country; an overall picture, as on a map or a philosophical chart. The principles developed by Montesquieu allow a hundred different peoples and countries to be reckoned up extempore on a political multiplication table. It is the same with all the fine arts, the crafts, and even the least of our daily labours. What need is there to dig down into the depths, to rummage around in vaulted cellars, when reason can afford perfect insights in bright daylight? We have dictionaries and philosophies about all subjects, but, even with these tools in our hands, we do not understand any of them. These digests and summaries of preceding pedantry are nothing but abstractions, a kind of instant philosophy produced by a mechanical process from a couple of general ideas.

Allow me to show you the intricate mechanism of this new philosophy. Is there a more elaborate language and syntax, that is to say, a narrower frame of thought, of the art of living, of genius and of taste, than that of the nation in which this philosophy has spread most brilliantly under a hundred different forms? Which drama comes closer to a marionette show of perfect regularity; which art of living to the mockery of gaiety in its frivolous mechanical courtesy? Which philosophy resembles more the display of a few sentiments and a treatment of everything in the world in terms of these few sentiments? To ape humanity, genius, cheerfulness, virtue, is to create imitations and, precisely because they are only imitations and can so easily themselves be imitated, the whole of Europe will follow suit.

III

This makes it easy to see in which direction civilization is going or is being driven: a philosophy of mechanized thinking! Cold reason exposes the very foundations of society, which formerly simply stood and bore its weight! After dozens of attempts, I find myself unable to comprehend how reason can be presented so universally as the single summit and purpose of all human culture, all happiness, all good. Is the whole body just one big eye? Would it not suffer if every part, the hand and the foot, had to serve as the eye and the brain? Reason, too carelessly, too uselessly diffused, may well weaken desires, instincts and vital activity—in fact, has already done so.

It is true that this lassitude may well suit the spirit of some countries, whose worn-out members have no energies left even to *think* of opposition. Each cog is kept in place by fear or habit or affluence or philosophy, and what are so many great philosophically governed herds but crowds held together by force like fenced-in cattle! They are supposed to be able to think, but perhaps thought is only spread among them, up to a certain point. From day to day they feel more like a machine, or else they feel according to the prejudices they have been fed with; they can do nothing but chew on these prejudices, though as a comforting delusion, they have free thought, this beloved, feeble, provoking, unprofitable free thought, a substitute for the things they perhaps have more need of, such as heart, warmth, blood, humanity, life.

Now let anyone cast the balance. Light is infinitely heightened and diffused whilst inclinations and vital instincts are infinitely weakened. Ideas of universal love for humanity, for all nations, and even enemies, are exalted, whilst warm feelings of family and friendship are allowed to decay. Principles of liberty, honour and virtue are commonplace; they are loudly acknowledged, and in certain countries everyone down to the lowest pays lip service to them, whilst at the same time lying in chains of cowardice, shame, luxury, servility and miserable desultoriness. Techniques and improvements are infinitely widespread, but all these techniques get into the hands of one person, or a few, who do all the thinking. The (human) machine has lost its zest to function; it has lost the ability to live nobly, benevolently and happily. Does it live at all? In its totality and in its minutest parts, it is entirely controlled by the thought of its master.

Is this then the ideal state into which we are being fashioned, to which all Europe, perhaps even the whole world, increasingly aspires? Is it the ultimate aim to organize, plan and control everything in order to create human beings, citizens, entities with their own *raison d'être*? And if so, surely this can only be determined by applying a most careful political calculus to the numbers involved, to the needs and to the purposes. And, let us not forget, each man is to wear the uniform of his station in life, to be a perfect cog in a perfect machine. Splendid marketplaces exist now for the edification of humanity, splendid pulpits and theatres, lawcourts, libraries, schools and, the crown of them all, the illustrious academies. What lustre! Inaugurated with splendour

for the eternal glory of the princes, for the education and enlightenment of the world, for the happiness of mankind. Here they
all are, and what are they doing? They are playing.

IV

A word now about some of the renowned means which are to serve
the great creative plan, and the pride of our century: the civilization and enlightenment of mankind. With it we come to at least
one practical aspect of this theme.

Unless all I have written has been in vain, it should now be
clear that the emergence and further development of a nation is
never other than a work of destiny, the result of a thousand concurrent causes and, in a way, of the entire element in which it
lives. And this being so, is it not childish to base this development
on a few bright ideas and to imagine that this constitutes a scientific
revolution? Should this or that book, author, or whole library,
further this development? Should the product of them all, the
philosophy of our century, do likewise? To bring this about
effectively it would have to arouse and strengthen *dispositions*
which genuinely animate mankind. Alas, what an abyssmal gulf
it would have to bridge to achieve this! Ideas yield only ideas. To
be sure, they give more clarity, accuracy and order to thought,
but that is all one can count on with certainty. Yet how does all
this affect the mind? How does it affect that which it finds in need of
change? How thorough and lasting are these changes to be? And
finally how does all this apply to the thousandfold occasions and
contingencies of one single human life, let alone to an era, a whole
nation, all Europe, or even the entire universe? Oh ye gods, what
another host of questions!

A man who would learn the artificial way of thinking of our
century, who would read all the books we read and praise from
childhood on, and from which we claim to educate ourselves, who
would collect the principles which we expressly or tacitly profess
or work over in our minds, who would wish to draw inferences
from these principles concerning the living and active totality of
this century—how pitiably in error he would be! Just because these
principles are so commonly held and passed on from hand to hand
like a toy, from lip to lip like gossip, we may well doubt their

worth and efficacy. Do we *use* what we *play* with? Do we have so much seed that we cannot sow or plant the field in the ordinary way but have to load it like a granary—a parched, dry granary? What can take root in this manner, or grow? Can a single seed reach the soil?

What should I take as an example to illustrate a truth to which, unfortunately, almost everything, from religion and morals to legislation and popular customs, seems to point? How inundated we are with fine principles, elaborations, systems, interpretations— inundated to the extent that almost nobody can see the bottom of the floodwaters, or keep his feet, and for that very reason merely floats on the surface. The theologian leafs through the most touching descriptions of religion, learns, knows, proves, and— forgets. We are all brought up to be such theologians from child- hood on. The pulpit resounds with principles which we all agree with, know, feel the beauty of—and which we abandon beside the pulpit. It is the same with literature, philosophy and morals. Are we not all more than tired of reading them? What author does not make it his prime concern to dress things up, to sugar the placebo? The head and the heart are completely separated: man has unfortunately reached the point where he acts not according to what he knows but according to what he desires. What good does it do an invalid to be provided with all the delicacies which his sickness prevents him from enjoying, and of which indeed a superfluity had made him sick?

We could always leave to the diffusers of this culture, their talk and their illusions of civilizing mankind, especially the illu- sions of the philosophers of Paris who claim to civilize 'toute l'Europe' and 'tout l'univers', though we know that such talk amounts to no more than good manners, clichés, a pretty turn of phrase or, at best, satisfying self-deception. If, however, they think that by such bookish means, or any other they may devise for the diffusion of culture, they are likely to liberate men's hands and hearts, they are deplorably mistaken. For all they succeed in doing is to envelop this century in a haze of refinement and to misdirect men's eyes by its seemingly brilliant but ineffectual light.

This is a time when the art of legislation is considered the sole method of civilizing nations. Yet this method has been employed in the strangest fashion to produce mostly general philosophies of the human race, rational axioms of human behaviour and what-have-you! Doubtless the undertaking was more dazzling than useful. Admittedly, we could derive from it all the commonplaces about the right and the good, maxims of philanthropy and wisdom, views of all times and peoples for all times and peoples. For all times and peoples? That means, alas, precisely *not* for the very people whom the particular code of law was meant to fit like clothing. It could be that all these tired generalities are nothing but a foam which dissolves in the air of all times and peoples. How different this is from nourishing the veins and sinews of one's own people, from strengthening their hearts and refreshing them to their very marrow.

What an abyss there is between even the finest general truth and the least of its applications to a given sphere, to a particular purpose and in any one specific manner! The village Solon who abolishes just one bad custom, who initiates just one current of human sentiment and activity, has done a thousand times more in the way of legislation than all our great rationalists who believe in the miserable general illusion that everything is either true or false.

This is a time when the institution of academies, of libraries and of art galleries, is seen as the creation of a truly universal culture. Splendid! Certainly, every such academy added lustre to the courts, was a worthy Prytaneum for men of merit,[3] a support to valuable learning, and a magnificent setting for the monarch's birthday celebrations. But what did it do for the education of the country, the people, the subjects? And if it did everything for it, to what extent did that bring happiness? Can these statues, even placed by the roadside and on the doorsteps, transform each passer-by into a Greek so that he sees them as a Greek, identifies himself with them as a Greek? Hardly! Can these poems, these fine lectures in the Attic manner, create an epoch in which these poems and discourses will do wonders and work miracles? I think not. The practitioners of the so-called revival of learning, popes and cardinals though they might be, went on playing with Apollo, the Muses and all the gods in their neo-Latin poetry, when they knew

---

[3] A public building or hall in ancient Greece in which the members of the council or senate (the Prytanes) met, and which also served as a place for entertaining distinguished citizens and visitors.

quite well that it was only a game. The statue of Apollo could stand beside that of Christ or Leda; all three had the same effect, which was no effect at all. If our theatrical performances really produced Roman heroism and created a Brutus or a Cato, do you think that any of our theatres, or pulpits, would be tolerated [by our rulers]? In the noblest of the sciences we pile Ossa on Pelion—a great enterprise—and hardly know to what purpose we are doing it. Treasures lie around and are not used; at least it is certainly not mankind which is using them at the moment.

This is a time when everyone enthuses about education, interpreted as meaning a good knowledge of the exact sciences, instruction, enlightenment, clarification, and the polishing of manners. As if all that could change and develop dispositions! No thought is given to ways of restoring or creating afresh the attitudes and even prejudices, the practices and energies, whereby alone it is possible to build a 'better world'. The essay, the plan, is written, printed, and—forgotten! A textbook of education, just like a thousand others! A codex of good precepts, of which we already have a million, and which will leave the world just exactly as it is.

When, in former times, nations were so much more parochial, they thought quite differently about these matters. Every cultural development originated from particular individual needs and in turn fostered other such needs; the process was one of genuine experience, achievement and practical life in a circumscribed sphere. In the patriarch's hut, the humble homestead, or the local community, people knew and clearly perceived what they talked about, since the way they looked at things, and acted, was through the human heart. Hence our enlightened century is justified in reproaching the less-enlightened Greeks for giving no really general and purely abstract philosophy to the world but speaking always of small needs limited to a narrow range of activity. The Greeks spoke with practical application, each word found its place; and in the best times, when men scarcely spoke through words at all but through deeds, customs, example and a thousand different kinds of influence—how different education was then, for it was certain, strong and enduring. We speak about a hundred social classes, periods, human species, in order to avoid speaking about each of them individually. Our wisdom is so delicate and insubstantial; it is a volatile abstraction which evaporates without having been put to use. Theirs, on the contrary, was and remained a civic wisdom, a matter of concrete human substance, full of sap and nourishment.

If, therefore, my voice had power and scope enough, I would appeal to those who contribute to the civilization of mankind: let us have no more generalizations about improvement, no more paper-culture, but wherever possible, implementation and action! Leave the talking and stargazing to those who have the misfortune to be able to do nothing else. Does not the bride's beloved have a finer place in her heart than the poet who sings her praises or the match-maker who seeks a suitor for her? The very man who is loudest in praise of philanthropy, love of countrymen and family loyalty, perhaps conspires to give them the deepest dagger-thrust for centuries to come. The noblest legislator in appearance may in reality be the most ardent destroyer of his age. With no thought for inner improvement, humanity and happiness, he swims with the tide of his century, deludes his century into acclaiming him its saviour, and claims the brief recompense for it all, the fading laurel of vanity which tomorrow becomes dust and ashes. But the really great and, indeed, divine work of civilizing mankind is quiet yet strong, hidden yet enduring, and has little in common with paltry vanity!

V

After what I have written, I will doubtless be accused of always praising the distant past and of complaining about the present, like children who, attracted by far-off tinsel which they know nothing about, exchange it for the apple they hold in their hand—but perhaps I am not such a child after all. I recognize all the great, fine, unique things of our century and, in spite of all my criticisms, I have always borne them in mind. Philosophy! Diffused light! Mechanical dexterity! Astonishing agility! Gentility! How high our century has risen since the revival of learning! With what remarkable ease it has attained this height, and how strongly it has anchored and secured these qualities for posterity! I believe the remarks I made in this respect are preferable to the gushing, self-congratulatory declamations that one finds in all the books now in vogue, especially in France.

205

It really is a great century, both in its means and its ends: without a doubt we stand at the very top of the tree in regard to the previous centuries! We have drawn from our roots, trunk and branches, as much sap as our slender topmost bough could contain. We look down on Orientals, Greeks, Romans, especially on the Gothic barbarians of the Middle Ages! From what a height we look down upon the world! In a sense, all peoples and continents stand in our shadow, and if a storm in Europe shakes two tiny branches, how the whole world trembles and bleeds! When has the whole world been so generally united by so few threads as now? What people have ever had more power and more machines, so that by pressing one finger entire nations could be thrown into turmoil? And to think that all this is precariously poised on the point of two or three ideas!

Likewise, when has the world been so generally enlightened as now, and gone on becoming more and more enlightened? Whereas formerly wisdom was never more than narrowly national—though firmer and more deep-rooted—how diffused its rays of light are now! Is there a place where Voltaire's writings are not read, in a world illumined by his clear light?

And so, it would appear, there is an ever-growing progress. Soon there will be European colonies everywhere! Savages all over the world will become ripe for conversion as they grow fonder of our brandy and our luxuries; they will soon approach our culture and become, so help me God, good, strong and happy men, just like us!

Trade and popery, how much have you already contributed to this great undertaking! Spaniards, Jesuits and Dutchmen: all you philanthropic, disinterested, noble and virtuous nations! How much of the development of mankind in the diverse parts of the globe is due to you?

If this should be the case in other continents, why not also in Europe itself? Shame on England, that Ireland remained wild and barbaric for so long: now it is policed and happy. Shame on England, that the Highlanders went so long without trousers: now at least they carry them with them on a pole and are happy . . .

To what perfection we have brought all skills, arts, and sciences! Can anyone think of anything more sublime than our art of government, our *system*, that great science for the development

206

of mankind?[4] We no longer require religion, (that childish sanction!) honour, spiritual freedom and human happiness as mainsprings for the existence of states, for these have effectively been replaced by fear and money. How well we know how to seize upon Mammon as our sole god, and to transform him into a second Proteus, so that by enlisting his aid we can acquire and enforce whatever we happen to want! All this we owe to that acme of perfection, the art of government!

Look at the armies; this archetype of human society! How free and comfortable they must feel in their motley apparel, being but lightly fed and lightly clad! They think in unison and their actions are most nobly inspired! What splendid tools they possess! In each of their daily tasks they add to their stock of virtue—in short, the very image of a perfected human mind and of world government!

Balance of Europe, thou magnificent invention, totally unknown to previous ages! Friction there might still be among our great political bodies—in which mankind is undoubtedly so much better cared for—mutual destruction, however, or even the possibility thereof, is now ruled out. How different from the miserable statecraft of Goths, Huns, Vandals, Greeks, Persians, Romans or any of the other sad examples of the past. In their noble and majestic progress our political monsters swallow up all the tiny insects that get into their paths and in return create for us uniformity, order and security. You poor town? You tormented village? Good for you, that we have maintained obedience, order, and security, supreme virtue and happiness. Mercenaries, allied soldiers! Hail to you! Hail to the balance of Europe! Hail to the eternal *peace, order, security* and *obedience* in Europe!

To depict the growth of these circumstances is the sole privilege of our political historians and of our historical eulogists of monarchy![5] How sad were the times when people acted according to needs and their innermost feelings; sadder still, when the power of rulers was still curbed, but saddest of all, when their revenues were not yet wholly arbitrary. For it provided the philosophical

[4] Herder refers here to Hume's *Essays, moral, political and literary* (1741–2), and his *History of England* (1754–62).
[5] Herder in a footnote remarks that he is 'commenting on comments' by William Robertson in his *History of the Reign of the Emperor Charles the Fifth* (1769).

and historical epicist with little scope for generalizing rationalizations and scant opportunity for painting the whole of Europe on one vast canvas! There were no armies in a position to threaten distant borders, no reigning princes who could afford to leave their countries in search of conquest. Military strategy was wholly based on the puny idea of self-defence. There was no political science, no searching ahead into remote times and distant lands, no speculations into the moon, no system of communication to bestow its philanthropic blessings upon mankind. Consequently, there could be no 'social life in Europe'—this latest word in fashion and taste! Fortunately, however, the distinct and individual members which once constituted the state have ceased to be of importance. In the course of the alternating victories and defeats of the free cities, the nobility, the peasants, these have all been successfully directed into the service of that miraculous invention, the state-machine. The result is that people no longer know, nor are permitted to know, what righteousness, dignity or self-determination really mean. Glory to us! What a social life we now have in Europe! A Europe in which monarchs completely dominate the state, a state which no longer has a purpose of its own, but is wholly the tool of the ruler in his foreign designs. Everything can now be foreseen, calculated, predicted and decided upon . . ., so that no state can even lift a feather without another promptly noticing it, without almost automatically causing a general blood-letting. Universality *par excellence!* Yet the wars to which they give rise are, of course, humane, scientifically limited and entirely passionless. Likewise, the ensuing negotiations are invariably fair, just and humane! How admirably this all furthers the greatest virtue of our times: the resignation of the individual human being. Oh, what a high social life we have in Europe!

And just consider by what glorious means we have come so far! In proportion as the distinct and individual members of the state have become enfeebled, so the strength of the mercenary has increased and, along with it, the power of the monarchy. We only have to study mediaeval and modern history, in particular that of France (the precursor of the rest of Europe) to discover by what means the monarchy enlarged its privileges, its revenues, how it succeeded in subjugating or controlling its internal antagonists and in extending its boundaries. How glorious the means, how great the purpose! Equilibrium of Europe! Happiness of Europe! Doubtless this equilibrium and happiness means the world to each individual grain of sand.

'Our system of trade!' This all-embracing, refined scientific system of ours, what do we really mean by it? How wretched were the Spartans to use their helots for field work, how barbaric the Romans to imprison their slaves in dungeons! In our Europe slavery has been abolished, because it has been actuarily established that slaves are far more costly and far less productive than free men. Nonetheless this did not prevent our raiding three other continents for slaves, trading in them, banishing them to silvermines and sugar plantations. But then, they are not European, not Christian! What is more, we get silver, precious stones, spices, sugar and—secret diseases, in return. For the sake of international trade, mutual brotherly assistance, and the common interests of all countries, therefore, let us forge ahead!

'System of trade!' The magnitude and uniqueness of the enterprise is manifest! Three continents are devastated, yet policed by us; we in turn are depopulated, emasculated and debauched as a result. Such is the happy nature of the exchange. Who does not have a hand in this grand European sponging enterprise? Who does not compete as a trader, even of his own children? The old name 'shepherd' has been changed into 'monopolist': Mammon is the god we all serve.

'Ways of living and mores!' How wretchedly primitive was the age in which nationality and national character still existed; and, with it, hatred and hostility towards the foreigner, self-centered parochialism, prejudice, attachment to the soil where one was born and in which one was buried; a native mentality, a narrow span of ideas—eternal barbarism! With us, thank God, national character is no more! We love each and every one, or rather, we can dispense with love; for we simply *get on* with one another, being all equally polite, well-mannered and even-tempered. To be sure, we no longer have a fatherland or any kinship feelings; instead, we are all philanthropic citizens of the world. The princes speak French, and soon everybody will follow their example; and, then, behold, perfect bliss: the golden age, when all the world will speak one tongue, one universal language, is dawning again! There will be one flock and one shepherd! National cultures, where are you?

'Ways of living and mores of Europe!' How late in maturing was the youth of the Gothic period of Christianity; a man was scarcely considered of age when he was thirty. Half of one's life was lost in miserable childhood. But what a new situation has been created by philosophy, education and good manners! We now mature when we reach the age of thirteen, and by the time we are twenty we are passed our prime, having indulged in sins of omission and commission during the dawn of our lives! . . .

'Fine arts and the sciences!' How different from those cruder forms which emerged under wretchedly unstable republican governments in the polities of ancient Greece. Just look at the coarse eloquence of a Demosthenes, the no less coarse Greek theatre; indeed, take the whole of classical antiquity: how crude it all was! . . . The real refinement and flowering of the arts had to wait for the establishment of our glorious monarchies! At the courts of Louis, Corneille showed us what heroes should be like and Racine instructed us about the true nature of sentiments. A completely new species of truth was here discovered, an entire revolution of taste was ushered in, the like of which cold, plain antiquity had not the slightest inkling of; what is more, the opera was invented! Hail to you, opera! You are the acme of the arts!

Our happy and glorious monarchy is the cradle of the really great inventions.[6] In place of the old pedantic universities, brilliant academies now arose. Bossuet created for us a history full of dates, declamations and sermons, vastly superior to that of simple-minded Xenophon and Livy.[7] Bourdaloue devised a rhetoric infinitely better than that of Demosthenes![8] Music was now being written with a completely novel type of harmony, one which could dispense with melody! New architecture was produced of a sort which was thought impossible hitherto; gardens were created replete with symmetry and mathematical proportion!

[6] Herder's sarcastic remarks aim, as his footnotes indicate, at Millar's *Observations concerning the Distinction of Ranks in Society* (1771), Hume's *Essays, moral, political and literary* and *Political Discourses* (1752), and Voltaire's *Le Siècle de Louis XIV* (1751).

[7] Bossuet, Jacques Bénigne, 1627–1704. French preacher and writer. His *Discourse on Universal History* (1681), is an attempt to vindicate the workings of Providence in human history.

[8] Bourdaloue, Louis, 1632–1704. French Jesuit theologian; professor at Bourges, court preacher (from 1670), known for saintly character and fervid eloquence.

A delightfully new nature *minus* nature! And all this we owe solely to the establishment of the monarchy!

Lately we also started to philosophize again.[9] But on what new lines! Without any systems or theorems, so that there was not the slightest difficulty in saying one thing at one time and quite the opposite at another. There was no longer any need of proof or empirical verification. *Esprit* wholly made up for this. After all, 'rigorous philosophy has never done the world any good.'[10] Last not least—the most splendid invention! We have memoirs and dictionaries where everyone can read what and how much he will— and the splendour of splendours: the Dictionary, the Encyclopaedia of all the sciences and arts. If all books, arts and sciences, were to perish through fire and water, thou, Encyclopaedia, would still nourish the human spirit! What the art of printing is to the sciences, the Encyclopaedia is to the art of printing: the highest peak of proliferation, perfection and durability.

Now I should celebrate our best achievement, the enormous progress we have made in the field of religion (for have we not begun to count the variants of the Bible!), and in the principles of honour (for have we not suppressed the ridiculous orders of chivalry and replaced them by bribes and gifts of court!); but above all I should celebrate the perfection achieved in the domestic virtues. But who could possibly celebrate everything in a century such as ours? It is enough that we are the tree-top quivering in the breeze, that the golden age is at hand.

SECTION 3

[v, 554–86]

The breeze is so refreshing that one would be tempted to hover too long over the tree-tops. However, we must go down to the sad earth to cast a glance over the whole or as much of it as we can.

God's wonderful creation! The work of three continents and almost six thousand years! The tender root full of sap, the slender,

---

[9] Herder refers in a footnote to d'Alembert's *Discours préliminaire de l'Encyclopédie* (1751).

[10] Herder refers here to Hume, who deals with this point in several of his essays. See, for example, Essay VIII. 'Of Parties in General' in *Essays, moral and literary*, where he writes: 'general virtue and good morals in a state . . . can never arise from the most refined precepts of philosophy.'

flowering shoot, the mighty trunk, the thrusting intertwined branches, the spreading, airy twigs—how all these rest on one another, grow out of one another! God's wonderful creation! But to what end or purpose?

That this growth, this progress from one thing to another, is not tantamount to perfection in the restricted sense of the schoolman, should be obvious by now. The seed ceases to exist with the coming of the shoot, the tender shoot is no more when the tree comes into being. The trunk is topped by the corona; if each of its branches and twigs wished to be the trunk and the roots, what would become of the tree? Orientals, Greeks, Romans, only existed once; only at one point, one place, were they to touch the electric chain held out by destiny. Hence we are heading for failure if we wish to be Orientals, Greeks and Romans all at once.

It is said that there must now be more virtue in Europe than there has ever been in the whole world. And why? Because there is more enlightenment? I think that for that very reason there must be less.

Perhaps we could ask the flatterers of the century what *is* this greater virtue that Europe is supposed to have acquired through enlightenment? Enlightenment! We know so much more nowadays, hear and read so much, that we have become tranquillized, patient, meek and inactive . . .

Why do we not realize that if we do not have all the vices and virtues of by-gone ages it is surely because we are not in their position, do not have their strength and savour, nor breathe the same air. To be sure, this is not a fault, but why fabricate false praise and absurd pretensions? Why delude ourselves about our means of education as if they had achieved something? Why deceive ourselves about our own trifling importance? Why, finally, drag into every century the story of a partial, derisory lie which ridicules and belittles the customs of all peoples and epochs, so that a healthy, modest, unprejudiced man finally comes to read nothing more into all the so-called pragmatic histories of the world than the nauseating rubbish of 'the loftiest ideals of his time'. The whole earth becomes a dung-heap on which we, like crows, scratch for grains of corn. Such is the philosophy of the century!

'We have no more highway robbers, no more civil wars, no more crime'—but where, how and why should we have them? Our lands are so well policed, so traversed by highways, so well garrisoned, the fields so judiciously apportioned, wise justice so vigilant— where could the poor rascal practise his nefarious trade even if he had the heart and strength for it? And why practise it at all? He can, according to the mores of our century, become in a far more convenient, nay respectable and illustrious, fashion a domestic bedroom thief, and even receive state payment for such services. Why should he not rather accept this payment? Why— and this is the heart of the matter—should he take up an uncertain trade for which he has neither heart nor strength nor opportunity? God have mercy upon our new voluntary virtue!

Do we have 'no civil wars' because we are all such peaceable, satisfied, happy subjects? Or is it not indeed for reasons which often accompany quite the opposite condition? Do we have 'no vices' because we are all so full of charming virtue, Greek liberty, Roman patriotism, oriental piety, mediaeval chivalry, and possess these in the highest degree? Or is it not rather because we have none of these and therefore cannot have their corresponding vices either? Feeble, trembling twigs that we are!

As such, it is presumably part of our excellence that we should be able to boast of a philosophy second to none in its insipidity, myopia, arrogance, complacency and, above all, its futility. The Orientals, Greeks and Romans could not boast of such achievements.

We are far too modest in assessing and valuing the strides we have made in perfecting our methods of educating mankind. Surely the clergy can be more than satisfied that the world has never been so well enlightened in both secular and ecclesiastical matters; the laity, that there has never been so much love for humanity, so much order, uniformity and obedience; our justice, that it has never been so fair and peace-loving; and, finally, our philosophy, that it has never been both so human and so divine, as now. Thanks to whom? Everyone claims the credit for himself! 'We are the physicians, the saviours, the enlighteners, the new creators—the age of feverish frenzy has passed.' Ah yes, praise be, the consumptive invalid lies peacefully in bed, whimpers and—gives thanks! But is he really grateful? And if he is, could not this very gratitude be considered a symptom of his decline, his despondency and extreme timidity? Indeed, our very enjoyment of the things we boast of may cut us off from experiences which might have proved superior. Perhaps, as I write, I am exposing myself to the most venomous and sarcastic misinterpretations. Surely, it could be said, I should write with pride of our advances in ideas, in industry, trade, and the arts; of having attained peace, security and order; of possessing governments able to rule without internal strife, constitutions that are almost perfect, and, above, all, infinite foresight! No time could look so far ahead, or more skillfully toy with predictions! At least this is what our political histories and our histories of commerce and trade tell us. And we have no reason to think that we are reading satire. For these histories are the most faithful expression of wholly sincere opinions. Need I say any more? We are faced here with a disease which precludes remedy. Since opium dreams help to ease the agony of death, should I disturb the ailing patient if I cannot hope to cure him?

Hence it is better to say what will please the patient. To be sure, even in adopting this stance, we are, each in his place, the purpose and instrument of destiny.

*　　*　　*

As a rule, the philosopher is never more of an ass than when he most confidently wishes to play God; when with remarkable assurance, he pronounces on the perfection of the world, wholly convinced that everything moves just so, in a nice, straight line, that every succeeding generation reaches perfection in a completely linear progression, according to *his* ideals of virtue and happiness. It so happens that he is always the *ratio ultima*, the last, the highest, link in the chain of being, the very culmination of it all. 'Just see to what enlightenment, virtue and happiness the world has swung! And here, behold, am I at the top of the pendulum, the gilded tongue of the world's scales!'

The philosopher has not considered what the faintest echo from heaven to earth could have taught him: that in reality man always remains man and nothing but man, after the analogy of the universal order. To see the form of angel or devil in man is only a fiction. For he is but half-way between them, daring and timid, striving in need, though wearying in idleness and opulence. Man—a mere tool—lacking motive and the exercise of your

214

talents you are nothing, but with them you advance, however imperceptibly, in almost everything—a hieroglyph of good and evil in the annals of history!

The philosopher has not considered that this elusive double creature can be modified in a thousand ways and almost has to be, given the structure of our earth; that climate and the circumstances of the time create virtues peculiar to a nation or a century, flowers which under one sky grow and thrive untended and under another die out or wither miserably; (a physics of history, psychology and politics, about which our century certainly has already indulged in much fantasy and brooding); that all this can and has to be does not rule out that, within the ever-changing husk, the same kernel of human substance and happiness can, and in all probability does, remain virtually the same.

The philosopher has not considered what an infinitely greater care on the part of the Father of us all it would reveal if an invisible germ of susceptibility to happiness and virtue were to be found in mankind throughout the whole earth and in all ages, which, though it developed differently, or appeared in different guises, was but one single inward measure and mixture of energies.

He has not considered—this omniscient philosopher—that there can be a great, divine plan for the whole human race which a single creature cannot survey, since it is not he, philosopher or monarch of the eighteenth century though he be, who matters in the last resort. Whilst each actor has only one role in each scene, one sphere in which to strive for happiness, each scene forms part of a whole, a whole unknown and invisible to the individual, self-centered actor, but evident to the spectator from his vantage point and through his ability to see the sequence of the total performance.

See the entire universe from heaven to earth! What are the means, what the ends? Is not everything a means to a million ends? Is not everything an end for a million means? The chain of an almighty and omniscient goodness is twisted and tangled a thousand times: but each link in the chain has its own place—it is attached to the chain, but is unaware of the end to which the chain is finally attached. Everyone is under the illusion that he himself is the centre, is sensitive to everything around him only so far as it directs its rays or its waves towards this centre—a fine illusion! But where is the outer circumference of all these waves, rays and apparent centres? What is it for?

Is it likely to be otherwise in the history of the human race? Are all the waves, and all the times to come, likely to be something other than the blueprint of the almighty wisdom? If the dwelling down to its smallest detail manifests itself as the handiwork of God, would it not be so with the history of its inhabitants? The dwelling is only décor, a painting of one scene, one view! The history of its inhabitants, on the other hand, is an unending drama with many scenes, God's epic through all centuries, continents and generations, a fable with a thousand variations full of immense meaning . . .

The so-called enlightenment and civilization of the world has really only touched and affected a narrow strip of the globe, the trend, condition and pervasiveness of which can scarcely be altered without changing everything at the same time. What if, for example, the introduction of learning, of religion and reformation had taken place differently; if, say, the Nordic peoples had combined in a different way and their succession been otherwise; if the Papacy had not for so long been the prime *vehiculum*? I could pose such questions and a hundred more, but they would be mere chimeras! The fact is that it was not so, and may we not, as a rule, with a little hindsight, establish why it was not so?

We can see that no nation succeeding another, even inheriting all its adjuncts, ever becomes what the other was. All the rudiments of its culture might be the same, but the culture itself would not be so, lacking the original influences which had helped to shape its former nature. Greek learning, absorbed by the Romans, became Roman; Aristotle became an Arab and a Scholastic and as for the modern Greeks and Romans—what a comedown! Marsilius, are you Plato? Lipsius, are you Xeno? Where are your Stoics, your heroes who accomplished so much? All you new Homers, orators and artists—where is the world of your miraculous achievements?

There is no country whose civilization has been able to take a backward step and become for the second time what it was before. The path of destiny is as inflexible as iron: the scenes of that time, of that world, have passed by; the aims, whatever they were, are gone—can today become yesterday? Since the passage of God over the nations takes place with giant strides, how could human forces tread a backward path with the steps of a toddler? Your Ptolemies could never again create an Egypt, your Hadrians a Greece, nor your Julians a Jerusalem! How wretched you are, Egypt, Greece and the land of God, with your bare mountains, without a trace or whisper of that genius which formerly passed over you and spoke to all the world! Why? It has said what it had to say. It has placed its imprint on the ages: the sword is worn out and its empty scabbard lies there in pieces. This might well be the answer to so many useless doubts, wonderings and questions.

*   *   *

The passage of God over the nations! The spirit of laws, times, manners and arts, and how they succeed each other, prepare for each other, develop from each other and disperse each other! If only we had a mirror of the human race to reveal all this with the fidelity, completeness and perception of a divine revelation. There is no lack of preliminary attempts, but these are as yet crude and unsystematic, enclosed, as it were, in husks and confusion. We have ransacked and rummaged through almost all nations of our present age and through the history of all previous ages, almost without knowing what we were looking for. Historical facts and researches, descriptions of discoveries and travels, are available in plenty, but who will sort them out and sift them?

Montesquieu's monumental work, the valiant effort of one man, could scarcely hope to meet this requirement. It is a Gothic edifice in the philosophical taste of the century! Often nothing more than a *jeu d'esprit*! Words torn from their context and heaped up in three or four market-places under the banner of three wretched generalizations—mere words, empty, useless, imprecise and all-confusing words, however spirited. The work is a frenzy of all times, nations and languages like the Tower of Babel, so that everyone hangs his goods and chattels on three weak nails. The history of all times and peoples, whose succession forms the great, living work of God, is reduced to ruins divided neatly into three heaps, to a mere collection even though it does not lack noble and worthy material. O, Montesquieu!

217

Who will restore for us the temple of God, which is being built continuously through all centuries? The earliest times of man's childhood are past but they have left enough relics and monuments—including the most magnificent of all relics, the teachings of the Father Himself to mankind in its childhood—Revelation! If you say, O man, that Revelation is too archaic for you, in the wisdom of your gray hairs, just look around you. You will see that the bulk of the nations of the earth are still in their childhood, speak the language of childhood, possess its manners and offer examples of its level of culture. Wherever you travel among, and listen to, so-called savages, you hear sounds that illustrate Holy Writ and catch a breath of living commentary upon Revelation.

The idolatry which the Greeks and Romans enjoyed for so many centuries; the often fanatical zeal with which everything pertaining to them has been sought out, brought into the light, praised—how much preparatory work has been put into it, how many contributions made! If the spirit of excessive veneration were dampened, if the partisanship with which each scholar caresses his favourite people like a Pandora were brought into a reasonable state of equilibrium—*then* we would really be able to know the Greeks and Romans, and assess them.

A byway leading to the Arabs has been opened up, revealing a world of monuments by which to learn about them. Monuments of mediaeval history have been discovered, though for quite different purposes, and part of what still lies in the dust will certainly soon be discovered, perhaps within half a century. (If only everything else in our enlightened century could be hoped for with so much certainty!) Our travelogues are multiplying and improving: our Europeans find nothing better to do than to run all over the globe in a kind of philosophical frenzy. They collect materials from the four corners of the earth and will someday find what they were least looking for: clues to the history of the most important parts of man's world.[11]

Our age will soon open more eyes: before very long we will be impelled to seek spiritual springs to quench the thirst of the desert—we will learn to value the epochs we now despise—the

[11] This alludes to contact with primitive cultures, which, in Herder's view, would puncture the pride of his philosophical century.

sentiment of general humanity and happiness will be stimulated: vistas of a higher than human existence will emerge out of this ruin-crammed history, and reveal to us a design where we found only confusion: everything will be found in its proper place—a history of mankind in the noblest meaning of the term! Until then, let the great teacher and lawgiver to kings both lead and mislead us. He has given us such a fine example, of how everything can be reduced to two or three forms of government, in spite of the limitations of dimension and time these are manifestly subject to. How agreeable it is to follow him in the Spirit of the Laws not only of his own people but *of all times and peoples*—that, too, is destiny! Often one holds a ball of thread in one's hand, glad that one can at least pull out single ends, but all one does is to tangle it up even more. Fortunate the hand, therefore, which succeeds in untangling the thread gently and slowly, so that it runs out long and smooth. History of the world! The smallest empire and the largest, and the smallest bird's nest, contribute to it . . .

* * *

Liberty, sociability and equality, as they are sprouting everywhere at present, have caused, and will cause, a thousand evils to be committed in their name. Anabaptists and fanatics devastated Germany in Luther's time, and now, with the general mixing of classes, with the lower pressing upwards to take the place of the flabbier, prouder and less useful higher, to become shortly even worse than these were, the strongest, most indispensable fundamentals of humanity are being depleted: the poison has gone deep into the body. And whether a guardian of this huge body, on account of a momentary increase in appetite or an apparent amplification of forces, throws an approving glance of encouragement—or whether he opposes strenuously, he will never destroy the motive for the increasing refinement and the impulse to reason, opulence, liberty and effrontery. How far the genuine, spontaneous esteem for authority, parents and the upper classes has fallen in the world within one century, cannot be expressed by a feeble comparison. In a dozen different ways the great and near-great of our day have had their share in this. Barriers and turnstiles have been demolished; prejudices, as they are called, of class, education and even of religion have been trodden under foot and even ridiculed to the point of injury: we will all become brothers, thanks to our uniform education, philosophy, agnosticism, enlightenment, vices, and, into the bargain, thanks to the oppression, bloodthirstiness and insatiable avarice which arouse our passions and satisfy our amour propre. We will all become brothers—hail to us!—and after many disorders and miseries, the aim and boast of our philosophy will be attained, that master and servant, father and child, the young man and the girl least known to him, will be one big fraternity. These gentlemen prophesy like Caiaphas, but is it at their own risk or that of their children?

It would already herald substantial progress if our 'art of government' had succeeded in at least *appearing* to adopt the sort of language, principles, attitudes and order of which every book is full and which every young prince, as if he were a living book, has on the tip of his tongue. If anyone, in particular our philanthropic philosopher, tried to read Machiavelli and the Anti-Machiavel together,[12] he would venerate the latter, willingly overlook the dungheaps disguised with flowers and green shrubs and the open wounds which one would prefer not to probe too deeply, and would say: What a book, and what a prince who should think according to such a book, and consciously observe it, and approximate in his actions the spirit in which it was written; what a prince he would be, both for our world and for posterity! To be sure, we might only exchange a coarse, inhuman and cruel madness for diseases which are even more oppressive and harmful because they creep furtively upon us. They would be praised and not recognized as diseases, but they would utterly devour the soul. The garment of generalities which characterizes our philosophy and philanthropy can conceal oppressions, infringements on the true personal freedom of men and of countries, of citizens and peoples, in a manner that would have appealed to Caesar Borgia. These concealments can and almost have to be contrived in accordance with the accepted principles of the century, with all the proper virtue, wisdom, philanthropy, and concern for peoples. But to praise them as if they were positive actions is beyond me! Doubtless Machiavelli would not have written in our century as he

---

[12] One of the best-known works of Frederick II. It was issued by Voltaire in The Hague in 1740, and contains a generous exposition of some of the favourite ideas of the eighteenth-century philosophers respecting the duties of sovereigns.

wrote in his own, and Caesar in other circumstances would not have been able to act as he did; nevertheless, basically, there has only been a change of clothing. But even such a change is gratifying. For if in our century anyone wrote what Machiavelli wrote, he would be stoned. No, I take back my words. One whose writings are far more harmful to virtue than Machiavelli's has not been stoned; for he writes as a philosopher, a wit, a Frenchman, and— an atheist; in other words, he writes as one of our century! And he even disavows his own writings.[13]

The licence accorded to thought, provided it is accompanied by certain *conventions* of good breeding (which may well be remote from real good breeding) may bring fruits even from a venomous and dissolute tree. Is it not conceivable that the sense and nonsense which is now so freely proferred against religion may one day have more significant effects than all the explanations, justifications and proofs advanced in its support, which, alas, prove very little? Yet it is equally conceivable, as some great man may indeed have prophesied, that the next century may be one of superstition, in reaction against the perverse scepticism of ours. Whatever the course of things (and it would be sad if only superstition could succeed to unbelief, and this wretched vicious circle never be broken) religion, reason and virtue are in time bound to defeat the maddest attacks of their adversaries. Wit, philosophy and free-thought have certainly served as a scaffolding for this new throne, though very much against their knowledge and inclination: once the cloud is suddenly dispersed the most brilliant sun in the world will be there in its full glory.

Even the amplitude and generality in which all this takes place can obviously become a concealed scaffolding. The more we Europeans invent methods and tools with which to subjugate the other continents, the more we defraud and plunder them, the greater will be their final triumph over us. We forge the chains with which they will bind us: the upturned pyramids of our constitutions will stand erect on their soil; they, along with us— but, enough, everything tends visibly towards a great end! We encircle the globe, with whatever it may be, and what follows can probably never more diminish its foundation. We are approaching a new stage in our development, even if it is only one of decay!

[13] This is an obvious reference to Voltaire.

Where does it take us, if our way of thinking—good and evil—becomes refined and our strongest, most vital, principles and stimuli consume themselves without the mass of men having either desire or strength to put anything in their place? The strong, vital ties of the old republics and eras are long since loosened (much to the glory of our century!); as for the more delicate ties of our time, everything tends to erode them: philosophy, free thought, opulence and an education leading to these, spreads from individual to individual, increasing in both intensity and extensiveness. The effect of this erosion is evident already in much of our politics where our motives cannot be judged as other than contemptible and despicable if examined calmly and objectively. It is evident also in the conflict that has raged for so long between Christianity and the secular world with little benefit to either and much reproach to both. Thus, since weakness can only lead to further weakness, must we not expect the acceleration of this process leading eventually to complete exhaustion as a result of so intense an abuse of our energies? But it is not my business to prophesy!

Still less is it for me to prophesy about what alone can be, will be, or even must be, substituted as a new source of vital energies on such an expanded stage, or how a new spirit could ensure that degree of warmth, stability and universal happiness of which human enlightenment and human sentiment are capable. No doubt I am speaking of still distant times!

Let us forge on, then, brethren, with courageous and cheerful hearts, even under a cloudy sky, for we are working towards a great future.

And let us choose a goal as clear, as bright and as pure as we can, instead of chasing a will-o'-the-wisp in twilight and fog . . .

* * *

The very limitation of my little corner of the globe, the blinding of my vision, the failure of my aims, the enigma of my dispositions and my desires, the defeat of my energies: these can only be measured in terms of one day, one year, one nation, one century. This indeed is a testimony that I am nothing, that the whole is everything. How vast the design, which includes nations and times, like fleeting shadows, colossal figures without point of view or perspective, so many blind tools who act under the illusion of freedom and yet do not know what they are doing or why they are doing it, who take a wide view of nothing and yet thrust themselves into action as zealously as if their ant-heap were the universe! The smallest detail contains so much order along with so much confusion, so many perplexities along with the means for their solution, and both the order and the confusion are a security and a guarantee for the rapturous splendour of the whole. It would have to be a miserable, little thing if I, insect that I am, could survey it all! Would it not contain very little wisdom and diversity if someone reeling through the world, who has trouble enough in holding on to a single idea, found no complexity in it?—In a short span, which is nothing, and yet holds a thousand ideas and germs of ideas striving together; in half a musical measure of two beats in which perhaps the most difficult notes are those which produce the sweetest harmony—who am I to judge, only crossing the huge room diagonally and casting a side-glance at the large, veiled painting in the flickering dusk? If Socrates maintained that neither he nor any other man could put into words more than his human frame would permit, who am I to comment upon the great book of God extending over worlds and times, seeing that I myself represent scarcely one letter in the book and am barely conscious of the letters on either side of me.

Our short span is infinitely minute in relation to the pride which claims to be everything, to know everything, achieve everything and develop everything, but infinitely great in relation to the pusillanimity which does not dare to be anything. But both the pride and the pusillanimity are nothing but tools serving individual purposes in the plan of an immeasurable Providence.

Yet when in the fullness of time we gain a position from which we may survey at least the whole of our own species, shall we be able to discern the end of the chain which links peoples and continents, observe how it forged its links hesitantly at first, then with increasing vehemence and clamour, until it began to weld the nations together, more firmly though less perceptibly? Shall we then see the ripening of the seed sown at random among the peoples, its strange germination, its manifold flowering, and finally its harvest of an uncertain fruit? Shall we then savour the product of the long, leavening process: the fermentation of the culture of man?

DISSERTATION ON
THE RECIPROCAL INFLUENCE OF
GOVERNMENT AND THE SCIENCES

Crowned by the Royal Academy of Sciences and Arts
for the year 1779

BERLIN 1780

[PART I]

DISSERTATION ON THE RECIPROCAL INFLUENCE OF GOVERNMENT AND THE SCIENCES

HOW FAR AND IN WHAT WAY HAS GOVERNMENT HAD AN EFFECT ON THE SCIENCES, AMONG THE PEOPLES WHERE THESE FLOURISHED?

[IX, 311–77]

With every age, with every people and climate, conditions for scientific development differed. Its noblest expression was attained only here and there, now and then, and for the most part briefly. The light of learning has touched only a narrow strip of the earth, and even that it merely tinges sporadically.

What causes this irregular and fitful change? Is it the climate? The countries where the sciences flourished and faded changed their climate not at all, or but slightly: Egypt, Rome and Greece stand where they stood, yet how different is the condition of their literature, sciences and arts to what it once was! The changes which have taken place in France, England, Germany and Sweden since the times of Caesar and Tacitus are greater than any which could be attributed to agriculture and deforestation alone. Likewise, the ancestral character of a people cannot be the origin of such changes, for that is constant; it is still discernible in Greeks, Romans, Gauls and Germans beyond ancient times; abilities and genius are the same and yet their productions and fruits are different—in short, why should we wish to separate what nature united? Climate may be regarded as the soil in which the seed of human knowledge grows, where it thrives better in one place than in another; national character may more closely determine the kind of seed; whilst the political constitution of a nation in its widest sense—its laws, government, customs, and civic traditions —undoubtedly represents the close tilling of the soil, the sowing of the seed and the influence of all those natural factors without which nothing can prosper and grow. The spirit and the blossom of the sciences has varied in direct proportion to them, as the history of the world shows.

Put in such general terms, these facts are pretty well known and undeniable; but now, considered more closely, what was it in the political constitution of a people, in their legislation and government, which furthered the sciences and brought them into bloom? Was it the same for all sciences? Or does each science perhaps have a particular government, a particular time, a favourite place, in which it best prospers? Do events repeat themselves in history or do they occur only once, and does each science, like each peculiar moment of government, have a single, unique existence? Can general principles be found to explain the relationship between certain kinds of government and certain kinds of learning, or between government and learning at particular points of time? Or is everything in the history of the human spirit, of a people, to be likened to the chaos of the jungle? Since this is not a likely supposition, can the principles referred to earlier be applied here too? Can one bring back again times, sciences and arts which are no more? And which sciences are being nourished by the contemporary spirit of government and politics? How do we compare with the ancients in this? Have we won or lost? And what have we to hope or fear for the sciences in the future, after the political wheels of destiny have turned?—I am deeply sensitive to the implications, niceties, depths and extent of these questions: they are the knot which interweaves political history with the history of the sciences, the realm of invisible human energies with the whole visible structure of its occasions, motives, impediments, changes and the like, in the strangest way and in a manner so peculiar to each period that perhaps nowhere does the paradoxical omnipotence and impotence of human endeavours become more apparent than in this troublesome, vast and intricate progress. However *in magnis voluisse sat est!* is the motto of my history as of my meditation. The Royal Academy is better acquainted with the difficulties of the proposition than I am; and yet it set the question. It expects the answer of a man, not an elucidation by the Genius of the sciences and of the various governments.

ON THE INFLUENCE OF PATERNAL GOVERNMENT ON THE ORIGIN OF THE SCIENCES

[IX, 313-15]

We could boldly accept the thesis that where there is no government, no learning exists either, even if no evidence for such a thesis were provided by history. The human race has never been without government; it is as natural to it as its origin and as the grouping together of its members within families. As soon as there is a family there is a form of government. Even peoples without developed sciences have governments, albeit imperfect ones . . .

Utopian dreams aside, let us observe the history of human government as it is, as it must be. Man is born under the very mild government of father and mother, consequently in the bosom of society, which his weakness makes necessary to him and from which he receives as an inheritance the germ of learning in the easiest and most natural way. He learns language from his parents, and with the language he acquires knowledge, information, laws, and rights. The ideas of his father, the precepts of his mother, enter into him with his mother's milk, with his observation of daily habits, with training and youthful games; and since no authority transcends the parental authority, no wisdom the parental wisdom, no kindness the parental kindness, this government in miniature is the most perfect which can be found. What is more, it makes the deepest impressions on the hearts of children and grandchildren, especially in the age of innocence and early simplicity. The sayings of the fathers were always the fountainhead of all wisdom; their judgment and their verdicts were accepted as final, as the old Book of Job shows with telling examples. The father bequeaths his treasure of experience, knowledge of nature, instruction and teaching, through tradition: this is received as a holy relic, and either increased or adulterated. The prime essays and embryos of human learning are words, meaningful, powerful sayings and proverbs, customary morality, rules of wisdom and rules of living, mostly recited imitatively and held in perpetual memory. Then came fables, genealogies, songs celebrating great deeds or virtues, the moral precepts of the fathers, their blessing, their last words, prophecies predicting the fortune and the future of the people—

all these are imprints of early paternal rule. Even religion took this form. From the father of the family came the analogy of the Father of mankind: the God of their fathers appeared, as it were, in the friendly guise in which he was first perceived; the hut became a temple, the table an altar, and the fathers, along with their first-born, became the priests. All the oldest religions are full of these family traits, and how could mankind be more gently introduced to, and improved by, the learning, wisdom, custom, religion and virtue, which was so necessary to it, than through these gentle ties of paternal rule? Everyone has been educated and taught by it. The first legislator was Nature, the first allegiance to learning was induced by inheritance, upbringing and kindness.

The paternal homestead, the rank of the fathers, the region, the way of life, the activity, the experience: all these determined the emergence of the germ of learning and the manner in which it was passed on. If the region is a natural garden in which its children play around like lambs in the meadow, if the climate, the activities, the temperament, the life itself, is agreeable, the customs pleasing, then the first offshoots of its spirit will flower and bear fruit. A field of sheep lead to pastoral song: a Tempe,[1] an Arcadia, lures an Apollo down from Heaven. Brothers and sisters who love each other, bride and bridegroom who serve one another lovingly, beautiful scenes of nature, more beautiful scenes of the heart and unaffected sentiment, produce idylls, love songs, tales of innocence, pastoral hymns, an anthology of rural wisdom. Everywhere in the world, where there are nooks and crannies in such a happy state, one sees the same flowers, often thriving near the sceptre of the severest despotism. From time immemorial, Sicily was the land of idylls, whatever kind of government ruled in the cities. Ireland up to the time of the conquest was the land of pastoral song, knowing almost no other memorial of its ancestors. The shepherd in Spain, happy in his poverty and his beautiful desert, sings and knows nothing of the stress and turmoil of the cities. Even in Turkey and in the heat of Africa there are many such beautiful spots which lie remote from the despotism of the pashas, in their deserts, like happy islands in the sea, and where, though yielding no fruits, flowers of such a kind are to be found—flowers

[1] Valley in Greece sacred to Apollo.

which here grow according to their nature but, in the schools and in the artistic fog of the city, often wither away. The bouquet of flowers to which we may liken such feelings and language grows pale when the breath of nature no longer blows upon it. In the end one puts coloured paper-flowers in their place, well-made and well-arranged, yet devoid of vitality and vigour. Art can create everything, except nature; these sort of natural scenes from the earliest antiquity of the world, full of childish simplicity, pastoral innocence and maidenly beauty, will remain unique, unless and until such a time returns again . . .

ON THE INFLUENCE OF DESPOTIC GOVERNMENT ON THE SCIENCES

[IX, 319–24]

It appears that nature has prescribed the condition of paternal government only as an introduction to human life, as a gentle preliminary to accustom men to harder conditions and greater activity. Soon tribes get together; and then through pride or through benevolence they acquire a common father, a common ruler. Should this ruler be ambitious, he will drive the defenceless shepherds themselves like sheep before him and gradually begin to treat children like slaves. Deluded by his talents, his supremacy and greatness, men become accustomed to bearing his yoke, nay in time they also kiss it and bedeck it with flowers; from being a man he becomes a god, from being a father a sultan.

All despotism of the Orient (where for many reasons it is most at home), has in it something of the divine, for the Sultan's will is respected as a command of fate and a Mufti always stands at his side. The main field of learning in such a state must therefore to some extent always be theology, and its only official textbook a Koran. The Iman explains it verbally; the Kadi with his executive authority carries it out. There is no question of argument here, nor yet of philosophy; for they are the pronouncements of God and of his ambassadors. What need is there for an art of politics, a philosophy of legislation, under a Sultan? The tender plant cannot grow under the oppressive shadow of the tree: the Sultan is God, his will is law, his word is life and death. What good would it be to discover anew a profoundly sophisticated art of war, if it

had not been passed down from the fathers? Fortune and misfortune lie in the hands of destiny, fluttering in the banners of the
prophets. Even the art of medicine, where it was not the com-
mandment of the fathers, is powerless: life and death come from
the hand of God and Islam, resignation to his will is the height of
learning and wisdom. To what riches and eminence this can lead
when combined with courage, resolution, intelligence, boldness and
good fortune, but also to what a rapid fall! All extremes run
together here, height and depth, courage and cowardice, everything and nothing. There is nothing between these extremes, no
permanence, and therefore such plants as the sciences, requiring
as they do conditions of permanence, of quiet care and nurturing,
cannot prosper. What is not the loudest hymn will be the most
puzzling conundrum; what does not bloom as a plant of God and
the king must seek a quiet valley for itself in which it may live in
retirement and be consumed neither by the oppressive shade nor
the burning heat of the sun.

Among the later writings of the Orient I know of no finer book
than the Persian Valley of Roses by Schich-Sadi;[2] it contains in my
opinion, the most delicate flowers which can grow in a Sultan's
garden. Its moral is true, simple, noble, elegantly-dressed and, if
I may say so, human with a spark of the divine. Its table of
contents reads: 'Of the mind and manners of the king, Of the
nature and manners of the dervish, Resignation, Discretion, Love
and Youth, Weakness and Old Age, the Upbringing of Children
and Good Manners, Courtesy and Proverbs'—it seems to me
that these eight chapter-headings are superscriptions of the best
philosophy and morality that can be found under a Sultan's rule.
The preface begins with the finest hymn to God and with fables
so singularly characteristic of the Orientals since antiquity; but it
ends with a dedication 'to Abubekr, the son of Sadi, the king who
is the shadow of God in the world, King of all kings, mightiest
among the peoples, ruler of the earth and the sea, the heir of
Salomo's empire, etc. etc.'. This dedication, along with what he
adduces of his life's circumstances, throws light on much that is
in the book. Anyone seeking the finest hymns, fables, pictures,

[2] Sadi, 1184–1291, Persian poet. His masterpiece, *Gulistan* (Pers. 'the garden
of roses') is a collection of moral sayings and stories, partly in poetry and
partly in prose.

proverbs, enigmatic wisdom and the like, may well find them associated with such government. Here the most richly aromatic flowers blossom under the densest, most spreading leaves; here the cedar and the palm-tree reach upwards next to the thorn and the hyssop and around them is a vast desert——

Judaic theocracy was probably intended by the Mosaic constitution to become the purest form of despotism. Moses rescued them from the fiery furnace of Egyptian servitude and gave them for their laws a divine constitution in order to protect them in future from tyrants and Pharaohs. The God of their fathers was to be king, the high priest His first servant and the people His obedient children. The ideal of this constitution was not attained, however, and hence the constitution never became fully operative. Moses' plan remained a patchwork. Since, however, it could not be wholly discarded even under the kings (who according to it should never have come into existence), we can still witness the beneficial effects of the old theocratic commandments, especially in matters of government and learning. Thus the kings were only thought of as the fathers of the people in place of God. Moral sayings and teachings, even if they flowed from the mouth of the richest, most magnificent, most voluptuous king, had to clothe themselves in the fear of God as the beginning of wisdom and show this as the end of all human meditation and questing. In evil times there could still be prophets who spoke out against the despots with pronouncements from the statute-book of the nation on how Israel's king should act. They claimed to receive blessings and curses from the lips of God and at least kept the eyes of the people open to what was right and good and permissible. Their prophecies took the place of statecraft and political sagacity, where in many a complicated case the result sufficiently proved how badly things went if one departed from them. In short, we have to thank Moses, his great mind, his legislation and his covenant, for a subsequent series of excellent writings, poetry, history, instruction and wisdom, which no other people possessed. Prophets, sages, teachers of the people, priests, even the good among the kings, followed in his track; his theocratic statute-book was the first bulwark against the abomination of idolatry, barbarity and oppression, as well as a nursery of pure ideas about God, of noble hymns, psalms, exhortations and precepts—how wonderful if it

233

could have reached complete fulfilment! However, many of their kings, in spite of the statute-book, were weak despots and petty tyrants, and so, through the contrast between principles and practice, the Jewish state necessarily came to an end before it reached political maturity.

Of the government as well as the sciences of the Chaldaeans, Egyptians and other ancient monarchical peoples, we know too little to be able to judge. In both nations sciences and arts were hereditary: whatever was deemed of value was handed down from father to son and to that extent did not depend on the monarchy. Moreover, among the Egyptians the sciences were also preserved by the priestly class who, though they were close to the throne, were quite independent of it, and in fact frequently acted as a restraint upon it. Thus the monarch could not claim credit for their efforts, concealed beneath their religious functions, in the service of the arts and sciences. It was the same with the Egyptian public administration and its much-vaunted distribution of land. If it really was as it is reputed to have been, it was not at all despotic but paternalistic, giving to each his own and administering it on his behalf. Consequently, the arts and sciences also felt the benefits of a just paternalism. Thirdly and lastly, the things for which one needs despotism, namely, the building of cities, the erection of pyramids, obelisks, colossa and labyrinths, truly leave their own mark. What are these monstrous heaps for? What need of the land do they serve? You say: 'the renown of the monarchs'; but, which monarchs? Who denominates them? Who knows their names? Who calls them by any other name than that of oppressors, acquainted with their subjects only in so far as they could make use of them and, moreover, achieving nothing themselves. Or did they 'build their tombs by it'? We could ask who lies in these tombs, or whether a pocket-size despot could lie under nothing less than a pyramid.—In short, the history of ancient Egypt is too uncertain for me to venture to say anything about it. It is the same with the walls of Semiramis, the ruins of Persepolis, and the gigantic buildings of India and China. The more one extols China the more obvious it becomes from everything that is said that the boasted excellences are a product of the laws and foresight of the ancient paternal rule; where this stops and despotism begins, all the good things come to an end. Language, laws, sciences, and arts remain the same for a thousand years: they cannot and will not progress, being walled up and embalmed in—old customs.

In general the most decisive influence which despotism exerts on the sciences is expressed by splendour, excess, colossal size, and arbitrariness. Whatever supports these, in ideas as in architecture, in regulations as in fortresses, carries favour and earns the despot's approval. Everything must be extraordinary, wonderful and supernatural, and thus is out of proportion to the needs of the state and the happiness of its members. Despotism has led to the same results, when in later times it partly returned to the west wrapped in a fine cocoon. Pope or Sultan, Shah or Emperor—the same hymns are always to be found, only garbed according to the taste of the age. The legends and chronicles of the monks under the yoke of superstition contain as many marvels as the history of Tamberlaine, Afrasiab or Rustem.[3] The feudal times, abounding in armies and slaves, were naturally dressed in the magic of knights and giants who strove with winged serpents and dragons. Louis's despotism loved splendour in the sciences and arts and everything which fostered it. Even the character of ordinary individuals is reflected in the manner in which they cultivate the sciences. There can be *despotism in individual tastes*, just as in government, in *ideas* as in laws and manners, and mostly it is accompanied here, too, by splendour, colossal size and excess.—The only government under which nature, true proportion and balance is maintained is freedom.

ON THE INFLUENCE OF FREE CONSTITUTIONS ON
THE SCIENCES AND ARTS

[IX, 324–9]

As much as Homer praised the monarchy, he yet showed himself at the same time to be a singer and herald of freedom. Nothing is obscure, incomprehensible or immense with him, except what

---

[3] Tamberlaine, 1336–1405, Mongol conqueror of a large part of Asia, renowned for his cruelty and ambition. Afrasiab was a semi-legendary king of ancient Persia. He is supposed to have conquered Persia with an army of Tartars and ruled despotically for many years until Zal (the father of Rustem) drove him out and restored the lawful line to the throne. Rustem was the most illustrious of Persian heroes, supposed to have lived about A.D. 600.

ought to be. Everything is measured and appropriate, full of distinction and character. Even his marvels have a human touch; his repetitions are sweet and childlike. The beautiful setting, the happy Greek outlook which marks his heroes, the wisdom and humanity with which he softens rough passions and scenes, are characteristic not of a servile slave but of a singer of nature, of humanity and of freedom—Greece was the first country in the world to break loose eventually from its petty tyrants and which with a new government, also brought new sciences and new arts into being.

Lycurgus drew his people together to the stern principle of sacrifice and patriotism. The sciences, too, had to conform to this; even the laconic style was formed by it. Wealth, drama, sumptuous verses, disappeared; vain orators, sophists and babblers went into voluntary exile, finding the air of Sparta unsuited to them. The art of war was its science and its practice, the flute was its instrument and Tyrtaeus its poet[4]——Sparta is the strongest example of the extent to which a state chooses its sciences, forms them and has to keep a tight rein on them. Indeed, in its ability to restrain the sciences, what a counter-image to Athens was Sparta! And yet it was perhaps Lycurgus who collected Homer's rhapsodies in Asia and gave them to the Greeks; he did not, however, give them to his Sparta, at least not as an example to be followed.

Solon took quite another path, seeking to couple wealth with freedom and plenty with patriotism. He left deliberation to those of high rank and decision to the people, and so, as Aristophanes says, made his republic into an old man who was clever at home and childish in public[5] . . . With this constitution Solon necessarily aroused everything which one could call political science, oratory, poetry, philosophy, arts. I include oratory since the orator was a demagogue and the state itself supported him. What a field—or what a school—for eloquence this was. All public affairs concern-

---

[4] Greek elegiac poet. The victory of the Spartans over the Messinians in the seventh century B.C. has been attributed to the inspiration of his songs.
[5] *The Knights*, 755–8.
    ' . . . The old fellow
    Is, when at home, the brightest man alive;
    But once he sits upon his rock, he moons
    With open mouth, as one who gapes for figs.'
        (trans. B. B. Rogers. Loeb Classical Library ed., 1938)

ing the people were openly discussed and matters were decided on the spot according to the feeling of the meeting. The debates ranged over business affairs, military matters, and the weal and woe of the state, and were not mere verbal disputations. Arguments were put forward for immediate decisions, in all seriousness and not just out of habit or jest; they were not intended to be ignored or forgotten. The orator spoke to his own people, to a circle he knew, not to strangers or despots; to the Athenian people, a multitude who were educated through poetry, songs, art, drama in the finest language in the world, not to Scythians or Lombards. Can one possibly compare this with any other eloquence, any other circle of orators, any other institutional form of debate (with the possible exception of the Romans)? More especially, how can one compare it with a completely disparate kind of oratory, harangues without point or purpose intended merely to flatter despots or curry favour with the mob? Let us create an Athens here; then the Demosthenes and Pericles will come by themselves——

So it was also with the Greek theatre. It too served democracy as oratory did. The people were to be wooed with ideas of freedom, tyrants threatened through the tragedies which acted as a mouthpiece of freedom. The people were to be educated about old heroes and nourished on their deeds and destinies; they were to be made to feel their Greek superiority and the grandeur of their race. That is how their national sagas came to life so magnificently on the stage. The theatre originated in religious ceremonies; in a short time it became the necessity of an idle state, thirsting for enjoyment. Trade and welfare flourished in Athens, and had to flourish there according to the founder's plan; consequently all the entertainments, the Muses and the Graces, were called in to amuse the born lover of music, of the dance, of song and of joy. Although Solon, who himself was a poet, indignantly testified against the first play which he saw and prophesied evil results from it, yet it was basically suited to his constitution and to the nature of the people. An Athenian theatre will not revive again except under similar circumstances——

The philosophy of the Greeks thrived in social intercourse, in the circles of Attic society, and was closely connected with their oratory, sophistry, art of politics, poetry and declamation. As is known, Socrates deflated the wisdom of the orators, poets and sophists of his time. His ironic genius and precise command of language divested the stage of its ornamental armour, the orators of their tittle-tattle, the sophists of their spurious political wisdom, in order to teach the people (the circles of youths, the houses in which he spoke) to find a true and practical wisdom. A man like Socrates admittedly could only fit into an Athens where the people were prepared for something like this and were receptive to such talk. Our societies would call it an insult to be questioned socratically on such matters. We rarely succeed in catching the tone of such conversation in our books, simply because it is foreign to our ordinary life. So much socratic sense in such a short time, among so few people, in so easy and natural a manner! Instead we prefer proofs, callow judgments, declamations: there, we really believe we have something!——To be sure, Greek, and especially Athenian, levity also made everything overflow into empty loquacity of systems and small-talk. The philosophers became dealers in second-hand words, sophists of empty systems, and it is due to the wilfulness of fate and the unfortunate piety towards the Greeks and ancients, that we have read vastly more into some of their words than they themselves probably put there. Much of their philosophy was conversational hypothesis, a Greek kind of wisdom——

Just as the *history* of a people is the reflection of its way of thinking and government, so also is the *writing* of such history. Certainly the Athenian state had no difficulty in supplying some of the finest historians. Xenophon and Thucydides were themselves commanders-in-chief and men of affairs; only such could write of war and of affairs of state. In Athens everything was closely connected, philosophy and public activity, the art of rhetoric and grammar. It was one spirit, one and the same Atticism, which conferred a silvery clarity or a golden oratory on their style, their oratory and their reflections, and knew how to unify the most heterogeneous talents with the greatest simplicity. In later times, also, it was political and military people, in short, men of affairs, who re-established the history and spirit of Xenophon, in order to examine state and history and, occasionally, to make necessary innovations. It was a happy republic for the sciences when a disciple of Socrates was both a military commander and a statesman!

Without discussing the other states of Greece I cannot analyse the general effect on the sciences of the number and variety of competing cities and states. So many cities and republics, which were closely linked to one another through the language and honour of Greece, and in part by kinship or political ties, had necessarily to be more or less in competition over what they considered the glory of their race. And since this glory consisted (apart from military prowess) in the freedom of the fatherland, and love for the sciences and the fine arts, no state remained wholly a stranger to the muses. They competed with statues and buildings, plays and poetry. Since the communal Greek games to some extent attracted everything flourishing and noble, contests other than the purely athletic took place there. Herodotus read his history there, and acquired a rival. There artists displayed their works to the admiration of all Greece. The games themselves provided an opportunity for song and arts: the collective hand of Greece has, as it were, woven the most beautiful lyrical garlands worn by a Greek. The many cities, the many peoples, the generation of ever-glorious victors, the many gods and heroes who were interwoven with them, form the leaves and the blossoms of this garland. Who will give us another Olympia with its games and its victories and at the same time assemble the whole of Greece with its interests, its glory and its language? . . .

From all that is said, it is evident that the specifically Greek sciences and arts, unsurpassed by those of any other age or peoples after more than two thousand years, have been daughters of Greek legislation, Greek political institutions and especially of Greek freedom, activities for the common good, enterprise and competition. I do not exclude national character, language, climate, situation, historical accident, and so on. These factors were indeed essential for the emergence of Greek political life. They were, so to speak, concurrent factors which helped to maintain it. Meanwhile history shows that as soon as freedom was lost (language, climate, the genius of the people, their abilities and character remaining) the spirit of the sciences likewise disappeared. Their poetry was gone, the theatre became the empty pastime of a vanquished and idle people. Demosthenes was their last voice of freedom; Aristotle and Theophrastus their last philosophers. The former was exiled. After his death a law was even promulgated that no one should publicly teach philosophy without the permission of the senate, and consequently all philosophy was to some extent banished for a time. The teachers of their sciences soon became grammarians, sophists, *literateurs*, and whatever of their sciences now migrated to Asia or to Egypt were like a transplanted flower in a foreign land which misses its native soil. Under the Romans Athens preserved its sciences, but they lacked vitality. It trafficked with them as with grains of seed for which perhaps only the vendor has the planting instructions. The most well-meaning Roman emperor could not create a new Greece in Greece. The freedom which the Romans bestowed on Athens was only a shadow, and the learning and oratory which grew out of it was only the shadow of a shadow, nothing but the echo of better times. Mount Athos has plenty of monks, but no orators, poets or philosophers. The loveliest ruins of all provinces inspire no artists in the old tradition. Why are they no more? The air, the climate, the culture, the character of the Greeks is the same, but the constitution and the government is lacking. Without these, they can never be what they were. The spirit which favoured their talents and members is gone, so the talents and members are dead...

ON THE INFLUENCE OF GOVERNMENT ON LEARNING
AFTER THE RENAISSANCE
[IX, 349–57]

... May I, who am appearing with this writing before the most renowned German Academy, humbly express some ideas about how the objections which are raised against this Areopagus of learning could perhaps be met?—At times a deficiency in invention has been imputed to it; now and then the limited horizons of its propositions, and perhaps the biassed judgments of the answers, have been criticized. Charges of imperfections, which are inseparable from any human institution, or commonplace reproaches which refute themselves, which concern the misuse of a thing and not the thing itself, have been levelled. Each man has his own perspective, and consequently so has each assembly of even the most enlightened men. The perspective determines both the questions posed and the solutions preferred. Hence they cannot but be biased, and the public, society and posterity, are the umpires. If no God on earth has ever devised uniform minds, why should it be expected of the God of the sciences. He plays on a many-stringed, many-toned lyre. More than once Academies have refuted themselves, sometimes in a short time, sometimes in the course of their history: the Academy of Inscriptions supplies us with a striking example of this, and the truth of it comes freely and extensively to light. Moreover most of the sciences, for which the Academies certainly act as a sanctuary, are less inclined to be biased: mathematics, physics, history, observation, are cases in point. Opinion, on the other hand, remains opinion and each man stands freely behind his own. Each of the Academy's prize competitions usually produces a quantity of writings which in rivalry follow or accompany or outstrip the winner. The public can enjoy and choose them all; the Academy caused them to be written. However it would not be unprofitable if we had an Academy which would set its questions in broad rather than specific terms and which would be prepared to accept writings, works, inventions, observations on this basis, and then to crown them as it deems fit. Perhaps many a quiet genius would come out with a masterpiece by which the Hall of the Academy would not be dishonoured. For all inventions have to be discovered, all masterpieces have to be completed, freely and in quiet seclusion. The best prize question (too specifically formulated), whilst it may succeed in upsetting this seclusion, may not necessarily touch upon the area in which the invention is to be made or do so only obliquely. The most splendid ideas of the human spirit were always accomplished in quiet seclusion.

Would it not be gratifying if the hidden genius knew of an Olympia where it could exhibit its work, the labour of its best energies and its finest hours, to an assembled Greece; where it could be judged, anonymously and secretly, without danger of shameful exposure, and where it could receive its garland of merit? And what if the Academy should light upon a series of such competing masterpieces, all free, all of original invention, in the sciences as in the field of art, and should be taken by surprise by them, should not have prizes enough for the rewards and should establish a free competition of the best and most renowned kind? At present perhaps the best brains have no inclination or time to participate. The questions posed are answered by the mediocre and the Academy must crown the best among the inferior . . .

I would now like to discuss the means by which governments in more recent times have sought to influence the sciences, and here I must first name the educational methods about which legislation has finally learned to be more closely concerned. Among the ancients education was everything. It was perceived as the prime means towards the development of the state; the smallest things, even amusements, music, mode of life, did not go unnoticed; the most important and decisive matters were attributed to changes in these. Even in the Papacy we still see what was achieved by education, partly in general and partly by some Orders. Should not therefore, better principles take root also in secular matters in our time? Should the principles and methods of a Rousseau, Locke, Fenelon, Chalotais, remain ineffective?[6] To be sure, their institution is a task for the government. As long as the appointment of teachers and the form of schools is left to incapable subordinate officials who have neither understanding nor desire for ideas of this kind and serve the base, infamous God Hercomannus, so long will our schools remain places where nothing but Latin is learned and even that badly. The best institutions, which enlightened regents and governments have set up (and, thank God, they have been set up in more than one place!) are of real value to the sciences just as they are to the state and the happiness of its citizens, human beings, generations——

The higher places of learning perhaps await the concern of the government. If many of them are in effect old barbaric scaffolding which remained standing into our times; if conditions cause so much flagrant embarrassment to the teacher, if so many crying defects characterize their teaching methods, if so many failed hopes exist among the youth they instruct . . ., if all this, or only one single part of it, is true, should we not be impelled thereby to change the innermost spirit of these institutions? Should we not provide a better link between these universities and our schools, academies, seminars, business activities and public administration? Indeed, should we not transform them into schools and colleges concerned with actual affairs and practical

---

[6] La Chalotais, Louis René de Caradeuc de, 1701–85. French magistrate and procureur général to the parliament of Brittany. Author of an attack on the Jesuits, *Comptes rendus des Constitutions des Jésuites* (1761–2) and of *L'education nationale* (1763), a work which Voltaire admired.

pursuits and organize these on the basis of different categories where each category serves the best interest of those capable of profiting from that level and type of education, instead of our present chaotic jungle of faculties? A university course would then not last for two years but for as long as it takes to become ready for the business of life, and likewise the teachers would not be vain oracles, but fathers and masters, each in his profession and office. Whole provinces would join with each other in learning as in practical matters and, as it were, teaching and learning would form one Academy of Education.—I concede that these few lines, so uncertainly stated, must seem obscure and perhaps impractical; however, if I detailed them more closely they would not remain so, for I think they are easy and practical in the highest degree. Only the unnatural is difficult; only a false classification causes confusion. Each faculty would also serve as a practical academy to meet the specific needs of the locality. Where is the Lycurgus or Solon who would bring about this new Atlantis?

Finally, governments in recent times have especially affected the sciences by encouraging their practical, mechanical side, applied physics, economics, navigation, mechanics, trade, the arts and military science. Substantial developments in the sciences have received their impetus from military leaders and the art of war; indeed they seem to approach a point where as a result of some further changes and decisions the arts of war and the sciences would, as it were, enter into a duel which may well bring advantages to either or the end to both. Less equivocal has been the contribution of the arts of peace, especially to the development of the practical sciences. Academies of economics compete with each other; and so do the richest and poorest regions after their fashion. Where academies are lacking, the governments themselves intervene, by offering prizes for one invention or another; so that in theory one could almost call our century the economic century. The culture of individual lands and provinces is promoted and encouraged, especially in Germany, by the example of a great monarch. Here and there, what formerly lay buried is sought after; what formerly would have remained despised is made known. The national history of some provinces, the sources of their wealth and resources, trade proposals, plans for the encouragement of industry, calculation of the number of the inhabitants and their abilities etc. frequently come to light, partly instigated by the government and partly tolerated by it. The most idle prince wants to gain renown through his encouragement of the sciences, even if much which receives this encouragement turns out to be nothing but tinsel, vanity and empty imitation. It is true, too, that a good many useful things have been invented and worked on in vain because they have not been applied, and it is in this respect that the greatest defect appears to lie. Whole eras compete in ideas, others will compete in deeds, the former in invention, the latter in execution; and it is undeniable that already much has usefully been accomplished, especially for the comforts of every-day life. Competition in international trade and the rivalry of interests between nations have become sciences in themselves, aspiring to reach a degree of precision comparable to that of the most exact sciences. The political sciences search for more clarity, order and security in the affairs of state, and legislation itself seeks to strike a note of humanity and conviction. Gross infringements of international law now are so much more publicly apparent and have to be camouflaged by governments in terms of truth, justice and humanity—a thing which previously was both unheard of and uncalled for . . . In short, the more wisdom, kindness and real love of humanity are enlisted in the service of government, the more the sciences are also animated by such a spirit and accompanied by such a purpose. Whole sciences and professions will be made more useful, they will be more united than they have been, they will root out old prejudices and use enlightenment to increase kindness and happiness.

Having wandered through the ages and having, as it were, drawn the external elevations of the building, I shall now turn my attention to aspects of its inner structure.

GENERAL OBSERVATIONS ON HOW THE GOVERNMENT
INFLUENCES THE SCIENCES

[IX, 357–61]

It can influence them in no other way than through licensing, opportunity, education, standards, training and rewards. We will examine these constituent parts and prove them with historical examples. The best way is by the *Nihil Obstat*, the license to pursue a good thing, above all, freedom of thought. All inquisition is prejudicial to the republic of learning. A book which must first be passed by ten censors before it reaches the light of day is no longer a book but the hackwork of the holy Inquisition, a mutilated thing, scourged with rods, a muzzled wretch and always a slave. It is known throughout the world that the realms of the Inquisition are as backward in sciences as they are rich in superstition, obscurity and edifying writings. In the sphere of truth, in the realm of ideas, no earthly power should or can give judgment; the government cannot do it, let alone its cowled censor. In the domain of truth he is not the judge but a party, just as the author is. He must make as good and exact a case for his deletions, for his 'No', as the author does for his 'Yes'. Otherwise he enters the lists arrogantly, as an oppressor. In fact, he is the oppressor of the noblest sap of mankind, of the best that creation has to offer, light, freedom of thought and of mind. All improvement can only come about through enlightenment; neither hand nor foot can move without the head and the brain.

I am far from advocating an unbridled licentiousness or moral indifference. Moreover, where it publicly stops the wheels of state, license defeats its own principle and so interferes directly with its purpose and with the general happiness. Well-being is worth more to man than speculation; the well-being of many, likewise, is worth more than the speculative happiness of one. Hence I believe it is permissible and even necessary for the state to directly exclude certain sciences as well as certain amusements and occupations, if it cannot rely on being able to combine them with its principle of efficacy. Everything may not grow everywhere.—He who will allow a weed to grow undisturbed because it looks pretty at times and even may be good after its kind, may not be able to sow and reap a harvest . . .

But, having conceded the wisdom of restrictive laws under certain circumstances, we would nonetheless reiterate that to reject everything which is new, simply because it does not accord with our habitual way of thinking, is the blindest form of stupidity, comparable to the Inquisition. For it does not take the state as its criterion but serves another mistress, the blind and leaden goddess of dullness with her oppressive regulations. There is also a great difference between regulating established sciences where one is aware of the benefits and dangers associated with them, and refusing to admit sciences simply because they are new or appear strange. If a government is set on closing its eyes to everything new, and takes as its maxim: 'Nothing must be changed, everything must remain just as it is!' then, in doing so, it does not reveal wisdom but apathy, not law and order but weakness and cruelty. Yet surely one thing is beyond question: nothing in the world remains as it is. Once, therefore, the sinews of the state slacken and its mainsprings run down, it will inevitably come to a standstill. Even the greatest masterpiece requires constant checking and frequent overhaul. It certainly applies to the sciences in a given polity; the prosperity or decline of the latter will have a direct bearing upon the former. The balance is here so delicate, the degree of relationship so various and manifold, that certainly no drowsy censor nor proudly stupid, stupidly proud Inquisitor is a suitable judge. And I always think that, precisely on account of this complexity and the weakness of human decision, it is better to be free than enslaved, better to be gentle than narrow and cruel, especially when it does not at all affect the most urgent needs of the state. That king of France in the Middle Ages who wanted to decide between the scholastic's nominal and real, between *quisquis* and *kiskis*, and needed *lettres de cachet* for it, cuts a ridiculous figure. Ridiculous too was the Pope who excommunicated Bishop Vergerius because he accepted the Antipodes.[7] The judges of Rome who threw Galileo into prison because he found the world beneath the stars to be other than they wished it to be were both senseless and cruel. (Their competence did not reach *above* the stars, neither they nor Galileo could get advocates from there). It is ludicrous that Harvey had to defend himself at law over the circulation of the blood, and atrocious that the best people in the Middle Ages were prosecuted, decried and burnt as wizards and atheists over the truest of discoveries, opinions and hypotheses. This is what we think now; at the time, however, people thought differently. Should not, therefore, such hateful and horrible mistakes at least serve as a warning to posterity? Much will be discovered which has not yet been discovered; many prejudices will be discredited which are still accepted as truth. If we cannot remove them our-

---

[7] Vergerio, Pietro Paolo, the younger, *c.*1495–1565. Bishop of Capo d'Istria who was converted to Protestantism about 1544.

selves, let us at least not prevent better and stronger hands from doing so; let us at least not close windows and keyholes to light and free air which is anxiously trying to reach us. The more firmly a state is based on its principles, the more orderly, clear and strong it is in itself, the less risk it runs of being shaken and blown about by every breath of opinion, by every lampoon of an angry writer; and all the more will it allow freedom of thought and (with some limitations according to situation and circumstances) freedom of writing, by which, after all, truth wins in the end. Only tyrants are suspicious; only secret evil-doers are timorous. A candid and honest man, who sticks to his principles, can afford to ignore evil tongues. He travels in daylight, and profits by even the most malicious lies of his enemies. It is the same with a government based on law, freedom and the welfare of its citizens; it is the same with a state religion which, if it is true, can only gain in the end by every examination and scrutiny. All monopolies of thought are pernicious; all oppressive guilds and corporations are no less so. The truth will not wait on them; they must serve the truth or else prove unworthy of their existence. Freedom of thought is the fresh air of heaven in which all the plants of a government, especially the sciences, thrive best. Since the ruler of a state should be almost neutral in his preferences in order to encompass, tolerate and clarify the opinions of everyone in his state and direct them to the common good, it is not surprising that great rulers of this kind are so seldom to be found...

GENERAL REMARKS ON CHANGES IN SCIENCES RESULTING FROM CHANGES IN GOVERNMENT

[IX, 371-7]

Change is a condition of everything on earth, including the sciences and states. Learning, like government, in the abstract, has not yet appeared on our ever-rotating globe and probably is nowhere likely to appear. To imagine such an abstract image, to cherish it as an ideal, is good and perhaps even profitable, but in the real world all we can expect to find is this or that characteristic, occasioned by such or such a factor, arising from particular developments and local circumstances. The more favourable these are, the longer, more actively and better they are developed, the greater the profit to the sciences and the government. The most brilliant monarch is not always the greatest; the heyday of a science is not always its most meritorious period. He who has sown the seed, who has ploughed the field and produced the fruit, does more than he who merely reaps the harvest.

It is easy to follow the thread of these changes on our earth, but difficult to label them clearly and more difficult still to calculate the effects they produced on governments at the time. We are wont to speak in such general terms as 'republic', 'monarchy', 'despotism', when talking about polities. When we discuss learning we imagine we do justice to it by distinguishing between such broad categories as 'poetry', 'rhetoric', 'philosophy', and 'the arts'. In both cases we fail to realize that such general words rarely, if ever, retain the meaning which they originally had. Often, after the briefest of periods, even in the same place, they assume a completely different significance. No two republics or monarchies have yet been identical, nor any two sciences, which are the mainsprings of a government. Time itself changes each of these at each moment, and philosophical history has no choice but to observe each detail most carefully and take account of it. I wish we had such a philosophical history of the sciences as well as of governments, and also of their influence on each other! We have some fine fragments, particularly in political history, in the treatment of individual periods, but we lack a picture of the whole tree, showing its branches and fruits in the order and position in which they appeared and revealing the occasions which brought it to life.

Paternal government seems to have initiated the most necessary kinds of human knowledge, especially religion, which later achieved a greater splendour under despotism, sitting, as it were, at its side. Despotism seems at first to have made good use of the knowledge which was established under paternal government and bound to the laws of the land, but later, especially through its excess, brutality and arbitrariness, to have infinitely injured it. The tree of knowledge stood still and grew no farther. The republics restored moderation and a sense of proportion in the relationships of the citizens to each other and of the sciences to the state. They differ among themselves, however, in nature, in their conception of human or political truth, in matters of everyday utility and circumstances. If the republic was a democracy, it was the popular sciences which flourished, poetry, oratory, popular philosophy, and those arts which appealed to the eye or the ear. If it was an aristocracy, the sciences were the more abstract ones of reflection, politics, philosophy and history. If both forms were mixed, then the sciences were also intermingled with each other. If a republic is built on diligence, stable industry, agriculture and the like, then the practical arts and thriftiness will hold sway. If it is a trading republic, the kind of knowledge which will be sought is that which favours commerce, or which commerce stimulates. The arts will be those of luxury if the republic itself enjoys the profits of its trade; should it only serve as a middleman, this characteristic will also spread to its learning and way of living. To all these observations the Greek republics and in modern times Venice, Florence, Switzerland, England (in so far as it may be considered a republic), and Holland, bear witness. If a republic is based on warfare, either it applies this principle to its own defence, as Sparta did, and hence supports all the sciences and arts pertaining to defence; or it wishes to attack, conquer and occupy, and may then share in the fate of Rome, which declined in the sciences as in political importance through its very size. If a monarchy is established in place of a republic as a result of foreign conquest, as happened in Greece, the bloom of the sciences may be preserved yet awhile if the internal conditions of the republic are left virtually unchanged or if the conqueror assimilates its culture. If, on the other hand, the monarchy originates from the internal destruction of republican freedoms, as in Rome, it scarcely deserves to be called a monarchy, since it is usually more like some form of tyranny or despotism. Then the blossoms of the republic fall swiftly to the ground, perhaps even more swiftly the stronger had been the force of their flowering. If circumstances combine to restrict this tyranny in time, and to give to the state, if not renewed freedom at least a stable, constitutional monarchy, then it can recover and bring forth fruit of another kind. If not, and the state remains shaky, with no partition between law and arbitrariness, then every-thing (setting aside a few fine exceptions) is lost, as the history of Rome shows. The load was too great to be easily rearranged, the borders too extended to protect the state from ruin. Nothing

remained but for the barbarians, to whom the weaknesses were
revealed, to destroy it and, with it, the empty cobweb of its
learning.—A monarchy based on Christian despotism is a weak
thing, in perpetual conflict with itself and its sciences, as the
history of Constantinople shows. Not only is Christianity intrinsically incompatible with despotism, but the interminable bicker-
ing of the priests is likely to deprive it of power to accomplish
its ends. Hence states and sciences based on such foundations
deteriorate through weakness, quarrelling and abstract disputations. The feudal monarchy of the barbarians was a weak arrangement both for itself and for the knowledge it fostered. Instituted
only for warfare, it had to be in perpetual stress, in continual
activity, or it became restless and annihilated itself. Sciences are
conspicuous by their absence, and the clerical estate is called upon
to fill the void. From monarchies of this kind arose despotism or
freedom as the die was cast; but many a despotism, becoming
eroded, had to give way to constitutional monarchy albeit against
its will. If for no other reason, this happened because despotism
finds no place or security between states with better constitutions.
This is the history of European monarchies in recent times and
consequently also of their sciences and arts. Having first of all
served a feudal regime, they then for a short time came under
a subtler form of despotism which progressively turned into a
more constitutional type of monarchy. Friction in time causes the
clattering wheels to run more smoothly, the monarchy becomes
an oligarchy in which finally, because of the feebleness or the true
greatness of the rulers, laws have to rule rather than princes.
Then the sciences too will obey the laws to the extent that these
promote the welfare of the state. The state will establish schools,
academies, seminars, and professional institutes, indicate their
subjects and methods of teaching and regulate them in relation to
itself and the whole. The monarchy will become a pyramid in
which laws form the base, industry the stones, the sciences its
cement, the prince the summit which rests on everything and
co-ordinates it all. And one day the sciences will probably succeed
in attaining that degree of truth and usefulness towards which
they strive.

Each state has its period of growth, maturity and decay, to
which its sciences and arts conform. In the early paternal govern-

ment their genius is to be found at its purest; subsequently it becomes adulterated by factionalism and contention, and through
the warping of traditions sinks into either oblivion or despotism.
A despotism is usually most brilliant under its founder. The very
circumstances and predominant talents which made him into a
despot, also ensured their speedy expression in splendour, excess
and grandeur. The Egyptian pyramids, the buildings of Semiramis,
date from the most ancient times; the ruins of Persepolis almost
transcend historical chronology and are lost in the abyss of time.
With succeeding generations, despotism declines into weakness,
confusion and disorder. Republics are like plants which are grown
from seed; their flowering does not take place on the day of
sowing. Instead, they grow and last as long as their vital energies
last, then they shrink and die. Learning appears sooner or later
according to how closely it corresponds to the purpose of the
republic, but mostly it accompanies the time of power, of prosperity, of the greatest efforts, of respect, of peace, the usually
short period of flowering. Then the sciences flourish along with
all else that flourishes with them. If a legislative aristocracy
succeeds in prolonging this state of affairs, or if the republic is
transformed into a constitutional monarchy, then the flower of
learning survives longer as the new republics, Florence, Venice,
Holland, Switzerland, England and Sweden, show. Otherwise, all
blooms, including the sciences, are quickly past. In general, it
seems that the new states gain in strength and permanence what
they lose in swifter flowering. None of them have achieved so
much in the arts and literature in so short a time as Rome and
Athens did; none in so short a time completed such a masterpiece.
But perhaps they deserve a place in history for having achieved a
good deal in a quieter, more pedestrian manner and, above all,
for having benefited an incomparably wider range of humanity by
their achievements. Even the light of the revival of learning would
have been only a short ephemeral flame, if monarchies had not lit
their lights by it and thus carried it on, albeit less brilliantly;
nonetheless, republics would have been the best kindling for the
flame at this happy conjuncture. The boldest, most sublime ideas
of the human spirit have been conceived in republics and likewise
the finest plans and works have been accomplished in them. Both
in mediaeval and modern times, the best history, the most humani-

tarian philosophy and the most sophisticated political science are invariably republican in origin . . .

We might now be able to establish with some degree of certainty our views on the struggle for position between the old learning and the new, which has been conducted with perhaps more heat than light. That nature never dies, can be taken as fact. That it can raise noble seed at all times even among different peoples with different national characters is just as certain and often demonstrated amidst the greatest misuse. Only the fact that this seed often falls on poor soil, that it lacks the conditions for exercising this or that talent, the opportunity for action or competition, makes, in my opinion the greatest difference between the sciences of different ages, not excluding the influence of climate and national character. Just as one cannot control the stream of years and world conditions so that it flows backwards, so no legislator with a magic wand can conjure up a Rome, Athens or Greece and expect it to reach maturity in its new surroundings. It would be unreasonable, then, from affection for old times to undervalue and neglect one's own, to set fire to Rome in order to watch Troy burn and read a new Homeric stanza. The popular government of Athens, the constitution of Rome, under which the sciences enjoyed their greatest flowering, had aspects which we would not wish to bring back even for the sake of their orators and poets, and the turbulent times which in Italy produced Dante and Petrarch are equally unenviable. Some sciences are the showy blossoms of a thorny plant, the splendid grapes of a weak vine. A rich cornfield is more useful and better for us though it is not so fine to look at. We are a mixture of peoples and tongues, and our circumstances and aims are likewise mixed. The pure Greek national character, with its simplicity in learning and culture, can never be for us. Let us emulate the Greeks as far as our constitution allows and in this way become what they could not be. Perhaps we will make up in fruit for our poor show of flowers; perhaps we shall achieve by permanence and pervasiveness what they attained by vitality and fervour.

IDEAS FOR A
PHILOSOPHY OF THE HISTORY
OF MANKIND

1784–91

[Books III–V, VII–IX]

IDEAS FOR A PHILOSOPHY OF THE HISTORY OF MANKIND

BOOK III

VI. ORGANIC DIFFERENCE BETWEEN ANIMALS AND MAN

[XIII, 109–14]

The human species has been praised for possessing in the most perfected form all the powers and capacities of every other species. This is patently untrue. Not only is the assertion incapable of empirical proof; it is also logically insupportable, for it is self-contradictory. Clearly, if it were true, one power would cancel out the other and man would be the most wretched of creatures. For how could man at one and the same time bloom like a flower, feel his way like the spider, build like the bee, suck like the butterfly, and also possess the muscular strength of the lion, the trunk of the elephant and the skill of the beaver? Does he possess, nay does he comprehend, a single one of these powers, with that intensity, with which the animal enjoys and exercises it?

On the other hand, man has also been, I will not say, degraded to the level of the beast, yet altogether denied a character *sui generis*. He has been depicted as a degenerate type of animal who, forever striving for perfection, has in the process wholly lost the characteristics originally peculiar to him. But this, too, flies in the face of truth and of all the evidence that human biology and human history provide. Manifestly, man has qualities which no animal possesses and acts in a manner which, for good or for ill, is entirely his own. No animal devours a member of its species for the sheer fun of it; no animal murders its kind in cold blood at the command of a third party. On the other hand, no animal has a language, still less writings, traditions, religion or rights and law of its own making. Finally, no animal has the education, clothing, habitation, arts, indeterminate mode of life, unrestrained propensities, and fluctuating attitudes, which distinguish almost every human being. We are not enquiring if all this is to the advantage or detriment of our species. It suffices to observe that it constitutes its character. Whilst animals on the whole remain true to the qualities of their kind, man alone has made a goddess of *choice* in place of *necessity*. It is this difference which calls for investigation. And the investigation must be as factual as the subject of inquiry. *How* man came to differ in this way is quite another question, being essentially historical in orientation. And that goes also for the question whether the difference is an original characteristic or an acquired one, whether it is real or only feigned. But that man's perfectibility or corruptibility (a propensity not shared by the animal world) is closely bound up with this distinguishing difference can scarcely be doubted. Let us, however, set aside all metaphysics and approach the problem from an empirical and physiological point of view.

1. *The posture of man is upright; in this he is unique upon earth.* Admittedly, the bear has a broad foot and fights in an erect position, and apes and pygmies sometimes run or walk upright. Yet only man is naturally and continuously in the erect position. His foot is firmer and broader than an ape's, with a longer big toe. His heel, too, is on a level with the sole of his foot, and all his bones, organs and muscles are adapted to the upright posture. The calf of his leg is less curved, his pelvis is drawn back and his hips are spread outward from each other. His spine is less curved, his breast wider. His shoulders have clavicles, and his hands have fingers with a sense of feeling. And to crown the structure, his head does not droop forward [like an ape's], but is raised on the muscles of his neck. Man is *anthropos*, a creature looking far above and around him . . .

2. *The upright posture of man is natural to him alone; indeed it is the organizing determinant of man's activities and the characteristic which distinguishes him from all other species.*

No nation upon earth has been found walking on all fours. However close some aborigines may appear to border on the beast by their mode of thinking and living, they nonetheless walk erect. Even the insensitive beings in Diodorus[1] and other legendary creatures found in ancient or mediaeval writings walk upon two legs . . . Had man been a quadruped, and had he been so for

[1] Diodorus Siculus. Sicilian historian (d. after 21 B.C.), author of a world history ending with the Gallic Wars.

thousands of years, surely he would have remained so to the present; and nothing short of a miraculous new creation could have made him what he now is and for what we have come to know him from history and experience.

Why, then, should we give credence to unproved and wholly contradictory paradoxes, when the structure of man, the history of his species, and, as it seems to me, the whole analogy of terrestrial organization point to quite a different hypothesis? No creature, that we know of, has departed from its original organization or has developed in opposition to it. It can operate only with the powers inherent in its organization, and nature knew how to devise sufficient means to confine all living things to the sphere allotted to them. In man everything is adapted to the form he now bears; from it, everything in history is explicable; without it, we are left completely in the dark . . .

With grateful eyes let us contemplate the blessing of the hallowed act by which our species became a human species. We cannot but note with a sense of wonder the peculiar organization of powers, deriving from the erect posture of man by which, and by which alone, he became what he is: *man*.

BOOK IV

I. MAN IS ORGANIZED WITH A CAPACITY FOR REASONING

[XIII, 115–28]

Internally and externally the orang-outang resembles man. Its brain has the form of ours; it has a broad chest, flat shoulders, a similar face and a skull of the same shape. Its heart, lungs, liver, spleen, stomach and intestines are like those of man. Tyson has pointed out forty-eight parts in which it resembles our species more than it does the ape.* Likewise, the actions attributed to it, even its vices and follies, are not unlike those of man, and the female menstruates like the human female.

Unquestionably, therefore, it must have some resemblance to

---

* Tyson, Edward. *The Anatomy of a Pygmy, compared with that of a Monkey, an Ape, and a Man*, London, 1751.

man also in its interior characteristics, in the operation of its mind. Those philosophers who would debase the orang-outang to the level of the smaller 'mechanical' animals seem to me to miss the basis of comparison entirely. The beaver builds, but instinctively; its whole mechanism is constructed for this. It cannot, however, do anything else; it is incapable of associating with man, of taking part in his thoughts and passions. The ape, on the other hand, has no determinate instinct; its mode of thinking almost approximates the process of reasoning, whilst its behaviour is highly imitative. The ape imitates everything and hence its brain must be fitted for a thousand combinations of sensitive ideas, of which no other animal is capable. Neither the wise elephant, nor the tractable dog, is capable of doing what the ape can perform. Moreover, *the ape seems anxious to perfect itself*, though this is precisely what it cannot do; the door is shut against it. Its brain is incapable of combining the ideas of others with its own, or of making what it imitates its own. The female ape, described by Bontius, possessed a sense of modesty, and covered herself with her hand when a stranger entered; she sighed, wept, and seemed to perform human actions.[2] The apes, described by Battel, go out in groups, arm themselves with clubs, and chase the elephants out of their precincts.[3] They attack the negroes and sit around their fires; but they do not know how to keep the fire going. The ape, which de la Brosse[4] placed at table, used a knife and fork, and was susceptible to anger, sorrow and all the human passions. The love of the mothers for their children, their education and initiation into the arts and tricks of an ape's life, the order that pervades their republics, the punishments they inflict on their criminals, their droll artifices and pranks and many other traits, provide enough evidence that they resemble man in their inner lives no less than they do in their external. Buffon wastes the torrent of his eloquence in vain when he disputes [in his *Histoire naturelle*] the natural uniformity of the external and internal organs of these creatures. The facts which he himself adduces refute his own argument. One simply cannot but infer from those facts that there

[2] Bontius, Jacob, *Historiae naturalis & medicae Indiae Orientalis* (Amsterdam, 1658) (Bk. VI, pp. 84–5).

[3] Battel, Andrew, fl. 1589. His account of his adventures in Angola was included in: Purchas, Samuel, *Purchas his pilgrimage* . . . (London, 1617).

[4] Brosse, M. de la. Author of a *Voyage à l'Angola* (1738).

is an unmistakable uniformity in the relationship between external and internal organs throughout nature in all living beings.

What is it, then, that the humanlike creature lacks to be fully human? Is it language only? To be sure, every effort to train apes to imitate human language has failed, so far; this is startling since one would expect creatures which so eagerly imitate everything to copy human speech first of all and do so without waiting for instruction. Is this deficiency due solely to their organs? I doubt it. For why is the ape, assuming it can grasp what is said, unable to converse by mime in spite of its propensity to gesticulate? Surely, there must be something else which prevents this poor creature entering the domain of human reason however closely it may approach it.

What is this 'something'? It is remarkable that upon dissection almost the entire difference is found to lie in *the parts pertaining to walking*. The ape is formed to be able to walk erect and thereby is more similar to man than its brethren; but it is not formed wholly for this, and this difference seems to deprive it of everything . . .

All the experiments hitherto collected by Haller,[5] the most learned physiologist any nation has yet produced, show how futile it is to analyze the *indivisible process of the formation of ideas* in terms of individual material parts distributed in the brain. Indeed, I am convinced that, even in the absence of these experiments, the very manner in which ideas are formed must have led to this realization. We name the powers of thought according to their different relations, imagination and memory, intellect and judgment; we distinguish the impulse of desire from the pure will, and the power of sensation from that of movement. But the most casual reflection tells us that these faculties are not locally separated as if judgment resided in one part of the brain, memory and imagination in another, the passions and sense perceptions in a third. For the thought processes of our mind are undivided entities, producing in their totality the diverse effects or manifestations which we treat as separate faculties. It would, therefore, be almost absurd to attempt to dissect abstract relations as if they were material bodies and to scatter the mind as Medea did the limbs of her brother. If the stuff of simple sensation, which

---

[5] Haller, Albrecht von, 1708–77. Swiss scientist noted for his researches in experimental physiology.

incidentally is quite distinct from the fluid of the nerves (if such exists), escapes our observation, how much less likely are we to detect the far more complex inter-connections of all our ideas, senses and perceptions, especially if we are not only to observe or to feel them, but to excite them at will in the different parts of the brain, as easily as if we ran our fingers over the keys of a harpsichord! To cherish such expectations strikes me as a very odd idea indeed.

It strikes me as even odder when I consider the structure of the brain and the nerves. How different is the economy of Nature from what our abstract psychology with its separation of senses and faculties, would like us to believe! How different is all this metaphysical nonsense about the origin, the division and the joining up of nerves from what we actually perceive? We know of the organic purposes of the different parts of the brain only insofar as we know their effects from our daily experience. Nothing remains for us, then, but to consider the brain as the sacred laboratory of ideas, where these and the senses converge, not unlike a womb in which the embryo of thought invisibly takes shape as one indivisible whole. If the womb is sound and healthy, if it affords the embryo not merely adequate psychological and physiological warmth but also ample space and favourable conditions in and through which the invisible organic power (*Kraft*), pervading everything, can thoroughly penetrate and engulf the perceptions of the senses and of the whole body, and combine them, if I may be allowed the metaphor, within that *luminous point* which we regard as clear *consciousness*, then the finely organized creature becomes capable of reason, provided, of course, external circumstances, such as education, help to facilitate the awakening and development of ideas. If the reverse is the case; if the brain is deficient in essential parts or finer fluids; if grosser senses overpower it; or if it gets warped as a result of other pressures; we may find that the subtle converging radiation of ideas will fail to take place, that the creature will remain a slave of the senses . . .

If, then, we arrive at the conclusion that man's superiority can be attributed to the structure of his brain, what can be said to determine the latter? Evidently, I would say, the *more developed organization of his whole being*, and, in the last analysis, his *erect posture.* The brain of every animal is fashioned after the shape of its head, or rather, since nature works from within to without, the reverse would be more accurate. To whatever gait, to whatever proportion of the parts, to whatever *habits* Nature destined a creature, to that purpose she combined and arranged its organic powers . . . What produces the organic difference between the head of man and the head of an ape? The *angle of direction.* The ape has every part of the brain that man possesses, but it has them thrust backward because, since the ape was not designed to walk erect, its head is set at a different angle . . . Thus everything depends on the *direction* in which the head was formed in relation to the organization of the whole body. I shall not proceed to any other examples, hoping that further anatomical research will turn its attention to this *inner relationship of the parts as regards their mutual proximity and the direction of the head within the organiza- tion of the parts,* especially in dissecting animals that resemble man. Here, I believe, lies the difference that predisposes a being to this or that instinct, that produces either an animal or a human mind. For every creature is in all its parts one living co-operating whole (*zusammenwirkendes Ganze*) . . .

III. MAN IS ORGANIZED FOR MORE COMPLEX SENSE
PERCEPTION, FOR THE EXERCISE OF ART AND THE
USE OF LANGUAGE

[XIII, 136–9]

If man were closer to the ground, his senses would be confined to a narrower sphere, and the inferior senses would dominate the superior ones, as has been found in those instances where man was forced to live under non-human conditions. Smell and taste then became his leading guides. In man, raised as he is above the earth and plants, smell gives way to sight. As a result, he surveys a wider area around him and his eyes are trained from early infancy to distinguish the finest geometry of lines and colours. The ear, placed deep beneath the projecting skull, is close to the inner 'chamber' where man's ideas converge and take shape, while with animals it stands on guard, as it were, almost outside the head and is almost wholly centred on what goes on around it, as its pointed form often visibly indicates.

With his erect gait man becomes a creature endowed with art. Because he is formed to walk erect, man has free and skilful hands. Thus he can manipulate objects and feel his way, as it were, towards new and clear ideas. Helvetius was right in saying that the hands are great assistants to man's reason . . .

It has often been said that man was created defenceless and that one of his distinguishing characteristics is his complete helplessness by himself. This, however, is not so. Man has weapons for defence like other creatures. Even the ape handles the club and defends himself with sand and stones . . . The freedom of his hands has made man a tool and weapon-making creature. Thus even in a wild state he is by the nature of his organization neither helpless nor defenceless. What animal has the multifarious implements of art which man possesses in his arms, his hands, the rigidity of his body, in all his powers? Art is the most powerful weapon; man is all art and in this sense the very personification of organized defence. To be sure, he lacks claws and teeth for attack; but, then, he was designed to be a peaceable creature. Man was not meant to be a cannibal.

What range of artistic propensities lies hidden in each of man's senses! Frequently this becomes evident only by some mishap, some deficiency or other, by disease or deformity. We may well speculate how many more capacities are concealed in us, how many more human senses have not yet unfolded. Some blind people have raised their sense of feeling or hearing, their memory or power of calculation and reasoning, to a degree that seems almost uncanny to men of ordinary faculties. It is hardly fanciful, therefore, to assume that in our complex machine worlds of variety and subtlety may lie dormant awaiting discovery by senses undeveloped so far. What subtlety of perception has man already attained in the eye and ear! In higher stages of development he will surely perfect it even further, since, as Berkeley observes, light is the language of divinity which our finest sense does but continually spell in a thousand forms and colours. Melody perceived by the human ear and developed by art is the purest form of symmetry which the mind obscurely practises by means of the senses, just as it evidences the most sublime geometry by the manner in which the rays of light act upon the eye. How infinite would be our astonishment if, having reached a higher stage of development, we could clearly see what we now with all our senses and power but darkly perceive in our complex divine machine.

However, all these implements of art, brain, senses, arms and hands, even the erect posture, would not have carried us very far, if the Creator had not provided us with the means to set them in motion. By the divine gift of speech dormant reason was aroused or, more precisely, the very capacity of reasoning which by itself would for ever have remained dead acquired through speech vital power and efficacy. Only by speech did the eye and the ear, nay the perceptions of all senses, become united, thus giving rise to creative thought, to which the hands and the other members were subservient tools . . . The delicate organs of speech must, therefore, be considered as the rudder of our reason, and speech itself as the heavenly spark that gradually kindled our thoughts and senses into flame . . .

IV. MAN IS ORGANIZED FOR FINER INSTINCTS AND HENCE FOR FREEDOM

[XIII, 142–50]

It has become a widely accepted view that man is devoid of instinct and that this is his distinguishing characteristic. But in actual fact man has every instinct that any of the animals around him possess, only he has them, in conformity with his organization, more delicately proportioned and hence in a reduced intensity.

The infant in the mother's womb seems under a necessity of going through every state that is associated with the life of a terrestrial creature. He swims in water; he lies prone with open mouth; his jaws are large before the lips, which are not formed till late, can cover them. As soon as he comes into the world, he gasps for air, and sucking is his first untaught act. The whole process of digestion and nutrition, of hunger and thirst, proceeds instinctively, or by some still more obscure impulse. The muscular and procreative powers strive in the same manner towards further development. All the animal instincts are observable here as also in cases where violent emotion or disease deprives man of his reason. Hardships and dangers unfold in some men, nay in whole nations, especially at a primitive level, the capacities, sensations and faculties of beasts.

Man, therefore, is not deprived of instincts as such. It would be more correct to say that they are *repressed* in him, that they are brought under the control of the nerves and the finer senses. Without instincts life would be impossible for the creature, since he is still in large measure an animal.

But how are they repressed? Let us observe their development from infancy and investigate this so-called human weakness which has given rise to so many foolish laments.

. . . Before the child learns to walk, he learns to see, hear and grasp things, and to practice the delicate mechanism of his sense apparatus. In this he is no different from the animal, since he exercises his senses in the same instinctive manner, only in a somewhat more delicate fashion. And he does so *not* as a result of innate skills or aptitudes. If these were predominant from infancy, man would remain a brute. Being able to do everything without having to learn it, he would learn nothing of what constitutes his human essence. Either reason must be born in him as an instinct, which appears a contradiction in terms, or he must come into the world feeble as he does *in order to acquire reason* . . .

It now becomes evident what human reason is. Far from being an innate automaton, as so many modern writings tend to imply, reason, in both its theoretical and practical manifestations, is nothing more than something *formed by experience*, an acquired knowledge of the propositions and directions of the ideas and faculties, to which man is fashioned by his organization and mode of life. An angelic reason is as inconceivable as the claim to perfect insight into the inner states of lower beings is presumptuous. Man's reason is the creation of *man*. From infancy man compares the ideas and impressions, particularly those of his finer senses, according to the delicacy, accuracy and frequency of his sense perceptions, and in proportion to the speed with which he learns to combine these. The result of these combinations constitutes thought, a newly created unity. And the result of the various combinations of thoughts and perceptions constitutes the process of distinguishing the true from the false, the good from the bad, the beneficial from the harmful. This ongoing process, which fashions our lives as human beings, is reason. Instead of viewing it, then, as an inborn *a priori* faculty, we have to see it as the accumulation or product of the impressions that are received, the examples that are followed, and the internal power and energy with which they are assimilated within the individual mind. They determine whether a man's reason—just as his body—is rich or poor, sound or diseased, stunted or well-grown. If Nature deceived us by false perceptions of the senses, we have to suffer the natural consequences. All those affected in this manner would share the same experience. If men deceive us, and we lack organs or faculties to perceive the deception and order our impressions in more correct proportion, our reason is crippled, frequently for life. Man has to learn everything. This is his destination, his 'instinct'. He even has to learn to walk upright and he does so by trial and error. He has to fall in order to walk, to encounter falsehood in order to appreciate truth. An animal, on the other hand, moves securely on his four feet, guided by his instinct alone. Man enjoys the royal prerogative of seeing far and wide with his head high above the ground; yet, at the same time, much of what he sees, he sees but darkly and mistakenly. Indeed, often he forgets his steps, and only by stumbling is he reminded of the narrowness of the base on which the whole structure of his ideas and judgments rests. Nonetheless, in accordance with his high *rational destination*, he is and remains what no other terrestrial creature is, a son of the gods, a sovereign of the earth.

In order to appreciate the eminence of this destination, let us consider what is involved in the great gifts of *reason* and *freedom*, and how daring, as it were, Nature was to entrust them to such a feeble and complex terrestrial creature as man. The animal is a slave, bent down to the ground. Even though some of the nobler species carry the head erect, or at least reach for freedom with uplifted neck, their minds, not quite ripened into reason, must submit to the impulses of necessity, and as a result they scarcely get an inkling of any independent use of their senses and propensities. Man is the first of nature's creatures to be set free; he stands erect. He can weigh up good against evil, truth against falsehood; he can explore possibilities and choose between alternatives. Nature has given him two free hands as instruments and a surveying eye to guide his progress; she has also given him the power, not only of placing the weights in the balance, but of being, if I may put it thus, *himself a weight* on the scale. He can, if so inclined, delude himself to such an extent as to choose deception and revel in it. He can, against his very nature, come to love the chains which fetter him, and even adorn them with flowers. What we said earlier about deceived reason, applies equally to abused or shackled freedom. With most men freedom is the *ratio* between certain powers and impulses established simply by habit or convenience. They rarely look beyond these and hence it is not uncommon for man to be subject to the basest instincts and prone to the vilest of habits. Thus fettered, he compares most unfavourably with the worst of brutes.

Yet even when he most despicably abuses his freedom, man is still king. For he can still choose, even though he chooses the worst; he can rule over himself, even if he legislates himself into a beast. To be sure, before the Omniscient, who conferred on him these powers, his liberty and reason are limited. But this does not in the slightest alter the fact that man, by his very nature, is and remains a free creature. In error and in truth, in rising and in falling, he still remains man: feeble indeed, but freeborn; not fully rational, though capable of reasoning. His human essence— *Humanität*—is not ready made, yet it is potentially realizable. And this is true of a New Zealand cannibal no less than of a Fenelon, of a wretched gypsy no less than of a Newton, for all are creatures of one and the same species.

It seems, indeed, as if every possible variety in the use of these gifts were to be found upon our globe. Evidently, we can trace a progressive scale, from the man who borders on the brute to the purest genius in human form. At this we ought not to wonder, since we can observe the vast gradation of animals below us, and the long course Nature had to take to prepare in us organically the tender sprouting flower of reason and freedom . . . But the greatest misanthrope can scarcely deny that the noble plants of reason and freedom have produced beautiful fruits when nourished by the celestial beams of the sun in spite of the many wild branches. It would be almost incredible, if history did not confirm it, to what heights human reason has ventured, attempting not merely to trace but also to imitate the creating and sustaining deity. In the chaos of beings, which the senses reveal, it has sought and discovered unity and meaning, order and beauty. The most hidden powers, of whose inner forces reason admittedly has no notion, have been observed in their external manifestations in terms of motion, quantity, duration, efficacy and substance, wherever it has perceived their effects on earth or in the heavens . . .

Freedom, too, has produced noble fruits in mankind, revealed both by what men pursue and by what they shun. That men have renounced the unsteady reins of blind appetite and voluntarily assumed the bonds of marriage, of friendship, of social co-operation and loyalty unto death; that they have given up their own wills to be governed by *laws*; that they are prepared to establish and defend with their own life's blood *the rule of man over men*, imperfect though it is; that noble-minded men have devoted their lives to their *country* and not just for one tumultuous moment but—and this is far nobler still—for days, months and years on end, in uninterrupted labour to confer what they at least thought to be welfare and peace on a blind ungrateful multitude; that divinely inspired visionaries voluntarily submitted to slander and persecution, poverty and want, from a noble thirst for *truth*, *freedom*, and *happiness*, cherishing the idea that they were promoting the highest boon of which they were capable, for the benefit of their brethren: if all these manifestations of human virtue are not expressions of the most powerful strivings for *self-determination* inherent in us, then I am at a loss to conceive of any other explanation. It is true that the number of those who have thus led the way and who, like physicians, have urged the multitude to do for their own good what they would not of themselves have chosen, has always been but small. Yet these few have been the flower of mankind, the free immortal sons of God upon Earth. Their names outweigh those of millions.

VI. MAN IS CONSTITUTED FOR HUMANITY (HUMANITÄT) AND RELIGION

[XIII, 154–64]

I wish I could include in this word *Humanität* everything that I have said so far about the noble constitution of man for reason and freedom, finer senses and impulses, the most delicate and most robust health, the realization of the purpose of the world and the control over it. For man has no nobler word for his destiny than that which expresses the essence of himself as a human being, and which thus reflects the image of the Creator of our earth. We need only sketch his structure and constitution to trace his noblest duties.

All the instincts of a living being are reducible to *self-preservation* and *sympathy*. The whole organic structure of man is by superior guidance most carefully adapted to these two basic instincts.

1. Man has for his protection the smallest circumference without, and the most varied velocity within. He stands on the most confined base and thus he can most easily cover his limbs. His centre of gravity falls between the most supple and powerful haunches that any creature on earth possesses, and no animal has in these parts the mobility and strength of man. His flat, steely chest, and the position of his natural weapons, i.e. his arms, give him the widest possible scope to defend his heart and all the vital parts from the head to the knees. It is no fairy tale that men have fought with lions and have overcome them. The African native, by combining prudence and cunning with strength can cope with more than one. It must be conceded, however, that man's body is primarily geared for defence and not for attack. In defence man is by nature the most powerful creature upon earth. But for purposes of attack he needs artificial aids. Thus his very structure teaches him to live in *peace* and not from robbery, murder and destruction. It is the first characteristic of his humanity.

2. Of the instincts that imply a relationship with others, the sexual instinct is the most powerful. In man it assumes a form appropriate to his humanity. No animal has lips like man; their delicate rim is the last part of the face formed in the womb. And that man's sexual drive is not subject to the seasons, as it is with animals, (though no accurate observations on the cycles of the human body in this respect have yet been made) indicates that it is not determined by blind necessity, but rather depends for its excitement on love which springs from affection tempered by reason. Sex, like everything else about man, was designed, accordingly, for voluntary control. Like love, with which it is intimately related, it was intended to be *human*. For that purpose Nature not only adapted his physical structure, but also his later development, the duration and form of his sexual relations, by bringing these under the law of a *voluntary social alliance* and the most intimate communion between two beings who feel themselves united in one for life.

3. This intimate sentiment of love apart, tender emotions express themselves in the form of sympathy, empathy or participation. Among all living creatures, man was chosen by Nature to possess these emotions to the highest degree. The texture of his fibres is so fine, delicate and elastic, his nervous system so diffused throughout every part of his vibrating body that, like an analogue of the all-sentient Deity, he can put himself in the place of almost every creature and share its feelings even at the risk of his own well-being. Even a tree arouses our sympathy, especially one in the prime of growth. Some people literally cannot bear to see a young green tree being cut down or destroyed; they feel pity for its dried-up crown. Indeed, we often grieve over a wilting flower. A sensitive man cannot pass a writhing, crushed worm with indifference. And the more developed a creature is, the closer its organization resembles our own, the more sympathy is excited in us by its sufferings. One has to have nerves of steel to dissect a living creature and watch its convulsive movements. Only an unquenchable thirst for fame and science can gradually deaden a man's organic sensibility . . . Man's vibrating fibres, his sympathetic nerves, need not the call of reason; they not only often precede reason but, indeed, frequently are in opposition to it . . .

It is noteworthy that our sympathy is much more powerfully evoked and increased by what we hear than by what we see.[6] The sigh or scream of an animal in pain attracts others of his kind, making them want to help, and causing them sorrow if they are unable to do so. The sight of suffering is often repellent to man rather than conducive to his tender compassion. But let the voice of a sufferer reach him: it pierces his heart, he cannot but rush to help. Sound seems to impart living reality to what we see, inducing us to share the feelings of others and linking their experience with recollections of our own. There may well be, as I am inclined to believe, even deeper organic forces at work. Suffice it to note that experience amply suggests that the human *voice and language* is the principal source of human sympathy . . .

4. Maternal love is most highly developed in the human species and represents a vital rung in the ladder of upright humanity. It humanizes the most depraved member of our race. Among animals even the lioness is affectionate to her young. The first human

[6] Cf. *Essay on the Origin of Language*, v, 64–6 and *passim*.

society originated in the family and was cemented by ties of blood, mutual trust and love. To prevent the wildness of men and to habituate them to domestic intercourse, it was essential that the human infant should require parental nourishment for some considerable time. Nature thus compelled men by tender bonds to keep together so that they might not disperse and forget each other like animals whose maturity is reached at a much earlier age. The father becomes the instructor of his son, as the mother had been the nurse of the infant. In this way a new link in the chain of humanity is forged. Here lies the essential basis of *human society*, without which no man could grow and develop and no collectivity of men could emerge. Man, then, is *born* for society. This is brought home to him by the affection of his parents and by the protracted period of his infancy.

5. Man's sympathy cannot, however, be extended to everything indiscriminately, since it could easily prove an uncertain and unreliable guide for so restricted and complex a creature in matters that are more remote and less familiar to him. For this reason wise Mother Nature drew together all his various interwoven tendencies under a safer guiding rule, that of *justice and truth* . . . : *Do not unto others what you would not wish them to do unto you;* but *what you expect others to do unto you, do unto them too.* This incontestable rule is written even in the breast of the human monster; for when he eats the flesh of others, he expects to be eaten in turn. It is the rule of true and false, of the *idem et idem*, of reciprocity, founded on the system of all our propensities, and attributable perhaps also to man's upright posture. If I press someone to my bosom, he presses me also to his; if I risk my life for him, he risks his for mine. It is on this principle of reciprocity that the laws of man and of nations are founded . . .

6. If *justum* and *honestum* are attributes of man's upright posture, so is *decorum*. Decorum demands the preservation of man's physical integrity as the necessary condition of his moral integrity. It demands the cultivation of inward form and wholesomeness. True beauty is nothing but the pleasing manifestation of such inner perfection. In this sense *decorum* is the dearest friend and servant of *justum* and *honestum*. Consider the divine image of man disfigured by carelessness or false art, by capricious fashion, affected manners and actions, customs, arts and language.

One and the same *human essence* (*Humanität*) pervades them all; yet how few of the nations of this world have realized it so far, whilst hundreds succeeded in distorting it by barbarism or pseudo-civilization. To trace this human essence in its manifold expressions, in social intercourse, in politics, in scientific and artistic pursuits, is the true function of *social philosophy*.

Finally, *religion* is the most exalted mark of man's humanity. No one needs to be startled by my referring to religion in this manner and mentioning it in this context. The human understanding is the most exquisite gift of man, the business of which is to trace the connection between cause and effect, and to divine it where it is not apparent. The human understanding does this in every action, occupation and art, for even where it follows an accepted practice, some understanding must originally have settled the connection between cause and effect, and thus have established it. To be sure, we cannot discern the inner cause of natural phenomena. There is little or nothing that we know about how things operate even within ourselves. In a sense, therefore all the phenomena around us are but a dream, a conjecture, a name, though we regard it as reality if and when we observe the same effects linked with the same occasioning circumstances, often and constantly enough. This is how philosophy proceeds, and the first and last philosophy has always been religion. Even the most primitive peoples have practised it, for there is not a single people upon earth that has been found entirely without some form of religion, just as there is no human society without the capacity for reasoning, without language, without connubial relations, or some traditional morals and customs. Where men could see no visible author of events, they supposed an invisible one; yet in spite of the darkness they continued to search into the causes of things. It is true that they focused more on the external manifestations of phenomena than on their intrinsic nature, and were more impressed by the terrifying and transitory aspects of things than by their more lasting and beneficial elements. Similarly they rarely succeeded in subsuming a multiplicity of causes under one basic cause. Nonetheless, man's first endeavours along these lines were religious in character. To maintain that religion originated in *fear*, that fear invented the gods of most people, is to say very little indeed, and to explain even less. Fear, as such, invents nothing. It merely rouses the mind to seek an understanding of given phenomena, to venture into the unknown by conjecture, by true and false hunches. As soon as man, therefore, learned to apply his mind at the slightest prompting, that is to say, as soon as he looked upon the world differently from an animal, he was bound to believe in more powerful invisible beings that helped or injured him. These he sought to make his friends or to keep as his friends, and thus religion was born. True or false, right or wrong, it served man as guide and comforter in a life full of perplexity, danger, and sizeable areas of darkness . . .

It is not difficult to see why in all religions of the world either God has been invested with human, or man with divine, properties; for we know of no form that is superior to our own. Whatever was to move man and make him more human had to be capable of being thought and felt in human terms. Thus nations that thought and felt in essentially aesthetic terms exalted the human form to divine beauty; whilst others, more inclined to abstract thought, represented the perfections of the Invisible by means of symbols. Even in those instances where God is said to have revealed Himself to man, His words and actions were interpreted in *human* terms and in accordance with the prevailing temper of the times.

BOOK V

II. NO POWER IN NATURE IS WITHOUT AN ORGAN; BUT THE ORGAN IS NOT POWER ITSELF, BUT MERELY ITS MEDIUM

[XIII, 172–6]

Priestley[7] and others have objected to the spiritualists that no such thing as pure spirit is to be found throughout Nature and that we know far too little about the intrinsic structuring of matter to rule out the possibility of thought or other spiritual powers being material. Both points seem valid to me. We know of no spirit capable of operating apart from, or without, matter. What is more, we observe in matter so many powers of a spirit-like nature,

[7] Priestley, Joseph, 1733–1804. English clergyman, chemist, and writer. His numerous works include *An Essay on the First Principles of Government* (1768), and *Disquisitions relating to Matter and Spirit* (1777).

that a complete *opposition* and *contradiction* of these admittedly different elements strikes me as at least unproven if not self-contradictory. For how could we account for the fact that two elements that were fundamentally dissimilar from, and essentially opposed to, each other, would succeed in working together in the closest possible harmony? How, indeed, could we assert that they *are* essentially different or incompatible if we know nothing of the inner nature of either?

Wherever we observe a power in operation, it is inherent in some organ and in harmony with it. For power as such is not open to investigation, at least not by our senses. It only exists for these by its manifestations in and through material forms which, if we may trust the analogy pervading nature as a whole, have been fashioned by it to meet its particular requirements. Seeds *in posse*, lying dormant since Creation, are not evident to our eyes; all that we observe from the first moment of a creature's existence are acting *organic powers*. If an individual being contains these within itself, it propagates its species without assistance. If the sexes are divided, each must contribute to the organization of their progeny, and in different modes according to the diversity of their structure. . . . The more complex the organization of a creature, the less recognizable is what we call its seed or genetic origin. It is *organic matter* which, in order to attain the form of the prospective creature, requires the addition of vital powers or life forces. What processes take place in the egg of a bird, before the young acquires and completes its form! The organic powers must destroy while they arrange; they attract parts together and separate them in turn. Indeed it seems as if several powers were in conflict and on the point of causing a miscarriage until an equilibrium is established between them and the creature becomes what it has to become by virtue of its species. Bearing in mind these transformations, these living operations in the egg of the bird or in the womb of the mammal, I feel we speak imprecisely if we talk of seeds that are merely evolving in the manner of an *epigenesis*, according to which limbs are superadded from without. For what really takes place is *creative and total development* or *genesis*, i.e., the operation of internal powers within a mass which Nature supplies and which is being fashioned by these powers in the manner that is manifest to us . . .

The reader would, however, misinterpret my meaning were he to ascribe to me the view that, as some have put it, our *rational mind* forms its structure in the womb by means of its inherent reason. We have noted earlier how late reason develops within us; that, though we are born with a capacity for it, we are not capable of possessing or acquiring it by our own unaided power. How could something which is so highly dependent in its maturation on *conscious* human development possibly come into being at a time when the major part of our vital functions are performed without any conscious volition of our mind, when we are wholly incapable of comprehending any part of its internal or external operations? It was not our reason that fashioned the body, but organic powers, the finger of creative Divinity . . .

If, therefore, we follow the course of Nature, it is evident that:

1. *Powers and organs are indeed intimately connected, but they are not one and the same thing.* The matter of our body existed, but it was shapeless and lifeless until fashioned and vitalized by the organic powers.

2. *Every power operates in harmony with its organ.* For it has fashioned it in such a way as to manifest its essential nature in and through it. It assimilated the parts supplied by the Almighty and used them, as it were, as its husk.

3. When the husk falls off, *the power, which existed before it,* though in an inferior state, *remains.* If it was possible for the power to pass from its original state into a later one, it should not be inconceivable that it might be equally capable of a further transition when it loses its husk. He who has brought it into being originally, albeit in an imperfect form, will take care to provide a medium for its further transformation . . .

Thus, I believe, the fallacy of the arguments by which the materialists imagine they have refuted the notion of immortality becomes evident. Granted that we know nothing of our soul as pure spirit; we even have no wish to know it as such. Granted, too, that it acts only as an organic power; for it is not supposed to act otherwise. Indeed, I would add, our mind only acquired reason and an essentially human character (*Humanität*), by means of organic powers such as the brain and the nerves which enabled it in the first place to learn how to think and feel. Finally, let us grant also that mind and matter, and all the powers of matter, of attraction and repulsion, of motion, of life, originally form one single entity. Does it, however, follow from this that even such basic powers as attraction and motion are one and the same thing as the material organs through which they manifest themselves? Moreover, is it conceivable that these powers simply vanish or perish? Has anyone ever witnessed the complete destruction of any one single power inherent in nature? Is it not feasible to assume that the combination of matter and power is capable of undergoing a series of mutations from its original state to a more developed and subtle organization? . . .

IV. THE SPHERE OF HUMAN ORGANIZATION IS A SYSTEM OF CREATIVE MENTAL POWERS

[XIII, 181–8]

The principal doubt usually raised against the immortality of organic powers stems from confusing the media through which these powers operate with the powers themselves. I venture to assert that by casting light on this doubt I can not only brighten a hope, but even kindle a certain assurance concerning the efficacy and continuity of their creative propensities. No flower blossoms as a result of the external dust or the mere structure of its material particles. No single activity of so complex an organization of powers as the human mind can be simply resolved into the component parts of the brain. Even physiology bears this out. The external picture that is painted on the eye does not reach the brain; the sound that strikes the ear does not mechanically enter the mind as sound. To imagine the brain, therefore, to be self-cogitative, the neural fluids to be self-sentient, is poor physiology indeed. Surely it is more in keeping with general experience to posit *specific psychological laws* according to which the mind combines ideas and performs its other functions. That it performs these functions in conformity and harmony with its organs is not disputed. If the tools are defective, the greatest artist will fail to produce great works of art. But all this does not in the slightest affect the point I am trying to make here. For I am concerned with the *manner* in which the mind operates and with the *essential nature of its ideas*.

1. It cannot be gainsaid that the *thought* and, indeed, the first

perception, by means of which the mind forms an 'image' of an external object is *something totally different from what the sensation itself conveys to the mind*. For what we call an image is not the speck of light which is reflected in the eye and does not even reach the brain. The image in the mind is the product of an intellectual process; it is the creation of the mind itself in response to the stimuli received by the senses. From the chaos of things that surrounds it, the mind calls forth a configuration (*Gestalt*) on which it focuses its attention and in this manner creates by means of its intrinsic power a unity out of multiplicity, a whole *sui generis*, entirely of its own making. The mind can recall or reconstruct the image, once formed, even when the object to which it refers is no longer present. Dreams and the imagination can and do form it according to laws very different from those underlying normal sense perceptions. The frenzies of disease, which have so often been adduced as proofs of the materiality of the soul, actually attest its immateriality. Listen to the mentally disturbed and observe the progress of his mind. He starts off from the idea which touched him so deeply and as a result deranged his intellectual make-up to such an extent that the connection between the idea and other sensations is broken. Everything is referred by him to the one idea because it dominates him, he is possessed by it and cannot shake it off. In the light of it he creates a world of his own, a concatenation of thoughts of its own peculiar kind, and all the wanderings of his mind and the manner in which it combines ideas is *mental* in the highest degree. It is not the result of a peculiar position of the cells of his brain, nor of the sensations as such, but is wholly determined by the affinity other ideas bear to his *idée fixe* and by the degree the latter warps the former. All the associations of our thought proceed in the same way. They are characteristic of beings capable of recalling past experiences by their own energy and of doing so quite frequently with a particular idiosyncracy. Ideas are connected, not by some external mechanism, but by feelings of internal affection or repulsion. I wish that ingenious men, especially physicians, would make known the qualities they observe in their patients. If this were done, I am convinced we should have clear evidence of the operations of an admittedly organic, but nonetheless self-powered being, acting in conformity to laws of mental inter-relation.

2. The same thing is demonstrated by the *artificial formation of our ideas from childhood on* and by the slow process through which the mind acquires consciousness of itself and the effort it expends in learning the use of the senses. More than one psychologist has observed the ingeniousness with which a child acquires the idea of colour, figure, magnitude and distance and thus *learns to see*. The sense organ as such learns nothing. For the image is depicted in the eye as faithfully on the first day of life as on the last, but it is the mind which learns to measure, to compare and to absorb the stimuli of the senses. In this the mind is assisted by the ear and by language. That language is an intellectual, and not a material, tool in the formation of ideas seems to me beyond doubt. One must be wholly devoid of intelligence to regard sounds and words as one and the same thing, for they are as disparate as body and mind, organ and creative power (*Kraft*). A word evokes a corresponding idea and transmits it to our mind from that of another person. But a word by itself is not an idea, anymore than a material organ is a thought. As the body gains by taking in food, so our mind is enlarged by absorbing ideas. And we observe in the latter the same laws of *assimilation, growth,* and *production,* only not in a physical manner but in a mode peculiar to itself. Nonetheless, the mind can, like the body, take in food in excess of what it can absorb and convert into nourishment. It must, therefore, preserve a balance of its intellectual powers if it is not to succumb to disease and enfeeblement, i.e., to madness . . . It is not a fanciful exaggeration to say that within everyone of us an *inner man of intellect* is continuously taking shape, with a nature of his own, who uses the body only as his implement, and who acts in conformity with this nature even if the bodily organs are seriously impaired. The more the mind gets separated from the body by disease or by violent emotional upsets and is thus forced to move as it were within its own world of ideas, the more we can witness its own power and energy in the creation and connection of ideas. In despair it wanders through the scenes of its earlier life and, unable by its very nature to forego forming ideas, it creates a new world for itself.

3. That great distinguishing feature of the human mind, clear *consciousness,* has been *acquired by it only gradually in the course of a process of intellectual humanization.* A child possesses little

consciousness, even though its mind incessantly attempts to attain it in order to gain awareness of itself and of its sense perceptions. All its endeavours to acquire ideas serve this process, whereby the growing individual strives to ascertain his place in, and relationship to, God's world, so that he can come to enjoy his existence and the use of his human energies. The animal, by contrast, goes through the world as if in a dark dream; its consciousness is diffused through the parts of the body receiving stimuli, and is indeed so powerfully enveloped by these that the progressive emergence of a clearer self-awareness never takes place. Man, too, it is true, is conscious of his sensual nature only by means of his senses; when these suffer injury in any way, his mind may be affected to the extent that one dominant idea can cause his self-awareness to be impaired. In this state he becomes an actor in a drama of his own choosing whether it be a comedy or a tragedy. But even when he is thus transported into a region of phantasy, his consciousness is still operative, his internal power of self-determination is still in evidence in however misguided a manner. . . . He may forget himself, become unaware of the lapse of time and indifferent to the promptings of his senses. Yet he is conscious of the high calling of his dominant idea and determined to pursue it. The most dreadful sufferings of the body have often been suppressed by one such vivid idea prevalent in the mind. Men imbued with a strong sentiment, particularly that of the love of God—which may well be the purest and most intense—have shown a complete disregard for life and death. With all their other ideas submerged under one dominant thought, they feel themselves to be in Heaven . . . Even the most primitive and the most savage peoples display the power of ideas. Irrespective of what they fight for, they fight under the impulse of ideas. The cannibal, no doubt, expresses his craving for revenge and bravery in an abominable manner, but this does not make his craving any less *spiritual*.

4. Thus, whatever the circumstances, whatever the organic disabilities or peculiarities, it is not they which constitute the *primary* power . . . When, one day, the same systematic study that is now devoted to the cure of physical diseases will be applied to disorders of the mind, it will be found that many of the former are in fact attributable to the latter. The realization of this fact will

shatter the dogmas of the materialists and cause them to vanish like mists before the sun. Those who are convinced of an *inner life of the self* cannot but regard the external circumstances which continually bring about change in the body, as in all other matter, as secondary and transitory factors that do not affect its essence . . .

Of this the Creator has given us ample evidence in our daily experience. We are closest to death when we are asleep, since most of the important functions of life are then in abeyance. Nerves and muscles repose; the senses cease to perceive; yet the mind continues to operate in its own domain. It is no more separated from the body than when it is awake, as the perceptions often interwoven in our dreams bear out. Even in deep sleep—of the dreams of which we have no recollection unless we are suddenly awakened —the mind operates according to laws of its own. Many people have observed that in undisturbed dreams their mind pursues the same series of ideas uninterruptedly, in a manner different from that of waking hours . . . The perceptions in a dream are more vivid, the emotions more violent, the connection between a thought and its realization more direct, our sight is keener, and the light surrounding us more brilliant. In healthy sleep we often fly rather than walk, our dimensons are enlarged, our resolutions have more force, our actions are less confined. And though all this depends on the body with which the most minute operation of the mind must necessarily harmonize (in view of their close structural interrelationship), all the phenomena of sleep and dreaming—which would greatly astonish us were we not so accustomed to them—reveal that not every part of our body is equally involved. Certain organs of our machine may be quite inactive, yet this in no way affects the power of our mind to think connectedly, vividly and freely, and to do so, frequently, with greater intensity than when they are active. Now, since all the causes that induce sleep, and all its physical symptoms, are physiologically, and not merely metaphorically, *analogous to those of death*, why should the spiritual symptoms not be likewise? . . .

VI. THE PRESENT STATE OF MAN IS PROBABLY THE CONNECTING LINK OF TWO WORLDS

[XIII, 194–9]

Everything in nature is connected: one state strives towards and prepares for the next. If, then, man be the last and highest link, closing as it were the chain of terrestrial organization, he must also begin the chain of a higher order of creatures as its lowest link. He is, therefore, probably, the middle ring between two adjoining systems of Creation. Since no living power can stand still or retreat in the realm of nature, it must push forward, it must progress. This means that for man to progress there must be a further step before him which is at once close to and exalted above him, just as, in the other direction, he is at once bordering on the animal and elevated above it. This view of things, which is supported by all the laws of nature, alone gives us a key to the wonderful phenomenon of man and hence also to a possible *philosophy of human history*.

For if we bear this view in mind, it helps us to throw light on the peculiar contradiction that is inherent in the human condition. Man considered as an animal is a child of the earth and is attached to it as his habitation; but considered as a human being, as a creature of *Humanität*, he has the seeds of immortality within him, and these require planting in another soil. As an animal he can satisfy his wants; there are men who wish for no more and hence can be perfectly happy here below. But those who seek a nobler goal find everything around them imperfect and incomplete, since the most noble has never been accomplished and the most pure has rarely endured on this earth. This is amply illustrated by the history of our species, by the many attempts and enterprises that man has undertaken, and by the events and revolutions that have overtaken him. Now and then a wise man, a good man, emerged to scatter ideas, precepts and deeds onto the flood of time. They caused but ripples on the waters, which the stream soon carried away and obliterated; the jewel of their noble purposes sank to the bottom. Fools overpowered the counsels of the wise and spend-thrifts inherited the treasures of wisdom collected by their fore-fathers . . . An animal lives out its life, and even if its years be too few to attain higher ends, its innermost purpose is accomplished;

its skills are what they are and it is what it is meant to be. Man alone of all creatures is in conflict with himself and with the world. Though the most perfect among them, in terms of potentialities, he is also the least successful in developing them to their fullest extent, even at the end of a long and active life. He is the representative of two worlds at once, and from this derives the apparent bipolarity of his nature.

It is not hard to see which part is likely to predominate in most men of this world. The greater part of man is his animal nature. He has brought into the world only a capacity for realizing his human essence (*Humanität*). It requires the utmost effort and diligence to transform this capacity into an operative principle of human behaviour. How few have achieved this, or been helped to achieve it, in the right manner! And how delicate and slender is the divine plant even in the best of us! Throughout life the brute strives to prevail over the man and there are not many who resist the former's dominance. It drags him down when his human spirit and his human heart crave for elevation and a freer sphere. And since the present appears more real and vivid to a sensual creature than the remote, since the visible affects him more powerfully than the invisible, it is not difficult to guess which way the balance tilts. Of how little pure joy, pure knowledge and virtue is man capable! . . . A man who has experienced things deeply, has also learned from them; the careless and indolent learns nothing. He is ignorant of himself and incapable of assessing his actual or potential abilities. Human life, then, is a conflict, and the realization of pure immortal humanity the hard-won crown of a ceaseless struggle . . .

This much is certain: in each of man's powers dwells an infinity which cannot be developed in his present state where it is repressed by other powers, by animal drives and appetites, and weighed down, as it were, by the pulls and pressures of our daily chores . . . The expression of Leibniz, that the mind is a mirror of the universe, contains perhaps a more profound truth than is commonly realized. For the powers of the universe that seem to lie concealed in the mind require only an organization, or a series of organizations, to set them in action . . . To the mind, even in its present fetters, *space* and *time* are empty concepts. They only measure and denote relations of the body and do not bear upon the internal capacity of the mind which transcends time and space . . .

BOOK VII

I. IN SPITE OF CONSIDERABLE DIFFERENCES BETWEEN MEN IN DIFFERENT PARTS OF THE WORLD, THERE IS BUT ONE AND THE SAME HUMAN SPECIES

[XIII, 252–8]

No two leaves of any one tree are exactly alike in nature; still less two human faces or two human constitutions. Of what endless variety is the intricate structure of our body capable! . . . 'No man', says Haller, 'is exactly similar to another in his internal structure; the system of the nerves and blood vessels differs in millions and millions of particulars, so that amidst the variations of these delicate parts, we are scarcely able to discover in what they agree.'* If the eye of the anatomist can perceive this infinite variety, what about the possibly even greater variety that may characterize the invisible powers inherent in so intricate an organization? Is not every man, in spite of his external resemblance to other men, in the last analysis (because of this uniquely individual internal structure) a cosmos in himself and, as such, a wholly incomparable being?

Yet man is not an independent entity. All elements of nature are connected with him. He cannot live without air, without nourishment from the many products of the soil, without other diverse foods, and without drink. And whilst he is thus formed and changed with the help of the universe around him, he, in turn, whether he be awake or asleep, at rest or in motion, contributes towards its change. As he makes use of fire, as he absorbs light and contaminates the air he breathes, he continually inter-acts with the elements of his environment. It is scarcely an exaggeration to compare him to an absorbing sponge, or to a glimmering tinder. Man constitutes a multitudinous harmony, a multiplicity and a unity, within his living self, acting, and acted upon, by the harmony of the forces surrounding him.

A man's life is one continuous series of change and its phases read like sagas of transformation. The species as a whole goes

* In his Preface to Part 3 of the German translation of Buffon's *Histoire Naturelle*, 1749–1804.

through a ceaseless metamorphosis. Flowers drop and wither; others sprout and bud. According to calculations based on perspiration, a man of eighty has renovated his whole body at least twenty-four times.* If this is so, who can trace the change of matter and its forms through the entire realm of mankind upon earth, by its diverse causes, when not a single point on our diversified globe and not a single wave in the stream of time is like any other? Only a few centuries ago the inhabitants of Germany were giants; but they are so no longer, and their inhabitants in future periods and climates will be equally unlike us . . . Thus the history of man is ultimately a theatre of transformations which only He, who animates these events and lives and feels Himself in all of them, can review . . .

But since the human understanding seeks unity in diversity, and since its prototype, the divine mind, has everywhere combined the greatest possible multiplicity with unity, we are brought back to our original proposition which simply asserted that, in spite of the vast realm of change and diversity, *all mankind is one and the same species upon earth.*

I wish the affinity of man to the ape had never been pushed so far as to overlook, while seeking a scale of Being, the actual steps and intervals, without which no scale can exist . . . Most of these apparent resemblances happen to be found in countries where apes never existed, as the reclining skulls of the Kalmucks and Mallicollese, the prominent ears of the Pevas and Amikwa, the small hands of some savages in Carolina, and other instances, show.[8] Moreover, as soon as one has got over first appearances, one finds that the resemblances are quite illusory and actually reveal very little that is of an ape-like nature. Kalmucks and Negroes are entirely human, including the structure of the head and the brain, and the Mallicollese display abilities that many other natives do not possess. It seems quite manifest that apes and men never were one and the same genus. I have yet to come across any

---

* According to Bernouilli. See Haller's *Elementa physiologiae corporis humani* 8 vol., Lausanne, 1757–1766, Vol. VIII, Bk. 30, which contains many observations on this point.

---

[8] Kalmucks. A branch of the Oirat Mongols, an Asiatic people. The Pevas and the Mallicollese are two South American tribes, and the Amikwa a North American tribe.

evidence that could verify the tiniest remnants of fables which purport that somewhere men and apes have formed sexual relations and lived in joint communities.* For each genus Nature has done her share and to each she has given its proper progeny. She has divided the ape into as many species and varieties as possible, and extended these as far as she could. But thou, o man, honour thyself: neither the pongo nor the gibbon is thy brother, but the American [Indian] and the Negro *are*. These, therefore, thou shouldst not oppress, or murder, or rob; for they are men like thee; with the ape thou canst not enter into fraternity.

Lastly, I should like to express the hope that distinctions that have been made—from a perfectly laudable zeal for scientific exactitude—between different members of the human species will not be carried beyond bounds. Some, for instance, have thought fit to employ the term *races* for four or five divisions, according to regions of origin or complexion. I see no reason for employing this term. Race refers to a difference of origin, which in this case either does not exist or which comprises in each of these regions or complexions the most diverse 'races'. For every distinct community is a *nation*, having its own national culture as it has its own language. The climate, it is true, may imprint on each its peculiar stamp, or it may spread over it a slight veil, without destroying, however, its original national character. This originality of character extends even to families and its transitions are as variable as they are imperceptible. In short, there are neither four or five races, nor exclusive varieties, on this earth. Complexions run into each other; forms follow the genetic character; and *in toto* they are, in the final analysis, but different shades of the same great picture which extends through all ages and all parts of the earth. Their study, therefore, properly forms no part of biology or systematic natural history but belongs rather to the anthropological history of man.

* In the *Aufzügen aus dem Tagebuch eines neuen Reisenden nach Asien* (Leipzig, 1784), this is asserted anew, still only from report.

II. THE HUMAN SPECIES HAS EVERYWHERE BEEN
EXPOSED TO, AND AFFECTED BY, CLIMATIC INFLUENCES

[XIII, 258–65]

. . . The Arab of the desert belongs to it as much as does his noble horse and his patient, indefatigable camel.* As the Mongol wanders over his heights and steppes, so does the Bedouin over his Afro-Asian deserts. Both are nomads, but each in *his own* region. The Bedouin's simple clothing, his mode of life, his manners and his character are adapted to the particular climate and region in which he lives. Even after the lapse of a thousand years, his tent still preserves the traditions of his forefathers . . ., and unless a foreign climate has gradually over a period begun to affect these, an Arab found on the Nile or the Euphrates, in Lebanon or Senegal, in Zanzibar or the islands of the Indian Ocean, will still display the characteristics that he originally acquired in the desert . . .

Some sensitive people feel so intimately close to their native country, are so much attached to its soil, that they can scarcely live if separated from it. The constitution of their body, their way of life, the nature of work and play to which they have been accustomed from their infancy, indeed their whole mentality, are climatic. Deprive them of their country, and you deprive them of everything.

'It has been found', reports Cranz, 'that six Greenlanders who were brought over to Denmark were exceedingly unhappy, in spite of all the friendly treatment they received and the plentiful supply of stockfish and train-oil. Their eyes frequently turned towards the North, towards their native country, with the most melancholic expressions and the most pitiful sighs. In the end they fled in their canoes . . .'†

No words can express the sorrow and despair of a bought or stolen Negro slave when he leaves his native shore, never to see it again in his life. 'Great care must be taken', says Römer, 'that the slaves do not get hold of a knife, neither before nor during the voyage. To keep them in good humour on their passage to the West Indies is indeed no easy task. To this end the usual European

---

* Besides the many ancient accounts of Arabia, see Pagès, Pierre Marie François de, *Voyages autour du monde . . . pendant les années 1767–1776*, 2 vol., Paris, 1782, vol. 2, pp. 62–87.

† Cranz, David, *Historie von Grönland . . .* Leipzig, 1765.

stock in trade is invoked. Drums and pipes are provided and dancing is permitted. The slaves are assured that they are going to a pleasant country, where they may have as many women as they want and plenty of good food. Yet many deplorable instances have been known of their attacking the crew, murdering them, and letting the ship run ashore.'* But how many more deplorable instances have been known of these poor kidnapped wretches committing suicide in their despair! . . . What gives you the right, you despicable slave-drivers, you inhuman brutes, even to approach the lands of these unfortunates, let alone to tear them away from it by cunning, fraud and cruelty? For ages these regions were theirs by heritage; it belonged to them just as they belonged to it. Their forefathers acquired it, paying the highest and heaviest price to preserve their integrity and the integrity of their kind: their Negro constitutions and Negro complexion . . .

The ferocious way the American natives are fighting for their country and for their brethren and children that have been deprived of it and cruelly degraded and oppressed, is another example worth citing. Even when the natives are reasonably well treated by the European, they feel cheated, and can scarcely conceal their hatred. 'You have no business here, for this land is ours', is a thought they cannot suppress. Hence the 'treachery' of all the so-called savages. They may appear docile enough, once they have been conquered by European arms or European diplomacy. But the very moment their inherited national feeling awakens again, the fire, that for so long had been assiduously kept smouldering in the ashes, will burst out into open flames. And it will in many cases not be extinguished until the flesh of the foreigner has been torn by the teeth of the natives. To us this seems horrible; and so it is, no doubt. Yet it was the European who first induced them to this monstrous deed. Why did they come to their country? Why did they enter it as despots, arbitrarily practicing violence and extortion?† For thousands of years it had

* Römer, Ludevig Ferdinand, *Nachrichten von der Küste Guinea*, Kopenhagen & Leipzig, 1769.
† See the editor's remarks on the unfortunate Marion's *Voyage à la Mer du Sud* [Crozet, Julien. *Nouveau voyage à la Mer du Sud, commencé sous les ordres de M. Marion* . . . Paris, 1783]; also Reinhold Forster's Preface to the *Tagebuch der letzten Cookschen Reise*, Berlin, 1781, and the Europeans' own accounts of their conduct.

been the universe to its inhabitants; they had inherited it from their fathers, together with the most ferocious determination to destroy in the most savage manner all who would deprive them of their land, tear them from, or cheat them out of it. The foreigner and the enemy seems to them one and the same thing. The native is like the *muscipula* which, rooted to its soil, attacks every insect that approaches it. But the right of devouring unwelcome and insulting guests is no more monstrous an institution than many a European excise duty.

Lastly, I cannot pass over the joyful scenes caused by the return of a Negro slave—this alienated son of nature—to his native land. When the worthy Negro priest, Job-Ben-Solomon returned to Africa, every Negro he met embraced him with brotherly affection, 'being only the second of their countrymen that had ever returned from slavery'.* How ardently he had longed for this moment! How little was his heart satisfied with all the tokens of friendship and respect which he had received in England, though as an enlightened and fair-minded man he had gratefully acknowledged them. He was not really at ease until he was certain of the ship that was to carry him home. This longing does not depend on the advantages and amenities that a man's native land has to offer him. The Hottentot Coree dispensed with all his European clothes and European refinements to share again the hard life of his kinsfolk.† Instances might be cited from almost any part of the world to show that often the most inhospitable countries have the strongest attraction for their natives. Hardships, or rather their challenge to mind and body from early youth on, inspire in the native (of desert or mountain areas) that love of country and climate, which the inhabitants of fertile and populous plains feel much less, and which the citizen of a European metropolis almost does not perceive at all any more. It is time, however, to enquire more closely into the term 'climate'. Whilst some philosophies of history have attached considerable importance to it and others have almost wholly denied its influence, I merely wish to pose some problems.

* *Allgemeine Historie der Reisen zu Wasser und Lande . . .*, 21 vol., Leipzig, 1747–74, Part 3, p. 127 ff.
† *Ibid.*, Part 5, p. 145. For other examples see Rousseau, in the notes to his *Discours sur l'inégalité parmi les hommes.*

III. WHAT IS CLIMATE? HOW DOES IT AFFECT MAN'S
MIND AND BODY?

[XIII, 265–73]

. . . We are still in the dark concerning the basis of the diverse
climates in different regions. One day, perhaps, the compass will
guide us in this sphere of physical powers as well as it has done—
quite unexpectedly—on sea and land for quite some time.

The revolution of our globe around its own axis and around
the sun enables us to classify climates more accurately. But the
application of even generally accepted laws proves more difficult
here and highly deceptive. The zones of the ancients have not been
confirmed by our later knowledge of foreign parts; they were
drawn up on the basis of their relative ignorance of physical
science. The same applies to mathematical calculations of heat and
cold which are based on measuring the quantity and angle of solar
rays. As a mathematical problem, the effect of these has been
industriously calculated with the greatest accuracy. But the
mathematician himself would consider it an abuse of his rule if the
philosopher of history, in dealing with the question of climate,
were to build conclusions on it, without admitting exceptions.*
In one place the proximity of the sea, in another the direction of
the wind, here the altitude of the land, there its vicinity to mountains, and so forth, necessitate so many local qualifications to the
general law, that we frequently find the most opposite climates in
places that closely border on each other. Moreover, recent
experiments have shown that every living being has its own mode
of receiving and emitting heat. Indeed it has been found that the
more complex the organic structure of a creature and the more
strongly it evidences the activity of an intrinsic life force, the greater
is its capacity of generating relative heat and cold.† The notion
that man can only live in a climate, the temperature of which does

* See Kästner, Abraham Gotthelf, 'Erläuterung der Halleyischen Methode,
die Wärme zu berechnen', in *Hamburgisches Magazin, oder Gesammelte
Schriften, aus der Naturforschung und den angenehmen Wissenschaften über-
haupt*, 26 vol., Hamburg, 1747–63, p. 429 ff.
† Crell, Lorenz Florenz Friedrich, *Versuch über das Vermögen der Pflanzen und
Thiere, Wärme zu erzeugen und zu vernichten*, Helmstadt, 1778. Crawford,
Adrian, 'Experiments on the Power of the Animals to produce Cold', in
Philosophical Transactions, Vol. LXXI, Part II, Art. 31.

not exceed that of his own bodily heat has been refuted by experience. On the other hand, modern theories about the origin and effect of animal heat are not perfected enough to justify our speaking in any way of a climatology of the human anatomy, let alone of a climatology of the human mind in its diverse and un-predictable operations. Everyone indeed knows that heat extends and relaxes the fibres, that it attenuates the fluids and promotes perspiration, so that it is capable in time of rendering solids slack and spongy, and so on. Without disputing the validity of this principle* (which in its application to cold, too, has helped to explain a number of physiological phenomena),† I would hesitate to deduce from it, or from any particular part of it (concerning relaxation or perspiration, for instance), general inferences applicable to whole nations and regions, nay to the most delicate functions of the human mind and the most contingent of social institutions. The more thoroughly and the more systematically we enquire into these matters, the more acutely we come to realize the doubtful value of sweeping generalizations. For we shall find them contradicted, step by step, by examples from history, or even by physiological principles. There are far too many forces at work, some of which, though opposed to each other, nonetheless operate in conjunction. Even the great Montes-quieu has been charged with erecting his climatic system of the spirit of the laws on the basis of inconclusive experiments carried out on a sheep's tongue. It is true that we are like pliable clay in the hand of Climate; but its fingers mould so variously, and the forces counteracting it, are so numerous, that perhaps only the genius of mankind is capable of combining the relations of all those forces into one basic equation.

Heat and cold are not the only forces of the atmosphere that act upon us, for the atmosphere is, according to recent researches, a vast store of other forces which combine with us to our detriment or advantage. Take, for example, electric currents, about the influence of which on man and the animal we as yet know very little. We are as ignorant about the forces inherent in electricity as

* See Gaubius, Hieronymus David, *Institutiones pathologiae medicinalis*, Lipsiae, 1771, chapts. v, x, etc., a logic of all pathologies.
† See Montesquieu, Castillon, Falconer; not to mention a number of less important writings, *Esprit des nations, Physique de l'histoire*, etc.

we are about the manner in which they are absorbed and worked up by the human body. We live by breathing air; but its balm, our vital food, is a mystery to us. If we now add the various and almost innumerable local modifications of its constituent elements caused by the diverse effluvia in different areas; if we bear in mind the instances of the most peculiar and frequently terrible diseases that have remained incurable over the ages and were caused by an invisible, malignant seed, to which the physician could give no other name than that of miasma; if we think of the secret poison that has brought us the smallpox, the plague, syphilis, and many other disorders which in the course of time have disappeared; if we consider how little we know not only of the *harmattan* and *simoon*, the *sirocco* and the north-east wind of Tartary, but also of the nature and power of our own winds, we cannot but realize how much preliminary research is yet to be done before we can arrive at a physiological pathology, to say nothing of a climatology, of man's powers of thought and feeling! In the meantime, every ingenious attempt deserves its laurels, and posterity will have many worthy ones to bestow on our times.*

We have to mention also the topographical characteristics of a region, its natural products, the food and drink men enjoy in it, the mode of life they pursue, their occupations, their clothing, even their habitual attitudes, their arts and amusements, and a host of other circumstances, which by their organic interaction palpably affect men's lives; all these belong to the picture of climate. What human hand can reduce this chaos of causes and effects to a world of order, in which every individual thing, and every individual region will be given its due, no more and no less? . . .

Since climate is a compound of forces and influences to which both plants and animals contribute, serving all that is alive within a relationship of mutual interaction, it stands to reason that man, too, has a share, nay a dominant role, in altering it through his creativity. By appropriating fire from Heaven and rendering iron obedient to his hand, by making not only animals but also his fellow men subservient to his will and by putting them, as well as plants, to his use, he has in several important ways participated in changing the environmental climate. Once Europe was a dank

* See Gmelin, Johann Friedrich, *Über die neueren Entdeckungen in der Lehre von der Luft* . . . Berlin, 1784.

forest and the same was true of other, now cultivated, regions. The forests have been cleared and, as a result, the climate and the inhabitants underwent a change. Without the creative skills of public administration, soil cultivation and architecture, Egypt would still be a mire of the Nile. It was reclaimed from the slime and both there and farther away, in Asia, natural creation has adapted itself to the artificially created climate. We may consider mankind, therefore, as a band of bold little giants, gradually descending from the mountains, to conquer the earth and change climates with their feeble hands. How far they are capable of going in this respect only the future will reveal.

. . . Finally: Climate promotes, but it does not compel, a given course of development. It imparts that elusive flavour which we can certainly detect within the total pattern of the life and manners of indigenous nations, but which it is exceedingly difficult to capture and isolate. One day, perhaps, a traveller may be found who will pursue without prejudice or exaggeration the *spirit of climate*. For the time being, it is our duty to note the living forces to which each climate is suited and which through their existence induce in it various changes and modifications.

IV. THE GENETIC FORCE IS THE MOTHER OF ALL CREATIONS ON EARTH: CLIMATE CAN ONLY CONTRIBUTE FAVOURABLY OR UNFAVOURABLY

[XIII, 273–7]

Imagine someone suddenly thrust into our world and faced with the wonder of seeing a living being coming into existence. How astonished he would be!* . . . What would he call it, seeing this wonder for the first time? This, he would say, is a *living organic force*. I cannot tell where it came from nor what it intrinsically is. But that it exists, that it lives, that it appropriated for itself organic parts out of the chaos of homogeneous matter: that I can see, that I cannot deny.

If he looked closer, he would discover that each of these organic parts was formed as it were *in actu*, by its own internal activity . . . If he observed this, would he not have to report that

---

* See Harvey, William, *Exercitationes de generatione animalium*, London, 1651. Cf. Wolff, Caspar Friedrich, *Theoria generationis*, Halle, 1759.

19-2

the invisible force did not operate arbitrarily, but that it rather *revealed* itself, as it were, according to its internal nature? This internal nature became visible, clothed in matter appropriate to itself, and must, therefore, be the *prototype of its appearance per se*, even if we cannot say how it formed or originated in the first place. The new creature is but the realization of a latent idea that was inherent in creative and forever actively thinking nature.

Let him continue his observations and he will find that, although the creative process is promoted by maternal or solar warmth and by the presence of material substances, these alone will produce no living fruit in the egg unless the latter has been fertilized by the paternal seed. Will our observer, therefore, not rightly infer that, whilst the principle of heat may certainly have an affinity to the principle of life, which it promotes, the cause which sets this organic force in action, to give the dead chaos of matter a living form, must actually lie in the union of two living beings? . . .

There is in all of us a vital force which assists us in sickness and in health, assimilates homogeneous substances, separates heterogeneous matter, and rejects the injurious. At length it grows feeble with age and lives in some parts even after death. Whatever this vital force intrinsically is, it is not the faculty of reason. For, assuredly, reason did not by itself fashion the body which it does not know and which it employs merely as an imperfect, extraneous tool of its thoughts. But whilst reason must not be identified with the life force, it is undoubtedly connected with it, since all forces of nature are connected. Its product, thought, is as much a force of nature, dependent on the health and organization of the body, as all the desires and propensities of our hearts, and inseparable from animal warmth. All these are natural *facts* which no hypothesis can shake and no scholastic logic can argue out of existence. Their recognition for what they are is basic to the most ancient philosophy of the world as it probably also is to the most recent.* I know for certain that I think, though I do not know the nature or source of my thinking power. I can see and feel with certainty that I am alive, yet I do not know the nature

---

* Hippocrates, Aristotle, Galen, Harvey, Boyle, Stahl, Glisson, Gaubius, Albinus, and many others of the greatest philosophers and observers of mankind, have, compelled by experiment, admitted this vital principle, only bestowing on it various appellations, or sometimes not sufficiently discriminating it from collateral powers.

and source of the life force. This vital power is innate, organic and genetic; it is the basis of my natural powers, the inner genius of my being. If the principles which we derive from incontestable experience are sound, it follows that all changes affecting man are organic in origin. Whatever the influence of the [external] climate, every man, every animal, every plant, has its own climate. For every living being absorbs all the external influences in a manner peculiar to itself and modifies them according to its organic powers.

V. CONCLUDING REMARKS ABOUT THE CONFLICT BETWEEN CLIMATE AND THE GENETIC FORCE

[XIII, 284–9]

If I am not mistaken, I have already, by what I have indicated so far, begun to draw the boundaries that mark the areas of conflict between climatic and genetic forces. No-one would, for example, expect that the rose should become a lily, or the dog a wolf in another climate. Nature has made them distinct genera, and prefers that they should perish rather than change so radically. But the rose can degenerate and the dog can acquire certain wolf-like characteristics. This lies in the nature of the historical process, and the mutation or degeneration always occurs as a result of more or less sudden and more or less violent changes effected by the opposing organic forces. Both contending forces exert considerable influence, yet each in its own manner. Climate is a chaos of heterogeneous elements, and hence acts in various ways. Gradually these diverse environmental elements penetrate the inner nature of a being, and bring about changes in its genetic and acquired characteristics. Its genetic life force, to be sure, offers resistance of varying duration and intensity in conformity to the uniqueness and inner homogeneity of its own organization. But as it is not independent of the heterogeneous external factors, it must accommodate itself to these in due course.

Instead of speculating about this conflict in general terms, I would prefer an instructive examination of particular cases, of which history and geography offer us a vast store. We know, for example, what effect the adoption of the mode of life of the natives, or the retention of their own European customs, has had in the

Portuguese colonies in Africa, or among the Spanish, Dutch, English and German settlers in America and the East Indies, and so on. Once all these cases were accurately investigated, one could then perhaps also attempt to investigate the more ancient trans-migrations, as for instance those of the Malays to the islands, of the Arabs to Africa and the East Indies, of the Turks to the countries conquered by them, and thus go on to the Mongols, the Tartars, and lastly the swarm of nations that covered Europe in the course of the great migration. One should, however, never overlook the climate from which a people came, the mode of life it brought with it, the country it settled in, the natives it mixed with, and the mutations it has undergone in its new abode. If these investigations were undertaken concerning those ages of which we have authentic records, we could probably arrive at some conclusions concerning the earlier migrations, of which we know only from the traditional tales of ancient writers or from coinci-dences of language and mythology. For there can be little doubt that most, if not all, nations changed their abode at some time or another. Thus, with the assistance of maps, we should obtain a *physico-geographical history of the descent and diversification of our species* according to periods and climates, which, step by step, should yield important results.

Without anticipating the labours of those enquiring spirits that might undertake this task, I will set forth a few empirical general-izations drawn from recent history. They may help to illustrate my preceding observations.

1. *Too sudden, too precipitate transitions to an opposite hemisphere and climate rarely benefit a nation,* for nature has not established boundaries between distant countries in vain. The history of conquests, of commercial companies and, above all, of missions, affords a melancholy, and in some respects a comic picture, if it is treated impartially both in its origins and consequences, even if we base it on records of participants in these various undertakings. We shudder with horror, when we read the accounts of many a European nation as it degenerated in body and mind in its affluence, arrogance, and insensitive pride, capable of neither enjoyment nor compassion. Bloated larvae in human form, lost to every active and noble pastime, they are creatures in whose veins lurks avenging death . . .

2. *Even in colonies where conditions did not deteriorate to so base a level, European enterprise was not always able to avert the effects of climate.* It is observed by Kalm that though the Europeans in North America arrive earlier at the age of puberty, they also grow old and die sooner than in their native country* . . . The women cease to bear children as early as the age of thirty, and the children born to them in the colonies tend to lose their teeth prematurely, in contrast to the native Americans [the Indians] whose teeth remain white and sound to the end of their lives . . .

3. *Let it not be thought, that man can by the sheer power of his will and by the application of his skills arbitrarily turn any foreign region into a second Europe.* By suddenly cutting down entire forests and cultivating the soil, the whole balance of nature—which ought to be considered with the utmost care—is disturbed. . . . The rapid destruction of the woods and the cultivation of the land in America not only lessened the number of edible birds which were originally found in vast quantities in the forests and on lakes and rivers, and the supply of fish; it not only diminished the lakes, streams and springs, but it also seemed to affect the health and longevity of the inhabitants. 'The Americans', Kalm reports, 'frequently lived a hundred years and upwards before the arrival of the Europeans. Now they rarely attain half the age of their forefathers. We must not attribute this, however, solely to the destructive effects of alcoholic spirits or to their altered way of life, but likewise to the loss of many odoriferous herbs and nourishing plants, which perfumed the air in the mornings and evenings as if the whole country had been a flower garden . . .' Although this account refers to a particular region only, it demonstrates that nature does not favour too rapid and violent changes, even if the aim, the cultivation of the soil, is a perfectly laudable one. May we not also attribute the feebleness of the so-called civilized Indians of Mexico, Peru, Paraguay and Brazil to the fact that, among other things, we have changed their country and mode of life, without being able or willing to give them a European nature? All those who have continued to live in the forests, after the manner of their forefathers, have remained strong and bold;

---

* Kalm, Per, *Beschreibung der Reise die er nach dem nördlichen Amerika . . . unternommen hat*, 3 vols., Göttingen, 1754–64 *passim.*

they live long and flourish like their trees. Those living in the cultivated areas, however, deprived of shade and moisture, decline miserably; their spirit and their courage left them with the trees . . . Such drastic changes of the natural environment may yield beneficial results in some places in the course of centuries, though I have my doubts even there. But for the first generations of both the civilizers and those to be civilized it appears to have none. For Nature is everywhere a living whole, expecting to be gently followed or improved, but not mastered by force . . .

O sons of Dedalus, emissaries of Fate upon earth, how many instruments were in your hands to confer happiness on nations by humane and decent means! But a proud, insolent love of gain led you almost everywhere into a different path. All newcomers from foreign lands who learned to adapt themselves to the situation they found by becoming native, as it were, not only came to enjoy the love and friendship of the original inhabitants, but also came to realize that their mode of life was not altogether unsuitable to their climate. Alas, there were not many of them! How rarely do we hear natives praising a European for being as reasonable as they themselves! Nature seems to avenge every insult inflicted upon her. Where are the conquests, the scenes of activity of former times, when remote foreign lands were invaded for no purpose other than their devastation and plunder? The still breath of climate has dissipated or consumed them, and it was easy enough for the natives to give the last push to the rootless tree. The quiet plant, on the other hand, which had accommodated itself to the laws of nature, has not only endured, but it has also succeeded in diffusing the seeds of culture in a beneficial manner. The next thousand years may decide what benefit or injury our genius has conferred on other climates, and other climates on our genius.

BOOK VIII

I feel like one who has taken to the air having learned only to navigate at sea if, having so far dwelt mainly on the physical structure and powers of man, I now venture to explore the workings of the mind and to investigate its diverse manifestations on earth from the admittedly indirect, defective and partly question-able accounts at our disposal. Here the metaphysician has the advantage. He starts out with a concept of the mind and deduces from it everything that can be deduced, wherever, or under what-ever circumstances it may be found. The philosopher of history cannot start off with an abstraction; his views must be firmly grounded in historical facts. At the same time he has to connect the innumerable facts within some generalizing framework in order to arrive at relatively meaningful conclusions. In charting my course, therefore, I shall not attempt to survey the world from an airship, nor to walk it by land, but instead coast along the shores. In plain language: I shall stick to undoubted facts, or at least to those generally accepted as such, distinguish them from my own conjectures, and leave it to my more fortunate successors to arrange and employ them in a better manner.

I. THE SENSUAL NATURE OF MAN CHANGES IN
CONFORMITY TO STRUCTURAL AND CLIMATIC FACTORS:
BUT ITS TRULY HUMAN APPLICATION RENDERS IT
UNIVERSALLY CAPABLE OF PROMOTING 'HUMANITÄT'

[XIII, 291–5]

All nations, with the possible exception of the albinos, possess the five or six senses commonly attributed to man. Yet we do not have to look far to observe how differently people respond to the same external stimuli. If this is so among ourselves, how much more so if we include the countless multitudes living under all the climates of the earth? We are faced, then, with an ocean where wave loses itself in wave. Every individual has a particular proportion, a particular harmony, as it were, between all his sense percep-tions . . . Even in the clearest sense, that of sight, these differences reveal themselves, not only with respect to distance, but also to the form and colour of things. Hence we find that almost every painter sees outlines in his own particular way and differs from every other in his particular style of colouring. It is not the task of a philosophy of history to exhaust this ocean of diversity, but merely to call attention to the most striking distinctions in the hope of making us more sensitive to the many subtle and elusive ones surrounding us.

The most general and most essential sense is the sense of touch. It is the basis of all the other senses and constitutes in man his most distinctive organic characteristic.* It has conferred on him all kinds of amenities, inventions and artistic skills, and contributes perhaps more to the formation of our ideas than we imagine. But how differently developed is this sense among the different peoples, according to its modification by the way of life, the climate, the genetic sensitivity of the body and the manner in which its powers are exercised and employed . . . Thus stoic apathy under bodily pain is to some a matter of natural habit, as a result of which many subjugated nations appear as in a waking dream. What brutes, therefore, are those who, from a still greater lack of human feeling, have abused, or put to painful trials, a want which nature bestowed on the former for their solace and comfort!

. . . What are the objects of our [European] obsession for ever-increasing luxury, which compels us to disturb and exploit all the other continents? New and pungent spices for a blunted palate; foreign fruits and foreign dishes the flavour of which we do not really appreciate since we often jumble everything up in a tasteless medley; intoxicating liquors that deprive us of our senses and our peace; in short, anything that one can think of to destroy our nature by over-excitement is the great goal of our daily lives. In this manner the [European] nations are to achieve happiness. In this manner class-distinctions are to be recognizably determined. But whose happiness are we talking about? Why do the poor suffer hunger, and with benumbed senses drag on a wretched life of toil and labour? To enable the rich and the great to deaden their senses in a more refined though tasteless manner and thus daily provide ever-increasing nourishment for their probably boundless brutality. Yet it is hardly feasible that nature has given us a tongue, so that the gratification of a few papillae on it should be the aim of a toilsome life, or the cause of wretchedness to others . . .

* See Metzger, Johann Daniel, *J. D. Metzgers vermischte medicinische Schriften*, 3 vols., Königsberg, 1782–84, vol. III.

II. THE HUMAN IMAGINATION IS SUBJECT TO ORGANIC
AND CLIMATIC FACTORS, BUT IT IS UNIVERSALLY
GUIDED BY TRADITION

[XIII, 299–309]

Of a thing that lies outside the sphere of our perception we can scarcely form a conception. The story of the Siamese king who considered ice and snow as non-things is in a thousand instances applicable to mankind as a whole. The conceptions of every indigenous people are confined to its own region. If it professes to understand words expressing things utterly foreign to it, we have cause to question the reality of this understanding.

. . . Compare the mythology of Greenland with that of India, the Lapp with the Japanese, the Peruvian with Negro mythology: it will provide you with a complete geography of the inventing mind. If the Voluspa of the Icelander were read and expounded to a Brahmin, he would scarcely be able to form a single conception from it; and to the Icelander the Veda would be equally unintelligible.

Why is this so? Have all the different nations invented their own mythology and thus become attached to it as their own property? By no means. They have not invented it; they *inherited* it. Had they produced them as a result of some deep thought, some further deep thought might well have improved on them. But this has not been so . . .

As I see it, the key to the mystery lies in this: were all notions as clear to us as those which we acquire by sight, and had we no other ideas than those which we derive from visual objects or can compare with them, the source of error and deception would soon be eliminated since it would be easily discoverable. Most national myths are, however, stories that reach our *ears*. The ignorant child listens with curiosity to the tales which flow into his mind like his mother's milk, and seem to explain to him what he has seen . . . Where there is movement in nature, where a thing seems to live and change without the eye being able to discern the laws of this change, the ear hears words which explain to it by something unseen the mystery of what is seen. The power of the imagination is aroused and releases by its own imagining the tension that existed before. The ear is in general the most timid and apprehensive of all the senses. It perceives things with great

299

intensity, yet obscurely; it cannot retain or compare them to render them clear, for they pass by at a bewildering rate. Designed to arouse the mind, it can rarely instruct it with clarity without the aid of the other senses, particularly the eye.

We find that the imagination is particularly vivid among peoples who live in solitude, or inhabit wild regions, the desert, rocky country, the stormy coast, the foot of volcanoes, or other areas full of movement and wonders. The deserts of Arabia have given birth from earliest times to the most sublime myths and those who cherished them have been for the most part solitary men filled with wonder and amazement. In solitude Mohammed began his Koran. His heated imagination caused him to imagine himself in Heaven where, in his ecstasy, he saw all the angels, saints and worlds . . . To what extent has the superstition of shamanism spread! It is true that it has been suppressed in Asian countries by religious and political cultures of a more positivist and sophisticated type; yet where it could appear again, in solitude or among the populace, it did so. The worship of Nature has gone round the globe. It manifested itself in the most diverse fancies according to those local circumstances which occasioned the most intense fear and horror of the powers of nature affecting our human needs. In ancient times it was the worship of almost all the nations on earth.

That the way of life and the genius of each nation have decidedly influenced the emergence and propagation of myths scarcely needs mentioning. The shepherd sees nature with different eyes than the fisherman and hunter. What is more, even these occupations differ with every region and are as divergent in their actual form as the diverse national characters . . . In short, the mythology of every people is an expression of their own distinctive way of viewing nature. The extent to which they found good or evil to prevail in nature and, in particular, how they sought to account for the one by means of the other, was essentially determined by their climate and their creative genius. Even in its most fanciful and absurd features, mythology is a philosophical essay of the human mind which dreams before it is awake, and which is readily inclined to revert to its state of infancy.

It is generally maintained that angekkoks,[9] conjurers, magicians,

---

[9] Eskimo conjurers.

shamans and priests invented myths to blind the people. By dismissing them as cheats one is inclined to think that one has explained everything. They may well have been cheats in many or most places, but this should not induce us to forget that they themselves were people too, and the dupes of myths older than themselves. They were born and brought up in a tribal setting permeated by traditional beliefs. Their consecration was attended by fasting, solitude, exhaustion of body and mind, and all this helped to excite their imagination. No one became a magician, until the spirit moved him to do for others what he had hitherto been doing in solitude. The work he was to perform for the rest of his life by repeated exaltations of his mind and fatigues of his body had ripened within him earlier. The most sceptical travellers have been amazed by the conjuring tricks they saw because they could not think it possible that the power of the imagination could successfully produce effects which they frequently found wholly inexplicable. Of all the powers of the human mind the imagination has been least explored, probably because it is the most difficult to explore. Being connected with the general structure of the body, and with that of the brain and nerves in particular—as many diseases remarkably reveal—it seems to be not only the basic and connecting link of all the finer mental powers, but, indeed, the knot that ties body and mind together. It is one of the first things that are passed down from parents to children . . .

The question of the existence of innate ideas has long been a subject of dispute. As these terms are usually understood, the answer must certainly be in the negative. But if we take them to refer to a predisposition to receive, connect and extend certain ideas and images, there seems a great deal to be said in favour of such a postulate and very little against it . . . The history of nations will show how Providence has employed this organic predisposition, as a result of which man's imagination can be so easily, yet so powerfully, influenced. But it will show also to our horror how deceit or despotism has abused it by rendering the limitless ocean of the human imagination and fancy subservient to its purposes . . .

III. THE PRACTICAL UNDERSTANDING OF MAN HAS ALWAYS
DEVELOPED IN ACCORDANCE WITH THE REQUIREMENTS OF
HIS PARTICULAR WAY OF LIFE: AT THE SAME TIME IT IS ALSO
THE BLOSSOM OF A PEOPLE'S GENIUS AND THE SON OF
TRADITION AND CUSTOM

[XIII, 310–18]

It is customary to divide the nations of the world into hunters, fishermen, shepherds and farmers, not only to determine accordingly their level of cultural development, but also to suggest that culture as such is a necessary corollary of a given occupation or mode of life. This would be most admirable, provided the diverse modes of life were defined in the first place. Since these, however, vary with almost every region and for the most part overlap, it is exceedingly difficult to apply such a classification with accuracy. The Greenlander who strikes the whale, hunts the reindeer and kills the seal, is engaged in both hunting and fishing, yet in quite a different manner from that of the Negro fisher or the Arancoan hunter. The Bedouin and the Mongol, the Lapp and the Peruvian are shepherds; but how greatly do they differ from each other, with one pasturing camels, the other horses, the third reindeer, and the last alpacas and llamas. The farmers of Whidoh are as unlike those of Japan as the merchants of England are to those of China.

Moreover, cultural development or progress does not solely or even necessarily depend on the stimulation of material needs. There may be ample powers and resources in a nation waiting to be developed to meet its needs, but there may be no urgency felt about doing so. Such is human indolence, at times, that it can easily come to terms with material deficiencies and thus married, as it were, produce an offspring by the name of Convenience. Man can remain in this condition for considerable periods and may only with difficulty be impelled to work for improvement. Thus the mode of life of a people comes to be determined one way or another by influences and circumstances other than those constituting its material requirements . . .

That men have learned most of their arts and crafts from nature and from animals seems to be beyond doubt . . . The hunter clothes himself like the game he pursues, and takes lessons in architecture from the beaver of his lakes. Others build their huts like nests on the ground or, like birds, fix them on trees. The beak of the bird was the model for arrows and spears; the form of the canoe was modelled on that of the fish. From the snake men learned the pernicious art of poisoning their weapons. The singularly widespread custom of painting the body was likewise an imitation of birds and beasts . . . The North Americans relate with gratitude that maize was brought to them by a bird, and the use of most indigenous medicines was apparently learned from animals. To be sure, all these adaptations required the perceptive spirit of free children of Nature who, living among animals, did not yet consider themselves infinitely exalted above them. For Europeans it is difficult even to discover what the natives in other continents find of use in their daily life. After many attempts of their own, they find themselves compelled in the end to obtain the secret from the natives either by force or entreaty.

Incomparably greater progress was made as soon as man succeeded in taming and domesticating animals. The immense difference between neighbouring nations living with or without these auxiliaries to their powers is truly striking. Why was it that America, on its first discovery, was so far behind the old world, and hence was no match for the Europeans who could treat its inhabitants like a flock of defenceless sheep? It was not chiefly a matter of sheer physical power and agility . . ., nor a question of intelligence . . . It was due to differences in the possession of crafts and skills, weapons, communications but, above all, to the absence of domesticated animals. Had the American only possessed the horse, the warlike majesty of which he tremblingly acknowledged, or fierce dogs like those which the Spaniard sent against him as fellow mercenaries of his Catholic Majesty, the conquest would have been far more costly. A nation of horsemen would at least have been able to retreat to the mountains, deserts and plains. Even now all travellers report that the horse makes the greatest single difference between the peoples of America. The horsemen in the northern parts, and still more in the most southern parts, are so superior to the conquered wretches of Mexico and Peru, that one would scarcely believe them to be neighbouring sons of the same continent . . .

The notion of private property, entailing the distinction between mine and thine, is a direct corollary of the introduction of agriculture which confined men to separate holdings . . . Generally speaking, no mode of life has effected so great a transformation in the minds of men as this parcelling out of land. Agriculture promoted the development of all kinds of special arts and crafts, of villages and towns, and facilitated the emergence of government and law. But, in so doing, it also paved the way for a despotism of the most terrifying kind. Now that every man was restricted to a fixed area of land, he was not hard to find, and it did not take governments long to realize this. In the end everyone was told exactly what he was permitted to do or to be on his allotted piece. The soil no longer belonged to man, but man to the soil . . .

IV. THE FEELINGS AND STRIVINGS OF MAN CONFORM EVERYWHERE TO HIS PHYSICAL ORGANIZATION AND THE CONDITIONS IN WHICH HE LIVES: BUT AT THE SAME TIME THEY ARE GOVERNED BY CUSTOM AND OPINION

[XIII, 319–33]

Everything that exists strives towards self-preservation; from the grain of sand to the solar system it strives to remain what it is . . .

Because of this instinct of self-preservation, some philosophers have inferred that man is a beast of prey and that the state of war is natural to him. This, evidently, is open to question. Man, it is true, is a robber, in picking the fruit from the tree; a murderer in killing an animal, and the greatest oppressor on the face of the earth, in that with every breath and with every step he destroys perhaps millions of invisible living things . . . But, leaving such speculative subtleties aside, let us consider man among his brethren. Is he by nature a beast of prey towards his fellows, is he an unsocial being? To judge by his physical constitution, he certainly does not qualify to be the former; and the circumstances of his birth make the latter even less likely. Conceived in love and nourished by affection, he is reared by his fellows who bestow on him a thousand kindnesses that he does little to earn. In this sense man is actually formed in and for society, without which he could neither have come into existence, nor grown to maturity. He starts to be unsociable when his own natural interests clash with those of other men. In this he wholly conforms to the great and universal principle of self-preservation, and hence is no different from any other being. But even here Nature has done her best to minimize the conflict and prevent a war of all against all. We may briefly mention some of her devices towards this end.

1. . . . . Men's dispositions, sensations and desires being so infinitely diversified makes it less likely for human pursuits to collide. What attracts one may be of little or no interest to the other . . .

2. Nature has provided ample space for men to develop their diverse interests under the most varied climates and modes of life . . .

3. Nature shortened, as far as she could, the time men must live together . . . It was not her object to crowd her children together but rather to encourage their diffusion . . .

Peace, then, and not war is the natural state of unoppressed humanity. War arises from exceptional pressures, from emergency situations, but not from a sense of enjoyment, a love of fighting. In the hand of Nature it is never an end (even cannibalism is no exception), but merely a severe and regrettable expedient, with which even the mother of all things could not entirely dispense . . .

Before we proceed to inquire further into the seeds of human enmity, let us dwell briefly on its more appealing opposite, human love. The whole world is its domain, yet everywhere it manifests itself in different forms.

. . . The age of puberty differs astonishingly in different regions and modes of life. The Persian female marries at eight and becomes a mother in her ninth year. Among the ancient Germans a woman attained the age of thirty before she thought of love.

. . . Since woman is the most tender plant of our earth, and love the most powerful motive force in Creation, the manner in which she is treated is a crucial criterion in the critical analysis of human history. Woman has everywhere been the first object of contentious desire and by her very nature the weakest cornerstone in the human edifice . . . There is, in my view, no circumstance which so decisively reveals the character of a man, or a nation, as the treatment of women . . .

. . . The feeling of paternal love is the basis of a tribal sense of honour and virtue; it makes possible an education that is both social and continuous and thus acts as an instrument for transmitting the values and prejudices of successive generations. Hence in almost all nations and tribes the attainment of manhood by the son is an occasion for joyful celebration . . ., just as the loss of a son causes the deepest sorrow to the father, for whom he was the proudest hope. Read the lamentations of the Greenlander upon losing his son,* listen to the wailings of Ossian on the death of his Oscar, and you will perceive in them the bleeding wounds of the paternal heart, the noblest wounds of the manly breast.

The grateful love of the son for his father is certainly but a slight return for the affection with which the father has loved him. But this, too, is the design of nature. As soon as the son becomes a father his affection centres on his children: it flows downward rather than upward. And this is as it should be. For only thus the growing chain of successive generations is maintained . . .

Finally we come to the third and most noble bond of man, *friendship*. Shared perils give rise to common fortitude and provide the most effective and lasting ties of social relationships. In countries and modes of life in which circumstances necessitate social co-operation, we invariably come across heroic minds devoted to the bonds of friendship through life and death. Of this there are many examples in the heroic ages of Greece, in Scythia, among all the hunting and warring peoples, in forests and deserts. In our days relationships are more remote: the links between bankers, intellectuals or civil servants are a far cry from the freely-chosen and intimate bonds of friendship between wanderers, prisoners and slaves. Even the farmer knows only a neighbour, the craftsman a fellow-worker, whom he helps or envies. Yet even now in times of need and common calamities minds unite . . . Indeed, the bloodiest wars that disgrace humanity, often spring from noble motives grounded in friendship between peoples and from a shared sense of injury committed against their honour.

I shall postpone a further discussion of this subject until I shall have occasion to speak of political government. Nothing I have said so far, however, helps to account for the existence of sovereigns, both male and female; nothing helps to explain why one man should rule over thousands of his brethren, merely by virtue of his birth; why he should exact from them obedience to his will without any contractual responsibilities, limitations,

* See the *Volkslieder* [edited by Herder], 2 vols., Leipzig, 1778 79, vol. 2, p. 128.

and controls, and be in a position to send thousands of them to death; to squander public funds without rendering any account, and to impose the heaviest tax burdens on the poorest members of his realm. We are even less capable of deducing from the original dispositions of Nature why a bold and valiant people, that is, thousands of worthy men and women, frequently kiss the feet of a weak creature, or worship the sceptre with which a madman tears the flesh from their bones. What god or demon has possessed them to submit their reason and faculties, nay frequently their lives and entire rights as men, to the will of one, and deem it their greatest joy and happiness that the despot should beget a future despot? Since all these phenomena appear to me at first sight to be the most puzzling enigma of humanity, and since fortunately they are unknown to the greater part of the globe, I feel justified in excluding them from an account of the first and most basic universal laws of nature concerning mankind. Husband and wife, father and son, friend and foe: these are determinate relations and meaningful words. But concepts such as leader, king, hereditary legislator and judge, arbitrary ruler and sovereign of states, associated with one person and his unborn heirs, require a different kind of exposition. Our purpose up to now has been to consider the earth as a nursery of natural dispositions and endowments, skills and crafts, mental powers and aspirations, in their considerable variety. Let us now inquire to what extent these enable man, or even entitle him, to enjoy happiness, and by what standards it may be measured.

V. THE HAPPINESS OF MAN IS INVARIABLY AN INDIVIDUAL GOOD: CONSEQUENTLY IT IS EVERYWHERE CLIMATIC AND ORGANIC AND THE CHILD OF PRACTICE, TRADITION AND CUSTOM

[XIII, 333–42]

The very concept of 'happiness' implies that man is capable of neither experiencing nor creating pure and lasting bliss. He is the child of chance; it is a matter of luck where he comes to live, when and under what circumstances. The country, the time, the total constellation of circumstances *happen* to decide both his capacity of enjoyment and the manner and measure of his joys and sorrows.

It would be presumptuous and foolish to imagine that all inhabitants of the world have to be Europeans in order to live happily. Would we ourselves have become what we are outside Europe? He who placed us here, and others there, gave to them as much right to happiness in this life as he gave to us. Happiness is an internal state; its standard or determination, therefore, is not outside ourselves but rather within the breast of every individual. No other person has the right to constrain me to feel as he does, nor the power to impart to me his mode of perception. No other person can, in short, transform my existence and identity into his . . .

We boast of the refinement of our mental powers; but let us learn from sad experience that every refinement does not promote happiness. Indeed some instruments become unfit for use by over-refinement. Speculative thought, for instance, can form the pleasure of only a few men of leisure, and even for them it is often what opium is for the oriental, an enervating, deceptive and stupefying form of pseudo-pleasure . . . Think not, sons of men, that a premature, disproportionate refinement or education constitutes happiness; or that the dead nomenclature of all the sciences and the pretentious parading of all the arts will help you in any way to enjoy life. The feeling of happiness is not acquired from words learned by rote, or a knowledge of the arts. A head stuffed with knowledge, even golden knowledge, oppresses the body, restricts the breast, dims the eye, and adds a morbid burden to one thus afflicted . . . Let us thank Providence, therefore, for refraining from over-indulgence in its distribution of refinement and from the treatment of mankind as a lecture audience and the world as a vast academy of the sciences . . .

Since our well-being is a quiet feeling rather than a brilliant thought, our lives are far more enriched with love and joy caused by the feelings of the heart rather than by the profound deliberations of reason . . . Every living being enjoys its existence; it does not inquire into, or brood over, the reasons of its existence. Its purpose is intrinsic to itself. No savage commits suicide, no animal destroys itself. They propagate their species without knowing why, and submit to every toil and exertion under the severest climate merely in order to live. This simple, deep-rooted feeling of existence, this something *sui generis* is happiness . . .

If I am not mistaken, a few lines could be sketched on the basis of these simple postulates (the truth of which seems self-evident enough) that would bear upon at least some of the doubts and fallacies concerning the destination of the human species. What, for example, is it supposed to mean that man, as we know him here, was formed for the infinite development and growth of his mental powers, for a progressive extension of his perceptions and actions? Does it mean—as some would have it—that he was made for the state? Or, that the individual existed merely for the good of the species, that he, his generation, and all subsequent generations were expected to forgo happiness for the benefit of posterity? The sight of our fellow-beings, nay even the experience of every single human being, contradicts this alleged plan of creative Providence.[10] Neither our head nor our heart is formed for an infinitely increasing store of thoughts and feelings, neither a part nor the whole of us is made to this end; our entire life is not geared for it. Do not our finest mental powers decay as well as flourish? Do they not fluctuate with years and circumstances? Who has not found that an unlimited extension of his feelings serves only to weaken and destroy them? It is impossible for us to love others more or otherwise than ourselves, for we love them only as part of ourselves, or rather ourselves in them. That mind which, like a superior spirit, embraces much within its sphere of activity as part of itself, achieves real happiness, whilst one which over-extends its feelings is bound to dissipate them into mere words and reaps nothing but misery for itself and everybody else. The savage who loves himself, his wife and child, with quiet joy, and in his modest way works for the good of his tribe, as for his own life, is, in my opinion, a truer being than that shadow of a man, the refined citizen of the world, who, enraptured with the love of all his fellow-shadows, loves but a chimera. The savage in his poor hut has room for every stranger; he receives him as his brother without even inquiring where he comes from. His hospitality is unostentatious, yet warm and sincere. The inundated heart of the idle cosmopolite, on the other hand, offers shelter to nobody . . .

---

[10] This refers especially to Kant who, in his *Idee zu einer allgemeinen Geschichte in weltbürgerlicher Absicht*, argues that the individual exists for the good of the species. Herder, by contrast, maintains that the striving for happiness is a process concerning the individual alone, where the *telos* does not lie beyond, but rather within the compass of, his own life.

I find it hard to believe that man should have been made for the state and that his happiness springs from its institution. For how many peoples of the world are entirely ignorant of this institution and yet are happier than a good many devoted servants of the state? I shall not elaborate upon the advantages and disadvantages which these artificial institutions of society bring in their train. However, it may be observed that, since every artefact is merely a tool, and since the most refined tool necessarily demands the most careful and discriminating handling, it stands to reason that, with the increasing size of states and the greater complexity and intricacy of their institutions, the danger of rendering individuals miserable is infinitely augmented. In some large states hundreds have to go hungry that one may feast and make merry; thousands are oppressed and hunted to death, that one crowned fool or philosopher may gratify his whims. Since we are told by the political scientist that every well constituted state must be a machine regulated only by the will of one, can there conceivably be any greater bliss than to serve in this machine as an unthinking component? What, indeed, can be more satisfying than to be whirled round all our lives on Ixion's wheel, contrary to our better knowledge and conscience, with no comfort other than that of being relieved of the exercise of our free and self-determining mind in order to find happiness in functioning as insensible cogs in a perfect machine? O, if we be men, let us thank Providence for not imposing on us a universal aim of that kind. Millions on this globe live without states. But even those who do have them, and have them in the most perfected form imaginable, must nonetheless, if they crave for happiness, start where the primitive peoples start: they must discover and maintain the sources of health in mind and body and of happiness in the individual and the family, within *themselves*, for they will not find them in the state. Father and mother, husband and wife, son and brother, friend and man: these are natural relationships in which we may be happy. The state can give us many ingenious contrivances; unfortunately it can also deprive us of something far more essential: our own selves.

Providence meant well, therefore, in giving preference to the natural attainment of happiness by individuals rather than to the attainment of the more complex ends required by unnaturally large societies, and thus saved generations as much as possible from the institution of these costly state machines. It has separated nations, not only by forests and mountains, seas and deserts, rivers and climates, but also, and more significantly, by languages, propensities and characters. And it did so in order to render the work of subjugation and despotism more difficult, to prevent all the four quarters of the globe being swallowed up within the belly of one giant wooden horse. No Nimrod has succeeded so far in driving all the inhabitants of the world into one meadow for his own use and that of his dynasty. And although it has for centuries been the aim of European alliances to impose their notion of happiness despotically on all the other nations of the earth, this happiness-dispensing deity is still far from having obtained her end . . . Men of all the quarters of the globe, who have perished over the ages, you have not lived solely to manure the earth with your ashes, so that at the end of time your posterity should be made happy by European culture. The very thought of a superior European culture is a blatant insult to the majesty of Nature.

If happiness is to be found on this earth, it has to be looked for within every sentient being. Every man has the standard of happiness within himself. He carries it within the form in which he has been fashioned, and it is only within this sphere that he can be happy . . .

BOOK IX

I. EAGER THOUGH MAN IS TO IMAGINE HIMSELF SELF-MADE, HE IS NONETHELESS DEPENDENT ON OTHERS IN THE DEVELOPMENT OF HIS CAPACITIES

[XIII, 343–8]

Philosophers have exalted human reason to a position of supremacy, independent of the senses and organs. But just as there is no such thing as an isolated faculty of reason, so there is no man who has become all he is entirely by his own efforts, as he is wont to imagine in his dream of life . . . Upon returning, however, from the world of fantasy to the world of empirical reality he, and the philosopher, cannot but recognize that the whole chain of human development is characterized by man's dependence on his fellows.

This indeed is the essence of the history of mankind: without it no such history could exist. Did man receive everything from himself, and develop everything independently of external circumstances, we might have a history of *one* man, but not of man as a species. Since our specific character derives from being born almost without instinct, it is only by training and experience that our lives as men take shape; they determine both the perfectibility and the corruptibility of our race. Thus the history of mankind is necessarily a whole, *i.e.* a chain formed from the first link to the last by the moulding process of socialization and tradition.

We can speak, therefore, of an education of mankind. Every individual only becomes man by means of education, and the whole species lives solely as this chain of individuals. To be sure, if anyone, in speaking of the education of mankind, should mean the education of the species as a whole and not that of so many individuals comprising it, he would be wholly unintelligible to me. For 'species' and 'genus' are merely abstract concepts, empty sounds, unless they refer to individual beings. Thus, if I were to attribute to such abstract concepts every perfection, culture and enlightenment of which man is capable, I should contribute to the actual history of man no more than if I were to speak of animal-kind, stonekind and metalkind in general, and decorate them with all the noblest qualities which, if they really existed, in any one single individual or entity, would cancel each other out.

Our philosophy of history shall not pursue the path of the Averroan system,[11] according to which the whole human species possesses but one mind (and that of a low order), which is distributed to individuals only piecemeal. On the other hand, were I to confine everything to the individual and deny the existence of the chain that connects one to the other and to the whole, I should equally fail to come to grips with the nature of man and his actual history. For no one of us became man by himself alone. The whole structure of man's humanity is connected by a spiritual genesis— education—with his parents, teachers and friends, with all the circumstances of his life, and hence with his countrymen and fore-

---

[11] Averroism. The doctrine of the Arab philosopher Averrhoes (1126–98) that the soul is perishable, the only immortal soul being the world soul from which individual souls went forth and to which they return.

fathers. Indeed, in the last analysis, he is connected with the whole chain of the human species, since some links of this chain inevitably come in contact with, and thus act upon, the development of his mental powers . . . Consequently, we are not the product of merely local circumstances. Beings like us, wherever they might dwell, contribute to our education. They help to instruct us and fashion our habits and attitudes. It is in the light of such considerations that I feel justified in speaking of an education of mankind and of a philosophy of the history of man. Their essential characteristic is the continuous interaction of individuals. This process alone makes man a human being in the proper sense of the word.

It must be evident by now that the principles underlying this philosophy of history are as simple and unmistakable as those underlying the natural history of man. They are *tradition* and *organic powers*. All education arises from imitation and exercise, by means of which the model passes into the copy. What better word is there for this transmission than tradition? But the imitator must have powers to receive and convert into his own nature what has been transmitted to him, just like the food he eats. Accordingly, what and how much he receives, where he derives it from and how he applies it to his own use, is determined by his own receptive powers. Education, which performs the function of transmitting social traditions, can be said to be *genetic*, by virtue of the manner in which the transmission takes place, and *organic*, by virtue of the manner in which that which is being transmitted is assimilated and applied. We may term this second genesis, which permeates man's whole life, *enlightenment*, by the light it affords to his understanding, or *culture*, in so far as it is comparable to the cultivation of the soil. But whichever term we prefer, its connotation is the same in two important respects: it is continuous and it is world-wide . . . The difference between the so-called enlightened and unenlightened, or between the cultured and uncultured peoples, is not one of kind but merely of degree. The picture of nations has infinite shades, changing with place and time. But as in all pictures, everything depends on the point of view or perspective from which we examine it. If we take the idea of European culture for our standard, we shall, indeed, only find it applicable to Europe. If, however, we establish arbitrary distinctions between cultures and modes of enlightenment, we are liable to lose ourselves in cloud-cuckoo-land . . .

[*Chapter II* deals with language in very similar terms to those elaborated at length in the *Essay on the Origin of Language*.]

III. ALL THE ARTS AND SCIENCES OF MANKIND HAVE EVOLVED THROUGH IMITATION, REASON AND LANGUAGE

[XIII, 367–74]

As soon as man was led by whatever god or genius to appropriate a symbol for an object as a distinguishing mark, he invented language. With this tool of reason, a basic start was made on the road leading towards the arts and sciences, for its operation essentially consists in observing and designating phenomena. In a very real sense, therefore, language, the most difficult of the arts, was a prototype of all that followed.

By conceiving a mark of designation for a given natural object such as an animal, man at the same time had to observe its chief characteristics, or at least those that were of use or relevance to him. In this way the foundations were laid for the domestication of animals. He noticed in the sheep, for instance, that it gave milk to the lamb and that its wool warmed his hand. Both observations prompted him to make use of the sheep. Hunger led him to try the fruits of the tree; he noticed leaves, with which he might clothe himself, and wood that could provide shelter. He observed the way Nature brought up her children and protected them from danger. He watched how the animals nourished and defended themselves. This was the path of development of all the arts and crafts of men, and their retention and transmission was made possible only by their conscious designation. This inner genesis of distinguishing symbols was the work of language . . .

With the development of the arts and sciences a new tradition began to pervade the human species. But only a few men were able to add new links to the chain of this new tradition. The rest clung to it like industrious slaves and mechanically dragged it along. Our intellect and erudition, our artistic accomplishments, the sciences of war and diplomacy, our whole mode of life, are a combination of the thoughts and inventions of others, which came to us from all parts of the world without any merit of our own. In these we have sunk or swum from our earliest youth.

Vain, therefore, is the boast of the European upstart who deems himself superior to the other parts of the world in what he is wont to call his enlightenment and his arts and sciences, claiming all the inventions of his continent his own just because he was born amidst the confluence of these inventions and traditions. Poor creature! Which of all these arts have you yourself invented? Have your own ideas added anything at all to the traditions you have absorbed? That you have learned to make use of them is the work of a machine; that you have sucked up the waters of science is the merit of a sponge that happened to grow in this humid soil. If you send your gunboats against the Otahites,[12] or allow your cannons to roar along the shores of the New Hebrides, you are in no way superior in skill or intelligence to the inhabitants of these islands, who with great skill navigate the boats they themselves have built with their own hands. All the primitive peoples soon perceived this, if only obscurely, as soon as they came to know the Europeans more intimately. At first these appeared superior to them by virtue of their tools and weapons, and were treated with awe and deference. But when the natives realized that the European was vulnerable, mortal, liable to disease, and indeed inferior in prowess to themselves, they reacted differently. They continued to dread the European's techniques, but they slew the European; for his techniques were no part of himself. This is applicable to the entire European culture. Just because the language of a people, especially in books, is clever and refined, it does not follow that everyone who reads these books and speaks this language is equally clever and refined. What matters is *how* he reads and *how* he speaks, though even then he only thinks and speaks in imitation of others; his ideas and his power of articulating them are also largely taken over from others. Primitive man in his narrower sphere knows how to think for himself and how to express himself with more truth, precision and force. Within this sphere of activity, he knows how to employ his mental and physical powers and his few implements, with skill, practical understanding and an instant presence of mind. Man for man, he is palpably more educated than the erudite, politically suave European, that machine of a

---

[12] Former name of the Tahitians.

man, or should I say child, that sits perched on a lofty edifice erected by the hands of others, by the labours of preceding generations. The man of nature, to be sure, is more limited in his accomplishments, but he is sounder and stands more firmly on the ground. No one will deny that Europe is the repository of art and the accumulated knowledge of man; the destiny of ages has deposited its treasures there; these have been both employed and augmented. But this is not tantamount to saying that everyone who made use of them has also therefore had the intellect of the inventor. On the contrary, the easy access to inventions has to some extent blunted the European's inventiveness. If I am provided by others with all the tools that I need, I shall scarcely take the trouble to invent them for myself.

It is difficult to determine to what extent the arts and sciences have increased man's happiness or, indeed, have contributed to it at all. I doubt whether a simple 'yes' or 'no' can settle this point. Here, as in everything else, all depends on the use that is made of human inventions. That there are now more intricate and sophisticated implements in the world, so that more can be done with less exertion, permitting the reduction of human toil where this is desired: of this there can be no question. It is equally incontestable that every art and science knits a new pattern of society, and that new common needs are created, the satisfaction of which modern man increasingly regards as imperatively necessary. But it is quite a different matter to establish whether or not an increase in wants is tantamount to an extension of the narrow sphere of happiness; whether art is capable of actually adding anything to nature rather than displacing or enfeebling it; and whether the diverse arts and sciences do not render the attainment of man's highest blessing, contentment, much more rare and difficult, by giving rise to an inner restlessness which incessantly conflicts with it. We may also wonder whether the bringing together of greater numbers of people and the increase of social activity have not also brought about the overcrowding of towns and countries, turning them into poor-houses and giant infirmaries, in the close atmosphere of which pallid human nature withers. Supported by so many unearned alms of science, art and political constitutions, have not men for the most part assumed the role of beggars with all the arts and tricks of begging, so that in the end they may also have to suffer the humiliating fate of beggars? These and many other questions are problems on which only History, the daughter of Time, can cast her revealing light.

Messengers of fate, men of genius and invention, on what beneficial yet dangerous heights have you exercised your divine calling! You invented, but not for yourselves. It was not in your power to determine how the world, how posterity, should apply your inventions . . . The inventor of gunpowder had no inkling of the destruction which the explosion of his black dust could cause in both the physical and the political realm of human activity. Still less could he foresee—since we ourselves can scarcely predict it—whether from this barrel of powder, which serves many a despot as a throne of terror, a different political constitution will one day emerge to benefit posterity. Does not thunder clear the air? Must not Hercules himself turn his hand to more beneficial works once the giants of this earth have been destroyed?

IV. POLITICAL ORGANIZATION CONSISTS OF SET RULES AND ORDERS AMONG MEN, GROUNDED, FOR THE MOST PART, IN TRADITION[13]

[XIII, 375–87]

The natural state of man is society. He is born and brought up in it, and his emerging impulses lead him to it during the years of adolescence. Words which are associated in his mind with the most tender feelings are father, mother, son, brother, sister, lover, and friend; all these entail natural ties which exist in the most primitive societies. The first forms of government arose out of these natural social relationships. They were, essentially, family rules and regulations without which human groupings could not persist;

[13] With this chapter Herder had by far the greatest difficulties. In a letter to Georg Hamann (April 1785), Herder complains that he had to rewrite it three times and even the final version did not really satisfy him. He submitted the second draft to Goethe for his comment and was advised that 'not a single word could be left as it is'. Goethe's advice was that of the prudent politician, for as the chief minister to the Duke of Weimar, he was concerned to keep both his friend and himself out of trouble. (See Suphan, XIII, 448; see also an earlier letter to Friedrich Jacobi [February 1785] in similar vein. H. Düntzer and F. G. v. Herder, *Aus Herders Nachlass*, Frankfurt a. M., 1856, II, 268.) Parts of the unpublished drafts have survived and reference will be made to these in subsequent notes.

laws formed and limited by nature. We could regard them therefore as representing *natural government of the first order*. It is the most basic political organization, and has proved the most lasting if not the best.

With this stage Nature considered her task accomplished: the foundations of society were laid. It was now up to man to build a higher structure on these foundations if reason or need were to call for it. In all the regions where particular tribes and kinship groups have less need of each other's assistance, they also take less interest in each other's concerns and, as a result, give little thought to the creation of large political systems. This is true of coasts inhabited by fishermen, of pastures and forests and their herdsmen and hunters. Where in these areas paternal and domestic governments cease to be effective, the extension of political organization usually takes the form of *ad hoc* arrangements contractually made for a given task. A nation of hunters, for instance, may feel the need for a leader when embarking on the chase. Such a leader, however, will only be a leader of the hunt. His election as leader will be determined by his reputation as a skilful hunter, and his electors freely choose to obey him because his expertise serves their common interests. For the same reason all gregarious animals elect a leader in such common concerns as migration, attack and defence. A political organization of this type we may classify as *natural government of the second order*. It will be found among those peoples whose chief concerns are common material needs and who are said to live therefore in a state of nature. Even the elected judges of a community come within this category of government; for they are elected to their office by virtue of their wisdom and sense of fairness, and for one specific task only. Their sphere of competence and range of power starts and ends in carrying out this limited task.

Yet how different is the *third type of political order*, hereditary government! For where do the laws of nature begin or cease to operate under such a system? That men in conflict should choose the wisest and most just among their fellows to resolve their disputes for as long as they proved competent was in keeping with the natural order of things. But if the old judge dies, is there any reason why his son should succeed him in office? Surely, the fact that he was begotten by a just and wise father does not constitute such a reason. For neither wisdom nor justice is hereditary. The son is not his father. The nation's recognition of the father's status for purely personal reasons does not commit it to extend the same recognition to his son. Now imagine that a law would be passed that all the descendants of the judge, as yet unborn, should enjoy the same recognition and prestige as he did, merely on account of their birth. Would it not be hard to reconcile such a piece of legislation, enshrining so blatantly the hereditary principle, with the very rudiments of reason and justice? Nature does not distribute her noblest gifts in families. The right of blood, according to which one unborn has a legitimate claim to rule over others yet unborn by right of his birth, is to me one of the most puzzling formulae human language could devise.

There must have been other grounds for the introduction of hereditary government among men, and history is by no means silent about these. What has given Germany, what has given civilized Europe, its governments? The answer is *war*. Hordes of barbarians overran the continent; their leaders and nobles divided the lands and their inhabitants among them. By these means principalities and fiefs arose; serfdom came into being. The conquerors were in possession; any alterations that have occurred since, have been the result of revolutions, wars, and mutual agreements between the powerful, that is to say, by the right of the stronger. This is the royal road of history, and the facts of history speak for themselves. What brought the world under the sway of Rome? What made Greece and the East subservient to Alexander? What has given rise to, or caused the ruin of, all the monarchies since the time of Sesostris and the fabulous Semiramis?[14] The answer again is *war*. Forcible conquests assumed the place of law. Only the passage of time or, as our political jurists phrase it, the tacit compact, conferred right upon might, and turned a feat of the sword into an act sanctioned by law. But the tacit compact in this case consists merely in the stronger taking what he wants, and the weaker giving what he cannot keep, or enduring what he cannot change. Thus the right of hereditary government, as that of almost any other hereditary possession, depends on a chain of traditions, the first link of which was

[14] Sesostris. The name of several kings of ancient Egypt of the 12th dynasty. Semiramis. Mythological queen of Assyria.

forged by force or accident and was followed, occasionally, by wisdom and goodness, but as a rule by more force or further accidents.[15] Heirs and descendants received what the ancestors had taken. That to him who has, more is given in abundance, scarcely needs explaining, for it is the natural corollary of the principle of first possession by the stronger. It applies alike to men and to lands.

As long as a father ruled over his family, he was a *father* (and not a monarch), permitting his sons to become fathers in turn, and seeking no mode of control over them other than that of advice. As long as several tribes chose in free elections their judges and their leaders for any given task, the incumbents of these offices were only servants of the common weal, like chairmen appointed to preside over a meeting. Names such as sovereign, king, absolute prince, arbitrary and hereditary despot, were unknown to these political associations. But if the nations fell asleep and allowed their fathers, leaders and judges to govern over them, in a fit of drowsy gratitude for imagined or real services, or out of fear of their power and wealth, and went so far as to endow them with an hereditary sceptre, they ceased to be adults and turned themselves into children or sheep in need of a tutor or shepherd. The result was utter weakness on the one side and a

[15] In one of his drafts, Herder puts forth another—and somewhat more sophisticated—explanation for the emergence and function of hereditary monarchy. 'The person of the first elected monarch', Herder writes, 'was, as it were, the abstracted symbol of the whole nation; all honours and distinctions that were conferred upon him were insignia, by means of which external recognition could be given to the collective values of the political artefact which the hereditary monarch represented. The philosopher, therefore, who spends his time examining the twentieth link in the chain of succession in order to decide whether the ancestors did right to elect the first link, foolishly misses the whole point of the matter. It was not the quality of the first monarch which determined that of his successors; here chance or fate took over. What *is* important is that the office of the monarch remains an *office*, a part of the machine of state, and to effect this is the task of all the other members of the state. It is in their interest to exert all their efforts to ensure that even the worst monarch does the least possible damage to the machine as a whole (XIII, 453). 'The more class distinctions wear down', Herder adds, 'the more obvious it will become even to the most misguided of subjects that the monarch is no god, but merely a component of the state machine. His service to the state is in kind no different from that of any other member, and the remuneration he receives in turn is of the same mechanical sort that is proffered to any citizen, taking the form of legal titles, protection, and pay; for no other reward can be expected from the state' (XIII, 454).

monopoly of power on the other; in short the right of the stronger. When Nimrod first killed animals and then subjugated men, he acted in both cases as a hunter. The leader of a colony or a clan, whom men followed like animals, soon treated them as such. Whilst they were employed in civilizing the people, they were its fathers and instructors, observing the laws for the general good. But as soon as they became absolute or, indeed, hereditary rulers, they became the personification of power over their powerless subjects. Frequently a fox took the place of the lion, and then the fox was the stronger. For strength does not consist in the force of arms alone. Cunning, trickery, and artful deceit achieve in most cases more than sheer physical power.

In short, the considerable differences in physical and intellectual endowments among men, or sheer accident, has established despotism and servitude on earth, varying in form according to areas, periods and modes of life. In many places change consisted merely in the transition of one form of despotism into another.[16] Warlike mountain peoples, for example, overran the peaceful plains; climate, hardship and want had made them strong and courageous. They spread themselves over the earth as its overlords until they in turn became the victims of luxury in milder climates and then fell under the yoke of others. Our old planet has been a prey to violence and its history presents a melancholy picture of man-hunts and conquests. Almost every little variation of a boundary, every new epoch, is inscribed in the book of Time with the blood of human victims and the tears of the oppressed. The most celebrated names are those of the murderers of mankind, crowned or crown-seeking executioners, and, even more distressingly, the worthiest of men have often been compelled by necessity to help in forging the chains of their brethren. We may well ask why the

---

[16] Herder explains in one of the earlier drafts that whenever he uses the term 'despotism', he does not confine it to monarchy. It applies 'to all arbitrary types of political rule and all kinds of abuse of political power' (XIII, 454). In another draft he elaborates this point further, by way of a criticism of Montesquieu's typology of governments. 'The terms applied to diverse forms of government, particularly in the case of modern states (since they are the most changeable political systems), are the most deceptive shadows on earth. What is often called a monarchy, is in actual fact the most oppressive aristocracy or oligarchy. A "republic" may in reality be a cloak for the worst form of despotism where the most stupid and extravagant of tyrants holds unbridled sway' (XIII, 451).

history of world empires displays such a dearth of rationality in their final achievements. The answer is not hard to find. The majority of history-making events did not spring from rational motives; passions, not humane reason, dominate the world and urge its peoples like wild beasts against each other. Had it pleased Providence to let superior beings govern humanity, its history would, no doubt, have been different. As it was, those who governed humanity have, for the most part, been *heroes*, that is to say, ambitious men, cunning or enterprising seekers of power and glory, who, prompted by passion, spun the thread of events which fate or accident wove into the cloth of history. If nothing else in the history of the world should point to the baseness of our species, the history of government would do so amply. Judging by it, our planet has been mis-named. More appropriately, it should be called Mars or child-devouring Saturn.

. . . The inequality of men is, however, not so great in nature as it has become through education; the nature of the very same people under different political regimes clearly bears this out. Even the noblest nation loses its dignity under the yoke of despotism. The very marrow is crushed in its bones; its finest and most exquisite talents are abused in the service of lies and deceit. Despotism creates slaves, cringing base creatures, shameless flatterers, and dissolute luxury. No wonder that the people eventually accustom themselves to the yoke, that they kiss their chains and decorate them with flowers. From such an abyss of habitual slavery a nation has rarely risen again without the miracle of a complete regeneration.

We may rightly lament this fate of mankind in both history and every-day life; but we must not delude ourselves into believing that it is the work of nature. Nature extended the bonds of society only to families. Beyond that stage it was left to man how to construct a polity, this most intricate work of art. If he built well, he fared well; if he chose, or endured, tyranny and bad forms of government, he also had to bear their burdens. His good mother, Nature, could do no more than instruct him by means of reason, the tradition of history, or his own perception of pain and misery. Some form of internal human degeneration, therefore, must be the cause of the vices and depravities of political government . . .

But even in man's deepest degeneracy, he is not forsaken by

322

his untiringly beneficient mother Nature. For she contrives at least to mitigate the bitterness of oppression by such palliatives as habit and oblivion. As long as nations retain some vigilance and vigour, or where they are nourished by Nature with the hard bread of industry, no effeminate sultans will stand much chance of success: the rugged land, the hardy way of life, are the pillars of their freedom . . .

Let me, finally, make some general observations.

1. The maxim, that 'man is an animal that needs a lord when he lives with others of his species, so that he may attain happiness and fulfil his destiny on earth',[17] is both facile and noxious as a fundamental principle of a philosophy of history. The proposition, I feel, ought to be reversed. Man is an animal as long as he needs a master to lord over him; as soon as he attains the status of a human being he no longer needs a master in any real sense. Nature has designated no master to the human species; only brutal vices and passions render one necessary. The wife requires a husband; the untutored child requires the instruction of the parents; the sick need the services of a physician; conflicting parties select an umpire, and the herd a leader. These are natural relations; they are inherent in the very notions themselves. The notion of despot, however, is not inherent in the notion of man. It presupposes man to be weak, under age, and hence incapable of managing his own affairs. As a result he needs a protector and guardian. Or, on the other hand, it presupposes man to be a wild, detestable creature, demanding a tamer or a minister of vengeance. Thus all governments of man arose, and continue to exist, because of some human deficiency. A father who brings up his children in a manner which keeps them under age for the rest of their lives and hence in need of a tutor and guardian, is rightly considered a bad father. A physician who contrives to keep his patient in a wretched state to the end of his days so that he will not dispense with his services, is hardly a credit to his profession. Let us apply this line of reasoning to the political teachers of mankind, to the fathers of nations and their charges. Either the latter are incapable of improvement, or it is odd that the thousands of years that men

---

[17] Kant, Immanuel, *Idee zu einer allgemeinen Geschichte in weltbürgerlicher Absicht* (1784), *Kant Schriften*, Preuss. Akademie der Wissenschaften edition, Berlin, 1923, vol. VIII, p. 23.

have been governed should have shown no more perceptible results or even revealed the aims of the educators.

2. It is nature which educates families: the most natural state is, therefore, *one* nation, an extended family with one national character. This it retains for ages and develops most naturally if the leaders come from the people and are wholly dedicated to it. For a nation is as natural a plant as a family, only with more branches. Nothing, therefore, is more manifestly contrary to the purpose of political government than the unnatural enlargement of states, the wild mixing of various races and nationalities under one sceptre. A human sceptre is far too weak and slender for such incongruous parts to be engrafted upon it. Such states are but patched-up contraptions, fragile machines, appropriately called state-*machines*, for they are wholly devoid of inner life, and their component parts are connected through mechanical contrivances instead of bonds of sentiment. Like Trojan horses these machines are pieced together, guaranteeing one another's immortality; yet since they are bereft of national character, it would only be the curse of Fate which would condemn to immortality these forced unions, these lifeless monstrosities. They were contrived by that kind of politics which plays with men and nations as if they were inanimate particles. But history shows sufficiently that these instruments of human pride are formed of clay, and, like all clay, they will dissolve or crumble to pieces.[18]

[18] In an earlier version Herder maintains, however, that 'every state as such is a machine'. Clearly, whenever he fears that his stress on the unity of a national culture could be interpreted as a sufficient legitimation of government or a denial of the uniqueness and freedom of the individual, he goes out of his way to reaffirm his belief in the essentially individualist ethic of the Enlightenment. Yet, while accepting this ethic, he nonetheless repudiates the political expression which it came to assume in the doctrine of enlightened absolutism. Thus he writes: 'Those who expect or even demand enlightenment from the state as such, who put their faith in an absolute ruler in the hope of receiving from him education and the means of happiness, cherish ideas that are wholly unintelligible to me. The state as an entity is an abstraction, incapable of seeing or hearing. Likewise "the public" as such is an empty notion; the public is neither wise nor foolish. Only individual men, in the state and as members of the public, see, hear, act, provide enlightenment or are provided with it' (XIII, 453). It would appear, then, that, though even the nation state is *qua* state a mechanical contrivance, it is less susceptible to breakdowns than the multi-national state, because in the latter, as Herder observes in one of the drafts, 'the causes of disintegration are inherent in its very structure' (XIII, 455).

3. Mutual assistance and protection are the principal ends of all human associations. For a polity, too, this natural order is the best; it should ensure that each of its members be able to become what nature wanted him to become. As soon as the monarch wants to usurp the position of the Creator and bring into being by his own arbitrary will or passion what God had not intended, he becomes the father of misrule and inevitable ruin. The distinctions of social rank, established by tradition, run counter to the forces of nature, which knows no ranks in the distribution of its gifts. Yet since these distinctions persist, it is not surprising that most nations, having tried various forms of government and incurred the inconveniences of each, finally returned in despair to that which wholly made them into machines: despotic hereditary government . . .

O, that another Montesquieu would come and really offer us the spirit of the laws and governments of our globe, instead of a mere classification of governments into three or four empty categories, when in fact no two governments are alike.[19] A classification of states, based on political principles, is also of little avail; for no state is founded on verbal principles, let alone invariably adheres to them at all times or under all circumstances. Least of all are we in need of a scissors and paste approach, where examples are assembled at random from all nations, times, and climates, until we can no longer see the wood for the trees; the genius of our earth as one entity is lost. What we do need is a vivid and philosophical presentation of civil history in which, despite the apparent

---

[19] That the writing of the chapter on political government was at least in part motivated (as so much else of what Herder wrote) by a polemical impulse is evident enough from the content of the last version, but it is even more plainly apparent from the earlier drafts. His two chief targets were Kant and Montesquieu. The very heading of a previous version openly challenges Montesquieu's close correlation between climate and forms of government. 'The various forms of government', he says there, 'are phenomena, the nature of which does not necessarily or invariably depend on climate or on the mode of life of a nation' (XIII, 448). In the same draft he later elaborates: 'It is contrary to the very nature of the thing, as also to history, to deduce types of government from climates and/or from some abstract principle or concept. I simply cannot accept that some such general concept as, for example, fear, honour, or patriotism, is inseparably linked to given degrees of longitude and latitude . . . It must be a source of comfort to humanity that the opposite has been proved by a succession of peoples and periods' (XIII, 451). We had occasion earlier to comment on Herder's criticism of Kant's political views.

uniformity, no one scene occurs twice. Not the external constitution as such will reveal the continuous change to which a state and its political institutions are subject, but rather the internal changes in the character and culture of a nation. It is only by tracing the historical process of these inner, and essentially traditional, forces, that we can hope to explain the continuous development of the boldest of man's mechanical works of art.[20]

[20] I have incorporated in this last passage some sentences from an unpublished earlier version.

INDEX

Orpheus, 72, 73
Ossian, 306

Peter I, 86–7
Petrarca, Francesco, 252
Pindar, 72, 73, 107
Plato, 9, 70, 76, 81, 106, 154, 216
Plutarch, 81
Poole, Matthew, 112, 113 n
Pope, Alexander, 94 n
Prémontval (André Pierre Le Guay), 94
Priestley, Joseph, 272

Racine, Jean, 100, 106, 111, 210
Rasles, Sebastien, 121
Reimarus, Hermann Samuel, 127, 128
Reinhard, Adolph Friedrich von, 94
Richelieu, Armand Jean du Plessis, duc de, 94, 103
Robertson, William, 45, 185, 191, 207 n
Römer, Ludevig Ferdinand, 285
Rousseau, Jean Jacques, 7, 8 n, 11 n, 12 n, 17, 18, 20, 33, 39 n, 45 n, 89, 91, 97 n, 101, 102, 108, 110, 126, 127, 133–4, 135, 139, 162, 164, 167, 177, 242, 287 n.

Sadi, 232
Saint-Foix, Germain François Poullain de, 111
Saint-Marc, Charles Hugues Lefebvre de, 63
Saint-Réal, Cesar Vichard, Abbé de, 63
Savigny, Friedrich Karl von, 53 n
Scaliger, Julius Caesar, 84, 85 n
Schlegel, Friedrich, 53 n
Schlegel, Wilhelm, 53 n
Schleiermacher, Friedrich Daniel Ernst 53 n, 55
Schlözer, August Ludwig von, 91
Schwartz, Berthold, 112, 113 n
Schwarz, Johann Christoph, 97
Sérionne, Jacques Accariague de, 98

Sévigné, Marie de Rabutin-Chantal, Marquise de, 63
Shaftesbury, Anthony Ashley Cooper 3rd Earl of, 33 n, 81
Socrates, 70, 119, 223, 238
Solon, 236, 237
Sophocles, 107, 111
Spinoza, Baruch, 33 n, 39 n
Stahl, Georg Ernst, 292 n
Stark, Werner, 32
Sumner, William Graham, 32
Süssmilch, Johann Peter, 17, 20, 120, 136–7, 138, 149, 151
Swift, Jonathan, 70, 73 n
Sydenham, Thomas, 112, 113 n

Tacitus, 189, 227
Tamberlaine, 235
Tesch, A. F., 97
Theophrastus, 239
Thomas Aquinas, St, 30–1
Thomasius, Christian, 34 n
Thucydides, 238
Torricelli, Evangelista, 63
Tyrtaeus, 236
Tyson, Edward, 257

Velly, Paul François, 63
Vergerio, Pietro Paolo, 246
Vergil (Publius Vergilius Maro), 72
Vico, Giovanni Battista, 33 n
Voltaire, François Marie Arouet de, 33, 35, 45, 63, 91, 94, 95, 97 n, 100, 101, 102, 106, 108, 185, 189 n, 191 206, 210 n, 220 n, 221 n, 242 n

Weber, Max, 9
Willebrand, Johan Peter, 96
Wolff, Christian von, 34 n, 94, 113, 137

Xenophon, 210, 238

Zeno, 216
Zwingli, Ulrich, 88, 97

CAMBRIDGE STUDIES IN THE HISTORY AND THEORY OF POLITICS

TEXTS

LIBERTY, EQUALITY, FRATERNITY, *by James Fitzjames Stephen.* Edited, with an introduction and notes, by *R. J. White*

VLADIMIR AKIMOV ON THE DILEMMAS OF RUSSIAN MARXISM 1895–1903. An English edition of 'A Short History of the Social Democratic Movement in Russia' and 'The Second Congress of the Russian Social Democratic Labour Party', with an introduction and notes by *Jonathan Frankel*

TWO ENGLISH REPUBLICAN TRACTS, PLATO REDIVIVUS or, A DIALOGUE CONCERNING GOVERNMENT (*c.* 1681) *by Henry Neville* and AN ESSAY UPON THE CONSTITUTION OF THE ROMAN GOVERNMENT (*c.* 1699) *by Walter Moyle.* Edited by *Caroline Robbins.*

STUDIES

1867: DISRAELI, GLADSTONE AND REVOLUTION. THE PASSING OF THE SECOND REFORM BILL, *by Maurice Cowling*

THE CONSCIENCE OF THE STATE IN NORTH AMERICA, *by E. R. Norman*

THE SOCIAL AND POLITICAL THOUGHT OF KARL MARX, *by Shlomo Avineri*